LABOR AND EMPLOYMENT
RELATIONS ASSOCIATION SERIES

Revaluing Work(ers): Toward a Democratic and Sustainable Future

Edited By

Tobias Schulze-Cleven

Todd E. Vachon

Cover photo credit: Photo 116747405 © Silvapinto | Dreamstime.com.jpg

First Edition
ISBN 978-0-913447-22-2
Price: $34.95

LABOR AND EMPLOYMENT RELATIONS ASSOCIATION SERIES

LERA *Proceedings of the Annual Meeting* (published online annually, in the fall)

LERA *Annual Research Volume* (published annually, in the summer/fall)

LERA Online Membership Directory (updated daily, member/subscriber access only)

LERA *Labor and Employment Law News* (published online each quarter)

LERA *Perspectives on Work* (published annually, in the fall)

Information regarding membership, subscriptions, meetings, publications, and general affairs of the LERA can be found at the Association website at www.leraweb.org. Members can make changes to their member records, including contact information, affiliations, and preferences, by accessing the online directory at the website or by contacting the LERA national office.

LABOR AND EMPLOYMENT RELATIONS ASSOCIATION
University of Illinois at Urbana-Champaign
School of Labor and Employment Relations
121 Labor and Employment Relations Building
504 East Armory Ave., MC-504
Champaign, IL 61820
Telephone: 217/333-0072   Fax: 217/265-5130
Website: www.leraweb.org
E-mail: LERAoffice@illinois.edu

Acknowledgments

For comments and suggestions on parts or aspects of LERA's 2021 research volume, we thank Ariel C. Avgar, Frances Benson, Jennifer M. Dixon, Adrienne Eaton, Janice R. Fine, Rebecca Kolins Givan, Alysa Hannon, Charles Heckscher, J. Ryan Lamare, Susan Schurman, and Heather Steffen.

Contents

CONCLUSION

Foreword

Like nothing we have experienced in our lifetimes, the interlocking health, economic, racial justice, climate, and democracy crises of the past year have placed workers and their well-being prominently in our minds and in the public discourse. The pandemic and related crises have exposed, highlighted, and exacerbated economic injustices and structural weaknesses that prevailed long before. They have made palpable the catastrophic consequences of decades of failing to address social problems, such as stagnating wages, disappearing jobs, declining worker power, and accelerating inequality of many dimensions. One of the many paradoxes of the pandemic is that essential workers, who are most at risk of getting sick, are those who are most precarious and poorly paid and are disproportionately African American, Hispanic, and female.

I welcome this year's LERA research volume, *Revaluing Work(ers): Toward a Democratic and Sustainable Future*, conceived before COVID-19 assaulted the world, but developed and published amid these cascading crises. Through a series of thoughtful essays, written by a diverse and knowledgeable group of contributors, the volume argues for a labor studies approach to addressing these crises and the future of work, including technological disruption: an approach that is worker centered, multidisciplinary, and normatively anchored, with an explicit commitment to upholding worker rights. The volume's premise is that labor studies provides a valuable source of ideas with unique advantages for building a democratic and sustainable future for work that advances workers' interests, a worthy alternative to long prevailing market-centered ideology.

The research volume underscores LERA's distinctive multidisciplinary forum. Even in today's polarized climate, labor, management, and government practitioners; scholars from many disciplines; advocates; and neutrals can come together, making LERA an ideal setting for dialogue about a way forward at this uncertain and difficult historical moment. Complementing the ideas explored in the research volume, LERA's June 2021 (virtual) annual meeting will also grapple with the challenges facing the nation. Its theme, "A Transformational Moment? Work, Worker Power, and the Workplace in an Era of Division and Disruption," was also conceived before the pandemic, but it has been made all the more relevant by the past year's ordeals. Whether this moment will be transformational remains to be seen.

For a long time, the United States has been at war over government, especially its role in regulating business and the market: for some, government is a social good; but for others, it is the enemy. With this deep divide, it has become nearly impossible for government to play its role, especially at the federal level.

Government can have a big impact on workers, their lives, and livelihoods, whether through action or inaction. The pandemic has unmasked the high costs of inaction.

In one view, America will not, indeed cannot, return to the pre-COVID state of affairs. Americans' feelings about government will be transformed, as they have witnessed what the virus has revealed and experienced the importance of government doing its job—and doing it well. Under this view, it is hard to imagine how anyone can still question the critical role of government as a social good.

And yet, in another view, these crises may turn out to be less of a watershed than many predict—with the weaknesses and injustices we had before still intact, with attitudes about government, including global governance, just as divided and entrenched. The jury is out on which of these views will prevail. Indeed, with poverty, misery, and social unrest on the rise, things could get even worse.

Faced with this dilemma, how do we seize this troubled moment to ensure a more secure, equitable, democratic, and sustainable future? To help struggling individuals and communities recover, policy makers must confront these challenges. It would be fanciful to expect these crises to be tackled on any meaningful scale without government intervention, relying solely on the market's ability to correct or regulate. With wise policy choices, we can do a better job to improve the lives and working conditions of America's workers, to better align the evolving realities of work with protective legislation, to minimize the health and safety risks of working, and to ease persistent market failures. For the good of the nation, government must be a major player to ensure a better future and shared prosperity for all American workers.

With its focus on a labor studies approach, this research volume aims to influence the debate over the future of work and the revaluing of workers. This is especially important given the suffering of the past year. I am privileged to be president-elect of LERA at this moment, and I welcome the opportunity to engage in the critical dialogue needed to emerge from these crises as a stronger nation.

Wilma B. Liebman
LERA President-Elect
Washington, DC
January 2021

INTRODUCTION

CHAPTER 1

Revaluing Work(ers) for Democracy and Sustainability

Tobias Schulze-Cleven
Todd E. Vachon
Rutgers University

ABSTRACT

How can we build a future of work that delivers for workers? How can we meet pressing challenges such as climate change, democratic erosion, and economic instability? This chapter outlines the necessary parameters for a debate on the future of work that faces up to the interlocking ecological, political, and economic crises currently engulfing societies. It argues that collective political action targeted at revaluing work and workers can greatly increase the long-term viability of contemporary social arrangements by curtailing capitalism's infringements on democracy, facilitating social reproduction, and reducing environmental exploitation. Rejecting the technological and market determinism characteristic of mainstream discussions about the future of work, the chapter calls for embracing the role of politics in adjustment and committing to workers' dignity as central to realizing the promises of democracy and improving sustainability.

INTRODUCTION

We live in a period of deep uncertainty, with one calamity seemingly chasing another. From climate change to democratic erosion to economic instability—ongoing and interrelated ecological, political, and economic crises have revealed deep imbalances in our contemporary social order, laying bare the inadequacies of the institutional arrangements that govern our lives. The arrival and mismanagement of COVID-19 has only further underlined this predicament. As the contradictions of contemporary democratic capitalism have grown, the system's ability to reproduce and sustain itself has come into doubt (e.g., Wallerstein et al. 2013).

This volume addresses these fundamental tensions by presenting a labor studies perspective on the future of work and workers. Critically examining the socially constructed and politically sanctioned processes through which workers are managed and empowered, it explores how changes in the regulation of labor could help address today's multi-pronged systemic crises. The book argues that revaluing work—the efforts and contributions of workers—is crucial to realizing the promises of democracy and improving sustainability. Workers' collective agency is central to driving forward this revaluation agenda for the governance of work and workers. Moreover, the valuation of reproductive work—the labor efforts from care to education that sustain the reproduction of society—can function as a crucible of innovation. Success in this area is not only decisive for democracy and sustainability by itself, but it can also help expand the scope of potentially viable governance reforms more broadly.

This volume offers a deliberate counterpoint to the mainstream debate on the future of work, which fails to engage the real-world hurdles to building a future that serves the interests of workers (Gupta, Lerner, and McCartin 2018). Narrowly concerned with the effects of technological change on the division of labor, and usually assuming that market forces will be determinative, the mainstream debate has tended to ignore the crises that contemporary societies are already experiencing. Not even the well-documented corrosive effects of financialization on evolving employment relations have received much attention. While ongoing socioeconomic changes arguably provide new openings for labor organizations to advocate for the concerns of workers, they do so after shifts in power among capital, labor, and government across societies have left many workers and their collective voice weaker than before (Vachon, Wallace, and Hyde 2016). Attempts to chart a future without truly appreciating the present, much less the past, are bound to fail. Our strategy to face today's major tensions head-on is timely and unique among recent books seeking to challenge dominant narratives (e.g., Chamberlain 2018; Kochan and Dyer 2017; Peetz 2019).

This chapter introduces the volume and its broader agenda in three steps. A first section elaborates today's interlocking crises and sketches how contemporary debate on the future of work neglects to address them. The second section spells out the necessary parameters for a debate on the future of work that actually speaks to the current predicament. The third section lays out how the volume develops and sustains its core propositions, starting with a second introductory chapter that makes the case for the unique contribution of labor studies for understanding and addressing contemporary challenges. The context and reflections advanced in this first, introductory chapter provide a productive frame for the remainder of the book.

THE FUTURE OF WORK AMID INTERLOCKING CRISES

Current ecological, political, and economic crises are inextricably and inevitably interlocking because they frequently amplify and negatively affect each other. Most prominently, contemporary economic imbalances have undermined both the workings of political systems and efforts to battle climate change. Today's calamities are global phenomena that deeply challenge all countries, including the rich democracies across the Global North (Wallerstein 2001). This volume, in turn, speaks to the United States in comparative perspective.

Economically, record levels of within-country inequality, widespread precarity, and the financial sector's supremacy have left individual livelihoods, countries' macroeconomies, and global markets extremely unstable (Kalleberg 2018; Stiglitz 2013). Across the wealthy democracies, greater access to credit has at times helped compensate for lagging wage growth by expanding consumption (Baccaro and Pontusson 2016), but it has done so at the price of increased volatility and without addressing how rising inequality hurts well-being, social cohesion, faith in democratic institutions, growth, and employment (Boushey 2019; Galbraith 2012). Governments have, moreover, been deeply challenged in managing economic instability. As the monetary policy of central banks has come to carry an ever-larger share of responsibility, rounds of quantitative easing have not only decoupled financial markets from the real economy, they also undermine the ability of societies to adequately price risks, which is a precondition for the efficient functioning of market competition (Chwieroth and Walter 2019).

Politically, democratic institutions and norms have weakened, with some countries sliding back on democratization (Lührmann et al. 2020). Right-wing populism has been on the rise cross-nationally, with systems of interest intermediation increasingly hollowed out and governing institutions' legitimacy frequently eroded (Levitzky and Ziblatt 2018; Mair 2013). The labor market consequences of new economic realities in particular have arguably wreaked havoc on political engagement, whether it has been through the breakdown of career trajectories encouraging personal drift (Sennett 1998) or status anxiety and social marginalization feeding resentment (Cramer 2016; Gidron and Hall 2020). On top of this, government policies encouraging private investment—including in education, housing, or retirement provision—have frequently undermined support for the broader solidaristic public approaches that are necessary to curb rising inequality, or to at least buffer its effects on individuals and households (Ansell 2014).

Finally, ecologically, the continued exploitation of natural resources has produced environmental degradation, loss of biodiversity, and climate change, all of which exacerbate existing economic, health, and social inequalities (Latour 2018; Purdy 2015). Current levels of fossil fuel consumption are stretching planetary limits by raising greenhouse gas (GHG) emissions and air pollution to dangerous levels that are negatively affecting the well-being of billions and disproportionately affecting marginalized populations and those who have contributed the least to the problem (Intergovernmental Panel on Climate Change 2013). Record global temperatures and warmer ocean temperatures are increasing the odds of devastating hurricanes and extreme rain events in some locations and prolonged droughts and wildfires in others. If unchecked, climate change will deprive millions of people access to the bare necessities of life—food, clean air, and water—leading to increased conflict, migration, and widespread humanitarian crises. Yet many workers rely on fossil fuel extraction, production, transportation, and consumption for employment. Without easy access to alternatives that offer equivalent pay and benefits, they often display anti-environmental attitudes and behaviors that slow or prevent solutions to the ecological crisis (Vachon 2021).

All of this is true around the world, but nowhere is it as striking as in the United States, a country struggling with relative decline after dominating the 20th century. As patterns of population growth and economic development shift the center of the world economy elsewhere, the United States has lost leverage to turn external hegemony into domestic stability. In the process, the United States' frequently invoked exceptionalism has taken on a new meaning. These days, the country stands out among rich democracies in rather unappealing ways, whether it is runaway income and wealth inequality at the top, hyper-partisanship, climate change denial, or forceful resistance to the overdue reckoning with institutionalized racism and its myriad consequences.

Having adopted lax neoliberal stances across policy areas, the United States not only vividly illustrates global crises, it frequently leads the world in producing them. Whether it is hands-off anti-trust policies that allow large firms to buck competition and maintain high consumer prices (Philippon 2019), loose financial regulations permitting corporations to binge on share buybacks that have filled the coffers of CEOs (Lazonick 2018), public supports for entrepreneurial ventures that socialize risk but allow rewards to be privatized (Mazzucato 2015), tax policies that have contributed to greater concentrations of income and wealth (Bargain et al. 2015), welfare-state retrenchment that has shifted the financial responsibility for life risks onto households and increased individuals' insecurity (Hacker 2019), or labor market policies that have grown the ranks of the precariat well beyond levels found in other rich democracies (Thelen 2019)—they have all helped contemporary American capitalism work for the few rather than the many. And this list does not even include high barriers to the availability of healthcare, which other wealthy countries provide via social citizenship, but which individuals in the United States, for all practical purposes, can only access in meaningful ways once they have submitted themselves to the disciplining effects of the labor market. Research tracking 50 metrics of well-being to assess the quality of life worldwide has found the United States to be one of only three of 163 countries—joined by Brazil and Hungary—for which scores have fallen since 2011. In access to healthcare, the United States now ranks 97th, and the country's overall standing on the composite "social progress index" has fallen from 19th in 2011 to 28th in 2020 (Kristof 2020).

Facilitated by politicians whose actions reflect the preferences of the elite and powered by Republicans who have been extremely adept at enlisting outrage-focused populism in the service of shoring up plutocracy, the resulting "winner-take-all politics" in the United States are literally killing people (Hacker and Pierson 2010, 2020). Well before producing an uncoordinated COVID-19 response that drove up fatalities during 2020, including disproportionately among communities of color and particularly for African Americans, they have nurtured "deaths of despair" among working-age White men and women without four-year college degrees. Having lost opportunities, meaning, and structure in their lives, the latter have succumbed to drug overdoses, suicides, and alcohol-related liver disease at increasing rates. As a result, life expectancy in the United States has been falling since 2014 for the first time in a century while continuing to rise in other rich democracies (Case and Deaton 2020).

Facing up to the toll of current arrangements and addressing their lack of sustainability is difficult—and, arguably, inconvenient for those who have benefited so much from them. As such, it should not be surprising that the ongoing debate about the future of work has stayed well within the parameters set by the neoliberal orthodoxy that has helped create the current predicament (Britton-Purdy, Grewal, Kapczynski, and Rahman 2020). Self-styled "thought leaders" on the impact of sophisticated digital tools—including advanced robotics, data analytics, machine learning, and the Internet of Things—have usually proceeded from assumptions of technological and market determinism. Whether they emphasize rapid automation or a far-reaching global reallocation of tasks, they agree that many workers will be subject to displacement and dislocation, including those far up the skill ladder and those in high-status jobs (Baldwin 2016; Susskind and Susskind 2015). One study estimates 47% of US employment to be at risk through computerization (Frey and Osborne 2013). Yet, despite the social instability implied by these scenarios, debates about appropriate policy responses have generally centered on how to facilitate technical disruption to enable potential productivity increases (Brynjolfsson and McAfee 2014; Frey 2019).

The desire to ease opposition to disruption has admittedly helped the once-marginal policy option of universal basic income (UBI) gain some traction in mainstream debates (e.g., Van Parijs 1995). One of the candidates in the Democratic Party's presidential primary in 2020, Andrew Yang, built his entire campaign around it, and the former president of the Service Employees International Union, Andy Stern, has also strongly endorsed it. Some of the short-term policies in response to the pandemic, moreover, have functioned not unlike UBI provisions and may well have changed public perceptions of this policy. Yet, beyond that, policy makers have generally failed to implement UBI schemes, and the discussed plans would not fundamentally challenge the labor market dynamics that have produced ever-greater inequalities. Effectively combating inequality requires "pre-distribution" policies to alter the market-based distribution of incomes, such as through active support for collective bargaining, raising minimum wages, instituting punitive taxes (or even limits) on high incomes, and embracing a host of other actions that would challenge inequalities of power in the contemporary economy.

Ultimately, policy recommendations have tended to continue along well-trodden paths. Returning to the mantra of a "race between education and technology" (Goldin and Katz 2008), these recommendations have largely left the pressure of adjustment on the shoulders of individual workers, perceiving a successful transition to depend on the ability of workers to be lifelong learners. In contrast, there has been little discussion of how to turn adaptation into a collective effort and how to build a human-centered future of work that would re-envision the role and nature of work in the interest of workers. Such an effort would explore how to channel the use of technologies to the benefit of the greatest number, including the use of technology to augment—rather than replace—labor across the skill spectrum.

SHIFTING THE DEBATE ON THE FUTURE OF WORK

It is thus eminently clear that addressing contemporary interlocking crises requires different discussions about the future of work. Three changes appear particularly advisable: addressing concurrent threats to the sustainability of contemporary societies, accepting the role of politics in adjustment, and honoring the dignity of work and workers.

Addressing Threats to Sustainability

Any productive debate about the future of work needs to engage with pressing questions about the long-run viability of contemporary social arrangements, including capitalism's increased dominance over democracy, challenges to social reproduction, and the consequences of environmental exploitation.

Capitalism's Increased Dominance Over Democracy

The contemporary imbalance between capitalism and democracy is a central issue to tackle (Rothstein and Schulze-Cleven 2020). As a governance system, democratic capitalism is by its very nature never free from tensions, given that it brings together quite different logics of individual valuation. Generally speaking, the value of an individual (or, more precisely, the value of that individual's labor effort) under capitalism is never higher than whatever another entity (whether an employer or customer) is willing to pay, which in turn can result in great divergences among people's market value and the accumulation of capital among the few. In contrast, democratic principles prescribe equal voice and treatment—typically secured through the rule of law, structures of political representation via parties and elections, and a system of checks and balances among different branches of government. Historically, the development of welfare states has done much to mediate tensions when claims to freedom and equality pulled into different directions, often by using social programs to provide greater equality of opportunity in the spirit of "positive liberty."

Yet market liberalization over the past few decades has arguably strengthened the forces of capitalism while weakening those of democracy, whether in terms of global financial markets constraining democratic governments' fiscal leeway or market logics increasingly pervading how governments relate to democratic citizenries. In Europe, events such as the Eurocrisis and Brexit have illustrated how negative policy feedback from market-led political integration—including the partial pooling of monetary sovereignty—has undermined the provision of effective political counterweights to market forces (Schulze-Cleven 2018). In the United States, the simultaneous growth of public and private debt illustrates the limits of recent strategies to manage contemporary imbalances (Streeck 2016), as does the rise of plutocratic populism, which has significantly recast central features of one of the United States' two major political parties and upended inherited patterns of partisan competition (Hacker and Pierson 2020). As scholars of capitalism established long ago, without effective democratic controls stabilizing the system, capitalism's internal contradiction will put it on a road to deepening crises. To avert this outcome, societies need to take more assertive steps to shore up democratic controls, including in the governance of the workplace, where capitalist and democratic logics often clash most immediately.

Challenged Social Reproduction

The changing ability of societies to reproduce and sustain themselves across time should be an important concern, particularly in terms of how they provide the labor that is necessary for reproduction, not just biologically but socially. Following World War II, the institutions of Fordist capitalism encouraged a gendered division of labor, with welfare states and industry tending to support male-breadwinner arrangements, including by aiming to ensure wage levels and wage-replacement benefits that could support entire households (Lewis 1992). Most of the labor necessary for social reproduction was provided by women within the family. Much of it revolved around the raising of children—including ensuring their comfort, literacy, and sociability. But social reproduction always involved a broader scope of unpaid activities, including feeding family members engaged in paid work; maintaining the safety, shelter, and emotional well-being of the entire household; caring for the sick, the elderly, or other family members unable to work; and building and maintaining relationships within the community, including the extended family (Briggs 2017).

As capitalism entered its post-Fordist phase, the demand for literate workers quickly opened pathways for increased labor force participation by women, typically in gendered occupations. Women of color and those from lower positions on the socioeconomic ladder more generally have always participated in forms of paid labor, but the rapid growth of female labor force participation beginning in the 1960s represented nothing short of a revolution in the labor market. The rising share of employment in services and simultaneous stagnation in wages helped fuel this transformation as families increasingly required two earners. At the same time, strong gender norms around domestic work endured, leaving many women doing double duty, with a "second shift" of care work waiting at home once the day's paid work was done (Hochschild, with Machung [1989] 2012). As these strategies have run up against physical limits, increased external provision of reproductive labor has become functionally necessary. Yet many families do not possess the resources to pay for such care work. Moreover, those performing the work, whether as home health aides or childcare workers, often do so at poverty wages, in line with the long-standing low status of these activities.

The strain is particularly large in the United States, with its rampant job insecurity, falling access to in-work benefits such as paid sick leave or vacations, high share of low-wage work, and employers' growing practice of paying for part-time work while expecting full-time availability. Led by the social democratic welfare states in Scandinavia, European countries have increasingly moved toward socializing both the cost and the organization of care provision, including making publicly sponsored (or at least state-subsidized) daycare universally available. These nations have done so in the name of "social investment," driven not only by equity considerations but also by the realization that it helps reap the productive potential of all citizens for higher economic growth (Hemerijck 2017). The United States, by contrast, lacks a comparable care infrastructure, despite federal programs such as Head Start and innovations at the state level. In turn, it faces a veritable "crisis of care," characterized by "time poverty," the lack of work–family balance, and widespread "social depletion" (Fraser 2016).[1]

It is crucial that the valuation and financing of reproductive labor (or work) receive wider attention. The social costs of contemporary arrangements—including their associated gender and racial inequities—provide great hurdles to sustainability. There is much scholarship to build on. Marxist feminists have not only long critiqued the traditional division between "productive" work for men on the one hand and women's relegation to supporting and servicing the current and future workforce on the other, they have also argued that reproductive work is just as central to capitalist accumulation and tends to be particularly exploitative (Bhattacharya 2017). Historical research illustrates this very well, particularly as it has explored the centrality of enslaved women for the 19th century's Atlantic economy, emphasizing their role in reproducing the predominant "capital" of the era (Morgan 2004; White [1985] 1999). Finally, research on contemporary migration has elaborated continuing global patterns of domination, with mothers from poorer countries leaving behind their own offspring to fill the childcare needs of richer nations (Parreñas 2015).

Last, but not least, it is important to conceptualize reproductive work broadly to include personal social services such as education and healthcare, which now fulfill functions once provided in the household. Just as is the case with care work, they—and public services in general—are crucial for sustaining the effective renewal of societies' workforces through time.

Consequences of Environmental Exploitation

Environmental sustainability has often been an afterthought in social science scholarship, leaving research on climate change solidly rooted in the natural sciences, with little attention to its social implications (Bjurström and Polk 2011; Frankel 2018). This is both perplexing and injurious, considering that human economic activity has been identified as the leading contributor to the GHG emissions that have contributed to the global warming process (Intergovernmental Panel on Climate Change 2013). Tellingly, the current era has been termed the "Anthropocene," acknowledging the extent to which human activity has become interconnected with natural forces so that the fate of one is interconnected with the fate of the other (Zalasiewicz, Williams, Steffen, and Crutzen 2010).

In 2017, the US government's Global Change Research Program issued its Fourth National Assessment, reaffirming the established scientific consensus that (1) global surface air temperature has increased by 1.0°C (1.8°F) since 1900, (2) sea levels have risen 8 inches in the same period, (3) our weather is already being impacted by the warming climate, and (4) the warming is caused primarily by human activity, particularly the combustion of fossil fuels such as oil and coal (US Global Change Research Program 2017). Among the key contributors to warming, electric power generation is the single largest, accounting for 25% of total GHG emissions annually. To keep global temperature increases below the 2.0°C limit prescribed by climate scientists and enshrined in the Paris Climate Accord, energy-related GHG emissions would have needed to peak before 2020 and need to fall by more than 70% by 2050. In other words, to prevent catastrophic climate change, a rapid and massive switch to renewable energy sources is required.

However, real commitments to renewable energy have proven politically difficult in the face of the entrenched power of the fossil fuel industry and the strong free-market ideology that influences economic policy making throughout the world. The most common efforts to reduce GHG emissions that are currently under way include various forms of carbon pricing (usually either taxation or, even more frequently, emissions trading schemes). Unfortunately, these efforts have not been aggressive enough and have generally proven inadequate. Private investment in renewable energy sources has also been insufficient in terms of meeting climate targets. According to the International Energy Agency, if all government commitments to clean energy were met by 2035, renewable energy would still stand at just 16% of all energy consumed globally (International Energy Agency 2017).

Current market-based solutions also reinforce or often exacerbate existing social and economic inequalities. Despite more energy being generated every year, 1.2 billion people still do not have regular access to electricity. Small island nations, which have contributed less than 1% of total GHG emissions, are confronting the very real prospects of annihilation due to rising sea levels. Polluting fossil fuel plants in wealthy countries are disproportionately located near lower-income communities and communities of color, while new green technologies, such as rooftop solar, are more likely to emerge in affluent areas. In sum, the current energy system and menu of solutions to climate change have created an unequal distribution of environmental benefits and risks and are proving incapable of adequately reducing GHG emissions to the levels required to prevent serious harms from climate change.

In response, climate activists such as the Sunrise Movement have come to call for a Green New Deal (GND) to address the interconnected crises of climate and inequality (Aronoff, Battistoni, Cohen, and Riofrancos 2019). Unlike current market-based solutions, the GND explicitly confronts existing social inequalities and the job impacts of rapid decarbonization by calling for a "just transition" for workers and communities through massive government investment in physical and social infrastructures that offer low-carbon jobs, such as in healthcare, eldercare, and childcare and in education. Many fossil fuel workers and energy unions that comprise the AFL-CIO's Energy Committee have come out in opposition to such efforts for fear of job loss among their membership; however, other unions noting the impacts of climate change and environmental injustice at workplaces and across communities have come out in support of the GND, including the Service Employees International Union (SEIU) and the American Federation of Teachers. Many labor–climate activists echo Naomi Klein's call for the revaluation of low-carbon reproductive work, which has frequently been undervalued but will play such an important role in building and maintaining a more sustainable economy. Some labor groups such as the Minneapolis Janitors, SEIU Local 26, have worked with community partners to develop climate justice demands and then engaged in Bargaining for the Common Good campaigns (Vachon, Hudson, LeBlanc, and Soni 2019). Groups like the Extinction Rebellion and Fridays for Future and youth activists such as Greta Thunberg have brought a laserlike focus on the ways in which climate change interacts with issues of social, economic, and environmental injustice.

Accepting the Primacy of Politics

A second, no less crucial, element for a productive reorientation in the debate on the future of work is accepting the inevitable role—even "primacy" (Berman 2006)—of politics in societies' adjustment to changing external environments and internal pressures. One can pretend that markets decide how resources are used, but this ignores that all markets are political creations. Only rudimentary exchange is possible without political intervention, which—at its most basic—includes the provision of currency and the definition and protection of property through enforcing the rule of law but which—in practice—always extends to a much wider range of regulatory policies (e.g., Balleisen and Moss 2010). Historically, the "market revolution" that spelled the practical end of feudalism and propelled the rise of capitalism was the result of policy decisions, such as launching the enclosures that turned English common land into private property. Far from being spontaneous, it was a revolution that was "made" (Polanyi [1944] 2001).

Moreover, particularly when it comes to labor, there are strong social limits to using markets for the allocation of resources. We can treat labor as a commodity, but in the end, it remains the labor effort of human beings, who have physical and emotional needs and are subject to social obligations. These sellers of labor will never behave entirely as economics textbooks assume. Frequently, they provide more labor when wages fall (to make ends meet) and decide to work less when wages rise (to enjoy more leisure), meaning that individual labor supply curves bend backward rather than slope steadily upward as economic theory predicts. Moreover, in today's context, workers enjoy many rights as democratic citizens. In turn, treating labor as a commodity is always "fictitious" (Polanyi [1944] 2001) and naturally comes with side effects that can threaten social and political stability. During the 1930s, those countries that recognized the social limits of markets and shored up social protection systems were best able to protect their democracies. Others, notably Italy and Germany, succumbed to fascism, an antidemocratic ideology that promised an altogether different version of breaking with market rule.

Distributional questions are the essence of politics (Lasswell [1936] 1958). How the costs associated with the implementation of technological change are distributed (i.e., whose jobs get eradicated or who gets laid off) is by definition political. In turn, it is important to recognize assumptions of market determinism in the debate on the future of work for what they—perhaps unwittingly—tend to be: expressions of "market fundamentalism," even "free-market utopianism," that fail to acknowledge the "reality of society" (Block and Somers 2014: 98, 218). This is not to deny that such assumptions about market dynamics are defensible in certain types of economic research. But using them as foundations in policy debates while failing to address long-standing market failures—including the inability of the price mechanism to put an end to labor shortages in the provision of care[2]—turns them into neoliberal policy prescriptions: conservative in character and seeking to elevate the role of markets in governing the social order so as to shrink and limit the room for collective political efforts.

Neoliberal approaches to governance gained traction—and ultimately hegemony—as a political answer to questions about the "governability" of advanced societies during the 1970s, which had brought increased unemployment and inflation (Hall 2013). Emphasizing the *theoretical* (albeit not necessarily *practical*) efficiency benefits of a decentralized market system, neoliberalism is deeply skeptical of the political voice of citizens. Powered by academic theorizing in such fields as "public choice" or "law and economics," furthered by a well-organized conservative legal movement, and pushed by the legal, accounting, and lobbying firms serving wealthy clients, this approach has become enshrined at different levels of governance, usually with great advantage to the holders of capital (Pistor 2019; Teles 2010). Whether it is internationally through the World Trade Organization or domestically, neoliberalism has pushed the use of markets for social coordination while isolating their operation from political pressures, often institutionalizing strong biases against underprivileged workers and marginalized communities.

In the United States, neoliberalism's influence is ubiquitous. Contemporary competition policy wields the axe against the attempts of "self-employed" gig workers to collectively represent their interests, but it has allowed increasing concentration among businesses, including the platform companies contracting gig workers, in the name of securing consumer benefits. In environmental policy, the rise of cost–benefit analyses and the trading of rights to pollute have replaced regulation of performance standards, yet the estimates of costs and benefits are often off, and the market-based pollution control of American cap-and-trade schemes has frequently concentrated pollution within poorer communities (e.g., Berman, forthcoming). Moreover, in the workplace, the lack of worker protections has allowed employers to curtail and control workers' rights in ways that are inconsistent with democratic values (Anderson 2017). Crucially, even where neoliberalism's ascendancy has not led to new laws, its pernicious consequences have been felt in the ossification and drift of old ones, including labor laws. These have come to represent mighty barriers for the attempts of union and "alt-labor" activists to promote the goals of equity and voice and move toward practices of efficiency improvements that price in negative social and environmental externalities (Budd 2003; Galvin 2019).

To be sure, accepting the primacy of politics does not automatically generate desirable results. Fascism's version of overcoming market rule sacrificed individual rights, and its rationalizations of social exclusion provided the ideological grounds for Nazi death camps. Moreover, even "social democracy," the 20th century's most successful progressive political movement in support of limiting market rule, has had its own limitations. Welfare states naturally stratify, and all social programs include, an element of social control (Piven and Cloward 1971). At any moment in history, among all the undeniable good that collective efforts at limiting market rule have had, there has been a tendency for them to express underlying patterns of domination, including racism. Take the New Deal in the United States, which depended on the assent of Southern Democrats who opposed policies that could upset the racial order in their states. In 1935, this political reality translated into excluding agricultural and domestic workers, among whom were a majority of Southern Blacks, from the benefits of both the National Labor Relations Act and the Social Security Act. Most social programs passed during the 1930s and 1940s disproportionately benefited White Americans. For instance, under the G.I. Bill of 1944, Whites received support for college attendance and home ownership at much greater numbers (Katznelson 2005). While New Deal programs provided unprecedented assistance to many African Americans, they did so in the context of highly unequal treatment that often increased disparities while relieving deprivation.

Whether one wants to simply understand or even improve society, there is no alternative to working from its political realities. Failing to acknowledge them only feeds capital's patterns of subjugation, whether with respect to class or race (Johnson 2018). For the debate on the future of work, this political perspective offers a more realistic take on the labor market as a social institution (Solow 1990) and concedes that inequalities in the market are often not justified by individual workers' abilities or efforts (Offe 2010). Finally, normatively, it boosts the case for extending democracy into the firm, with a focus on limiting the authoritarian power of employers over workers' lives and promoting genuine "economic democracy" (Dahl 1985: 111).

Once this foundation is laid, there are many important discussions to be had about how to manage the inevitable tensions in labor markets and how to remedy existing inequities, particularly as they relate to cumulative disadvantage. On the one hand, an intersectionality lens emphasizes how class, gender, and racial inequities tend to concentrate and amplify each other, thus raising the need for policies targeted at those in greatest need. On the other hand, universal policies have frequently had greater long-term effects because of their broader political buy-in (Korpi and Palme 1998).

Emphasizing the Dignity of Work and Workers

A final necessary shift in the debate on the future of work, and a logical corollary of the discussion above, is the need to emphasize the dignity of work and workers. References to the imperative of respecting human dignity in the world of work have a long lineage. Laying an important baseline, lesson-learning from years of destruction during World War II produced international declarations that stressed the basic respect that all people are due by virtue of their common humanity, from the 1944 "Philadelphia Declaration," which spelled out the aims and purposes of the International Labour Organisation, to the United Nations' 1948 "Universal Declaration of Human Rights."

Two decades later, at the tail end of the United States' mid-century civil rights movement, striking sanitation workers in Memphis called for such respect. Keen to minimize the cost of public service provision, many American municipalities had relied on cheap, pliant, and heavily African American labor toiling in atrocious working conditions. When he spoke to striking workers, Martin Luther King Jr. emphasized the protection that the reproductive character of their labor deserved in particular, emphasizing that "whenever you are engaged in work that serves humanity and is for the building of humanity, it has dignity, and it has worth" (Jones 2020: 2).

More recently, social philosophers have come out strongly against the "tyranny of merit" (Sandel 2020), questioning the injustices involved in the construction of merit and calling on societies to emancipate themselves from the social Darwinism that contemporary market dominance entails. According to this line of reasoning, respecting human dignity at work would have far-reaching consequences. For instance, one prominent voice calls for acknowledging unemployment as an act of violence, given that it expels human beings from participation in crucial social relations against their own will; breaking with the recent acceleration of work because it undercuts creativity, productivity, and cultural heritage; and providing opportunities for workers to identify with the product of their labor because doing so meditates against alienation (Negt 2002). Increasingly, discussions on economic reforms also display concerns about workers' dignity, whether in international development or domestically (Anner, Pons-Vignon, and Rani 2019; Sperling 2019).

It is in the threefold spirit of sustainability, democratic politics, and human dignity that this volume argues for revaluing work and workers. The case for raising the wages of many working people is so strong that it does not even require us to refer to the millions of "working poor" who are obviously without the economic means to lead a dignified life. Widening inequality powerfully illustrates the increased scope for domination and humiliation at the workplace, which a dignity-led reform agenda would seek to address. At the largest 350 American firms, CEO pay has crept up to 320 times that of typical workers, having grown 1,167% between 1978 and 2019 as compensation for the typical worker increased by only 13.7% (Mishel and Kandra 2020). Moreover, in line with an intersectionality lens, the evidence for the widespread accumulation of disadvantage is strong. Wages of Black women working full time in the United States display a "double gap" of both gender and race, reaching a mere 61% of wages received by White men working full time in 2017. This amounts to an estimated $50 billion of wages per year that African American women have involuntarily forfeited, benefiting the bottom lines of private, for-profit corporations (Holder 2020).

Yet, of course, the agenda of revaluing work and workers is an even broader one, extending to other employer responsibilities, such as healthy and safe workplaces; sufficient opportunities for collective worker voice, including via collective bargaining or through works councils; and publicly provided social protections, including transfer or social insurance systems that cover workers during illness, unemployment, old age, and disability.

There hardly could have been a better demonstration of this agenda's worth than the effect the United States' weak labor protections had on producing an overly harsh impact of COVID-19 on the working population (Leibenluft 2020). Sick workers often could not afford *not* to work, which helped increase community spread of the virus. Moreover, frequently, "essential" workers could count on only woefully inadequate safety protections, if any at all. Unemployment shot up quickly, within a few months reaching twice the level in Europe, where publicly financed work-share and short-time work arrangements successfully kept workforces employed (MacGillis 2020; Müller and Schulten 2020). By the end of summer 2020, an estimated 12 million people in the United States had lost their employer-sponsored health insurance coverage as they were laid off—right when many of them needed it most (Bivens and Zipperer 2020). Furthermore, while some large corporations introduced temporary hazard pay or more-generous sick leave provisions, they rescinded these measures quickly as the initial wave of the virus slowed. Finally, in line with long-standing patterns, the impact of the pandemic was highly unequal. Low-income workers; communities of Black, Indigenous, and People of Color; and women disproportionately bore the brunt of pandemic-induced unemployment (Groeger 2020), and immigrant workers, particularly undocumented ones, often had the hardest time.

It is now time to take COVID-19 not merely as a lens for what has gone wrong—but to treat it as a catalyst for change. Attention to the deficiencies of contemporary valuations of work has markedly increased, moving from expert circles to mainstream newspapers (Ferreras et al. 2020; Kobayashi 2020). Of course, the demonstrations against police brutality and for racial justice have also elevated the themes elaborated here, forcing onto mainstream discussions a broader reckoning with systemic racism and its far-reaching influences on people's lives—both at work and beyond. From physical insecurity and criminal justice (Pettit 2012; Walker 2020) to housing (Desmond 2016; Rothstein 2017) and the distribution of wealth (Baradaran 2017), awareness of the astounding and cumulative racial disparities in the United States has significantly spread. At least in some quarters, there now appears to be growing recognition of the multiple interconnections between the different forms and realms of oppression that sustain racial hierarchy.

ROADMAP TO THE VOLUME

Having established the need for a very different debate about the future of work, the book elaborates a labor studies perspective on the topic. In Chapter 2, Tobias Schulze-Cleven reviews the advantages of labor studies for understanding and shaping the future of work. He emphasizes how the field provides much-needed new intellectual direction to challenge the hold that the "market fundamentalism" of neoclassical economics has had on discussions about the future of work to date. With its focus on the struggles of working people, interdisciplinary inquiry, and upholding workers' rights, labor studies brings a greater appreciation of the power of collective action and the role of politics to the debate. The latter part of the chapter lays out the book's main arguments about revaluing work, workers' collective agency, and innovations in reproductive work, which act as a foundation for any further claims put forth in the volume.

The remaining chapters, which will be described briefly below, make the case for revaluing work and workers in three parts. Part I ("Articulating the Labor Studies Perspective") explores different elements of the labor studies perspective on the future of work, including input from different disciplines, a focus on worker voice, and placing the revaluation agenda in the context of climate change. Part II ("Evolving Forms of Collective Agency") zeros in on the role of workers' collective agency in shaping the evolving world of work. Part III ("Reproductive Work as a Crucible of Innovation") investigates how such collective agency has produced innovation in labor processes that help reproduce and sustain society, focusing on domestic work and education. The individual contributions are arranged with an eye toward allowing the volume's argumentation to unfold steadily and relatively seamlessly throughout the book.

Articulating the Labor Studies Perspective

In Chapter 3, Michael Merrill and Dorothy Sue Cobble set the stage for Part I of the volume with a historical perspective on technological disruption that compares the scale and effects of the current labor market disruption in the United States to three previous transformations: colonization, commercialization, and industrialization. The authors contend that the massively disruptive changes accompanying today's "smart machines" are not unprecedented in either scale or scope and that managing the effects of such changes requires that we pay as much attention to sociological as to technological possibilities. Building a more just and sustainable future of work, the authors conclude, requires fixing the social structure and power arrangements in which it occurs.

Chapter 4, by Tod D. Rutherford, extends the critique of technological determinism by deploying a geographer's perspective to examine the differentiated negotiation over the adoption of Industry 4.0 technology across three countries—Germany, Italy, and the United States. Rutherford contends that many perspectives on the future of work ignore how Industry 4.0 will develop in a geographically uneven or variegated fashion and that there is, and will continue to be, experimentation by unions and firms around the processes of adopting new technology. Upon documenting both successes and challenges in the exercise of worker voice, the author acknowledges that the ability to "scale up" and sustain such experimentation within the context of neoliberalism remains an open question.

In Chapter 5, J. Mijin Cha and Todd E. Vachon focus on societal-level adjustments against the backdrop of climate change. The necessary transition away from a growth-oriented "extractive" economy toward a sustainable and "regenerative" one will completely reshape existing labor markets, undermine the gains made over generations by workers in historically unionized sectors, and further shift employment into sectors where unions have been unable to gain a foothold. The authors explore three cases of recent socioecological transitions and consider the ingredients of and prospects for a "just transition" for workers and communities. They conclude that the inclusion of worker and community voice in shaping and implementing transitions is paramount to ensuring the potential for just outcomes.

Evolving Forms of Collective Agency

The collective action of workers has often been crucial in shaping outcomes, not least because it pushed both employers and the state into action. In Chapter 6, Naomi R Williams and Sheri Davis-Faulkner open Part II of the volume by using a critical race theory and intersectionality lens to examine key moments within US history when workers managed to shape the political landscape and expand democracy and economic citizenship. Critically reassessing the tendency of the dominant historical narrative to treat the struggle for civil rights and worker activism as separate processes of contention, the authors emphasize the vital role of Black workers in building interracial coalitions. When such mobilization was matched with activist/interventionist federal policy, workers' agency increased, income inequality declined, and real wages rose. These experiences, the authors contend, provide valuable lessons on building, maintaining, and adapting class solidarity through a broad social justice view today.

Chapter 7, by Joel S. Yudken and David C. Jacobs, continues the pushback against technological determinism by exploring various mechanisms through which worker voice can be expanded in the development and deployment of technologies in order to support the retention and creation of skilled, high-paying jobs while promoting a broadly shared economic prosperity. After first tracing the evolution of labor's response to technological change historically, Yudken and Jacobs elaborate a contemporary model of craftwork to guide labor's strategy on technology. In conclusion, the authors propose a robust program to restore worker voice that honors workers' skills and empowers them across nodes of decision making.

In Chapter 8, Joseph A. McCartin, Erica Smiley, and Marilyn Sneiderman engage with two major focal areas of innovation in organizing collective worker voice: sectoral bargaining and Bargaining for the Common Good (BCG). Proponents of sectoral bargaining advocate for laws that empower workers to bargain for a whole sector rather than with individual employers. BCG efforts have sought to transform bargaining in terms of its participants, processes, and purposes by bringing union members and community allies together to develop joint demands that are presented not only to the direct employer but also to the web of corporate and financial relationships that influence or control the employer. The authors consider the range of new possibilities that might emerge from an effort to combine the broadening impulse of sectoral bargaining with the deepening impulse of BCG.

In Chapter 9, Victor G. Devinatz and Robert Bruno explore the role that US labor education and worker education can play in examining and shaping the future of work. A historical analysis of US labor education programs reveals an initial focus on both "tools" classes as well as classes oriented toward "social transformation." Following World War II, the normalization of labor relations led to a predominant focus on tools classes in the university-based labor education programs taking hold during the period. The authors contend that the erosion of a stable and widespread system of labor relations in recent decades necessitates returning labor education to focus on topics of social transformation, including a greater emphasis on issues of race, class, gender, immigration, and young workers, in order to help workers develop a vision and plan for shaping a more just future of work.

Reproductive Work as a Crucible of Innovation

Part III focuses on reproductive work as a crucible of innovation. We chose to focus on this realm in part because of its strategic importance for sustainability. No longer can we pretend that this work is less "useful" for our society; moreover, it is central for reflecting about work's value for the public good rather than merely satisfying the immediate demand of markets. Finally, as a personal service, it is not subject to international competition, a constraint often invoked to shut down reform attempts in other contexts. As we shall see, this area of work has served as a trial ground for promising new forms of collective action that have led to substantial changes in the governance of labor.

Chapter 10, by Elaine Zundl and Yana van der Meulen Rodgers, explores how domestic worker organizations are innovating, including through organizing Domestic Worker Bill of Rights campaigns as well as creating new digital platforms with portable benefits, strengthening efforts to prevent wage theft, and reconceptualizing collective bargaining strategies to address the poor working conditions experienced by domestic workers. Such innovations in pursuit of benefits and protections for domestic workers, the authors argue, could also benefit other low-wage workers struggling with precarious and nontraditional work arrangements.

In Chapter 11, William A. Herbert and Joseph van der Naald explore how precarity has not only affected domestic workers and care workers but increasingly those working in higher education as well, including graduate student employees. While legal rights to unionize have come and gone for private sector graduate workers, and universities have largely opposed unionization, graduate student employees have nonetheless voted overwhelmingly in favor of representation between 2012 and 2019. The authors find that militant and sustained organizing led to a variety of positive changes, with even unsuccessful efforts inspiring sustained cultures of resistance. These experiences, the authors contend, can provide lessons for workers in other industries facing similar obstacles.

Chapter 12, by Saul A. Rubinstein and John McCarthy, explores how neoliberal governance in secondary education has failed and how collaboration with teachers can improve school outcomes. The authors argue that collaborative school reform is a proven alternative to neoliberal governance and report on promising approaches to scaling the model. The focus is firmly on collective experimentation, including how experimentation might change the valuation of labor in the sector.

Chapter 13, by Alysa Hannon, Heather McKay, and Michelle Van Noy, critically assesses the role of education and training in the changing labor market. The infrastructure for skills development in the United States is complicated and involves a myriad of systems, institutions, government agencies, and policies that are all heavy influenced by employers operating within a liberal market economy. After reviewing the conceptual parameters of skilling in the United States, the authors highlight key strategies that can promote worker interests within the country's existing systems and empower workers to better buffer against the challenges of the liberal economy's labor market.

In the final chapter, Tobias Schulze-Cleven looks toward the future. Rather than further summarizing the volume, he takes stock of the book as a product of the contemporary American academy and reflects on how labor studies can help enlist public research universities in support of building a human-centered future of work. As the chapter emphasizes, American universities have long been intricate bundles of contradictions, but recent trends have left them at a crossroads: Will they be able to reform and connect with a progressive reading of the original land-grant vision to support a future in the interest of workers? Or will their practices further drift away from a public-serving mission as they succumb to neoliberal expectations? Schulze-Cleven contends that the three constitutive features of labor studies illuminate crucial steps for realizing the much-needed innovations in higher education that can support the revaluation agenda developed in this volume.

We hope that this volume can serve as inspiration for broadening the debate on the future of work and re-centering it around people's needs. As the contributions to the book elaborate, labor studies provides fruitful guidance on *how* to do so. With its interdisciplinary and normatively anchored focus on the struggles of working people, the field can help publicly engaged scholarship deliver on its promises to support social change. We encourage readers to join the conversation.

ENDNOTES

1. Public discourses have also shown little recognition of how children, and appropriate care for them, sustain the long-term well-being of even the childless. The latter would not be able to receive pensions if it were not for children-turned-workers paying into public pay-as-you-go systems or using their purchasing power to sustain the corporate profits and stock-market valuations that ensure annual returns in private funded systems.

2. We thank Adam Seth Litwin for this point.

REFERENCES

Anderson, Elizabeth. 2017. *Private Government*. Princeton, NJ: Princeton University Press.

Anner, Mark, Nicolas Pons-Vignon, and Uma Rani. 2019. "For a Future of Work with Dignity: A Critique of the World Bank Development Report, *The Changing Nature of Work*." *Global Labour Journal* 10 (1): 2–19.

Ansell, Ben. 2014. "The Political Economy of Ownership: Housing Markets and the Welfare State." *American Political Science Review* 108 (2): 383–402.

Aronoff, Kate, Alyssa Battistoni, Daniel Aldana Cohen, and Thea Riofrancos. 2019. *A Planet to Win: Why We Need a Green New Deal*. New York, NY: Verso.

Baccaro, Lucio, and Jonas Pontusson. 2016. "Rethinking Comparative Political Economy: The Growth Model Perspective." *Politics & Society* 44 (2): 175–207.

Baldwin, Richard 2016. *The Great Convergence: Information Technology and the New Globalization*. Cambridge, MA: Harvard University Press.

Balleisen, Edward, and David A. Moss, eds. 2010. *Governments and Markets: Toward a New Theory of Regulation*. New York, NY: Cambridge University Press.

Baradaran, Mehrsa. 2017. *The Color of Money: Black Banks and the Racial Wealth Gap*. Cambridge, MA: Harvard University Press.

Bargain, Olivier, Mathias Dolls, Herwig Immervoll, Dirk Neumann, Andreas Peichl, Nico Pestel, and Sebastian Siegloch. 2015. "Tax Policy and Income Inequality in the United States, 1979–2007." *Economic Inquiry* 53 (2): 1061–1085.

Berman, Elizabeth Popp. Forthcoming. *Thinking Like an Economist: How Economics Became the Language of U.S. Public Policy*. Princeton, NJ: Princeton University Press.

Berman, Sheri. 2006. *The Primacy of Politics: Social Democracy and the Making of Europe's Twentieth Century*. New York, NY: Cambridge University Press.

Bhattacharya, Tithi, ed. 2017. *Social Reproduction Theory: Remapping Class, Recentering Oppression*. London, UK: Pluto Press.

Bivens, Josh, and Ben Zipperer. 2020. "Health Insurance and the COVID-19 Shock." Report. Washington, DC: Economic Policy Institute.

Bjurström, Andreas, and Merritt Polk. 2011. "Physical and Economic Bias in Climate Change Research: A Scientometric Study of IPCC Third Assessment Report." *Climatic Change* 108: 1–22.

Block, Fred, and Margaret R. Somers. 2014. *The Power of Market Fundamentalism*. Cambridge, MA: Harvard University Press.

Boushey, Heather. 2019. *Unbound: How Inequality Constricts Our Economy and What We Can Do About It*. Cambridge, MA: Harvard University Press.

Briggs, Laura. 2017. *How All Politics Became Reproductive Politics: From Welfare Reform to Foreclosure to Trump*. Berkeley, CA: University of California Press.

Britton-Purday, Jedediah, David Singh Grewal, Amy Kapczynski, and K. Sabeel Rahman. 2020. "Building a Law-and-Political Economy Framework: Beyond the Twentieth-Century Synthesis." *The Yale Law Journal* 29 (6): 1786–1835.

Brynjolfsson, Erik, and Andrew McAfee. 2014. *The Second Machine Age: Work, Progress, and Prosperity in a Time of Brilliant Technologies*. New York, NY: Norton.

Budd, John W. 2003. *Employment with a Human Face: Balancing Efficiency, Equity and Voice*. Ithaca, NY: Cornell University Press.

Case, Anne, and Angus Deaton. 2020. *Deaths of Despair and the Future of Capitalism*. Princeton, NJ: Princeton University Press.

Chamberlain, James A. 2018. *Undoing Work, Rethinking Community*. Ithaca, NY: Cornell University Press.

Chwieroth, Jeffrey M., and Andrew Walter. 2019. *The Wealth Effect: How the Great Expectations of the Middle Class Have Changed the Politics of Banking Crises*. New York, NY: Cambridge University Press.

Cramer, Katherine J. 2016. *The Politics of Resentment: Rural Consciousness in Wisconsin and the Rise of Scott Walker*. Chicago, IL: University of Chicago Press.

Dahl, Robert. 1985. *A Preface to Economic Democracy*. Berkeley, CA: University of California Press.

Desmond, Matthew. 2016. *Evicted: Poverty and Profit in the American City*. New York, NY: Crown.

Ferreras, Isabelle, Dominique Méda, and Julie Battilana et al. 2020 (May 15). "Work: Democratize, Decommodify, Remediate." Op-ed published in 43 newspapers in 36 countries. https://democratizingwork.org

Frankel, Boris. 2018. *Fictions of Sustainability: The Politics of Growth and Post-Capitalist Futures*. Melbourne, Australia: Greenmeadows.

Fraser, Nancy. 2016. "Contradictions of Capital and Care." *New Left Review* 100 (July/Aug): 99–117.

Frey, Carl Benedikt. 2019. *The Technology Trap: Capital, Labor, and Power in the Age of Automation*. Princeton, NJ: Princeton University Press.

Frey, Carl Benedikt, and Michael A. Osborne. 2013. "The Future of Employment: How Susceptible Are Jobs to Computerization?" Working Paper. Oxford, UK: Department of Engineering Science, University of Oxford.

Galbraith, James K. 2012. *Inequality and Instability*. New York, NY: Oxford University Press.

Galvin, Daniel J. 2019. "From Labor Law to Employment Law: The Changing Politics of Workers' Rights." *Studies in American Political Development* 33 (1): 50–86.

Gidron, Noam, and Peter A. Hall. 2020. "Populism as a Problem of Social Integration." *Comparative Political Studies* 53 (7): 1027–1059.

Goldin, Claudia, and Lawrence F. Katz. 2008. *The Race Between Education and Technology*. Cambridge, MA: Harvard University Press.

Groeger, Lena V. 2020. "What Coronavirus Job Losses Reveal About Racism in America." *ProPublica*. https://bit.ly/2ODJ9qj

Gupta, Sarita, Stephen Lerner, and Joseph A. McCartin. 2018 (Aug. 31). "It's Not the 'Future of Work,' It's the Future of Workers That's in Doubt." *The American Prospect*. https://bit.ly/3vF5JiL

Hacker, Jacob S. 2019. *The Great Risk Shift: The New Economic Insecurity and the Decline of the American Dream*, 2nd ed. New York, NY: Oxford University Press.

Hacker, Jacob S., and Paul Pierson. 2010. *Winner-Take-All Politics: How Washington Made the Rich Richer and Turned Its Back on the Middle Class*. New York, NY: Simon & Schuster.

Hacker, Jacob S., and Paul Pierson. 2020. *Let Them Eat Tweets: How the Right Rules in an Age of Extreme Inequality*. New York, NY: Liveright.

Hall, Peter A. 2013. "The Political Origins of Our Economic Discontents." In *Politics in the New Hard Times*, edited by Miles Kahler and David A. Lake, pp. 129–149. Ithaca, NY: Cornell University Press.

Hemerijck, Anton, ed. 2017. *The Uses of Social Investment*. Oxford, UK: Oxford University Press.

Hochschild, Arlie, with Anne Machung. (1989) 2012. *The Second Shift: Working Families and the Revolution at Home*, rev. ed. London, UK: Penguin.

Holder, Michelle. 2020. "The 'Double Gap' and the Bottom Line: African American Women's Gap and Corporate Profits." Report. New York, NY: The Roosevelt Institute.

Intergovernmental Panel on Climate Change. 2013. "Climate Change 2013: The Physical Science Basis." Fifth Assessment Report of the Intergovernmental Panel on Climate Change. Cambridge, UK: Cambridge University Press.

International Energy Agency. 2017. *World Energy Investment 2017*. Paris, France: Organisation for Economic Co-operation and Development.

Johnson, Walter. 2018 (Feb. 20). "To Remake the World: Slavery, Racial Capitalism, and Justice." *Boston Review*.

Jones, William P. 2020. "The Dignity of Labor." *Dissent* 67 (3): 93–96.

Kalleberg, Arne L. 2018. *Precarious Lives: Job Insecurity and Well-Being in Rich Democracies*. Cambridge, UK: Polity.

Katznelson, Ira. 2005. *When Affirmative Action Was White*. New York, NY: Norton.

Kobayashi, Michiko. 2020 (Jul. 20). "Service Workers Are Still Undervalued During Coronavirus." *The Philadelphia Inquirer*.

Kochan, Thomas A., and Lee Dyer. 2017. *Shaping the Future of Work: A Handbook for Action and A New Social Contract*. Cambridge, MA: MIT Press.

Korpi, Walter, and Joakim Palme. 1998. "The Paradox of Redistribution and Strategies for Equality: Welfare State Institutions, Inequality, and Poverty in the Western Countries." *American Sociological Review* 63 (5): 661–687.

Kristof, Nicholas. 2020 (Sep. 9). "We're No. 28! And Dropping!" *New York Times*.

Lasswell, Harold. (1936) 1958. *Politics: Who Gets What, When, How*. New York, NY: Meridian.

Latour, Bruno. 2018. *Down to Earth: Politics in the New Climate Regime*. Cambridge, UK: Polity.

Lazonick, William. 2018 (Jun. 25). "The Curse of Stock Buybacks." *American Prospect*.

Leibenluft, Jacob. 2020 (Aug. 19). "The Pandemic Hurts Countries That Don't Value Workers." *Foreign Affairs*.

Levitzky, Steven, and Daniel Ziblatt. 2018. *How Democracies Die*. New York, NY: Crown.

Lewis, Jane. 1992. "Gender and the Development of Welfare Regimes." *Journal of European Social Policy* 2 (3): 159–173.

Lührmann, Anna, Seraphine F. Maerz, Sandra Grahn, Nazifa Alizada, Lisa Gastaldi, Sebastian Hellmeier, Garry Hindle, and Staffan I. Lindberg. 2020. "Autocratization Surges—Resistance Grows." Democracy Report 2020. Gothenburg, Sweden: Varieties of Democracy Institute.

MacGillis, Alec. 2020 (Jun. 3). "How Germany Saved Its Workforce from Unemployment While Spending Less per Person Than the U.S." *ProPublica.*

Mair, Peter. 2013. *Ruling the Void: The Hollowing of Western Democracy.* London, UK: Verso.

Mazzucato, Mariana. 2015. *The Entrepreneurial State.* New York, NY: PublicAffairs.

Mishel, Lawrence, and Jori Kandra. 2020 (Aug. 18). "CEO Compensation Surged 14% in 2019 to $21.3 Million." Report. Washington, DC: Economic Policy Institute.

Morgan, Jennifer L. 2004. *Laboring Women: Reproduction and Gender in New World Slavery.* Philadelphia, PA: University of Pennsylvania Press.

Müller, Torsten, and Thorsten Schulten. 2020. "Ensuring Fair Short-Time Work—A European Overview." Policy Brief 7/2020. Brussels, Belgium: European Trade Union Institute.

Negt, Oskar. 2002. *Arbeit und Menschliche Würde.* Göttingen, Germany: Steidl.

Offe, Claus. 2010. "Inequality and the Labor Market—Theories, Opinions, Models, and Practices of Unequal Distribution and How They Can be Justified." *Zeitschrift für Arbeitsmarktforschung (Journal for Labour Market Research)* 43: 39–52.

Parreñas, Rhacel Salazar. 2015. *Servants of Globalization: Migration and Domestic Work,* 2nd ed. Stanford, CA: Stanford University Press.

Peetz, David. 2019. *The Realities and Futures of Work.* Canberra, Australia: Australian National University Press.

Pettit, Becky. 2012. *Invisible Men: Mass Incarceration and the Myth of Black Progress.* New York, NY: Russell Sage Foundation.

Philippon, Thomas. 2019. *The Great Reversal: How America Gave Up on Free Markets.* Cambridge, MA: Harvard University Press.

Pistor, Katharina. 2019. *The Code of Capital: How the Law Creates Wealth and Inequality.* Princeton, NJ: Princeton University Press.

Piven, Frances Fox, and Richard Cloward. 1971. *Regulating the Poor.* New York, NY: Pantheon.

Polanyi, Karl. (1944) 2001. *The Great Transformation.* Boston, MA: Beacon Press.

Purdy, Jedediah. 2015. *After Nature: A Politics for the Anthropocene.* Cambridge, MA: Harvard University Press.

Rothstein, Richard. 2017. *The Color of Law: A Forgotten History of How Our Government Segregated America.* New York, NY: Liveright.

Rothstein, Sidney A., and Tobias Schulze-Cleven. 2020. "Germany After the Social Democratic Century: The Political Economy of Imbalance." *German Politics* 29 (3): 297–318.

Schulze-Cleven, Tobias. 2018. "A Continent in Crisis: European Labor and the Fate of Social Democracy." *Labor Studies Journal* 43 (1): 46–73.

Sandel, Michael J. 2020. *The Tyranny of Merit: What's Become of the Common Good?* New York, NY: Farrar, Straus and Giroux.

Sennett, Richard. 1998. *The Corrosion of Character.* New York, NY: Norton.

Solow, Robert M. 1990. *The Labor Market as a Social Institution.* Oxford, UK: Basil Blackwell.

Sperling, Gene. 2019. "Economic Dignity." *Democracy: A Journal of Ideas* 52 (Spring).

Stiglitz, Joseph E. 2013. *The Price of Inequality: How Today's Divided Society Endangers Our Future.* New York, NY: Norton.

Streeck, Wolfgang. 2016. *How Will Capitalism End? Essays on a Failing System*. London, UK: Verso.

Susskind, Richard, and Daniel Susskind. 2015. *The Future of the Professions: How Technology Will Transform the Work of Human Experts*. Oxford, UK: Oxford University Press.

Teles, Steven M. 2010. *The Rise of the Conservative Legal Movement*. Princeton, NJ: Princeton University Press.

Thelen, Kathleen. 2019. "The American Precariat: U.S. Capitalism in Comparative Perspective." *Perspectives on Politics* 17 (1): 5–27.

US Global Change Research Program. 2017. *Climate Change Impacts in the United States*. Fourth National Climate Assessment. https://nca2018.globalchange.gov/

Vachon, Todd E. 2021. "Skin in the Game: The Struggle Over Climate Protection Within the U.S. Labor Movement." In *Anti-Environmental Handbook*, edited by David Tindall, Mark C.J. Stoddart, and Riley E. Dunlap. Cheltenham, UK: Edward Elgar.

Vachon, Todd E., Gerry Hudson, Judith LeBlanc, and Saket Soni. 2019 (Sep. 2). "How Workers Can Demand Climate Justice." *The American Prospect*.

Vachon, Todd E., Michael Wallace, and Allen Hyde. 2016. "Union Decline in a Neoliberal Age: Globalization, Financialization, Regionalization, and Union Density in Eighteen Affluent Democracies." *Socius: Sociological Research for a Dynamic World* 2 (Jan.).

Van Parijs, Philippe. 1995. *Real Freedom for All: What (If Anything) Can Justify Capitalism?* Oxford, UK: Oxford University Press.

Walker, Hannah. 2020. *Mobilized by Injustice: Criminal Justice Contact, Political Participation, and Race*. New York, NY: Oxford University Press.

Wallerstein, Immanuel. 2001. *The End of the World As We Know It*. Minneapolis, MN: University of Minnesota Press.

Wallerstein, Immanuel, Randall Collins, Michael Mann, Georgi Derluguian, and Craig Calhoun. 2013. *Does Capitalism Have a Future?* Oxford, UK: Oxford University Press.

White, Deborah Gray. (1985) 1999. *Ar'n't I a Woman? Female Slaves in the Plantation South*, 2nd ed. New York, NY: Norton.

Zalasiewicz, Jan, Mark Williams, Will Steffen, and Paul Crutzen. 2010. "The New World of the Anthropocene." *Environmental Science and Technology* 44 (7) 2228–2231.

Chapter 2

Beyond Market Fundamentalism: A Labor Studies Perspective on the Future of Work

Tobias Schulze-Cleven

Rutgers University

ABSTRACT

The debate about how to build a desirable and sustainable future of work appears stuck. While skepticism of neoliberalism's emphasis on free markets and individual choices has grown, most contributions to the debate on the future of work remain denominated in the "market fundamentalism" codified in neoclassical economics. This chapter argues that the academic field of labor studies can provide much-needed new intellectual direction. With its focus on the struggles of working people, interdisciplinary inquiry, and upholding worker rights, labor studies brings a much better appreciation of the power of collective action and the role of politics to the debate. Both the analytical choices and normative commitments of labor studies are well aligned with the tasks looming ahead. The latter part of the chapter lays out the book's main arguments about revaluing work, the collective agency of workers, and innovations in reproductive work.

INTRODUCTION

The debate about how to build a desirable and sustainable future of work appears stuck. On the one hand, today's interconnected economic, political, and ecological crises have nurtured widespread skepticism of neoliberalism's uniform emphasis on the promises of free markets and individual choices. Policy makers' reliance on simplistic—and often deeply normative—notions offered by economists in support of such policies has attracted particular criticism (e.g., Appelbaum 2019; Skidelsky 2020). On the other hand, most contributions on the evolution of work remain denominated in the neoliberal terms codified in economic theories. This includes the assumption that markets and technology will determine—rather than merely effect—the looming reorganization of social life.

Of course, the influence of economics on policy making has neither been absolute nor direct, given that a plethora of mediating circumstances across countries has conditioned the discipline's intellectual guidance. Yet the increased professional authority of economists, their institutional positions in government, and the diffusion of their styles of reasoning have had a profound impact (Hirschman and Berman 2014). Perhaps most crucially, economists have even come to speak for leftist political parties, calling on them to overcome long-held skepticism of market-led policy solutions and to embrace neoliberal policies as "modern" and context-appropriate approaches (Mudge 2018)—often with disastrous consequences for these parties' electoral prospects.

In the United States, recent empirical research has led many progressive economists to abandon core neoliberal beliefs, and a growing number of them now readily admit that the discipline has been wrong to push neoliberal policy prescriptions (e.g., Krugman 2019; Romer 2020). Yet economics textbooks and mainstream discourse frequently fail to reflect these reservations. For instance, the nation's best-selling introductory textbook flatly asserts neoliberal mantras without any qualifications, from the supposed trade-off between equity and efficiency to the negative effects of government redistribution on economic growth (Mankiw 2015: 5). This flies in the face of empirical realities, including the positive association between higher taxes at the top of the income distribution and faster growth across countries (Boushey 2020).

What guiding ideas can take the place of neoliberal assumptions, and what academic research can governments turn to in order to build a sustainable and inclusive future of work—i.e., one that is actually desirable for workers and thus for citizens? Credible alternatives, or at least complements, to economic theories are needed to loosen and potentially dislodge neoliberalism's hold on contemporary thinking about work, the economy, and their evolution. Without alternatives, there is little reason to think that neoliberalism's contemporary resilience will diminish (Schmidt and Thatcher 2013). The American debate certainly points in this dispiriting direction. Mainstream contributions generally fail to appreciate the role played by neoliberalism in facilitating populist plutocracy and have little to say on what it would take to keep democracy from fully degenerating into oligarchy (Purdy 2018; Winters 2011).

This chapter argues that the academic field of labor studies can provide intellectual direction. With its focus on the struggles of working people, interdisciplinary inquiry, and upholding the rights of workers, labor studies brings a much better appreciation of the power of collective action and the role of politics to the debate on the future of work. All social scientific analyses are selective in terms of the questions they ask, the data they interrogate, and the type of abstractions they strive for, which means that they highlight, even prioritize, some parts of a complex social reality over others (e.g., Immergut 1998). I contend that both the analytical choices and normative commitments of labor studies are well aligned with the challenges looming ahead.

In support of this contention, the chapter spells out the essential contribution of labor studies in three steps. A first section recounts the rise of neoliberalism and economics to illustrate the influence of ideas on policy making and to make the case for unchaining the future of work from the market fundamentalism that neoliberalism and economics have promoted. The second section presents labor studies as the source of an alternative set of ideas that comes with unique advantages for understanding what needs to go into building a democratic and sustainable future of work that delivers on workers' interests. A concluding third section builds on the preceding analysis to elaborate the volume's main arguments.

UNCHAINING THE FUTURE FROM MARKET FUNDAMENTALISM

While neoliberalism is an ideology and economics is a social science discipline, they share a commitment to the efficient management of scarce resources through markets, which generally means opposing collective political decision making that could undercut market efficiency. This joint normative vision has fundamentally shaped the world of work globally over the past few decades and now acts as a powerful constraint on a future of work that would address societies' interlocking ecological, political, and economic crises. This section sketches the historical trajectory of these ideas, before delving into three key hurdles that prevent many mainstream economists from productively engaging in the debate over building a democratic and sustainable future.

The Historical Trajectory of Neoliberalism

The main promulgators of 20th-century neoliberal thought borrowed heavily from Adam Smith, the 18th-century moral philosopher turned father of economics. According to Smith, free markets would challenge what he saw as the unwarranted political privileges and restrictions of feudalism. Allowing for a greater degree of specialization and a deeper division of labor, markets would provide greater opportunities on the individual level and promote the wealth of nations by aggregating individuals' self-interested decisions. Neoliberals turned Smith's arguments against the democratic welfare states and international institutions built after World War II. When progressive policy makers defended regulatory limits on markets' reach and devised Keynesian macroeconomic management in the name of serving the "common good" and the "public interest," neoliberals like August Friedrich von Hayek and Milton Friedman diagnosed political overreach and collusion. While Smith had objected to the monarchically sponsored monopolies of chartered trading companies, 20th-century neoliberals were skeptical of the organizational power wielded by both public authorities and labor unions.

As the post-war Keynesian regime ran into long-predicted trouble during the 1970s, with businesses rebelling against workers' newfound power that the full-employment strategies of governments had provided (Kalecki 1943), right-wing reformers successfully called on neoliberal ideas and popularized them in the political mainstream. In the words of Ronald Reagan, government was the problem not the solution. Britain's Margaret Thatcher was arguably the most outspoken critic of Keynesianism's worker-friendly policies. Thatcher stated flatly that there was no such thing as society, only individual men and women and families, thus denying the existence of the collectivity whose interests had motivated policy makers' post-war quest to more extensively flank the economic sphere with institutions of social protection.

The diffusion of neoliberal ideas has not been uniform, but labor market reforms were soon adopted across countries, as were broader deregulatory initiatives launched to spur economic adaptability (e.g., Schulze-Cleven, Watson, and Zysman 2007; Schulze-Cleven and Weishaupt 2015). Where the collective has remained a reference point, the relationships of individuals to it have been deeply transformed. While post-war welfare states had emphasized society's obligation to sustain individuals' well-being by expanding social citizenship, contemporary neoliberal discourses tend to stress the responsibilities of individuals to support their country's global competitiveness (Lessenich 2008).

Modern Economics Arrives

Economics itself moved quickly beyond Smith's underspecified notion of markets working as if an "invisible hand" led them. By the late 19th century, the outlines of neoclassical economics were established. This approach spells out with mathematical precision how—in a hypothetical state of "perfect competition"— variable prices can match supply and demand in market equilibria. This matching process, neoclassical theory argues, maximizes the utility of all (rational and self-interested) participants, given their preferences and resource endowments. According to the theory, an equilibrium price equals both a purchaser's marginal benefit and a seller's marginal cost. In the labor market, this translates into workers' wages representing their individual productivity rather than the results of bargaining processes.

In terms of assessing the worth of goods and services, the neoclassical approach decidedly breaks with the labor theory of value of classical economists. Embracing a thin utilitarian theory of worth, it views value as entirely subjective, expressed in the prices of transactions that themselves are a function of scarcity and individual preferences. No judgment of an activity's worth for the collective is necessary, given that outcomes are treated as revealed preferences, and the value of collective economic activity—including its growth—can be easily captured through the aggregation of transactions as the gross domestic product.

By the mid-20th century, a new neoclassical synthesis incorporated the macroeconomic insights of John Maynard Keynes. While this codification of knowledge further marginalized nonmathematical analyses, including the institutional tradition, it did not mean that disagreements had been removed from the discipline.[1] Yet whatever the discipline's shifting controversies were, they never cast doubt on the neoclassical model's main propositions, which meant that introductory economics courses could forcefully advance the case for the power of markets. Serious discussion of the long list of unrealistic assumptions underlying the neoclassical model (and, in particular, its general equilibrium formulation)—including a timeless economy with unlimited future markets, the ability of companies to flexibly adjust labor–capital ratios in production (i.e., the differentiability of the production function), complete information, and perennial full employment—became relegated to advanced courses. Moreover, when theorizing got a bit closer to real-life markets, such as with respect to the "non-accelerating inflation rate of unemployment," this did not appear to undercut economists' faith in neoclassical meta-theory. Notwithstanding the fictional character of the theoretical edifice provided by modern economics, right-wing politicians easily mobilized it to bolster their criticism of "labor market rigidities" and to promote deregulation.

The Left Turns to Neoliberalism

When progressives eventually embraced neoliberalism during the 1990s, they did so under the banner of offering a third way between popular neoliberal conservatism and old styles of socialism that had become further delegitimated by the fall of the Soviet Union. Intellectually, they drew from economists' theories about human capital, flanked by some reliance on endogenous growth theory, which offered a way out of the dual obstacles the left was facing by the end of the 20th century. In the realm of policy, the leaders of leftist parties were looking to maintain welfare state generosity and avoid the type of retrenchment that the right was implementing, even as progressives themselves came to think that fiscal expenditures had little room to grow. Moreover, politically, they were searching for ways to expand electoral support beyond the shrinking working-class vote, which deindustrialization and the weakening of unions had undermined, and to appeal to voters from the middle class, many of whom were more skeptical of redistribution because of their own wider asset ownership (Hall 2020).

Emphasizing the skill biases of technological change, human capital theory offers the expansion of education as the primary way to contain rising economic inequality in the context of increasingly knowledge-based capitalism. For the optimists on the left, this education-focused path promised to turn the tables on workers and companies, empowering individuals to have companies compete over them and enlisting the process of capital accumulation for the benefit of workers (Andersson 2010). Yet this modernization strategy also entailed significant shifts away from traditional social democratic conceptions of human progress, including moving to equate cultural and social values with economic ones, as third-way reformers embraced markets as the primary means of sociocultural inclusion and encouraged workers to conceive of themselves primarily as entrepreneurs focused on leveraging individual human capital (Bröckling 2015).

Assessing Neoliberalism's Impact

In hindsight, the limits of the left's neoliberal strategy are striking. Third-way reforms sought to support workers able to compete in the knowledge economy, but they had little to offer to workers who could not. Plans to socialize at least part of the costs associated with investments in human capital often fell short, and companies soon discovered that human capital was available around the world—often at lower cost than in the advanced democracies (Brown, Lauder, and Ashton 2011). Workers unable to compete increasingly fell behind, and many began to support right-wing populist parties and movements.

Moreover, just when the education sector was supposed to empower workers for successful market-based competition, policy makers increased the role of markets in the governance of higher education (Schulze-Cleven 2020). This produced "varieties of academic capitalism," which shifted power to individuals with the highest endowments of financial and human capital (Schulze-Cleven and Olson 2017). While the prospect of improved living standards for the next generation has dimmed for many workers, the marketization of education has left members of the financial elite with expanded "neo-feudal" opportunities to transfer their economic status to their offspring via the purchase of educational credentials (Schulze-Cleven, Reitz, Maesse, and Angermuller 2017). Unsurprisingly, parts of the left moved away from neoliberalism as the negative feedback of third-way reforms became evident, yet no agreement on how to re-regulate the economy or reconnect with former voters has emerged.

The impact of neoliberal thinking has been remarkable over the past half a century. Providing a new "software" to run the economy's "hardware," neoliberal ideas have starkly recast processes of market allocation (Blyth 2019). Most economists have tended to encourage this reorientation, whether it was policy makers' move from demand management to supply-side strategies, their abandonment of unemployment prevention in favor of inflation minimization, or their attempts to leverage liberalizing and assets-focused reforms—not just in education but in pension and housing policies as well—for encouraging workers to think more like capitalists. As an epistemic community, economists have had less to say about the distributional consequences of these decisions, given that the discipline has no conception of social relations beyond markets, generally ignores the role of ideas, and defines away social conflict (e.g., Rodrik 2015).

Barriers to Productive Engagement in a Debate on the Future

Economics continues to evolve, of course. Some high-profile economists have pushed hard against the limitations of their own discipline, emphasizing the role of democratic decision making in setting limits to market rule and containing increased inequalities (e.g., Banerjee and Duflo 2019; Stiglitz 2020). Innovation in teaching is particularly pronounced, with efforts to place abstract theories in real-world contexts, including the 2007–08 global financial crisis. In research, moreover, there is growing recognition that the entire edifice of modern macroeconomic policy is rather unstable, with scholars revisiting long-standing theories about fiscal and monetary levers (e.g., Blanchard and Summers 2019).

Nevertheless, the ontological and epistemological conventions of economics continue to contribute to a truncated debate on the future of work. First, and particularly problematic, some economists still aim to establish the total primacy of markets in social relations and erase all notions of the "social" (and the "political"). Practically, they seek to turn the fictional—and arguably dystopian—neoclassical model from a benchmark device for positive analysis into a normative framework that "messy" real life should approximate (Ackerman and Beggs 2013). One prominent voice recently presented this position as a "just deserts" perspective that aims to ensure workers' compensation "congruent with their contributions" and restricts government interventions to cases of market imperfections that prevent any individual earning exactly "the value of his or her own marginal product" (Mankiw 2013: 32).

Second, and more broadly, what is considered knowledge in the discipline continues to be tilted to what can be theorized through formalization in mathematical models, a phenomenon that Paul Krugman long ago described as the "remarkable extent to which the methodology of economics creates blind spots" (Krugman 1993: 26). Debate about the sources of global patterns of inequality—slowly decreasing among countries and rapidly rising within them as divergences between classes become more pronounced (Milanovic 2016)—is a powerful case in point. For instance, even after Krugman had modeled how the presence of increasing returns could undermine neoclassical theories of international trade, he fervently criticized nonmathematical analyses of trade policy that diverged from neoclassical conceptions (Krugman 1996). Only recently did Krugman admit that he was wrong on the benefits of free trade, and he now acknowledges the drawbacks of globalized markets. Rather than trade, economists emphasized technological change as a source of inequality, a reading that far better fit with the neoclassical reference model, even as evidence against it was mounting (Lauder, Brown, and Cheung 2018). Some economists have admittedly come around to acknowledging the importance of political decisions, including steps taken to weaken unions (Stansbury and Summers 2020). Yet this recognition appears largely limited to empirical analysis, making few inroads into theorizing.

Third, the discipline's narrow scope of analysis inhibits its ability to build knowledge over time in other ways as well. One important mechanism for such reduced capacity operates through the types of researchers that the discipline attracts and promotes, and the subset of research questions and empirical domains that the profession sees as relevant for the highest-profile journals. Centrally, the American economics discipline has long been overwhelmingly White and male. For instance, only about 20 of the more than 9,000 full professors of economics in the United States are Black (Child and Duffin 2020). The challenges associated with contemporary social selectivity were widely reported in the case of Lisa Cook, who sought to publish an article in a leading peer-reviewed journal about how violence had affected the filing of patents by Black Americans (Cook 2014). Not only did the process of placing her piece take a decade, it also exhibited her colleagues' restricted knowledge of history and required interventions from disciplinary leaders (Child and Duffin 2020). It appears that this "social" constraint on the discipline's aggregation of knowledge contributes to a less than steady process of continually challenging long-standing principles in the discipline.

Having elaborated the far-reaching influence and analytical limits of neoliberalism and economics, it is now time to turn to labor studies as an alternative source of ideas that proceeds from, rather than sidelines, the social realities of economic exchange.

THE UNIQUE ADVANTAGES OF LABOR STUDIES

The advantages of labor studies for clarifying and guiding how to move toward a democratic and sustainable future stem from the field's particular focus. In contrast to the organization of economics around the goal of maximizing efficiency, labor studies seeks to understand the experiences of working people, which it tackles through interdisciplinary inquiry and with a commitment to upholding worker rights. By challenging disciplinary biases stemming from the interdependence of theorizing and methodology, and by being explicit about its normative agenda, labor studies has the potential to provide a truly transformative understanding of work. Given the field's integrated, problem-focused and context-sensitive lens, it is well prepared to counter the increased uncertainty of the 21st century, allowing us to more clearly see the political and organizational challenges lying ahead. This section first provides some background on the history of labor studies, then discusses the field's main features and particular benefits for thinking about the future of work and its human impact.

A Short History of Labor Studies

As an interdisciplinary field, labor studies is naturally a broader tent than any specific social science discipline, particularly compared to the narrow grounding of economics in the neoclassical core. At times, the phrase "labor studies" is used so widely that the focus of the field might appear fuzzy.[2] Briefly skimming academic journals that carry the phrase in their titles around the world shows great variety, including labor economics and labor education, as well as both nationally specific and comparative analyses. Given this diversity, there are many ways to write the history of the subject and distill its essence.

From a North American vantage point, the field has strong roots in labor and worker education, first British and Danish, then later American, with US universities offering night-school classes since the late 19th century and more specialized innovative institutions being founded in the 1920s (Dwyer 1977; Gray 1966). The industrial relations programs launched on the heels of World War II to promote labor–management cooperation provided the immediate institutional context for the development of labor studies—e.g., Harvard in 1942; Berkeley, Cornell, Illinois, Minnesota, Rutgers, and UCLA between 1945 and 1947; and Indiana and Michigan in the 1950s (Wong, no date). These programs offered worker education in addition to, and sometimes in collaboration with, trainings that unions were running themselves.

Labor studies arguably came into its own in the United States during the 1960s, with the first graduate program launched at the University of Massachusetts in 1965 and the first undergraduate degree at Rutgers starting in 1967 (Dwyer 1977: 199). Social mobilization for civil rights, the federal government's sponsorship of the expansion of higher education, and academic professionals' rising power within universities arguably provided crucial background conditions for the field's emergence (e.g., Jencks and Riesman 1968). Parts of society increasingly recognized human differences, and universities moved to credential knowledge about how such differences were associated with distinct life experiences. While labor studies focused on the effects of class, other new fields such as Black studies or Hispanic studies explored those of race (Dwyer 1977: 198).

Labor studies thus represented more than simply the "academization" of labor education, as one critic insinuated (Lieberthal 1977). In addition to a stronger academic professionalization of the faculty, the birth of labor studies included a clear shift in emphasis away from the utilitarian "tool" courses offered in university labor education and extension departments at the time. Instead, labor studies embraced a liberal arts approach that sought to integrate knowledge from a range of (mostly social science) disciplines about the "nature of work, those who work, and the organizations they create to advance and defend their interests" (Dwyer 1977: 201). In its normative orientation toward advancing "industrial justice," moreover, labor studies set itself apart from the neighboring field of industrial relations, which focused more on functional cooperation across the class divide and remained dominated by institutional economists (Dwyer, Galvin, and Larson 1977).

By the mid-1970s, labor studies had experienced substantial growth, including at community colleges, with certificates and degree programs being offered at 43 institutions (Gray 1976: 35). The *Labor Studies Journal* launched in spring

1976. Arguably, the declining strength of American unions eventually weighed on the development of the field domestically (Parsons 1990), and there has been some organizational consolidation that more closely linked labor studies and labor education, as well as university-based and union-run programs. Specifically, since 2000, the United Association for Labor Education (UALE) has brought together labor educators from universities and unions, with the *Labor Studies Journal* acting as the UALE's official scholarly outlet. At the same time, the field successfully developed new audiences. While labor studies course offerings were initially aimed at working adults with union backgrounds, they today attract many younger students as well.

One area of labor studies where there has been substantial recent growth is cross-nationally comparative and even truly global research (Brookes and McCallum 2017; Burawoy 2009). Building on such path-breaking scholarship as Beverly Silver's study of shifting global patterns of labor unrest since 1870, contributors to global labor studies have produced in-depth research on workers' experimentation with new ways to build labor power and renew their agency repertoires in different parts of the world (Eaton, Schurman, and Chen 2017; Silver 2003). Occurring in parallel with the rise of "global labor history" (van der Linden 2012), the expansion of global labor studies has benefited from support by the International Sociological Association's research committee on "Labour Movements" (RC44). Another organizational pillar has been the Global Labour University—a network of trade unions, universities, the Friedrich Ebert Foundation, and the International Labour Organisation—that offers MA-level degrees in five different countries. Centered around the *Global Labour Journal*, the scholarly community of global labor studies is filling a space that had been left open by the disciplines. For instance, the political science subfield of international political economy has had little to say about labor, and it took the American Political Science Association's new organized section on "Class and Inequality" a while to embrace labor politics. At the same time, global labor studies appears to be consciously leveraging the particular advantages of specific disciplines, including wider and more analytically driven selection of cases, more conscious temporal anchoring, and broadened geographic reach (Schulze-Cleven, Herrigel, Lichtenstein, and Seidman 2017). Transnational labor alliances and the effects of transnational labor markets on worker strategies have been important recent themes, with the growth of precarity in the Global North providing an important linkage to long-standing patterns in the Global South (e.g., Brookes 2019; Mense-Petermann 2020).

Having briefly outlined the field of labor studies, let us now turn to the benefits of the field's core features for informing debate, policy, and scholarship on the future of work.

Working People at the Center of the Analysis

More than half a century after the first labor studies degrees were introduced in the United States, the field continues to focus on the experiences of working people, their shared struggles, and the organization of their collective voice— grounded in an appreciation of the social function of work (Budd 2011). Seeking to speak to people's "total labor effort" (Golatz 1977: 2), the field takes a holistic human-centered approach, examining both formal and informal, paid and unpaid work. The focus is on appreciating working people's lives in their complexity, paying attention to political, economic, and social contexts, and examining the governance processes through which workers are managed, empowered, and ultimately valued. This explicitly includes examining how workers make sense of their work situation and conceive of ways to change it, from individual strategies to collective efforts, whether through unions or other means.

Three aspects of this approach are particularly important for overcoming blind spots in the contemporary debate on the future of work and refocusing it on democracy and sustainability. The first is the ability of labor studies to speak directly to the perennial social question, which explores how to refashion formally free but substantially un(der)protected wage labor in the face of social crisis and heightened distributional conflict. While the social question is a product of the Enlightenment and the Industrial Revolution in the 18th and 19th centuries, it continues to be with us and poses itself forcefully for the future (Breman, Harris, Lee, and van der Linden 2019). Making substantive headway in addressing the drivers of contemporary economic instability, political backlash, and climate change turns significantly on improving protections for wage labor.

Historically, European nations were most successful in answering the social question during the 20th century, with pressure from industrial unions proving decisive for building genuine "welfare capitalism" that provided open-ended employment contracts and extensive public social protection programs (Castel 2003; Esping-Andersen 1990). Yet even this relatively successful strategy came with exclusionary tendencies domestically (such as on matters of gender and race) and internationally (e.g., encouraging brain drain from the Global South to the North). Moreover, the model has since lost much of its shine, as corporate strategies have shifted and former class compromises are becoming undone. Institutional retrenchment and drift (i.e., conscious cuts and the failure to update both public and in-work social protections to changing circumstances) have increased workers' precarity. The symptoms are widely known, including a declining wage share of GDP; the breaking apart of core features of long-term employer–worker relationships, as evidenced in the rise of outsourcing, self-employment, and gig work; increased contingency and a move to both part-time and fixed-term employment; and reduced coverage for collective bargaining.

The need for rethinking institutions at the work–welfare nexus has been clear for decades, yet private companies and state authorities have continued to shift financial responsibility for social risks onto the working population (Hacker 2019; Supiot 2001).

Apart from the very top of the income distribution, where wage growth has been strong, maintaining living standards has frequently depended on turning to cheap imports for consumption, which is a form of cost externalization given its frequent reliance on atrocious working and environmental conditions abroad (Lessenich 2016). Arguably, at this stage, the social question is not satisfactorily answered anywhere in the world. Recent experiences under COVID-19 and expectations of a K-shaped recovery from the pandemic-induced recession only further underline that. Moreover, as sectoral change has eroded strong industrial bases and working-class identities have become less coherent, weakened industrial unions alone are not able to push for the renewal of social contracts. Instead, new political pathways will have to be found to drive the resettlement of increasingly dysfunctional institutions—from workplace regulations and labor relations provisions to social security systems—across a variety of local contexts.

A second important benefit of the worker-centered approach taken by labor studies is that it reveals the contemporary crisis of social reproduction and the associated undervaluation of "reproductive work" in the United States. Paid and unpaid care work—which is one of the key forms of reproductive work—is a case in point. The closer one looks at the struggles of families unable to afford care and caregivers receiving poverty wages, the clearer become the individual and collective costs associated with the lack of a proper care infrastructure with paid parental leaves, public cost pooling, and regulated labor standards. In many cases, individuals and families simply cannot live up to the ever-greater expectations of personal responsibility that they have been tasked with under such slogans as "a hand up rather than a hand down" or an emphasis on "family values" (Cooper 2017; Mounk 2017). Attention to workers' lives on the ground also suggests that welfare state investment in expanding the care infrastructure is crucial for addressing the accumulation of multiple forms of disadvantage in the labor market for women, non-White populations and single parents (Mezzadri 2020). Yet the undervaluation of reproductive work is a broader phenomenon, and labor studies scholarship has made similar observations in other areas of reproductive work, from healthcare to education (e.g., Givan 2014).

Finally, there is a third advantage of the focus on working people: It reveals how the dynamics of workers' collective action are changing in response to contemporary gaps in worker representation (Rosenfeld 2019). In the context of lower union membership, the service economy, and the continued feminization of employment, and recognizing that racial and gender divisions frequently support processes of proletarianization, workers have increasingly embraced intersectional forms of organizing and solidarity that seek to build bridges with other social movements (Lee 2018; Tormos 2017). There is clear momentum among some parts of the labor movement to embrace a "noninstitutional strategy" of voice, focused on building "a mass movement that is broad, intersectional, yet ideologically coherent enough to replace postracial neoliberalism as the common sense of our times" (De Leon 2020: 8). At the same time, of course, there is innovation within more traditional institution-focused approaches. For instance, some unions seek to focus collective bargaining on the "common good" and broaden its reach toward whole sectors, as McCartin, Smiley, and Sneiderman review in their contribution to this volume.

An Interdisciplinary Lens

Since labor studies leverages tools from the entire breadth of the social sciences, it is conceptually more open than any particular discipline. Bringing to bear theoretical insights from quite different strands of academic inquiry allows for a deeper understanding of labor and work. One might even speak of labor studies as particularly—maybe even radically—empirical, not in the sense of being atheoretical but rather in terms of being committed to appreciating and addressing reality to the fullest degree possible.

Engagement across disciplines is an important corrective to any one particular discipline's conceptual biases. The goal of this engagement is explicitly not to displace disciplines, which rightly remain functionally differentiated pillars of the academic world by providing the main frames of reference for scientific inquiry and knowledge accumulation, as well as the reflexive interplay between scientific evolution and social organization (Stichweh 1984; Wagner, Wittrock, and Whitley 1991). But disciplinary discourse communities often operate with tight ontological and epistemological corsets that serve to defend and reinterpret an inevitable pattern of core principles (Abbott 2001; Heilbron 2004). With disciplines being less committed to any particular empirical realm, their mechanisms of control and foci of attention can translate into merely partial understandings of work and labor.

While labor studies thus provides more room for analytically eclectic approaches, drawing on the repertoires of various scholarly discourse communities to advance knowledge on work can be a conflictual process. Whenever scholars from different disciplines engage with each other, "tussles over turf" can be expected as the central terms of exchange are hammered out (Dixon 2020: 2). Yet with appropriate reflexivity about the distinct advantages of particular approaches, multidisciplinary scholarship can be an experience of mutual learning (Joas and Kippenberg 2005). The continual questioning and challenging of the appropriateness of particular preconceptions and assumptions can produce language that helps synthesize knowledge. Scholars of labor studies regularly engage in such efforts to bridge different theoretical camps—for instance with respect to comparative political economy, regulation theory, labor process theory, industrial relations, and global labor studies (e.g., Schulze-Cleven 2017; Vidal and Hauptmeier 2014).

There remain, however, untapped opportunities. For instance, the focus on workers' lives provides leverage to bring the humanities and social sciences more closely together, maybe even to push for a "rehumanization" of the social sciences through developing thicker theories of action that operate with a conception of worker interests as not just material but also ideational (e.g., Joas 2005). Whether it is Max Weber's humanistically informed historical sociology or works such as E.P. Thompson's analysis of the collective construction of working-class agency during British industrialization, there would be much to build on. Moreover, recent progress in comparative historical analysis bodes well for the successful pursuit of this agenda. As scholars have brought historians' sensibilities of the *long durée* to social science scholarship on cross-national similarities and differences in countries' welfare and employment regimes, they have significantly rethought causal processes in the world of work (e.g., Esping-Andersen 1990; Thelen 2014).

Crucially, with respect to debate about the future of work, labor studies can help elevate and integrate the work of economists who question their own discipline's mainstream. Alternatives to neoclassical conceptions of valuation—both in terms of process and goals—are a particularly important topic for which critiques of the neoclassical model by leading economists have laid important foundations (Stiglitz, Sen, and Fitoussi 2009). Fruitful cross-disciplinary engagement has since emerged on distinctions between value creation and value extraction, the role of nonmarket valuation processes in the face of existential ecological crisis, and the potential for post-growth or de-growth strategies (e.g., Gough 2020; Mazzucato 2018; Rosa and Henning 2018).

Finally, there is particular scope to engage Thomas Piketty and his collaborators, who have provided powerful new data on shifting patterns of income and wealth inequality (e.g., Alvaredo et al. 2018). Theoretically, Piketty's magisterial *Capital in the Twenty-First Century* challenges economists to think more broadly about markets and engage the dynamics of capitalism, in the context of which he argues that the long-term returns on capital exceed the long-term growth rate, thus structurally driving up inequality (Piketty 2014). In Piketty's recent follow-up, *Capital and Ideology*, he pushes even further beyond the conventions of the discipline by resolutely focusing on power and ideas (Piketty 2020). Delving into the changing ideologies that have driven the evolution of inequality throughout history, the volume makes the case for markets, profits, and capital not as natural but as historical constructs. He further identifies the struggles for equality and education as the main drivers of human history, not the establishment of property rights in pursuit of stability, as economists typically claim.

Scholars of labor studies would find much to agree with here, but a labor studies perspective would push Piketty's work further in at least three respects.

First, it would seek to draw more from other disciplinary approaches to arrive at the type of analysis that Piketty himself proposes—i.e., one that is "at once political and historical, multipolar and multidisciplinary" (Piketty 2020: viii). Deeper engagement with political science and greater attention to gender seem particularly important (Boushey 2020). Second, labor studies scholars would strive for a more realistic theory of change. Piketty hopes that better disaggregated measures of inequality can drive ideological renewal, which in turn could power a far more assertive social democracy to produce what he calls "participatory socialism" (Piketty 2020: 966). Yet, as contemporary responses to climate change highlight, hard evidence will barely suffice to shift the course in the face of winner-take-all dynamics and the decreasing legitimacy of political systems. Such a transformation will need a much better theory of collective action that addresses how diverse groups can cooperate at a time when institutional liberalization has reduced their capacity to do so (Ornston and Schulze-Cleven 2015). Finally, a labor studies perspective would move beyond a focus on reducing economic inequality to an emphasis on realizing substantive democracy. Strong labor organizations are important for pursuing this more encompassing goal, as illustrated by the association of declining union density with lower voter turnout, falling vote shares for progressive candidates, and reduced legislative responsiveness to the citizenry (Feigenbaum, Hertel-Fernandez, and Williamson 2018).

Anchoring in Normative Commitments

The third feature of labor studies to mention in terms of the field's power to inform debate on the future of work is its explicit commitment to upholding worker rights in the spirit of individual freedom, human dignity, and social justice. Given that the institutions for governing work are socially constructed and politically sanctioned, labor studies sees them as open to change through collective action. While the field acknowledges constraints, trade-offs, and conflicts in the quest to change governance systems, it emphasizes human beings' ability to remake their life worlds in line with particular goals. Two beliefs about how to implement substantive democracy anchor the field: work should be rewarding for all workers, and all workers should be able to exercise voice in the design of labor processes. In its focus on two kinds of rights, this normative grounding offers a stark contrast to the analytic focus in economics, which emphasizes usefulness over humanity and explores how market processes express differences in workers' purported marginal products through wage dispersion.

To some observers, concepts such as dignity and social justice might appear slippery, given that one could conceptualize them quite differently. Neoliberalism's progenitor Friedrich August von Hayek, for instance, thought of social justice as merely a "mirage" (Hayek 1976). Admittedly, there has been a proliferation of concepts that highlight different aspects of social justice, including economic justice, racial justice, intergenerational justice, and environmental justice. So, obviously, there are many considerations that would go into constructing a "just" solution to the valuation of any one worker's efforts. Yet Hayek's alternative of a "total market" is neither practical in the context of democracy nor free of normative preconceptions (Supiot 2012). Even economists operate with conceptions of "fairness" as spelled out in theorizing on "welfare economics." A key difference is that neoliberalism and economics tend to accept and proceed from the unequal distribution of resources, whereas labor studies is committed to realizing equality in core respects.

For labor studies, social justice is not merely an abstract principle but a substantive ambition about how human beings should be able to engage with real-world institutions. In that quest, labor studies focuses less on individual choices and more on how collectivities construct choices. This includes whether broader legal structures and labor market institutions provide human beings with the capacity to self-actualize based on their innate creativity rather than focus on turning individuals into human resources and human capital for the immediate productive use by corporations (Supiot 2012: 104–116). This particular attention allows labor studies to speak to the mediation of the social conflicts that are associated with the broader economic, political, and environmental crises faced by contemporary societies, and for which progress ultimately depends on engendering new forms of solidarity. This also includes addressing the challenges associated with overcoming institutionalized racism in the United States. In its focus on justice, labor studies has room both for arguments in favor of universal approaches to refashioning workers' social protections and for demands to address particular cumulative disadvantages through targeted initiatives.

Scholars of labor studies do not necessarily agree on how best to realize these normative commitments, but they tend to share a general sense of the necessary direction. In the spirit of scenario planning, or "envisioning real utopias," some have thought through particular reform pathways (Bregman 2017; Wright 2010). Expanding our imagination and defining potential prospective states of the world, these visions can be important guides for building the future and overcoming the limitations of past institutional settlements. Together with labor studies' other central tenets—placing workers at the center of analysis and embracing an interdisciplinary lens—the field's clear normative anchor can help policy makers better cope with contemporary uncertainty by facilitating rational problem solving. The world view of labor studies reduces complexity by defining clear priorities, which makes it possible to attach probabilities to particular future scenarios and turns an uncertain future into one with calculable risks (Blyth 2010).

TOWARD A FUTURE FOR WORKERS

As elaborated throughout this volume, a labor studies perspective on the future of work suggests a reorientation away from the strategies emphasized by neoliberal ideology and its purveyors in mainstream economics, and instead advocates for revaluing workers, exploring possibilities through collective agency, and appreciating reproductive work as a crucible of innovation. Below I elaborate on these three shifts.

Beyond Technology's Impact: Toward Revaluing Work(ers)

A labor studies lens suggests abandoning the almost singular focus in the current debate on the effects of technological change and instead paying more attention to strategies for revaluing work(ers). Undoubtedly, technology-facilitated automation has affected the task content of work and productivity growth (Acemoglu and Restrepo 2019). But this is a long-running story, and while it will continue in the future, its intensity might well have peaked already (Gordon 2016: 579). Methodological choices have arguably led to inflated predictions of technology's impact on job displacements (Arntz, Gregory, and Zierahn 2016). Moreover, technology is highly plastic, providing much room for users to shape and deploy it in different ways (e.g., Helper, Martins, and Seamans 2017). This is one of the main lessons from the "varieties of capitalism" literature that has explored cross-national differences in the organization of contemporary economic life, and there are many more examples throughout history (Hall and Soskice 2001; Merrill and Cobble, this volume). In any case, the impact of technology should be considered in the context of the economic, political, and environmental crises engulfing societies, as well as other overarching trends such as globalization, demographic change, the increasing concentration of capital, and the growing fragmentation of labor. How can we build a future of work that addresses interlinked systemic crises and strengthens the sustainability of social arrangements in the face of these broad trends?

As starkly illustrated by the coronavirus pandemic, it is at the intersection of multiple pressures that societies will have to find new ways of organizing and valuing different forms of work that are performed by diverse groups of workers. In addition to understanding how transformational processes interact to radically alter the foundations of work, it is important to address how to actively shape the world of work and move toward the revaluation of workers' efforts. Invariably, this is a discussion about how real-world markets, and labor markets in particular, function quite differently from the dynamics theorized in economic models of perfect competition among price-taking firms. Not only can market concentrations allow firms to exercise monopoly power in product markets and monopsony power in labor markets, but individual workers are generally structurally disadvantaged vis-à-vis their employers, given that they depend far more on a particular job than employers do on a particular worker. In turn, the governing institutions of democratic capitalist societies frequently restrict managerial control and regulate market competition to safeguard social stability, realize democratic principles, and prevent market failures associated with such phenomena as information asymmetries and increasing returns.

Dedicated to sustaining a "human-centered" world of work, a labor studies perspective openly acknowledges and directly engages with the democratic processes of rulemaking that govern markets and determine the direction and strength of market forces. Just as during the "golden age" boom years of the 20th century, when American manufacturing companies paid "family" wages to (typically) White and male breadwinners that diverged from ideal-typical scenarios of market-generated allocative efficiency, there continues to exist scope for the collective design of markets and organizations that function in accordance with evolving social goals. In exploring the room for such institutions at different levels of the polity, the field of labor studies emphasizes how individuals' productivity is rooted in the organization of work as much as it is in individual "human capital." Moreover, it acknowledges that perceptions of efficiency depend greatly on the attention paid to both market externalities and the allocation of property rights.

The scope of this agenda is broad, and it includes addressing the increasing monopolization of businesses, particularly in the platform economy, where monopolization's far-reaching effects on work are probably most direct and which, within niches, offers opportunities for worker cooperativism (Kenney and Zysman 2019; Scholz and Schneider 2016). Similarly, it concerns itself with new technologically driven forms of performance control, including the potential that insufficient regulation of data use can "automate inequality" and produce a form of "surveillance capitalism" (Eubanks 2018; Gerber and Krzywdzinski 2019; Zuboff 2019). To be clear, this is not a program to close off increases in efficiencies. Rather, it seeks to push the development of markets and platforms into the direction of decent working conditions and real room for worker voice, with empirical research on successful cases leading the way (Krzywdzinski and Gerber 2020). In terms of how technological advances are affecting work, this is the agenda that workers themselves would like to see. In addition to a lack of access to training, workers are most concerned with the decline of full-time jobs with benefits and increased employer surveillance (O'Dea 2020).

Beyond Constraints: The Power of Collective Action

Current debate about the future of work highlights structural constraints on the evolving world of work. In contrast, the labor studies perspective emphasizes the power of collective agency in recasting multiple structural transformations, shaping the interactions between them, and devising new approaches to absorbing the cost of transition. Rather than narrowing the options for coping with powerful technological change in the spirit of "managing the future of work" (as an initiative at Harvard Business School frames it), the labor studies perspective contends that there is scope to dramatically expand the range of responses appropriate for consideration.

Historically, the collective efforts of workers have often changed the valuation of work. Current attempts at worker agency have similarly shown success, from the fight for a $15 minimum wage in the United States to the transnational campaign for workplace safety after the 2013 Rana Plaza fire in Bangladesh. This volume goes over many more such efforts, from attempts of American, German, and Italian workers to negotiate the algorithm behind automation in industry (chapter by Rutherford) to efforts to achieve climate justice (chapter by Cha and Vachon), from worker-driven innovation in the home healthcare sector (chapter by Zundl and Rodgers) to attempts to leverage education for successful worker advocacy (chapter by Devinatz and Bruno). No doubt, the re-regulation of work has a lot further to go, but goals for job design have been proposed—such as on "recrafting" (Yudken and Jacobs, this volume)—and visions for how workers can exert collective agency have been refined with respect to new forms of social and sectoral bargaining in the United States (e.g., Andrias and Rogers 2018). Of course, progress is far from automatic. Rather, movement toward better answers to the social question is typically the result of active struggle, and success often depends on intersectional patterns of solidarity.

Beyond Production: Reproductive Work as a Crucible of Innovation

While care, education, and domestic work are crucial for enabling all other forms of work, the debate on the future of work tends to have little to say about the evolution of such "reproductive" activities. Labor studies, in contrast, sees them as a crucible of innovation. Tensions abound at the boundary of social reproduction and economic production, but so do opportunities for reform. For instance, paid reproductive work often takes the form of a personal service, which means that—to a great degree—it has to be provided in place. This leaves it much less affected by international competition and opens important room for political solutions that emphasize the dignity of work (Poo and Shah 2020). At the same time, reproductive work is important for achieving such goals as sustaining economic growth, providing jobs, targeting climate change, and addressing racial inequalities. Spending on healthcare and education already adds up to more than a quarter of GDP in the United States. Job growth, moreover, is particularly vibrant in home healthcare and personal care, which both feature small carbon footprints and thus are key areas for boosting environmentally sustainable employment. Finally, the substandard working conditions of paid care work disproportionately affect people of color. Yet, as international comparisons show, there is nothing inevitable about the designation of care work as low status and low paid in contemporary America (Gautié and Schmitt 2010).

Against this backdrop, there are already signs of the scope for innovation in reproductive work. Labor mobilization and coalition building in California have led to stronger public regulation and worker voice in healthcare (Eaton and Weir 2015). In Oregon, organizing and union representation have transformed the home care industry, the lives of caregivers, and the welfare of those who are served

(De La Cruz and Bussel 2018). After COVID-19 struck nursing homes particularly hard, with more than 40% of all reported virus-related deaths occurring in such facilities, we have seen pay increases for workers in long-term care across New Jersey (Stainton 2020). Moreover, improved labor standards and worker voice have paid off in better collective outcomes, including during the pandemic. The presence of healthcare worker unions in nursing homes significantly improved residents' chances of survival, with research on outcomes in New York State finding a 30% relative decrease in the COVID-19 mortality rate in unionized facilities compared to non-unionized facilities (Dean, Venkataramani, and Kimmel 2020). Finally, there is also important movement in the valuation of work and workers across different areas of education, as this volume elaborates with respect to high schools (chapter by Rubinstein and McCarthy), universities (chapter by Herbert and van der Naald), and workforce development (chapter by Hannon, McKay, and Van Noy).

Innovation can take many forms and paths, and key questions about mechanisms for valuation, forms of public intervention, and the role of markets remain to be settled with respect to reproductive work and other forms of work. In this context, there is much scope for pulling together new approaches anchored in the public interest and concern for individual dignity that could produce positive-sum solutions through greater collaboration, including labor–management partnership. Moreover, given investors' desire to co-locate production with particular available human capital and consumer bases—i.e., with global finance capital being less mobile than is often thought (Iversen and Soskice 2019)—there is room for the innovation in regulating reproductive work to inform approaches in other sectors of the economy as well.

It is time to briefly review and conclude. I have argued that labor studies can make an essential contribution to the debate about the future of work by challenging its market fundamentalism with a focus on the struggles of working people, interdisciplinary inquiry, and worker rights. Rather than approaching the evolution of work with a narrow analytical repertoire, the field acknowledges societies' interlocking crises, contextualizes the influence of technological change, and clarifies the enduring political construction of markets. On that basis, labor studies highlights the promise of collective action for revaluing work and workers, including in the much-overlooked realm of social reproduction. As recent history—including the fallout from COVID-19—has made it harder to ignore the long-standing concerns of labor studies, we have more than ever to gain from engaging with the field's propositions.

ENDNOTES

1. The Cambridge capital controversy on the nature of capital between Marx-inspired post-Keynesians Joan Robinson and Piero Sraffa from the United Kingdom on one side and neo-Keynesians such as Paul Samuelson and Robert Solow from the United States on the other,

was a prominent case in point. Neo-Keynesian macroeconomists also butted heads with monetarists on the right over government intervention. Later, after Robert Lucas successfully pushed for microeconomic foundations in macroeconomics, the central division became one between new classical economics on the right and new Keynesians on the center-left. Contemporary Marxist and heterodox economists tend to operate outside of the discipline's mainstream.

2. Compare references to labor studies in economics with those in sociology and industrial relations (Rosenfeld 2019; Viscelli and Gutelius 2020). The labor studies program at the National Bureau of Economic Research (NBER) is one of the largest and most active at the NBER, producing almost 200 working papers annually.

REFERENCES

Abbott, Andrew. 2001. *Chaos of Disciplines*. Chicago, IL: University of Chicago Press.

Acemoglu, Daron, and Pascual Restrepo. 2019. "Automation and New Tasks: How Technology Displaces and Reinstates Labor." *Journal of Economic Perspectives* 33 (2): 3–30.

Ackerman, Seth, and Mike Beggs. 2013 (Sep.). "Don't Mention the War." *Jacobin*. https://bit.ly/3bCqljJ

Alvaredo, Facundo, Lucas Chancel, Thomas Piketty, Emmanuel Saez, and Gabriel Zucman. 2018. *World Inequality Report 2018*. Cambridge, MA: Belknap Press.

Andersson, Jenny. 2010. *The Library and the Workshop: Social Democracy and Capitalism in the Knowledge Age*. Stanford, CA: Stanford University Press.

Andrias, Kate, and Brishen Rogers. 2018. "Rebuilding Worker Voice in Today's Economy." Report. New York, NY: Roosevelt Institute.

Appelbaum, Binyamin. 2019. *The Economists' Hour: False Prophets, Free Markets, and the Fracture of Society*. New York, NY: Back Bay Books.

Arntz, Melani, Terry Gregory, and Ulrich Zierahn. 2016. "The Risk of Automation of Jobs in OECD Countries: A Comparative Analysis." OECD Social, Employment and Migration Working Papers No. 189. Paris, France: Organisation for Economic Co-operation and Development.

Banerjee, Abhijit V., and Ester Duflo. 2019. *Good Economics for Hard Times*. New York, NY: Public Affairs.

Blanchard, Olivier, and Lawrence H. Summers, eds. 2019. *Evolution or Revolution? Rethinking Macroeconomic Policy after the Great Recession*. Cambridge, MA: MIT Press.

Blyth, Mark. 2010. "Ideas, Uncertainty and Evolution." In *Ideas and Politics in Social Science Research*, edited by Robert Cox and Daniel Beland, pp. 83–101. New York, NY: Oxford University Press.

Blyth, Mark. 2019. "A Brief History of How We Got Here and Why." Lecture, Department of Philosophy, McMaster University. https://youtu.be/tJoe_daP0DE

Boushey, Heather. 2020 (Apr. 27). "Which Side Are We On?" *Democracy—A Journal of Ideas*. https://bit.ly/3cmDtlP

Bregman, Rutger. 2017. *Utopia for Realists: How We Can Build the Ideal World*. New York, NY: Back Bay Books.

Breman, Jan, Kevan Harris, Ching Kwan Lee, and Marcel van der Linden. 2019. "The Social Question All Over Again." In *The Social Question in the Twenty-First Century: A Global View*, edited by Jan Breman, Kevan Harris, Ching Kwan Lee, and Marcel van der Linden, pp. 1–22. Oakland, CA: University of California Press.

Bröckling, Ulrich. 2015. *The Entrepreneurial Self: Fabricating a New Type of Subject.* London, UK: Sage.

Brookes, Marissa. 2019. *The New Politics of Transnational Labor: Why Some Alliances Succeed.* Ithaca, NY: Cornell University Press.

Brookes, Marissa, and Jamie K. McCallum. 2017. "The New Global Labour Studies: A Critical Review." *Global Labour Journal* 33 (3): 201–218.

Brown, Phillip, Hugh Lauder, and David Ashton. 2011. *The Global Auction: The Broken Promises of Education, Jobs, and Incomes.* Oxford: Oxford University Press.

Budd, John. 2011. *The Thought of Work.* Ithaca, NY: Cornell University Press.

Burawoy, Michael. 2009. "The Global Turn: Lessons from Southern Labor Scholars and Their Labor Movements." *Work and Occupations* 36 (3): 87–95.

Castel, Robert. 2003. *From Manual Workers to Wage Laborers: Transformation of the Social Question.* New Brunswick, NJ: Transaction Publishers.

Child, Mary, and Karen Duffin. 2020 (Jun. 12). "Patent Racism." *Planet Money,* National Public Radio. https://n.pr/3qBBhCj

Cook, Lisa. 2014. "Violence and Economic Activity: Evidence from African American Patents, 1870–1940." *Journal of Economic Growth* 19 (2): 221–257.

Cooper, Melinda. 2017. *Family Values: Between Neoliberalism and the New Social Conservatism.* New York, NY: Zone Books.

De La Cruz, Sonia, and Bob Bussel. 2018. *The Care Revolution: The Transformation of Home Health Care in Oregon.* Documentary. Eugene, OR: Labor and Education Research Center.

De Leon, Cedric. 2020. "Racial Capitalism and the 2020 Election: On the Presentism and Methodological Individualism of American Sociology." *Footnotes* 48 (5): 6–8.

Dean, Adam, Atheendar Venkataramani, and Simeon Kimmel. 2020. "Mortality Rates from COVID-19 Are Lower in Unionized Nursing Homes." *Health Affairs* 39 (11): 1993–2001.

Dixon, Jennifer M. 2020 (Aug. 11). "Multidisciplinarity and Comparison in the Study of Dark Pasts." Book Forum, *Dark Pasts: Changing the State's Story in Turkey and Japan. Journal of Genocide Research* (online first). https://bit.ly/3t5Ch3e

Dwyer, Richard. 1977. "Workers' Education, Labor Education, Labor Studies: An Historical Delineation." *Review of Educational Research* 47 (1): 179–207.

Dwyer, Richard E., Miles E. Galvin, and Simeon Larson. 1977. "Labor Studies: In Quest of Industrial Justice." *Labor Studies Journal* 2 (2): 95–130.

Eaton, Adrienne E., Susan J. Schurman, and Martha A. Chen. 2017. *Informal Workers and Collective Action: A Global Perspective.* Ithaca, NY: Cornell University Press.

Eaton, Charlie, and Margaret Weir. 2015. "The Power of Coalitions: Advancing the Public in California's Public–Private Welfare State." *Politics & Society* 43 (2): 3–32.

Esping-Andersen, Gøsta. 1990. *The Three Worlds of Welfare Capitalism.* Princeton, NJ: Princeton University Press.

Eubanks, Virginia. 2018. *Automating Inequality: How High-Tech Tools Profile, Police, and Punish the Poor.* New York, NY: St. Martin's Press.

Feigenbaum, James, Alexander Hertel-Fernandez, and Vanessa Williamson. 2018. "From the Bargaining Table to the Ballot Box: Political Effects of Right to Work Laws." NBER Working Paper 24259. Cambridge, MA: National Bureau of Economic Research.

Gautié, Jérôme, and John Schmitt, eds. 2010. *Low-Wage Work in the Wealthy World.* New York, NY: Russell Sage Foundation.

Gerber, Christine, and Martin Krzywdzinski. 2019. "Brave New Digital Work? New Forms of Performance Control in Crowdwork." *Research in the Sociology of Work* 33: 121–143.

Givan, Rebecca Kolins. 2014. "Why Teachers Unions Make Such Useful Scapegoats." *New Labor Forum* 23 (1): 68–75.

Golatz, Helmut J. 1977. "Labor Studies: New Kid on Campus." *Labor Studies Journal* 2 (1): 5–22.

Gordon, Robert J. 2016. *The Rise and Fall of American Growth.* Princeton, NJ: Princeton University Press.

Gough, Ian. 2020 (Apr. 28). "In Times of Climate Breakdown, How Do We Value What Matters?" *openDemocracy.* https://bit.ly/3cm9v7T

Gray, Lois. 1966. "The American Way in Labor Education." *Industrial Relations* 5 (2): 53–66.

Gray, Lois. 1976. "Labor Studies Credit and Degree Programs: A Growth Sector of Higher Education." *Labor Studies Journal* 1 (1): 34–51.

Hacker, Jacob S. 2019. *The Great Risk Shift: The New Economic Insecurity and the Decline of the American Dream,* 2nd ed. New York, NY: Oxford University Press.

Hall, Peter A. 2020. "The Electoral Politics of Growth Regimes." *Perspectives on Politics* 18 (1): 185–199.

Hall, Peter A., and David Soskice, eds. 2001. *Varieties of Capitalism.* Oxford, UK: Oxford University Press.

Hayek, Friedrich A. 1976. *Law, Legislation and Liberty: The Mirage of Social Justice, Volume 2.* Chicago, IL: The University of Chicago Press.

Heilbron, Johan. 2004. "A Regime of Disciplines: Toward a Historical Sociology of Disciplinary Knowledge." In *The Dialogical Turn: New Roles for Sociology in the Postdisciplinary Age,* edited by Charles Camic and Hans Joas, pp. 23–42. Lanham, MD: Rowman & Littlefield.

Helper, Susan, Raphael Martins, and Robert Channing Seamans. 2017. "Value Migration and Industry 4.0: Theory, Field Evidence, and Propositions." Unpublished Manuscript.

Hirschman, Daniel, and Elizabeth Popp Berman. 2014. "Do Economists Make Policies? On the Political Effects of Economics." *Socio-Economic Review* 12 (4): 779–811.

Immergut, Ellen M. 1998. "The Theoretical Core of the New Institutionalism." *Politics & Society* 26 (1): 5–34.

Iversen, Torben, and David Soskice. 2019. *Democracy and Prosperity: Reinventing Capitalism Through a Turbulent Century.* Princeton, NJ: Princeton University Press.

Jencks, Christopher, and David Riesman. 1968. *The Academic Revolution.* New York, NY: Doubleday.

Joas, Hans. 2005. "Neue Aufgaben für die Sozialwissenschaften. Eine handlungsteoretische Perspektive." In *Interdisziplinarität als Lernprozeß: Erfahrungen mit einem handlungsteoretischen Forschundsprogramm,* edited by Hans Joas and Hans G. Kippenberg, pp. 74–93. Göttingen, Germany: Wallstein.

Joas, Hans, and Hans G. Kippenberg. 2005. "Einleitung: Interdiziplinarität als Lernprozeß." In *Interdisziplinarität als Lernprozeß: Erfahrungen mit einem handlungsteoretischen Forschundsprogramm,* edited by Hans Joas and Hans G. Kippenberg, pp. 7–12. Göttingen: Wallstein.

Kalecki, Michał. 1943. "Political Aspects of Full Employment." *The Political Quarterly* 14 (4): 322–330.

Kenney, Martin, and John Zysman. 2019. "Work and Value Creation in the Platform Economy." *Research in the Sociology of Work* 33: 13–41.

Krugman, Paul. 1993. "How I Work." *The American Economist* 37 (2): 25–31.

Krugman, Paul. 1996. *Pop Internationalism*. Cambridge, MA: MIT Press.

Krugman, Paul. 2019. "Econ 101 Meets Labor Reality." Keynote Presentation, 46th Annual Conference, National Center for the Study of Collective Bargaining in Higher Education and the Professions, New York, NY, Apr. 8.

Krzywdzinski, Martin, and Christine Gerber. 2020. "Varieties of Platform Work: Platforms and Social Inequality in Germany and the United States." Weizenbaum Series #7 Working Paper. Berlin, Germany: Weizenbaum Institute.

Lauder, Hugh, Philip Brown, and Sin-Yi Cheung. 2018. "Fractures in the Education–Economy Relationship: The End of the Skill Bias Technological Change Research Program?" *Oxford Review of Economic Policy* 34 (3): 495–515.

Lee, Tamara. 2018. "From Melting Pots to Intersectional Organizing," *Perspectives on Work*, 70–71.

Lessenich, Stephan. 2008. *Die Neuerfindung des Sozialen: Der Sozialstaat im flexiblen Kapitalismus*. Bielefeld, Germany: Transcript Verlag.

Lessenich, Stephan. 2016. *Neben uns die Sintflut: Die Externalisierungsgesellschaft und ihr Preis*. Munich, Germany: Hanser.

Lieberthal, Mil. 1977. "On the Academization of Labor Education." *Labor Studies Journal* 1 (3): 235–245.

Mankiw, N. Gregory. 2013. "Defending the One Percent." *Journal of Economic Perspectives* 27 (3): 21–34.

Mankiw, N. Gregory. 2015. *Principles of Economics*. Stamford, CT: Cengage.

Mazzucato, Mariana. 2018. *The Value of Everything: Making and Taking in the Global Economy*. London, UK: Allen Lane.

Mense-Petermann, Ursula. 2020. "Interest Representation in Transnational Labour Markets: Campaigning as an Alternative to Traditional Union Action?" *Journal of Industrial Relations* 62 (2): 185–209.

Mezzadri, Alessandra. 2020. "The Informal Labours of Social Reproduction." *Global Labour Journal* 11 (1): 56–63.

Milanovic, Branko. 2016. *Global Inequality: A New Approach for the Age of Globalization*. Cambridge, MA: Harvard University Press.

Mounk, Yascha. 2017. *The Age of Responsibility: Luck, Choice, and the Welfare States*. Cambridge, MA: Harvard University Press.

Mudge, Stephanie L. 2018. *Leftism Reinvented: Western Parties from Socialism to Neoliberalism*. Cambridge, MA: Harvard University Press.

O'Dea, Colleen. 2020 (Sep. 25). "Workers Fear Losing Full-Time Jobs, No Training, Corporate Surveillance." *NJ Spotlight News*.

Ornston, Darius, and Tobias Schulze-Cleven. 2015. "Conceptualizing Cooperation: Coordination and Concertation as Two Logics of Collective Action." *Comparative Political Studies* 48 (5): 555–585.

Parsons, Michael D. 1990. "Labor Studies in Decline." *Labor Studies Journal* 15 (1): 66–81.

Piketty, Thomas. 2014. *Capital in the Twenty-First Century*. Cambridge, MA: Harvard University Press.

Piketty, Thomas. 2020. *Capital and Ideology*. Cambridge, MA: Harvard University Press.

Poo, Ai-Jen, and Palak Shah. 2020. (Jun. 24). "The Future of Work Isn't What People Think It Is." *New York Times*.

Purdy, Jedediah. 2018 (Summer). "Normcore." *Dissent*, 121–128.

Rodrik, Dani. 2015. *Economics Rules: The Rights and Wrongs of the Dismal Science*. New York, NY: Norton.

Romer, Paul. 2020 (Mar./Apr.). "The Dismal Kingdom: Do Economists Have Too Much Power?" *Foreign Affairs*, 150–157.

Rosa, Hartmut, and Christoph Henning, eds. 2018. *The Good Life Beyond Growth: New Perspectives*. London, UK: Routledge.

Rosenfeld, Jake. 2019. "US Labor Studies in the Twenty-First Century: Understanding Laborism Without Labor." *Annual Review of Sociology* 45: 449–465.

Schmidt, Vivienne, and Mark Thatcher, eds. 2013. *Resilient Liberalism in Europe's Political Economy*. New York, NY: Cambridge University Press.

Scholz, Trebor, and Nathan Schneider, eds. 2016. *Ours to Hack and to Own: The Rise of Platform Cooperativism*. New York, NY: OR Books.

Schulze-Cleven, Tobias. 2017. "Collective Action and Globalization: Building and Mobilizing Labour Power." *Journal of Industrial Relations* 59 (4): 397–419.

Schulze-Cleven, Tobias. 2020. "Organizing Competition: Regulatory Welfare States in Higher Education." *The ANNALS of the American Academy of Political and Social Science* 691: 276–294.

Schulze-Cleven, Tobias, Gary Herrigel, Nelson Lichtenstein, and Gay Seidman. 2017. "Beyond Disciplinary Boundaries: Leveraging Complementary Perspectives on Global Labour." *Journal of Industrial Relations* 59 (4): 510–537.

Schulze-Cleven, Tobias, and Jennifer R. Olson. 2017. "Worlds of Higher Education Transformed: Toward Varieties of Academic Capitalism." *Higher Education* 73 (2): 813–831.

Schulze-Cleven, Tobias, Tilman Reitz, Jens Maesse, and Johannes Angermuller. 2017. "The New Political Economy of Higher Education: Between Distributional Conflict and Discursive Stratification." *Higher Education* 73 (6): 795–812.

Schulze-Cleven, Tobias, Bartholomew C. Watson, and John Zysman. 2007. "How Wealthy Nations Can Stay Wealthy: Innovation and Adaptability in a Digital Era." *New Political Economy* 12 (4): 451–475.

Schulze-Cleven, Tobias, and J. Timo Weishaupt. 2015. "Playing Normative Legacies: Partisanship and Employment Policies in Crisis-Ridden Europe." *Politics & Society* 43 (2): 269–299.

Silver, Beverly J. 2003. *Forces of Labor: Workers' Movements and Globalization since 1870*. New York, NY: Cambridge University Press.

Skidelsky, Robert. 2020. *What's Wrong with Economics? A Primer for the Perplexed*. New Haven, CT: Yale University Press.

Stainton, Lilo H. 2020 (Aug. 15). "In Response to COVID, NJ Moves to Pay Long-Term Care Workers More." *NJ Spotlight News*.

Stansbury, Anna, and Lawrence H. Summers. 2020. "The Declining Worker Power Hypothesis: An Explanation for the Recent Evolution of the American Economy." NBER Working Paper No. 27193. Cambridge, MA: National Bureau of Economic Research.

Stichweh, Rudolf. 1984. *Zur Entstehung des modernen Systems wissenschaftlicher Disziplinen: Physik in Deutschland, 1740–1890*. Frankfurt, Germany: Suhrkamp.

Stiglitz, Joseph E. 2020. *People, Power, and Profits: Progressive Capitalism for and Age of Discontent*. New York, NY: Norton.

Stiglitz, Joseph E., Amartya Sen, and Jean-Paul Fitoussi. 2009. "Report by the Commission on the Measurement of Economic Performance and Social Progress." Paris, France: Commission on the Measurement of Economic Performance and Social Progress.

Supiot, Alain. 2001. *Beyond Employment: Changes in Work and the Future of Labour Law in Europe*. Oxford, UK: Oxford University Press.

Supiot, Alain. 2012. *The Spirit of Philadelphia: Social Justice vs. the Total Market*. London, UK: Verso.

Thelen, Kathleen. 2014. *Varieties of Liberalization and the New Politics of Social Solidarity*. New York, NY: Cambridge University Press.

Tormos, Fernando. 2017. Intersectional Solidarity." *Politics, Groups, and Identities* 5 (4): 707–720.

van der Linden, Marcel. 2012. "The Promise and Challenges of Global Labor History." *International Labor and Working-Class History* 82 (Fall): 57–76.

Vidal, Matt, and Marco Hauptmeier. 2014. "Comparative Political Economy and Labour Process Theory: Toward a Synthesis." In *Comparative Political Economy of Work*, edited by Marco Hauptmeier and Matt Vidal, pp. 1–32. London, UK: Palgrave MacMillan.

Viscelli, Steve, and Beth Gutelius. 2020. "Book Review Symposium: Technological Encounters: How New Writing on Technology Can Inform Modern Labor Studies." *ILR Review* 73 (3): 801–804.

Wagner, Peter, Björn Wittrock, and Richard Whitley, eds. 1991. *Discourses on Society: The Shaping of the Social Science Disciplines*. Dordrecht, Netherlands: Springer.

Winters, Jeffrey A. 2011. "Oligarchy and Democracy." *The American Interest* 7 (2).

Wong, Kent. No date. "Draft History of the UALE." Chicago, IL: United Association for Labor Education.

Wright, Erik Olin. 2010. *Envisioning Real Utopias*. New York, NY: Verso.

Zuboff, Shoshana. 2019. *The Age of Surveillance Capitalism: The Fight for a Human Future at the New Frontier of Power*. New York, NY: Public Affairs.

PART I
ARTICULATING THE LABOR
STUDIES PERSPECTIVE

CHAPTER 3

Deus Est Machina:[1]
Historical Amnesia, Methodological Myopia, and the Future of Work

MICHAEL MERRILL
DOROTHY SUE COBBLE
Rutgers University

Suppose that industrialism succeeds in replacing every type of human labor with machines.
… You then achieve the economist's ideal, production at the lowest possible cost, and
at the same time, the absolute triumph of Capital over Labor. But what will happen
to your huge output of products? Where will they go? Who will consume them? If
the people go willingly, peacefully, and legally to die of hunger, remaining respectful
to your notions of order and the sacred right of property, won't you see your production
system collapse on itself and crush you in the ruins?

—Victor Considerant (1843: 66)

ABSTRACT

The massively disruptive changes accompanying today's "smart machines" are not unprecedented in either scale or scope, and managing their effects requires that we pay as much attention to sociological as to technological possibilities. There is no fixing work without fixing the social structure and power arrangements in which it occurs. This chapter examines human work and social development over the long term to put past and present concerns about technology and technological unemployment into better perspective. It surveys the most significant upheavals in the history of the economy of the Atlantic world during the past 500 years, including colonization, commercialization, mechanization, and computerization, and it outlines their effects. The chapter concludes with a discussion of how humanity might best ensure a sustainable prosperous future, given that it now presses against the limits of the Earth's carrying capacity.

INTRODUCTION

The future of work—more precisely, "the future of formal sector employment"—has a long history.[2] Our goal is to recall some of it. We divide contributions to the discussion into two distinct groups. One catalogs the wondrous ways in which our tools have changed, and with what promising implications; the other concentrates on sounding alarms rather than issuing encomiums. Neither of these emphases has always been wrong. In the first section, we review some of the earliest 19th-century expressions of concern about the impact of technological change on the good order of society. In the second, we provide a perspective on the present by examining human work and social development over the very long term. The third section is a Eurocentric survey of the most significant upheavals in the history of work and workers in the past 500 years. The final section then concludes with our sense of how best to ensure a future for work, given that humanity now presses against the limits of the Earth's carrying capacity.

We argue, first, that the massively disruptive changes accompanying today's "smart machines" are not unprecedented in either scale or scope; and, second, that managing the effects of such changes requires that we pay as much attention to sociological as to technological possibilities. We hope to show that approaching "the future of work" with a more informed historical perspective and a more nuanced political–economic framework offers new insights. How we work is inseparable from how we live. "To work," in the most general sense, does not mean being employed. It means doing what we must do to survive and, if possible, to live well. A crisis in work is thus never just an economic crisis. It is also always a social one. There is no fixing work without fixing the social structure and power arrangements in which it occurs.

ON MACHINES AND STATIONARY STATES

More than 200 years ago, the celebrated manufacturer and socialist Robert Owen expressed both concern and astonishment at the rapid spread of labor-saving machinery and its implications. Invited on the strength of his renown as an enlightened businessman to serve with a group of civic-minded aristocrats and high-ranking churchmen on a "Committee for the Relief of the Manufacturing and Labouring Poor," Owen tried to focus their attention on "the depreciation of human labour ... occasioned by the general introduction of mechanism into the manufactures of Europe" (Owen 1818: 3). The machinery at one such establishment in Britain, he observed, produced "as much as the existing population of Scotland could manufacture ... fifty years ago," and there were several such establishments (Owen 1818: 5). "So steadily, yet rapidly" did industry advance that "there appeared to be no limit to [the nation's] acquirement of riches, and the description of [its] power" (Owen 1818: 8).

Owen's observations at once interested David Ricardo, who had published to great acclaim his *Principles of Political Economy and Taxation* in 1817. In response to the issues raised by Owen, Ricardo added a chapter, "On Machines," to the 1821 edition of his treatise. There he alerted readers to the fact that, yes, the new machinery might have negative as well as positive consequences for wage earners (Ricardo 1951: 386). But how to help all those superseded by the new methods of production? Owen proposed establishing state-funded farming villages to provide "advantageous employment ... for the unemployed working classes" (Owen 1818: 7). Ricardo voted for the plan in Parliament, arguing that it could do no harm and might do some good (Ricardo 1952: 31, 467–468). But Owen's advocacy otherwise fell on deaf ears, both at the toney Association for the Relief of the Poor and in Parliament. It did, however, launch his career as a social reformer and England's best known, home-grown socialist (Morton 1962).

Victor Considerant's fears, voiced a generation later and quoted in the epigraph to this chapter, testify to the continuing concerns of various observers. The changing structure of work and the increasing precarity of many traditional occupations were among the root causes of the great labor and social upheavals of the 1840s, including the Chartist movement in England and the revolutions of 1848 across Europe (Chase 2007; Marx and Engels 1998; Sperber 1994). To provide a framework for thinking about these changes was one of the primary objects of John Stuart Mill's *Principles of Political Economy,* which went through many editions between its first printing in 1848 and Mill's death in 1873. In theory, he acknowledged that "the laboring classes as a collective body" were likely to "suffer temporarily by the introduction of machinery." However, "as things [were] actually transacted," Mill did not believe improvements in production had that effect. When adopted gradually, as they usually were, and paid for by funds raised for the purpose rather than diverted from ongoing operations, he thought them rarely "injurious, even temporarily" (J.S. Mill 1917: 96–97). The worst one might say about such improvements, he wrote, was that they "enabled a greater population to live the same life of drudgery and imprisonment" that most had always lived. The best was that they made it possible for "an increased number of manufactures and others to make fortunes" and for "the middle classes" to enjoy more "comforts" (J.S. Mill 1917: 751).

Discussion of these issues has changed little from Mill's time to our own. Concern has continued, but hosannas in praise of economic growth and the newest machines still are the dominant notes. The American engineer David A. Wells captured the continuing emphasis in essays serialized in the 1880s in the monthly *Popular Mechanics* and later published as *Recent Economic Changes* (1889). "The continued increasing material abundance which follows all new methods for effecting greater production and distribution," Wells insisted, "is the true foundation for increasing general prosperity." Some of his contemporaries worried that continuing technical improvements might one day leave little gainful employment for those displaced by machines and other innovation. Wells did not share these worries. Every reduction in the labor required to meet the existing demand for goods and services, he predicted, would breed more demand. In his words, "The real truth is ... that the amount to be done is not limited; that the more [that] is done the more there will be to do." Nor did he share the fears of contemporaries, concerned that if the general population and prosperity continued to increase, the Earth might fill with people and see its resources exhausted. He refused to deal "with remote cycles and millenniums, of which we know nothing" and insisted that it was "sufficient for the present ... to believe [the world] will continue under substantially the same conditions as now exist" (Wells 1889: 394–395).

We know a great deal more about "remote cycles and millennium" than Wells did. We find ourselves at the end of one geological epoch and beginning another, needing to grow less if we are to grow better. Mill was aware of this problem and famously devoted an entire chapter of his *Principles* to a consideration "Of the Stationary State." No doubt some of Wells's pessimists had read it. Even economists, Mill noted, could see "more or less distinctly" that "the increase of wealth is not boundless" and that "what they term the progressive state" of continuing growth must end. Increased production, he thought, was important only "in backward countries of the world." In rich countries, "what is economically needed is better distribution." An unlimited increase of wealth might support more people, but it need not make them happier. He urged redirecting innovations from "serving no purpose but the increase of wealth" to "their legitimate effect, abridging labour" (J.S. Mill 1917: 746, 749, 751).[3]

How are we to secure this beneficent result? Mill's hope has blossomed into a large literature on various "paths to paradise," a post-work world "beyond the wage-based society," where robotic devices liberate humanity from toil and everyone lives wage, if not care, free (Gorz 1985, 1999; Mason 2015; Srnicek and Williams 2016; Weeks 2011). We leave paradise for another occasion and focus here on other concerns, repeated now in the world's highest circles, that "as technology races ahead it's leaving some people behind" (Brynjolfsson and McAfee 2014: xiii). In the interests of time and space, we will narrow our consideration to an early but influential contribution to the discussion, Erik Brynjolfsson and Andrew McAfee's *The Second Machine Age: Work, Progress, and Prosperity in a Time of Brilliant Machines*, which we believe fairly representative of the most commonly expressed views (cf. Carney 2018; Lund et al. 2019; Manyika et al. 2017; Schwab 2016; Susskind 2020).

The Second Machine Age invites a historical perspective. It begins with an account of the 18th-century Industrial Revolution, or what the authors call "the first machine age," and remains focused throughout on the trends and patterns of the past 50 years. Opening with a "history of humanity in one graph," Brynjolfsson and McAfee credit the new machines of the late 18th century, especially the steam engine and its associated technologies, with effecting the greatest, the most "astonishing," transformation human society had ever known. They then try to make a convincing case that the digital revolution of the 21st century—the "brilliant" machines of the "second machine age"—heralds another momentous break (Brynjolfsson and McAfee 2014: 4–8).

Below we argue that Brynjolfsson and McAfee, in common with other analysts, overemphasize the wonders of technology and underemphasize the importance of its historical and social context. Machines matter. But people matter, too. To begin with, people invent and build machines; machines do not invent and build people. Second, the impact of technology is *always* a social fact, an effect of its social context. Machines do not decide whether they will help or hurt. People do. Despite the many interesting things that *The Second Machine Age* reveals about the new digital technologies, it has little either new or terribly bold to say about how to spread their benefits more broadly or put them to better use.

In the following section, we look more closely at Brynjolfsson and McAfee's perspective on the Industrial Revolution and at their human history in one graph. Doing so throws into sharp relief the historical amnesia and methodological myopia we find in much of the literature on the future of work. The curve of human social development, drawn in different ways with the same data, tells a different story. Astonishing transformations to the human condition did not begin with the steam engine. They began with the fire pit and the wheel. The Neolithic Agricultural Revolution, in particular, played a much larger role in the human saga than most modern accounts allow, for it was then that human habitation changed from being mostly at home to being mostly at odds with the rest of nature.

We next review the history of the North Atlantic economy from the European discovery and conquest of the Americas down to the present day. We intend to show thereby that neither the scope nor the potential disruptions of "the second machine age" are unprecedented. Reviewing this history also underscores our conviction that the prosperity of the past 500 years is not principally a function of our technology, as Brynjolfsson, McAfee, and others would have us believe. The magic of machines has had something to do with it. But the entire process is inconceivable without the sudden acquisition of two vast continents and their resources by a few adventurous societies on the margins of a third, which unalterably changed the character of the world.

Finally, we conclude with what we take to be the principal lessons of this history: that the effects of modern technology are inseparable from the effects of modern capitalism, and that reckoning with the former requires reckoning with the latter. Brynjolfsson and McAfee, we find, hobble their prescriptions for how to respond to the current technological transition because they confuse "capitalism" with commerce. They dismiss structural alternatives to capitalist economies on the grounds that without capitalism there is no commerce. They are not alone in this confusion, which is both widespread and stultifying. Distinguishing capitalism from commerce not only provides a more illuminating perspective on the past, but it also suggests other, more promising ways to the future. We offer a different, more political perspective on economies, which suggests other ways of minimizing the impact of dramatic technological and social change.

WHERE DID WE COME FROM?

Consider the trajectory of human social development over the past 10,000 years. According to Brynjolfsson and McAfee, the brilliant devices of today's second machine age promise to "bend the curve of human history" as it has been bent only once before. To make their case, they enlist Ian Morris's definition of social development as "a group's ability to master its physical and intellectual environment to get things done" and sum it all up in a "history of humanity in one graph" (Brynjolfsson and McAfee 2014: 4).[4] "For many thousands of years," they write, "humanity was [on] a very gradual upward trajectory. Progress was achingly slow, almost invisible" (6). Then, 250 years ago, the steam engine "bent the curve of human history—of population and social development—almost ninety degrees" (6) (Figure 1). It was, they proclaim, "the most profound time of transformation our world has ever seen." For the first time, human progress "was driven primarily by technological innovation" (7).

Brynjolfsson and McAfee's foray into "deep history" provides them a standard by which to judge the relative importance of their "second machine age." They

Figure 1
What Bent the Curve of Human History? The Industrial Revolution

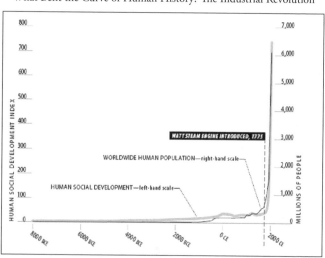

Source: Brynjolfsson and McAfee (2014).

are careful to note that no one yet knows whether the new technology "bends the curve as dramatically as Watt's steam engine." Regardless, it is, they insist, "a very big deal indeed." Computers and other digital machines "are doing for mental power—the ability to use our brains to understand and shape our environments—what the steam engine did for muscle power." These "brilliant machines" allow us "to blow past previous limitations and take us into new territory" (8).

We find Brynjolfsson and McAfee's faith in progress is as unfounded as it is unbounded. (For more sober assessments, see Rotman 2020, Smil 2019: 449–508, and Suzman 2020). Still, we applaud their attempt to ground their techno-optimism in something more substantial than mere enthusiasm. Granted the 18th-century Industrial Revolution was big, but how big was it? Their human history in one graph is one such measure, but every scale is arbitrary. If we use logarithmic rather than linear axes, the graph of human history has different bends and curves.[5]

We reproduce below one such plot (Figure 2), based on Edward Deevey's influential 1960 *Scientific American* essay on human population, which Joel Cohen discussed at length in his *How Many People Can the Earth Support?* (Cohen 1995: 95–96; Deevey 1960: 198). The most significant difference between a linear and logarithmic graph of human population is that the "boring" and the "astonishing" parts (Brynjolfsson and McAfee's words for "flat" and "steep") are not the same. In particular, the logarithmic plot reveals rates of change long before the modern era that were anything but invisible. The Industrial Revolution represented an advance and lies on a positive slope in each case. But neither the steam engine nor its ancillary and associated technologies launched the development process. It is more accurate to say that the development process launched them. From the standpoint of the rate rather than the volume of change, the first machine age occurs at the leveling end of humanity's second advance—not at the

Figure 2
Deevey's Schema of World Population History, Last Million Years

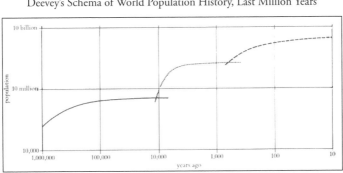

Source: Cohen (1995), from Deevey (1960).

start of its first. The newer methods of production were as much the results of prior astonishing changes as they were the drivers of later ones.

Another important datum has also escaped notice. The ancient Agricultural Revolution that occurred 6,000 to 8,000 years ago in several locations contributed a more significant increase to the supportable scale of human society than did the modern Industrial Revolution. Here is Deevey's 1960 account of that earlier revolution:

> The stepwise evolution of population size, entirely concealed in graphs with arithmetical [linear] scales, is the most noticeable feature of this diagram [Figure 2]. For most of the million-year period the number of hominids, including man, was about what would be expected by any large Pleistocene mammal. ... Then the food-gatherers and hunters became plowmen and herdsmen, and the population was boosted about 16 times between 10,000 and 6,000 years ago. The scientific-Industrial Revolution, beginning 300 years ago [i.e., with Isaac Newton], has spread its effects much faster, but it has not yet taken the number [of people] as far above the base line. (197–198)

Think about Deevey's last point for a moment. During the transition to settled agriculture, he estimated that human ingenuity managed a 25-fold increase in its life-sustaining outputs. More recent estimates put the relevant multiplier at 50 to 100 (Christian 2004: 185, 209; Smil 2002: 186–187, Figure 7.3). Humanity has managed to multiply the scale of its supportable population since then. But most of this multiplication occurred *before* the Industrial Revolution, not after. In short, the upward trajectory of humanity before the modern era was never "achingly slow" nor was the Industrial Revolution "the most profound time of transformation our world has ever seen" (7).

Brynjolfsson and McAfee provided their sketch of human history "to demonstrate how important technology has been" to the "sudden, sharp, and sustained jump in human progress" detectable in our population history (6). The "sudden, sharp, and sustained jump" of this conclusion, however, hangs on an optical illusion. When we graph the history of human population differently—the rate rather than the volume of change—we get a different picture. Technical innovations accompanied each of these advances. But association does not entail causation. As Colin Renfrew and David Noble have emphasized in ancient and modern contexts, technology is a function of social relationships, which are in their turn determined by shared values and rules of conduct—what Durkheim referred to as "social facts" (Durkheim 1974; Noble 2011; Renfrew 2007: 106). To understand what is happening, we need to be looking not only at the means but also at the modes of production.

HOW DID WE GET HERE?

Brynjolfsson and McAfee (2014) think the second machine age may be another inflection point in human history (9), another period of "astonishing progress" (2). They are also aware that the new machines bring "thorny challenges" (10). The best way to overcome these challenges, they assert, is to "grow the economy" (207). They favor common-sense interventions, which are echoed widely in elite circles: teaching children better, launching start-ups, abolishing burdensome regulations, eliminating labor market rigidities, supporting scientists, upgrading infrastructure, welcoming talented (but not, it seems, untalented) immigrants, and taxing wisely (214–228). Longer term, they are willing to consider more radical notions like a universal basic income or Milton Friedman's negative income tax (232–241). They also mention other "wild" or "out-of-the-box" ideas, including sovereign wealth funds, labor-enhancing rather than labor-saving technologies, an expanded nonprofit sector, a "made by humans" labeling movement, "vouchers for basic necessities," and expanded government hiring (246). They are only willing to go so far in this direction, however, and have nothing to say about how to mobilize the political power necessary to effect such changes. Indeed, they declare their lack of faith in any solution that depends on politics or government actions. Instead, they insist that the best solutions—"probably, in fact, the only real solutions"—to the looming challenges will come "from markets and capitalism, and from technology-enabled creations of innovators and entrepreneurs" (245).

We read the lessons of the past differently. The "technology-enabled creations of innovators and entrepreneurs" (245), not to mention those of artisans, operators, and homemakers, have expanded life's possibilities; so, too, have markets. But sociology and politics matter at least as much as machines and economics. Technology has beneficial effects when put to beneficial purposes. These effects depend on politics and government as much as on markets and capitalism. Left to chance, the second law of thermodynamics tells us that entropy will triumph over utopia. If the brilliant machines on our horizon are to put us on a more equitable and sustainable development path, sociological and political innovation are as necessary as technology.

In the last section, we offer our ideas about how best to meet the "thorny challenges" of the "second machine age." But first we undertake a short flyover of the North Atlantic economy in the modern era. We want to survey the many far-reaching social and economic disruptions that preceded and followed the Industrial Revolution and to observe how people responded to these disruptions, to what effect. Four major periods of transformative upheaval stand out: *colonization*, during which England invaded, subdued, and colonized the Atlantic Coast of North America and several Caribbean islands, destroying the settled lives of millions of American and African peoples; *commercialization*, during which the explosive growth of European public and private finance increased the supply and liquidity of money, fueled a rapid expansion of commercial institutions and practices, and overturned long-established ways of doing things in every corner it reached; *industrialization*, during which semi-automatic machine processes made a wide range of manual skills obsolete, while large, centralized organizations replaced the dispersed networks of households and smaller workshops that previously had been the principal locus of economic activity; and *computerization*, where we now find ourselves and which portends further profound changes.

Colonization

The modern age does not start for us, as it does for Brynjolfsson and McAfee, with the perfection of the steam engine and the invention of other mechanical marvels. It begins with the 16th-century conquest and genocidal depopulation of the Americas, the plunder of which sparked a commercial boom in the Atlantic economy. The rulers of Western Europe, which was already a populous and prosperous part of the world in 1500, had pioneered a new, more dynamic type of political and administrative formation, the nation-state, to meet their own local military, political, and economic requirements. Supplanting older, less dynamic imperial structures, the new entity proved effective for mobilizing Western Europe's resources to explore and control the globe (Anderson 1974; Mann 1986, 1993; Strayer 2005; Tilly 1990; Wallerstein 1974, 1980).

The "discovery" of the Americas magnified European power and prosperity many-fold. The actual windfall—perhaps we should say "landfall"—accruing from the Old World's invasion and conquest of the New is hard to overstate. The approximate landmass of Western Europe is 1 million square miles (European Countries 2020).[6] That of the Americas is 15 *billion* square miles, or 15,000 times that of the former (Continents 2020). A triumphant Spain, having driven the last of the Moorish emirates from the Iberian Peninsula and flush with unanticipated American treasure, claimed the fruits of first conquest. The Dutch and the English, the former a rebel, the latter a rival of Spain, followed in its wake. Portugal and France, too, enjoyed their share (Arrighi 1994; Boxer 1969; Braudel 1981, 1982, 1984; Elliott 2007; Findlay and O'Rourke 2007).

The invasion, conquest, exploitation, and settlement of the Americas involved significant labor market disruptions. A brutal slave labor system, fed by African warlords, European human traffickers, and American planters, expanded unchecked in the New World colonies. By the end of the 18th century, the system had entrenched itself throughout the hemisphere. To minimize the inevitable resistance that enslavement engendered, enslavers systematically stripped the enslaved of as many social connections and cultural assets as they could (Baptist 2015; Klein 1999; Morgan 1975; Rediker 2007). The process left what had been one of the most developed regions of Africa "depleted in population, divided irremediably among themselves, retarded economically, and despised as an inferior race in a world which had built a vision of racial hierarchy based on the inspiration of their enslavement" (Manning 1990: 2; Nunn 2008; Rodney 1982).[7] It also seeded the New World with brutal social practices and invidious social distinctions that still plague it. Slavery was not the only form of labor that flourished in the Americas, however. It existed alongside a household labor system, where family members and other dependents worked in an extended patriarchal homestead. Labor relations in this setting were personal rather than impersonal, customary rather than contractual. Most members of such households, though subject to the control of the family head, had considerable autonomy and freedom of movement. Local families formed customary relationships and associations with each another, marked by various kinds of obligations and requirements. Markets and commercial relationships existed and played their part. But the customary relationships, obligations, and associations, flattened by their removal from the Old World to the New, dominated "the economy" in British North America and elsewhere (Greene and Pole 1984; Hartman 2004; Jennings 1975; Nash 2015).

The legacy of Europe's conquest and colonization of the Americas was thus bipolar: on one hand, an expanding, evermore brutal slavery, which exploited millions of unwilling victims and impoverished their homelands, even as it enriched enslavers and their clients; and, on the other, a growing number of self-reliant, semi-autonomous households of farming and craft families, which liberated and made the fortunes of millions of immigrants and their descendants.

Commercialization

Such was the North American shore onto which broke a transforming wave of commercialization. From the middle of the 18th century forward, the rapid expansion of commercial enterprise disturbed both the dominant household organization of labor and the mutuality characteristic of their relationships. A thin web of trade routes, maintained by specialized merchant families and warlords, connecting the largely self-reliant islands of what Fernand Braudel has called "a vast world of self-sufficiency," predated the modern era (1977: 19). Within this world, persistent shortages of reliable currency left the great bulk of local, mundane transactions and relationships unmonetized (as we say today), though possessed of a dynamism all their own. The financial and banking revolutions in the North Atlantic heart of European oceangoing commerce lessened this constraint on a massive scale. The English constitutional settlement of 1688 put the state's finances on a new, self-sustaining foundation, while demand deposit banking expanded in urban areas, flooding markets with private bank notes, money orders, and other currencies. Similar developments in the United States after its own constitutional settlement in 1787 sparked a similar commercial "takeoff" (Acemoglu and Robinson 2012; McCusker and Menard 1991; Merrill 1990; Muldrew 1998; Polanyi 2001).[8]

Commercialization had clear economic and social benefits. In the United States, the real value (in 1860 dollars) of the GDP rose from an estimated $149 million to $4.3 billion between 1774 and 1860, an almost 30-fold increase. GDP per capita over the same period increased by almost 300% (Gallman 2000; Weiss 1989). At the same time, the American Revolution democratized the nation's governing institutions by expanding political participation, even as it protected slavery, refused the rights of man to women, and engaged in a genocidal war against the continent's original inhabitants (Drinnon 1980; Jennings 2000; Kerber 1980, 1998; Main 1965; Wood 1980).

On a list of commercialization's most disruptive labor market effects in the United States from the mid-18th to the mid-19th centuries, we would include (1) the continuing conquest and expulsion of the descendants of the first settlers of the Americas from their native lands; (2) the massive deportation of enslaved people from the coastal states to the interior of the United States, the utter destruction of their families, and the intensification of slavery regimes across the continent; (3) the continuing erosion of customary rural economies and traditional employments in Europe, which triggered mass migrations from the countryside to the city and abroad; and (4) a similar process in the United States, resulting in increased urbanization and mechanization, accompanied by declining standards of living and life expectancy for the migratory generation (Beckert and Rockman 2016; Berlin 2003; Blum 1978; Costa and Steckel 1997; Dowd 1992; Johnson 2013; Sellars 1991; Zakim and Kornblith 2012).

The literature on the rise of competitive commerce and political democracy is vast, both as regard their benefits and their costs. Every modern social science is in some sense an effort to understand the new commercial order. For example, the discipline of economics arguably developed to counter the conventional wisdom about what was possible and to explain why replacing familial, customary relationships with impersonal commercial ones had clear social and individual benefits. Sociology, political science, and even psychology developed under the aegis of similar concerns. After centuries of monarchial expansion and a shift to more centralized, top-down control, to think that society could operate on a decentralized, democratic basis and be efficient, peaceful, and stable withal, appeared revolutionary to many observers (Smith [1776] 1937; Tocqueville [1835, 1840] 2000).

The resistance to commercialization and its literature is also extensive. Every colonizer, enslaver, encloser, and exploiter, not to mention every innovator, encountered resistance of various kinds, including demands for more freedom, equality, independence, democracy, and broadly shared prosperity (Marx [1867] 1976). But commercialization swept all before it. By the mid-19th century, human social organization had broken through the structural and organizational barriers that had retarded the commodification of the familiar and the routine—and nothing would ever be the same.

Industrialization

The next 100 years, 1850 to 1950 or so, were similarly transformative, with machines replacing manual labor in an increasing number of occupations. David A. Wells, whom we met above, chronicled the first signs of this process in his *Recent Economic Changes*. He there declared the period from 1860 to 1885 the most important quarter century in the history of humanity (Wells 1889: 27–28). "The world has ... never experienced in so short a time such an expansion of all that pertains to what is called business," Wells wrote, "and has never before ... been able to accomplish so much in the way of production with a given amount of labor in a given time" (Wells 1889: 61–62). In Adam Smith's time, "it was considered a wonderful achievement for ten men to make 48,000 pins in a day, but now three men can make 7,500,000 pins of vastly superior character in the same period." Many "similar and equally remarkable experiences, derived from almost every department of industry except handicrafts, might be presented" (Wells 1889: 60–61).

In Wells's most important quarter century, "mechanization takes command." As explored at length in Siegfried Giedion's 1948 book of that title, the new machines did not just enhance humanity's ability to get things done. They affected every aspect of life from the most visible to the most intimate (Giedion [1948] 1969: v). During the second half of the 19th century in the United States, mechanical processes took the place of "complicated handicraft" for "the farmer, the baker, the butcher, the joiner, the housewife"—in fact, almost everyone (Giedion [1948] 1969: 5). The impulse to mechanize was never more in evidence than in these years:

> Invention was in the normal course of things. Everyone invented, whoever opened an enterprise sought ways and means by which to make his goods more speedily, more perfectly, and often of improved beauty. Anonymously and inconspicuously, the old tools were transformed into modern instruments. Never did the number of inventions per capita of the population exceed its proportion in [the] America of the [eighteen-]sixties. (Giedion [1948] 1969: 40)

Clearly, the cult of the new and its fascination with gadgets did not begin yesterday.

Several transformative disruptions of work during this period of "high mechanization" are worth noting: (1) the end of slavery in the South and the immediate emancipation of 4 million enslaved people; (2) the mechanization of manifold skilled tasks in the workshop and the household that shifted the balance of power between employers and employees, husbands and wives, parents and children; (3) the growing size of worksites and enterprises, consequent on other sources of energy (petrochemical and electrical) and new means of communication and transportation; and (4) the rise of various public agencies, institutions, and services (including schools, transportation networks, water systems, police and public health measures, building codes, etc.), which replaced the household and the neighborhood as the primary sites of social protection and regulation.

These transformations had winners and losers. Abolishing slavery, for example, certainly benefited the enslaved and radically changed their prospects. In an all-too-frequent pattern, however, having lost the most under slavery, those once enslaved lost again after emancipation (Blackburn 2011; Blackmon 2008). The mechanization of traditional household and workshop tasks also lightened labors and eliminated much drudgery. But doing so also rendered many long-valued household skills superfluous and impoverished many skilled workers and artisans. Viable options were often available for the affected men, though not always readily. The mechanization of household tasks presented other kinds of challenges for women. Mothers and married women had fewer options outside the household, and many found themselves trapped in and infuriated by a constricting domestic servitude (Boydston 1994; Cowan 1983; Dublin 1994; Jones 2010). The new mammoth enterprises were also sites of intense control struggles over both the work process and for the largest possible share of the value it added (Marx 1867/1976). This ongoing battle seeded decades of industrial strife in lethal and costly ways.

The ensuing conflicts resulted in new institutions of political representation, workplace regulation, and social governance (Brecher 2020; Chandler 1977; Montgomery 1980, 1987; Nelson 1975). The increasing scale of market enterprise spurred a parallel growth in the size of government enterprises, both to service the new, commercial behemoths and to provide adequate means of regulation and control (Bakija, Kenworthy, Lindert, and Madrick 2016; Lindert 2004; Robinson 2020). None of these adjustments were costless. They required conscious effort and considerable expense. Each new process displaced some of those dependent on or devoted to the now obsolete products and processes. Not everyone displaced found a substitute. Many struggled. Some died.

The question for us now is can we do better? Private and public means managed each of the transitions we have surveyed. Self-absorbed innovators with their technology-centered creations played their part, as did self-interested entrepreneurs and their income-maximizing opportunities. But community-based civic and political leaders, who invented novel forms of social responsibility, accountability, and action, were also indispensable. Civic associations and trade unions, along with other civil society initiatives, did at least as much to facilitate successful adaptations to the new ways of doing things as did the engines and enterprises.

Computerization

Tools, machines, and media have been changing from mechanical to electronic and analog to digital since World War II. The recent literature on the future of work focuses on this transition, and we will not review it here. We have surveyed prior transformations as a reminder that the scale of the current disruption is not unprecedented. The world has seen upheavals like this before. What it has not seen are upheavals like this in an environment where there is so little room for maneuver or error. We cannot now assume, as Wells did in the 1880s, that things will continue as they always have. We have changed them. Humanity is no longer just one among many dependent factors in the ecosystem. It *is* the ecosystem. Welcome to the Anthropocene (Vince 2014; Wallace-Wells 2019). The Earth will survive the epoch, of couse. But whether human civilization will do so is an open question. In truth, "the future of work" is not our most pressing problem. We must reduce our footprint on the planet or our future will be much less brilliant than we might hope (Downing et al. 2020). To ignore this imperative is no longer excusable.

WHAT NEXT?

What adaptations are possible and desirable? Our history suggests that those with the most to lose usually pay more of the costs of transition than those with the most to gain. Innovation, even when it produces better job prospects overall, leaves many people without work. Put another way, output-enhancing and labor-saving technologies are more likely to impoverish than to enrich those whose output they increase and labor they save. Humanity has tried to grow its way out of these difficulties for centuries. But growth is not the attractive option it once was. We can no longer solve our distribution problems by doubling down on our production solutions. Despite years of trying, inequality continues to widen, and our efforts to grow the curve of history in a more sustainable direction has barely registered in the data (Hickel and Kallis 2019; McAfee 2019; Otto et al. 2020; Ward et al. 2016; Wiedmann, Lenzen, Keyßer, and Steinberger 2020; Wiedmann et al. 2015).

If business as usual no longer serves, what might? Brynjolfsson and McAfee's most radical recommendation is some version of a universal basic income (UBI). They worry that proposals for an outright grant neglect the benefits of work for both individuals and communities, and we agree (234). (We also worry that an economics of dependency is never conducive to a politics of independency.) But Brynjolfsson and McAfee set strict limits on the range of social possibilities they are willing to entertain. To be sure, they are not Luddites. As they explain: "We do not think the right policy would be to try to halt the march of technology," which they equate with "locking all the schools and burning all the scientific journals" (231). Yet they do not have similar hesitations about halting the forward march of sociology. On the contrary, they are "skeptical of efforts to come up with fundamental alternatives to capitalism" and are more than happy to "let the technologies of the second machine age do their work" (231). This skepticism marks a limit to their social imagination. They are prisoners of the familiar, capacious, economists' definition of capitalism, which they render as "a decentralized economic system of production and exchange in which most of the means of production are in private hands (as opposed to belonging to the government), where most exchange is voluntary (no one can force you to sign a contract against your will), and where most goods have prices that vary based on relative supply and demand instead of being fixed by a central authority" (231). Defined this way, most economies have been "capitalist." The result is that Brynjolfsson and McAfee have a tough time going "wild," even as they call for their readers to do so (245–247). They may turn Thatcherite austerity away at the front door, but they let "there is no alternative" in through the back.

Happily, there are other ways to define capitalism than as a generic market economy. The best approaches capitalism as a political system, a way of organizing and controlling market economies. A political perspective on capitalism also yields more useful ways to think about alternatives to it (Ingham 2011; Kocka 2016; Merrill 2014a; Wallerstein 1995). From a political–economic perspective, capitalism—a commercial economy governed by or in the interests of capitalists—is not the only market economy imaginable. There are other types: for instance, one governed by or in the interests of wage earners. A "wage-centered market economy" maximizes wages not profits, but otherwise meets all the criteria of the most desirable economic system as defined by Brynjolfsson and McAfee. Calls for a UBI point the way there. But making an economic winner of everyone is not just about redistributing income. It is about redistributing power. Capitalists are not only powerful because they are rich; they are also rich because they are powerful. Anyone with assets to invest wants a range of acceptable options from which to choose. Capitalists use their power to create institutions that foster such options and make themselves better off. If wage earners used their power to foster an equivalent range of options and leverage for themselves, they too would be better off.

Devising such a democratic, worker-empowering competitive system, with adequate and serviceable choices available to all, requires a good deal of rethinking about how best to conduct the public's business. The goal of such rethinking is not to reduce but to multiply the options available to investors, consumers, and workers, to make available at the bottom a range of attractive alternatives equivalent to those available at the top. We need to set goals that ensure both a reasonable profit for the average entrepreneur and a reasonable wage for the average employee. Obscene wealth on one side of the scale and abject poverty on the other is unnecessary. When wage earners have as many acceptable options to choose from as investors and employers do, then and only then can we ensure a balance of economic power consistent with a fairer distribution of income. In other words, we will solve the problem of work only when we solve the problems of workers. A job for everyone who wanted to work—in the private sector at a premium wage, if possible, and in the public sector at a living wage, if not—would shift the balance of power in a fairer, more just direction. The surest way to adjust the balance and reduce the inequity of the present system is to give public enterprises the means to compete for employees with private businesses and then encourage them to do so. To get there, we need more clear thinking about "the entrepreneurial state" and "managing the commons" (Bollier and Helfrich 2012; Mazzucato 2015; Mitchell and Fazi 2017; Ostrom 2015). The key is to strike the right balance between reward, responsibility, and accountability.

Greater equity is also not the only good reason to give labor as many viable options to choose from as capital has. New public employment opportunities and wage stabilization policies would reduce the destructive volatility of labor markets, just as public investment opportunities and interest rate management have reduced the destructive volatility of capital markets. With such policies in place, labor-saving technologies, more renewable energy sources, and nonpolluting, biocompatible processes and materials would meet less resistance from those whose livelihoods are now dependent on older, more environmentally destructive and unsustainable employments. Government-backed securities have long been available to investors looking for a safe haven. A government-backed job guarantee ought to be available for every wage earner looking for steady work. These jobs must and can create value, providing services for which people are prepared to pay taxes and fees. Most importantly, however, they must be available to anyone who wants one. Everyone who works deserves a decent job (Elster 1988; Harvey 1989; Tcherneva 2020; Wray 1997, 1998).

As we read what the great American sociologist C. Wright Mills once called "the drift" of our time, we can see movement in this direction. The public sector is changing and growing alongside the private. Among our challenges is to continue to nurture both sociological and technological innovation. The current form of our societies is not the only one possible—and we hope not the last. Economic growth will not save us. It merely pushes the waste downstream and leaves the inevitable day of reckoning to later generations, probably even the next. We are running out of room and time to suffer such delusions. We need organizations and institutions now that enhance the way we work together, even more than we need "brilliant machines." Without a stable and sustainable equilibrium between nature's necessities and our desires, humanity's continued flourishing is impossible.

ENDNOTES

1. With apologies to Ms. Alice Vetter, Merrill's public high school Latin teacher in Boise, Idaho, for the ungrammatical construction that the word play required.

2. A Google Ngram of the "future of work" turns up only a few instances of that phrase before 1970. The history of the "end of work" is longer. It shows up often from the 1860s on.

3. All the quoted passages were in the first edition and carried forward through every subsequent printing. We wish to acknowledge that the closing remarks bear the unmistakable imprint of Mill's intellectual partner and frequent co-author Harriet Taylor (H.T. Mill 1998: 291ff.).

4. All parenthetical page numbers in the text refer to Brynjolfsson and McAfee 2014.

5. On a linear graph, the distance between any two points (A, B) is the difference between them (B − A) and measures the amount of change. The distance between any two points on a logarithmic graph, in contrast, is their ratio (B/A), which measures the rate not the amount of change.

6. For our estimate, we added the reported territories in square miles of the following modern European countries: Austria, Belgium, Czechia, Denmark, France, Germany, Hungary, Ireland, Italy, Netherlands, Portugal, Slovakia, Spain, and the United Kingdom.

7. Nathan Nunn's 2008 econometric study, "The Long-Term Effects of Africa's Slave Trade," supports Manning's summary description. Nunn found that the "African countries that are the poorest today are the ones from which the most slaves were taken," even though it was the "most developed parts of Africa, not the least, … tended to select into the slave trades" (Nunn 2008: 140, 168).

8. One of us has estimated the money economy of the United States at 10% of total economic activity in 1800. By 1850, it accounted for almost half of the total, and by 1870, as a direct consequence of the transforming effects of the Civil War, for 90% (Merrill 2014b).

REFERENCES

Acemoglu, Daron, and James A. Robinson. 2012. *Why Nations Fail: The Origins of Power, Prosperity, and Poverty.* New York, NY: Crown Business.

Anderson, Perry. 1974. *Lineages of the Absolutist State.* London, UK: Verso.

Arrighi, Giovanni. 1994. *The Long Twentieth Century: Money, Power, and the Origins of Our Times.* London, UK: Verso.

Bakija, Jon M., Lane Kenworthy, Peter H. Lindert, and Jeffrey G. Madrick. 2016. *How Big Should Our Government Be?* Berkeley, CA: University of California Press.

Baptist, Edward E. 2015. *Half Has Never Been Told: Slavery and the Making of American Capitalism.* New York, NY: Basic Books.

Beckert, Sven, and Seth Rockman, eds. 2016. *Slavery's Capitalism: A New History of American Economic Development.* Philadelphia, PA: University of Pennsylvania Press.

Berlin, Ira. 2003. *Generations of Captivity: A History of African-American Slaves.* Cambridge, MA: Belknap Press of Harvard University Press.

Blackburn, Robin. 2011. *The American Crucible: Slavery, Emancipation and Human Rights.* London, UK: Verso.

Blackmon, Douglas A. 2008. *Slavery by Another Name: The Re-Enslavement of Black Americans from the Civil War to World War II.* New York, NY: Doubleday.

Blum, Jerome. 1978. *The End of the Old Order in Rural Europe.* Princeton, NJ: Princeton University Press.

Bollier, David, and Silke Helfrich, eds. 2012. *The Wealth of the Commons: A World beyond Market and State*. Amherst, MA: The Commons Strategies Group Levellers Press.

Boxer, C.R. 1969. *The Portuguese Seaborne Empire, 1415–1825*. New York, NY: Knopf.

Boydston, Jeanne. 1994. *Home and Work: Housework, Wages, and the Ideology of Labor in the Early Republic*. New York, NY: Oxford University Press.

Braudel, Fernand. 1977. *Afterthoughts on Material Civilization and Capitalism*. Baltimore, MD: Johns Hopkins University Press.

Braudel, Fernand. 1981. *Civilization and Capitalism 15th–18th Century, Vol. I. The Structures of Everyday Life: The Limits of the Possible*. New York, NY: Harper & Row.

Braudel, Fernand. 1982. *Civilization and Capitalism, 15th–18th Century, Vol. II. The Wheels of Commerce*. New York, NY: Harper & Row.

Braudel, Fernand. 1984. *Civilization and Capitalism, 15th–18th Century, Vol. III. The Perspective of the World*. New York, NY: Harper & Row.

Brecher, Jeremy. 2020. *Strike!* 50th anniversary edition. Oakland, CA: PM Press.

Brynjolfsson, Eric, and Andrew McAfee. 2014. *The Second Machine Age: Work, Progress, and Prosperity in a Time of Brilliant Machines*. New York, NY: Norton.

Carney, Mark. 2018 (Sep. 14). "The Future of Work." Whitaker Lecture. Central Bank of Ireland. https://bit.ly/2LBqZDA

Chandler, Alfred D. 1977. *The Visible Hand: The Managerial Revolution in American Business*. Cambridge, MA: Harvard University Press.

Chase, Malcolm. 2007. *Chartism: A New History*. Manchester, UK: Manchester University Press.

Christian, David. 2004. *Maps of Time: An Introduction to Big History*. Berkeley, CA: University of California Press.

Cohen, Joel. 1995. *How Many People Can the Earth Support?* New York, NY: Norton.

Considerant, Victor. (1843) 2006. *Principles of Socialism: Manifesto of 19th Century Democracy*. Washington, DC: Maisonneuve Press.

Continents. 2020 (Dec. 11). *Wikipedia*. https://bit.ly/2K3tXQL

Costa, Dora, and Richard H. Steckel. 1997. "Long-Term Trends in Health, Welfare, and Economic Growth in the United States." In *Health and Welfare During Industrialization*, edited by Richard H. Steckel and Roderick Floud, pp. 47–90. Chicago, IL: University of Chicago Press.

Cowan, Ruth. 1983. *More Work for Mother: The Ironies of Household Technology from the Open Heath to the Microwave*. New York, NY: Basic Books.

Deevey, Edward S. Jr. 1960. "The Human Population." *Scientific American* September: 195–204.

Dowd, Gregory. 1992. *A Spirited Resistance: The North American Indian Struggle for Unity, 1745–1815*. Baltimore, MD: Johns Hopkins University Press.

Downing, Andrea S., Manqi Chang, Jan J. Kuiper, Marco Campenni, Tiina Häyhä, Sarah E. Cornell, Uno Svedin, and Wolf M. Mooij. 2020 (Jul. 17). "Learning from Generations of Sustainability Concepts." *Environmental Research Letters* 15, 083002. https://bit.ly/38vqYKq

Drinnon, Richard. 1980. *Facing West: The Metaphysics of Indian-Hating and Empire-Building*. Minneapolis, MN: University of Minnesota Press.

Dublin, Thomas. 1994. *Transforming Women's Work: New England Lives in the Industrial Revolution*. Ithaca, NY: Cornell University Press.

Durkheim, Emile. 1974. *Sociology and Philosophy*. New York, NY: Free Press.

74 REVALUING WORK(ERS)

Elliott, J.H. 2007. *Empires of the Atlantic World: Britain and Spain in America, 1492–1830.* New Haven, CT: Yale University Press.

Elster, Jon. 1988. "Is There (Should There Be) a Right to Work?" In *Democracy and the Welfare State*, edited by Amy Gutmann. Princeton, NJ: Princeton University Press.

European Countries. 2020 (Dec. 11). *Wikipedia.* https://bit.ly/3oC7IQT

Findlay, Ronald, and Kevin O'Rourke. 2007. *Power and Plenty: Trade, War, and the World Economy in the Second Millennium.* Princeton, NJ: Princeton University Press.

Gallman, Robert. 2000, "Economic Growth and Structural Change in the Long Nineteenth Century." In *The Cambridge Economic History of the United States, Vol. 2: The Long Nineteenth Century*, edited by S. Engerman and R. Gallman. Cambridge, UK: Cambridge University Press.

Giedion, Siegfried. (1948) 1969. *Mechanization Takes Command: A Contribution to Anonymous History.* New York, NY: Norton.

Gorz, André. 1985. *Paths to Paradise: On the Liberation from Work.* London, UK: Pluto Press.

Gorz, André. 1999. *Reclaiming Work: Beyond the Wage-Based Society* Cambridge, UK: Polity Press.

Greene, Jack, and J.R. Pole, eds. 1984. *Colonial British America: Essays in the New History of the Early Modern Era.* Baltimore. MD: Johns Hopkins University Press.

Hartman, Mary. 2004. *Households and the Making of History: A Subversive View of the Western Past.* Cambridge, UK: Cambridge University Press.

Harvey, Philip. 1989. *Securing the Right to Employment: Social Welfare Policy and the Unemployed in the United States.* Princeton, NJ: Princeton University Press.

Hickel, Jason, and Giorgos Kallis. 2019. "Is Green Growth Possible?" *New Political Economy* 25 (4): 469–486. https://bit.ly/3sfur7F

Ingham, Geoffrey. 2011. *Capitalism.* Cambridge, UK: Polity Press.

Jennings, Francis. 1975. *The Invasion of America: Indians, Colonialism, and the Cant of Conquest.* Chapel Hill, NC: University of North Carolina Press.

Jennings, Francis. 2000. *The Creation of America: Through Revolution to Empire.* Cambridge, UK: Cambridge University Press.

Johnson, Walter. 2013. *River of Dark Dreams: Slavery and Empire in the Cotton Kingdom.* Cambridge, MA: Harvard University Press.

Jones, Jacqueline. 2010. *Labor of Love, Labor of Sorrow: Black Women, Work, and the Family, from Slavery to the Present.* New York, NY: Basic Books.

Kerber, Linda. 1980. *Women of the Republic: Intellect and Ideology in Revolutionary America.* Chapel Hill, NC: University of North Carolina Press.

Kerber, Linda. 1998. *No Constitutional Right to Be Ladies: Women and the Obligations of Citizenship.* New York, NY: Hill & Wang.

Klein, Herbert A. 1999. *The Atlantic Slave Trade.* Cambridge, UK: Cambridge University Press.

Kocka, Jürgen. 2016. *Capitalism: A Short History.* Princeton, NJ: Princeton University Press.

Lindert, Peter H. 2004. *Growing Public: Social Spending and Economic Growth Since the Eighteenth Century.* Cambridge, UK: Cambridge University Press.

Lund, Susan, James Manyika, Liz Hilton Segel, André Dua, Bryan Hancock, Scott Rutherford, and Brent Macon. 2019 (Jul. 11). "The Future of Work in America: People and Places, Today and Tomorrow." Report. San Francisco, CA: McKinsey Global Institute. https://mck.co/39qp8cS

Main, Jackson Turner. 1965. *The Social Structure of Revolutionary America.* Princeton, NJ: Princeton University Press.

Manyika, James, Michael Chui, Mehdi Miremadi, Jacques Bughin, Katy George, Paul Willmott, and Martin Dewhurst. 2017 (Jan.). "A Future That Works: Automation, Employment, and Productivity." Report. San Francisco, CA: McKinsey Global Institute. https://mck.co/3sntURp

Mann, Michael. 1986. *The Sources of Social Power, Vol. I: A History of Power from the Beginning to A.D. 1760*. Cambridge, UK: Cambridge University Press.

Mann, Michael. 1993. *The Sources of Social Power, Vol. II: The Rise of Classes and Nation-States, 1760–1914*. Cambridge, UK: Cambridge University Press.

Manning, Patrick. 1990. *Slavery and African Life: Occidental, Oriental, and African Slave Trades*. Cambridge, UK: Cambridge University Press.

Marx, Karl. (1867) 1976. *Capital: A Critique of Political Economy*. Harmondsworth, UK: Penguin.

Marx, Karl, and Frederick Engels. (1848) 1998. *The Communist Manifesto: A Modern Edition*. London, UK: Verso.

Mason, Paul. 2015. *Postcapitalism: A Guide to Our Future*. London, UK: Allen Lane.

Mazzucato, Mariana. 2015. *The Entrepreneurial State: Debunking Public vs. Private Sector Myths*. New York, NY: PublicAffairs.

McAfee, Andrew. 2019. *More from Less: The Surprising Story of How We Learned to Prosper Using Fewer Resources—and What Happens Next*. New York, NY: Scribner.

McCusker, John J., and Russell Menard. 1991. *The Economy of British America, 1607–1789*. Chapel Hill, NC: University of North Carolina Press.

Merrill, Michael. 1990. "Anticapitalist Origins of the United States." *Review* XIII (4): 165–197.

Merrill, Michael. 2014a. "How Capitalism Got Its Name." *Dissent* Fall: 77–81.

Merrill, Michael. 2014b (Sep.). "The Monetarization of Everything: Gifted Credit, Commercial Exchange, and the Transition to Capitalism in the 19th-Century United States." Newberry Seminar on the History of Capitalism. Chicago, IL: The Newberry Library.

Mill, Harriet Taylor. 1998. *The Complete Works of Harriet Taylor Mill*, edited by Jo Ellen Jacobs and Paula Harris Payne. Bloomington, IN: Indiana University Press.

Mill, John Stuart. 1917. *Principles of Political Economy*. London, UK: Longman, Green, and Co.

Mitchell, David, and Thomas Fazi. 2017. *Reclaiming the State: A Progressive Vision of Sovereignty for a Post-Neoliberal World*. London, UK: Pluto Press.

Montgomery, David. 1980. *Workers' Control in America: Studies in the History of Work, Technology, and Labor Struggles*. Cambridge, UK: Cambridge University Press.

Montgomery, David. 1987. *The Fall of the House of Labor: The Workplace, the State, and American Labor Activism, 1865–1925*. Cambridge, UK: Cambridge University Press.

Morgan, Edmund. 1975. *American Slavery, American Freedom: The Ordeal of Colonial Virginia*. New York, NY: Norton.

Morton, A.L. 1962. *The Life and Ideas of Robert Owen*. London, UK: Lawrence & Wishart.

Muldrew, Craig. 1998. *The Economy of Obligation: The Culture of Credit and Social Relations in Early Modern England*. New York, NY: Palgrave.

Nash, Gary B. 2015. *Red, White, and Black: The Peoples of Early North America*, 7th ed. Boston, MA: Pearson.

Nelson, Daniel. 1975. *Managers and Workers: Origins of the New Factory System in the United States, 1880–1920*. Madison, WI: University of Wisconsin Press.

Noble, David F. 2011. *Force of Production: A Social History of Industrial Automation*. New Brunswick, NJ: Transaction Publishers.

Nunn, Nathan. 2008. "The Long-Term Effects of Africa's Slave Trade." *Quarterly Journal of Economics* 123 (1): 139–176.

Ostrom, Elinor. 2015. *Governing the Commons: The Evolution of Institutions for Collective Action.* Cambridge, UK: Cambridge University Press.

Otto, Ilona M., Jonathan F. Donges, Roger Cremades, Avit Bhowmik, Richard J. Hewitt, Wolfgang Lucht, Johan Rockström, Franziska Allerberger, Mark McCaffrey, Sylvanus S.P. Doe, Alex Lenferna, Nerea Morán, Detlef P. van Vuuren, and Hans Joachim Schellnhuber. 2020. "Social Tipping Dynamics for Stabilizing Earth's Climate by 2050" *PNAS* 117 (5), 2354–2365. https://bit.ly/2MVnfNW

Owen, Robert. 1818. "Report to the Committee of the Association for the Relief of the Manufacturing and Labouring Poor." *New View of Society: Tracts Relative to this Subject.* London, UK: Robert Owen.

Polanyi, Karl. 2001. *The Great Transformation: The Political and Economic Origins of Our Time.* Boston, MA: Beacon Press.

Rediker, Marcus. 2007. *The Slave Ship: A Human History.* New York, NY: Viking.

Renfrew, Colin. 2007. *Prehistory: The Making of the Human Mind.* New York, NY: Modern Library.

Ricardo, David. 1951. *Works and Correspondence of David Ricardo, Vol. I: On the Principles of Political Economy and Taxation,* edited by P. Sraffa and M. Dobb. Cambridge, UK: Cambridge University Press.

Ricardo, David. 1952. *Works and Correspondence of David Ricardo, Vol. V: Speeches and Evidence,* edited by P. Sraffa and M. Dobb. Cambridge, UK: Cambridge University Press.

Robinson, Marc. 2020. *Bigger Government: The Future of Government Expenditure in Advanced Economies.* Evolène, Switzerland: Arolla Press.

Rodney, Walter. 1982. *How Europe Underdeveloped Africa.* Washington, DC: Howard University Press.

Rotman, David. 2020. "When More Is Not More." *MIT Technology Review* November–December: 14–15.

Schwab, Klaus. 2016. *The Fourth Industrial Revolution.* Geneva, Switzerland: World Economic Forum.

Sellars, Charles. 1991. *The Market Revolution: Jacksonian America, 1815–1846.* Oxford, UK: Oxford University Press.

Smil, Vaclav. 2002. *The Earth's Biosphere: Evolution, Dynamics, and Change.* Cambridge, MA: MIT Press.

Smil, Vaclav. 2019. *Growth: From Microorganisms to Megacities.* Cambridge, MA: MIT Press.

Smith, Adam. (1776) 1937. *An Inquiry into the Nature and Causes of the Wealth of Nations.* New York, NY: Modern Library.

Srnicek, Nick, and Alex Williams. 2016. *Inventing the Future: Postcapitalism and a World Without Work.* London, UK: Verso.

Sperber, Jonathan. 1994. *The European Revolutions, 1848–1851.* Cambridge, UK: Cambridge University Press.

Strayer, Joseph. 2005. *On the Medieval Origins of the Modern State.* Princeton, NJ: Princeton University Press.

Susskind, Daniel. 2020. *A World Without Work: Technology, Automation, and How We Should Respond.* New York, NY: Henry Holt.

Suzman, James. 2020. *Work: A History of How We Spend Our Time.* London, UK: Bloomsbury Circus.

Tcherneva, Pavlina R. 2020. *The Case for a Job Guarantee.* Cambridge, UK: Polity Press.

Tilly, Charles. 1990. *Capital, Coercion, and European States.* Oxford, UK: Basil Blackwell.

Tocqueville, Alexis de. 1835 & 1940/2000. *Democracy in America.* 2 vols. Chicago, IL: University of Chicago Press.

Vince, Gaia. 2014. *Adventures in the Anthropocene: A Journey to the Heart of the Planet We Made.* London, UK: Vintage.

Wallace-Wells, David. 2019. *The Uninhabitable Earth: Life After Warming.* New York, NY: Tim Duggan Books.

Wallerstein, Immanuel. 1974. *The Modern World System, Vol. I: Capitalist Agriculture and the Origins of the European World-Economy in the Sixteenth Century.* New York, NY: Academic Press.

Wallerstein, Immanuel. 1980. *The Modern World System, Vol. II: Mercantilism and the Consolidation of the European World-Economy, 1600–1750.* New York, NY: Academic Press.

Wallerstein, Immanuel. 1995. *Historical Capitalism with Capitalist Civilization.* London, UK: Verso.

Ward, James D., Paul C. Sutton, Adrian D. Werner, Robert Costanza, Steve H. Mohr, and Craig T. Simmons. 2016. "Is Decoupling GDP Growth from Environmental Impact Possible?" *PLoS ONE* 11 (10): e0164733. https://bit.ly/3bwa2p0

Weeks, Kathi. 2011. *The Problem with Work: Feminism, Marxism, Antiwork Politics, and Postwork Imaginaries.* Durham, NC: Duke University Press.

Weiss, Thomas. 1989. "Economic Growth Before 1860: Revised Conjectures." NBER Working Paper Series, No. 7, Historical Factors in Long-Run Growth. Cambridge, MA: National Bureau of Economic Research. https://bit.ly/3qnPvaz

Wells, David A. 1889. *Recent Economic Changes and Their Effect on the Production and Distribution of Wealth and the Well-Being of Society.* New York, NY: D. Appleton and Company.

Wiedmann, Thomas, Manfred Lenzen, Lorenz T. Keyßer, and Julia K. Steinberger. 2020. "Scientists Warning on Affluence." *Nature Communications* 11, 3107. https://go.nature.com/3sfgIh3

Wiedmann, Thomas O., Heinz Schandl, Manfred Lenzen, Daniel Moran, Sangwon Suh, James West, and Keiichiro Kanetodo. 2015 "The Material Footprint of Nations." *PNAS: Proceedings of the National Academy of Sciences* 112 (20): 6271–6276. https://bit.ly/3qflWYD

Wood, Gordon. 1980. *The Creation of the American Republic, 1776–1787.* Chapel Hill, NC: University of North Carolina Press.

Wray, L. Randall. 1997. "Government as Employer of Last Resort: Full Employment Without Inflation." Working Paper No. 213. Annandale-on-Hudson, NY: Jerome Levy Economics Institute.

Wray, L. Randall. 1998. *Understanding Modern Money: The Key to Full Employment and Price Stability.* Cheltenham, UK: Edward Elgar.

Zakim, Michael, and Gary Kornblith, eds. 2012. *Capitalism Takes Command: The Social Transformation of Nineteenth-Century America.* Chicago IL: University of Chicago Press.

Chapter 4

"Negotiate the Algorithm": Labor Unions, Scale, and Industry 4.0 Experimentation

Tod D. Rutherford

Syracuse University

ABSTRACT

This chapter examines the experiences of American, German, and Italian unions and workplace employee representatives' negotiation in adopting Industry 4.0 technology within organizational and institutional experimentation over new forms of work and its governance. The chapter makes three distinct but related points. The first is that many perspectives on Industry 4.0 are characterized by technological determinism and ignore that it will develop in a geographically uneven or variegated fashion. Second, a critical factor shaping Industry 4.0 variegation is the role played especially by trade unions in negotiating its experimentation. Third, there is ongoing workplace or organizational experimentation by unions and firms around Industry 4.0, but union interventions are often late in the technology adoption process. Given this and an overall neoliberal context of slower growth, wage suppression, and bargaining decentralization, it is not clear that these organizational and institutional experiments can be "scaled up" or sustained.

INTRODUCTION

According to many commentators, we are undergoing a qualitative leap forward in automation that may increasingly displace even relatively complex and well-remunerated employment (Brynjolfsson and McAfee 2014; Frey and Rahbari 2016). As such, attention should focus on both the quality of employment and how best to facilitate adjustments by workers (International Labour Organization 2018). These issues are evident in debates around Industry 4.0, an emerging manufacturing paradigm that deploys an integrated suite of advanced technologies, including robotics, artificial intelligence, and digitalization and is attracting considerable business, scholarly, and policy attention (Edwards and Ramirez 2016; McKinsey & Company 2019). However, Industry 4.0 confronts very real technical and social challenges, making production workers and their representatives potentially critical agents in what Murray, Levesque, Morgan, and Roby (2020) term organizational experimentation around this paradigm (Helper, Martin, and Seamans 2019; Krzywdzinski, Jürgens, and Pfeiffer 2015).

To better understand Industry 4.0 challenges for workers, trade unions, and works councils, the purpose of this chapter is threefold. The first is to briefly review the debate around Industry 4.0 and especially the roles trade unions are playing in new technology adoption. The second is to examine what a cross-national labor geography may contribute to current debates about Industry 4.0 experimentation. Drawing on Wright (2000), labor geography emphasizes the constrained but multiscalar agency of workers that is linked to their (1) structural powers stemming from their position within global production networks (GPNs), (2) institutional powers based on their legal and other institutional embeddedness, and (3) associational powers, or the ability to develop solidarity among workers and importantly to *act on* their structural and institutional powers (Coe 2015). Murray, Levesque, Morgan, and Roby (2020) have argued that labor's agency can be important to both organizational/work experimentation and "scaling up" into wider institutional experimentation.

The third and main goal of this chapter is to examine via case studies of trade unions in the United States, Germany, and Italy how structural, institutional, and associational powers mediate union roles, especially through workplace representational institutions. These experiments are occurring across what the varieties of capitalism (VoC) literature terms "coordinated market economies (CMEs)," such as in Germany, which are distinguished by having strong formal workplace representational institutions. They are also being undertaken in liberal market economies (LMEs) and in Mediterranean varieties, such as in the United States and Italy, respectively, which largely lack the workplace rights and institutions found in CMEs. Unions in CME Germany have greater avenues of intervention than in non-CME United States and Italy, but this has not prevented American, and especially Italian, unions from developing significant Industry 4.0 organizational experimentation.

In this organizational experimentation around Industry 4.0, the workplace is an increasingly central forum. However, workplace negotiation hinges on whether, and how, labor actors can draw on structural, institutional, and associational powers that also operate on other scales. The evidence suggests that while these confer some advantages to German unions, in all cases, unions confront similar multiscalar challenges, including a lack of sufficient technological knowledge among workplace representatives, retention of GPN investment, and a neoliberal context of slower overall growth, wage suppression, and sectoral bargaining derogations. Such findings also illustrate that power asymmetries favoring firms still largely prevail in Industry 4.0 experimentation. As such, labor's organizational experimentation remains largely tentative, uneven, and focused on defensive bargaining around the effects of change rather than the proactive design of technology. Furthermore, even in Germany and Italy, scaling up initiatives by labor have resulted in at best, a "quasi" form of institutional experimentation that may be neither sustained nor generalized.

To address these issues, this chapter is divided into three sections. In the first section, I examine debates around Industry 4.0. In the second, I review how labor geography's emphasis on labor's multiscalar agency and the variegated nature of capitalism can offer important insights into Industry 4.0 experimentation. In the third section, I critically engage with VoC theorizing and scholarship on experimentation to examine how US, German, and Italian trade unions are negotiating Industry 4.0 adoption. In the conclusion, I review the lessons of these cases.

THE INDUSTRY 4.0 DEBATE

Over the past five years, many researchers have argued that a new production paradigm—Industry 4.0—is increasingly informing advanced manufacturing strategies (Helper, Martins, and Seaman 2019; Totterdill 2015). Industry 4.0 refers to the digitally driven integration of manufacturing, and it includes technologies such as robotics, automation, sensors, artificial intelligence (AI), "big data," cloud computing, virtual reality (VR), augmented reality (AR), and additive manufacturing (i.e., 3D printing) (Rainnie and Dean 2020: 18). These technologies are creating new forms of human–machine interaction, or "cyber-physical" production systems, including touch interfaces, augmented-reality systems, and big-data analytics (Edwards and Ramirez 2016: 110).

Industry 4.0 also involves a strong managerial discourse that emerged in the wake of the 2008–2009 financial crisis as a primarily German response to the challenge of increasing competitiveness from China (Pfeiffer 2017). As such, national context matters to the interpretation of Industry 4.0 (Lloyd and Payne 2019). Thus, in Germany, Industry 4.0 is viewed as the critical enabler of a deeper transformation not only in manufacturing but in all sectors of the economy (Rainnie and Dean 2020: 20).

Yet it is important to stress that the salience of Industry 4.0 as a coherent manufacturing paradigm is open to question. Many technology-employment prognostications have been criticized for their technological determinism and exaggerated predictions of employment loss (Moody 2018). Indeed, because of Industry 4.0's technological challenges, many firms remain in "pilot purgatory," with only 30% able to capture value at scale (McKinsey & Company 2019).

As such, Industry 4.0 must be viewed as inchoate and with an uncertain trajectory. Furthermore, whatever Industry 4.0 might become, managerial accounts often ignore the potential workplace role played by workers and their representatives (Helper, Martin, and Seaman 2019; Totterdill 2015). Indeed, because of its very uncertainty, like other new work forms, Industry 4.0 is viewed as open to organizational experimentation in which workers and unions can be critical agents (Edwards and Ramirez 2016: 111–112; Murray, Levesque, Morgan, and Roby 2020). For example, while Industry 4.0 may reduce worker autonomy by limiting their ability to establish their own rules in organizational and production processes, it may also increase the need for worker discretionary interventions during production (Cirillo, Rinaldi, Staccioli, and Virgillato 2019).

In other words, Industry 4.0 may create both positive and adverse possibilities for workers (Byhovskaya 2018; Totterdill 2015). Avogaro (2018) contrasts an optimistic "specialization" scenario in which workers experience major upskilling and the elimination of more physically demanding and sometimes dangerous work, with a more pessimistic "automation" situation in which new technologies intensify work, increase surveillance, erode work–life balance, and substitute for, and control, even higher-skilled workers. Which outcomes emerge is in part determined by worker agency itself, with some favoring a workplace partnership between labor and capital that "moves away from its traditional focus on industrial relations, emerging as a potentially important driver of, and resource for organisational innovation in the broadest sense" (Totterdill 2015: 72). In so doing, trade unions need to "shape innovation in ways supporting fair and affordable working conditions, and to strengthen their capacity for autonomous action and decentralised self-regulation [because] based on past experiences with automation processes, the degree of process stability produced under laboratory conditions is hardly achieved in practice" (Krzywdzinski, Jürgens, and Pfeiffer 2015: 22–23).

However, the challenges confronting workers and unions in negotiating Industry 4.0 are not simply around collective bargaining strategies. Because Industry 4.0 is itself embedded in much wider and longer-term structural changes in employment connected to globalization and neoliberalism, including increased outsourcing and work intensification strategies by employers, it also challenges the institutional architecture and scaling of industrial relations systems themselves (Moody 2018). Thus, unions are having to adapt their strategies within a disrupted if not adverse environment.

WHY GEOGRAPHY MATTERS

Union and worker responses to Industry 4.0 are inextricably bound up in existing geographically variegated conditions. Geographic variegation is the iterative outcome of how agents make use of institutions in which geographic space is an active element in capitalist socio-scalar processes of convergence and differentiation (Peck and Theodore 2007). A major actor in these processes is labor, and labor geography stresses the agency of workers defined as any individual or collective attempt to change the status quo of the capitalist landscape (Coe, 2015: 174; Herod 2001). Emphasis is placed on worker and trade union ability to use their structural, associational, and institutional powers to "scale up" their actions from the local to the global, including via the formation of international networks (Cumbers 2015; Herod 2001).

There has been increased recognition that worker structural power is both subject to and shaped by global production networks (GPNs) led by multinational enterprises (MNE) (Cumbers 2015). Workers and unions deploying these powers can lead to worker "social upgrading" in GPNs in terms of skills, wages, conditions, and overall collective bargaining rights (Coe 2015). Thus, labor's multiscalar agency is important in shaping the governance of the workplace, including via influencing state policies, firm strategies, and local labor control regimes (Rutherford and Holmes 2013).

Labor geography's emphasis on worker multiscalar, relational agency has important synergies with perspectives stressing how social agents are responding to uncertainty by engaging in organizational and institutional experimentation through a process of iterative adaption (Murray, Levesque, Morgan, and Roby 2020: 141). Like labor geographers, experimentation perspectives problematize both "top down" structural accounts of neoliberalism and national-centric VoC approaches in favor of a more "bottom up" agent-led focus—especially at the organizational scale. However, labor geography and scholarship on experimentation also recognize the challenges in scaling up organizational experimentation into wider institutional change (Herod 2001; Murray, Levesque, Morgan, and Roby 2020). Furthermore, even within the uncertainties of a dynamically scaled capitalism, organizational experimentation over Industry 4.0 is still shaped by nation-state institutions (Lloyd and Payne 2019). Finally, the formative impact of GPN restructuring and neoliberalism should not be underestimated. Not only have these augmented capital's powers, but they have made nation-state policies less supportive of workers and have contributed to both a narrowing of work system bargaining outcomes between nations and a deepening of differences within them (Howell and Givan 2011; Katz and Darbishire 2000). As such, while Industry 4.0 uncertainties may enhance labor's experimentation role, this could be offset by how restructuring is impacting both its organizational experimentation positionality and its scaling up capacity in institutional experimentation.

Based on this VoC and experimentation informed labor geography perspective, worker and union capacity to shape Industry 4.0 will be contingent on their respective structural, institutional, and associational powers. As we will see below, how these translate into organizational and especially workplace-scale Industry 4.0 experimentation is not a linear one but reflects how unions and workplace representatives are able to act on such powers within a context of firm restructuring and state neoliberal policies.

CROSS-NATIONAL TRADE UNION EXPERIMENTATION AROUND INDUSTRY 4.0

United States

From a VoC perspective, the United States is the defining LME that relies more exclusively on markets for economic coordination (Hall and Soskice 2001). However, the US federal state has intervened significantly in shaping economic development and has an adversarial industrial relations system in which there is no legal support for direct forms of employee voice (Groshen, Helper, MacDuffie, and Carson 2019). This means that while the main union representing auto workers—the United Auto Workers (UAW)—has some institutional power derived from being the legal agent for workers, what "co-management" arrangements exist, for example, board-level labor representation in automotive original equipment manufacturers (OEMs) such as GM and Fiat Chrysler, are tenuous and based solely on four-year contracts (Lippert, Huzzard, Jürgens, and Lazonick 2014).

Because of its role as a leading advanced capitalist nation and the size of its consumer market, the United States represents a strategic site for automotive GPN investment. Despite the rise of Mexico, the United States still wins by far the most automotive investment (77%) within North America. Between 2009 and 2019, the Great Lakes states—the traditional heartland of US auto manufacturing and trade unionism—received more than three times the investment ($76.8 billion) of the US South ($23.8 billion) (Dziczek 2020). However, most Great Lakes states investment is reinvestment in existing plants, and the region has had significant unionized assembly plant closures (e.g., GM in Lordstown, Ohio). Furthermore, the transition to Industry 4.0–linked electric vehicles has included the closure of conventional powertrain plants and is predicted to cost nearly 35,000 union jobs over the next five to ten years (Dawson, Naughton, and Coppola 2019).

Thus, even though the UAW has potentially strong strategic powers stemming from its overall GPN position, they have been weakened by restructuring, the loss of US OEM market share to nondomestic assemblers, job movements to southern "right to work" states, and outsourcing to Mexico. The UAW has never been able to unionize any of the expanding nondomestic OEMs in the US South. This, coupled with Michigan and Wisconsin becoming right-to-work states and the long-term erosion of rank-and-file confidence in UAW leadership over concessionary workplace strategies, has also adversely impacted the unions' associational power (Gindin 2019). Nonetheless, the 2019 strike by GM workers that won concessions from the OEM on multi-tier employment systems illustrates that rank-and-file associational power is still significant.

Given this relative weakness, it is not surprising that organized labor has been given little attention in government or industry pronouncements around Industry

4.0 or, as it is commonly termed in the United States, "smart manufacturing" (Rainnie and Dean 2020). Nonetheless, the UAW still has institutional power derived from being the legal bargaining agent for a workforce for which OEMs have an ongoing need for skills and cooperation. In fact, over the past two decades, the UAW has adopted an increasingly collaborative approach to workplace change, and Industry 4.0 has also been viewed as a way of enhancing labor–management cooperation (Cutcher-Gershenfeld, Brooks, and Mulloy 2015; Groshen, Helper, MacDuffie, and Carson 2019). Furthermore, union power also derives from US labor law that requires firms to consult worker representatives over any technological change that can displace represented employees (Kochan, Liebman, and Weitershausen 2018).

Based on such powers, the UAW has negotiated with OEMs such as GM to have skilled trades workers run 3D printing rooms as part of what Helper, Martins, and Seamans (2019) term "worker enhancing" strategies. Furthermore, the 2019 GM–UAW contract established a joint National Committee on Advanced Technology to meet quarterly and discuss how GM plans to implement new technologies, such as electric and autonomous vehicles and 3D printing (Noble 2019). This national committee will also directly liaise with existing plant-level new technology committees and the newly established joint Mobile Equipment Technology Specifications Committee (METSC). The latter will meet over new powered industrial vehicles technology, including automated guided vehicles and vehicles that are personally driven in a facility, "to ensure that any current or future work that belongs in the unit is done by represented workers" (United Auto Workers 2019a: 6).

The UAW is also concerned about problems of physical stress on workers that may be augmented by Industry 4.0 technologies (United Auto Workers 2019b). Thus, the 2019 GM contract also succeeded in reducing the threshold number of employees—from 2,000 to 1,500—to merit a second full-time UAW industrial hygiene technician–joint ergonomics technician (IHT-JET). In addition, plants with more than 2,000 members will gain a third full-time UAW IHT-JET (United Auto Workers 2019b: 11). The UAW also wants to increase its existing rights around technological change while developing continuous training and preventing contracting out (United Auto Workers 2019a: 58).

Despite such initiatives, the UAW's relatively weak structural, institutional, and associational powers impact its Industry 4.0 experimentation. Thus, the UAW's 2019 contract with Ford saw the union agree to a Taylorist strategy allowing the firm to deploy digital video recording and path-mapping technologies to surveil and better control worker movements (Brooks 2019). The UAW is thus still informed by Taylorism and largely defers to managerial prerogatives over Industry 4.0 that view labor in cost minimization terms rather than playing an active role in its implementation (Helper, Martins, and Seamans 2019). Furthermore, an ongoing concern is that its workplace representatives lack sufficient knowledge to effectively negotiate robotics and other Industry 4.0 technologies (Brown 2018: 363).

Germany

Germany is considered the archetype CME, with strong financial and industrial capital links and complementarities between codetermination institutions, incremental innovation, and trade unions and works councils in core manufacturing (Deeg and Jackson 2007). Germany is the largest manufacturing economy in the European Union and is extensively integrated into GPNs—especially for mid-range technology such as machinery, transportation equipment, and process industries (De Ville 2018).

This GPN positionality gives German unions a relatively high degree of potential structural power, which they have augmented through their institutional role in which German employees are represented in the codetermination system consisting of statutory works councils and employee board-level representation (EBLR) (Müller-Jentsch 2018). Unions can thus influence corporate investment strategy, and despite some outsourcing of lower value-added, labor-intensive components (mainly to Central and Eastern Europe), Germany has retained a relatively high share of GPN production (De Ville 2018). Works councils are also part of a dual system in which unions negotiate wages at the sectoral scale while the councils allow employee participation in decisions over mainly qualitative, personnel issues at the establishment level. While formally independent, most works council representatives are also trade union members and unions have developed strong supportive relationships with the councils (Bosch and Schmitz-Kießler 2020). Board representatives may be trade union members and, under German law, half the supervisory board members in firms with more than 2,000 employees must be appointed by the employees.

Finally, this relative degree of structural and institutional power has implications for German union associational power. While overall German union density has declined, most workers within core manufacturing sectors are represented by IG Metall—the largest metal workers union in the world, with over 2 million members (Müller-Jentsch 2018). Under codetermination, German strike levels have been relatively low, but as we will see, the 2018 IG Metall–led strike reveals that German unions have significant capacity for taking such action to advance their position (see Table 1 on page 93).

Given these relatively strong structural, institutional, and associational powers, it is not surprising that labor stakeholders were included in the 2016 "German Federal Ministry for Labor and Social Affairs White Paper on Industry 4.0" (Byhovskaya 2018). However, the German Trade Union Federation, which has prioritized enabling labor mobility, providing workers' training, curtailing intensification, strengthening codetermination, and enhancing work–life balance in Industry 4.0 adoption, has expressed concerns that the white paper will not lead directly to policy. As such, it has been through both sectoral bargaining and the works councils that German unions led by IG Metall are seeking to meet these union goals (Bosch and Schmitz-Kießler 2020).

At the enterprise scale, IG Metall has emphasized integrating worker requalification into the longer technical and organizational strategies of firms. Significantly, the role played by trade union officials is viewed as not only to manage conflicts but to "suggest different creditable solutions to management" (Avogaro 2018: 173). In IG Metall's case, strategy around Industry 4.0 must be coordinated with works councils, and it emphasizes intervening as early as possible in Industry 4.0 "to support works councils in '4.0'-change processes" (Vanselow 2017: 11).

Such coordination with works councils builds on both IG Metall's 2004 Pforzheim Agreement with firms regulating their derogations from sectoral agreements and the union's subsequent besser statt billiger (better rather than cheaper) campaign to combat outsourcing and assist works councils to deal with the impact of the 2008–2009 recession (Bosch and Schmitz-Kießler 2020). In these, IG Metall accepted that firms could deviate from sectorally negotiated wages and working times, but only if they presented a convincing long-term recovery strategy and made "counter-concessions," including augmenting worker codetermination rights around innovation and investment in ways that often went well beyond both codetermination law and pre-crisis precedent (Schulten and Bispinck 2018: 124).

Since the 2008–2009 crisis, IG Metall has adopted a strategy of "proactive modernization" because, during the besser statt billiger campaigns, firms in economic difficulties did not put sufficient investment into new technology early enough to offset job losses or plant relocation (Bosch and Schmitz-Kießler 2020). The subsequent Arbeit 2020 project, coordinated by IG Metall and other unions, targeted the North Rhine–Westphalia region for the first phase of the project (2015–2017) and supported works councils at 28 companies to negotiate agreements shaping workplace digitalization (Harbecke and Filipiak 2018). The aim of this project was to involve works councils at the earliest possible stage to design technology in a more humane manner, especially around workloads and the upgrading of work, technology design, and employee qualification development. This project has involved the extensive use of outside technical consultants to support works councilors and new forms of employee participation, including intercompany exchanges aiming to "proactively support and shape these technological processes in the companies" (Harbecke and Filipiak 2018: 24).

By December 2019, agreements on the digital future were concluded in 13 of the 28 selected plants, all of them represented by IG Metall. The unions' involvement in plant-level bargaining, previously conducted only between works councils and management, also included the intensive participation of the rank and file (Bosch and Schmitz-Kießler 2020). However, the other unions involved did not have the capacity to support the works councils or conclude agreements on their behalf. Furthermore, the project's limitations, including firm and works council resistance and an overall lack of works council's expertise in technological change, raised doubts about generalizing such initiatives beyond the initial pilot regions. Indeed, an IG Metall survey of 2,000 works councilors found that 62% were not involved in shop-floor change management projects, skills requirements were routinely assessed in only 35% of plants, and more than three quarters of councilors said they needed greater support to be able to carry out their codetermination functions (Bosch and Schmitz-Kießler 2020: 16). As a result, some 1,000 full-time and voluntary IG Metall officials are to be trained around supporting Industry 4.0 adoption (see Table 1 on page 93).

Thus, while the reformatting of union–work council relationships around Industry 4.0 may constitute a form of quasi-institutional experimentation, they confront real challenges in scaling up organizational experiments beyond individual workplaces. Furthermore, such a union and works council experimentation role is mainly in plants in higher positions in GPNs where new products and processes are being introduced (Krzywdzinski 2017). At plant sites lower in the value chain, the role of unions or works councils is much less significant.

These challenges to unions and works councils occur as their overall institutional power has weakened. German works council coverage has fallen significantly, and they now represent only about 9% of all establishments and 41% of all employees (Schulten and Bispinck 2018: 144). This decline has happened in a context of increasing collective bargaining derogations, while outsourcing and globalization have shifted strategic decision making away from the establishment scale (Müller-Jentsch 2008). Workplace managers have also increasingly "hollowed out" codetermination by marginalizing labor representatives (Schulten and Bispinck 2018: 143–144). As Bosch and Schmitz-Kießler argue,

> there is a world of difference between employers' assertions on co-determination in policy documents and the actual involvement of unions and works councils in the shaping of structural change in the workplace. In recent decades, the restructuring of value chains has also been used to revoke the social compromises of the past. The share of precarious employees has risen, and many activities have deliberately been outsourced to supplier firms without collective agreements or works councils, seriously weakening unions. (2020: 3)

Such workplace challenges mean that wider collective bargaining strategies and labor's associational powers may also be critical to both organizational and scaling up institutional experimentation. In early 2018, after 24-hour "warning" strike actions against Baden-Württemberg employers, IG Metall was able to win a significant pay increase for 900,000 employees and the option of employees to work a 28-hour week for up to a two-year period, to facilitate better work–life balance. Importantly for institutional innovation, Baden-Württemberg serves as a key "pilot agreement" region that may then be transferred to other bargaining areas (Schulten and Bispinck 2018: 118).

Italy

Italy is a Mediterranean variety of capitalism with weak industrial financial complementarities, relatively low research and development (R&D) investment, and industrial relations significantly more decentralized and less consensual than Germany's (Vallejo-Peña and Giachi 2018). Italy is second only to Germany in EU manufacturing, being highly specialized in machinery, motor vehicles, and high-end clothing and accessories. However, Italian firm GPN participation is very fragmented between a relatively small, internationalized core of large firms and a very large share of domestically oriented small and medium enterprises (SMEs). This divide was deepened by the 2008–2009 recession that disproportionately hurt domestically focused SMEs and Italian suppliers to GPNs (Agostino, Guinta, Scalera, and Trivieri 2016: 4). These trends adversely impact the structural power of Italian unions in GPN segments—most notably Fiat Chrysler, whose presence in Italy has long been subject to delocalization (Ciravegna 2006). After the 2008–2009 financial crisis, Fiat withdrew from the national employers' federation Confindustria and leveraged its credible threat to withdraw investment, to win significant concessions from unions over working time and labor flexibility (Pulignano, Carrieri, and Baccaro 2018: 668) (see Table 1 on page 93).

Furthermore, in contrast to the institutional powers that German unions derive from legally embedded codetermination, the Italian system is highly voluntaristic, without legally mandated employee board-level representatives or works councils (Leonardi, Ambra, and Ciarini 2018: 188). The main employee representative forums in manufacturing workplaces, the Rappresentanze Sindacali Unitarie (RSUs), are essentially union bodies that are elected by all employees. There are also Rappresentanze Sindacali Aziendali (RSA) at the company scale that are designated by unions and not elected by all employees. Collective agreements with firms are considered binding if they are approved by a majority of RSU members. However, not only have the rights of Italian workers to codetermination never been legally secured, but in Italian SMEs with 15 or fewer employees—the great majority of firms and workers—only 12% of firms have an RSU (Armaroli and Spattini 2018).

Italian labor's associational power is also less significant than Germany's. Italy's national collective bargaining coverage remains quite high, but it has significant levels of noncompliance and "pirate agreements" with increasingly decentralized secondary bargaining and territorial pacts. In addition, Italian worker associational power is also more problematic because of the multiplication of trade unions (about

12 in total) (Leonardi, Ambra, and Ciarini 2018). Moreover, the relationship between the main advanced manufacturing unions—the Italian General Confederation of Labour (CGIL) and the metal workers federation of the Italian Confederation of Workers' Trade Unions (FIM-CISL)—has often been characterized by rivalry rather than cooperation (Pulignano, Carrieri, and Baccaro 2018). Such fragmentation weakens overall union associational power. While rank and file workers have often displayed considerable militancy, it has declined significantly since the 1990s (Leonardi , Ambra, and Ciariani 2018). Finally, since 2000, Italian unions have also lost institutional power with the decline of tripartite social pacts (Pulignano, Carrieri, and Baccaro 2018).

The Italian national plan Industria 4.0, was developed in 2016 and focused on stimulating private investment in R&D, new technologies, and processes by using a mix of tax credits and super-depreciation rates on technology purchases (Seghezzi and Tiraboschi 2018: 5). Unlike Germany, however, it largely ignored the role of labor (Gaddi, Garbellini, and Garibaldo 2018). Nonetheless, the Economic Development Ministry subsequently established a working group that included trade unions, while the Ministry of Labor also held meetings on skill development with unions (Byhovskaya 2018: 19).

To address Industry 4.0, the CGIL and the FIM-CISL have developed Web discussion platforms and issued proposals calling for the strengthening of collective bargaining around skill development, training, and working time in conjunction with a broader social pact for industries. FIM-CISL has the more optimistic position on Industry 4.0, viewing it as an "enabler not only of Italian firms' territorial competitiveness," but also of FIM-CISL's desire for "a human-centered society and people's self-fulfillment within the experience of work, thanks to a special focus on workers' participation and knowledge" (Alioti 2018: 18). In late 2016, the union signed a national agreement with employers that included an "individual right to professional training," strengthened employee participation rights, and revised job classification systems (Armaroli and Spattini 2018: 44). This agreement included a "right to education" for 250 hours paid over a three-year period, including higher professional education leaves for up to 11 months and a continuing education chapter that features 24 hours of digital and organizational training (Alioti 2018). The agreement also ensured participation rights in companies with more than 1,500 employees via the creation of joint labor–management consultative committees that will convene to examine market trends and industrial strategies or when strategic employment decisions are to be made. Finally, with other European unions such as IG Metall, FIM-CISL has scaled up cooperation through a European Commission co-funded project on Industry 4.0 and unions, Smart Unions for New Industry.

The CGIL is more critical toward Industry 4.0 but, like FIM-CISL, it also views Industry 4.0 as an opportunity for labor and is seeking better skill development and employment security for its members and advocates a proactive strategy in which unions and workers actively shape Industry 4.0 technologies (Gaddi, Garbellini, and Garibaldo 2018). Importantly, despite past rivalries between Italian unions, they have come together to develop common protocols over Industry 4.0. For example, in 2016, there was an agreement among the CGIL, FIM-CISL, and UIL unions on developing a modern system of industrial relations based in new rules for collective bargaining, participation, and representation. This included protocols to better link company-level agreements to RSUs and local trade unions (Armaroli and Spattini 2018). In 2018, a five-point Pact for the Factory collective agreement among the CGIL, FIM-CISL, UIL and Confindustria—the Italian employers federation—was signed. It focused on worker health, security, and participation concerns, but it also represented the employer association's attempt to achieve a consensus with unions around Industry 4.0 (Alioti 2018).

Italian research also suggests the increasing importance of workplace RSUs in negotiating Industry 4.0 (Gramolati and Sateriale 2019). This also stems from the broader 2016 confederal agreement between the major unions because such agreements are valid only if they are signed by a majority of the RSUs. The RSUs are also vital because they are sites where unions bargain around Industry 4.0 technologies—not only for the requalification/training of workers but also to increase employee participation in work organization. For the CGIL, the need for increasing employee participation is considered consistent with the increased cognitive demands being placed on employees (Gaddi, Garbellini, and Garibaldo 2018). This includes asserting the RSU's right to "negotiate the algorithm"— which has often not been included in collective agreements (Gramolati and Sateriale 2019: 59). Thus, at a major General Electric plant, Nuovo Pignone near Florence, the union and RSU bargained for four years with the company to codetermine the input parameters, in part to prevent excessive surveillance of employee time and movements.

Industry 4.0 may also augment decentralizing trends such as territorial pacts that have been ongoing in Italian industrial relations since the 1980s (Leonardi, Ambra, and Ciarini 2018). Moreover, recent localization is also viewed as constituting "innovative forms of agglomeration" and hence the possibility of scaling up organizationally into wider institutional experimentation (Seghezzi and Tiraboschi 2018: 29). Armaroli and Spattini (2018) document several recent territorial collective agreements, including Confirmi Apindustria Bergamo representing regional metal-working SMEs with FIM-CISL and UILM-UIL, in which the unions secured increased worker participation, training, and pay and also agreed to develop with employers an online platform for better matching of local supply and demand, including reskilling protocols for redundant workers. Finally, the agreement also included measures for better protecting work–life balance.

Yet despite some examples of employers reaching out to unions and RSUs around Industry 4.0, these instances remain relatively few. Moreover, increasing bargaining fragmentation is having a deleterious impact on both organizational and more multiscaled institutional experimentation:

> The effects of these issues are particularly strong at local and company levels, where a polarization between the best and the worst practices of collective bargaining persists and industrial relations still rely on power and shows of strength. The lack of vertical coordination of collective bargaining and the proliferation of autonomous unions evidently exacerbate these problems, by nullifying the efforts made by representative social partners at the national level to establish common rules and achieve sustainable compromises applicable to all. (Armaroli and Spattini 2018: 8)

Furthermore, like the German situation, increased Industry 4.0 participation has put increased demands on workplace RSU representatives. To meet this challenge since 2009, funded by the joint union and Confindustria Fondimpresa, the CGIL and CISL-FIM have increased investment to assist union and RSU members to promote workforce lifelong learning and to better negotiate new technologies (Armaroli and Spattini 2018: 43). Finally, union and RSU responsiveness is hampered because Italian firms typically give very little notice about major technological change, and while there are some examples of codetermination of technology in Italy, they have been more reflective of individual firm cultures than union or RSU initiatives (Gaddi, Garbellini, and Garibaldo 2018; Gramolati and Sateriale 2018) (Table 1).

DISCUSSION AND CONCLUSIONS

How US, German, and Italian trade union and workplace representative's roles in Industry 4.0 experimentation are embedded in their structural, institutional, and associational powers provides some important insights. In all three cases, especially in Germany, trade unions have drawn on such powers to engage in organizational experimentation around Industry 4.0 (Table 1). Thus, German unions have institutional powers based on codetermination that are stronger and more multiscalar (i.e., workplace to board level) than both the UAW and Italian RSUs, which allow German unions to have greater structural power to retain more of GPN value chains in Germany (De Ville 2018: 17). Furthermore, while overall German unionization has declined, as was evident in the 2018 IG Metall strike, union associational powers are still strong within the automotive industry. Finally, while the UAW in the United States may in fact have greater formal institutional/legal power to negotiate the employment impacts of technological

Table 1
US, German, and Italian Union Structural, Institutional, and
Associational Powers and Industry 4.0 Experimentation

	United States	Germany	Italy
Structural power	Overall, UAW has limited power in North American GPNs and none in nondomestics except Fiat Chrysler and is increasingly weak in components.	Overall high. Germany is a strategic location for automotive GPNs, and unions have a strong presence, especially in assembly but less in components.	Italy increasingly has a marginal role in GPN unions strong in assembly (Fiat Chrysler) but uneven in components.
Institutional power	Relatively weak. UAW agency role and new technology-employment bargaining rights, but North American OEM board-level presence is based on time-limited contracts with little strategic influence.	Overall high. Union codetermination rights at supervisory board and via establishment works councils is legally embedded. Formal rights over new technology relatively are weak but there have been some recent more informal initiatives. Also, increased derogations in sectoral bargaining.	Relatively weak. No legal right to board-level presence but right to establishment scale input via RSUs, but only where there is a union presence. Advanced notification of technology is uneven and mostly determined by the firm.
Associational power	Overall relatively weak, especially workforce tiering but strong rank-and-file support for 2019 GM strike.	Relatively high, but divisions exist between core and peripheral (outsourced workers) within and between firms. Strong rank-and-file support for IG Metall's 2018 strike.	Uneven. Multiple and often divided unions, although more collaboration exists around Industry 4.0. Some strong rank-and-file mobilizations but also divisions with outsourced and temporary workers.
Workplace power and challenges	Overall weak and uneven, but there are new technology committees and increased role of ergonomics and health and safety representatives. Workplace representatives lack sufficient technological knowledge.	Overall strong, but uneven. Works councils require considerable union support. Lack of workplace representatives with technical knowledge. Employer resistance.	Overall weak but uneven. Dependent on workplace-specific union and RSU strength. Lack of workplace representatives with technical knowledge but increased training and also role of health and safety committees. Employer resistance.
Experimentation	Limited organizational experimentation, no institutional.	Extensive organizational experimentation in some instances and some local "quasi" institutional experimentation, but scaling up/generalizing these is problematic.	Some organizational experimentation and limited territorial "quasi" institutional experimentation, but in both cases are isolated in a few lead firms and regions.

change, the evidence suggests that IG Metall has taken greater initiatives around technology using a mix of institutional codetermination law, collective sectoral agreements, and more informal workplace organizational experimentation.

As such, despite the UAW having some structural advantages in GPN positionality and a monopoly over automotive union membership, their relative institutional and associational weaknesses have disadvantaged them in the workplace. Italy's less coordinated economy and voluntarist institutions combined with their increasingly peripheral GPN positionality and uneven associational capacity have also presented trade unions with challenges.

Despite such real differences, the cases also reveal similar union Industry 4.0 strategies, especially between Germany and Italy. Thus, Avogaro (2018) views both the Italian FIM-CISL and the German IG Metall as pushing firms to adopt a more specialized version of Industry 4.0, with FIM-CISL emphasizing the continued centrality of labor, involving developing the skills of a more "professionalized" worker through lifelong learning and via a "smart working" strategy limiting extended working hours stemming from excessive remote working.

It is also evident from the Italian and German examples that Industry 4.0 may be intensifying decentralizing tendencies and rescaling workplace governance, but the German case especially illustrates the importance of unions deploying their multiscalar powers. IG Metall's 2004 protocols around negotiating technological change and work reorganization with works councils and the Arbeit 2020 initiative reveals how critical the union is to upgrading establishment-scale works councils' capabilities in Industry 4.0 organizational and institutional experimentation (Bosch and Schmitz-Kießler 2020). To a lesser extent, this was also evident in the Italian case, where unions are supporting RSUs with investments in training of workplace representatives. However, as noted above, to counter Industry 4.0's potential negative impacts in 2016, all the major Italian unions signed an agreement to better coordinate national bargaining with the RSUs.

In the United States, the UAW has also adopted a multiscalar strategy via company-level collective bargaining and the establishment of joint national technology committees that also liaise with existing plant-level new-technology committees. However, more than German and Italian unions, the UAW has focused on securing skilled workers' positions rather than a more generalized professionalization strategy. The UAW is also paying attention to reducing outsourcing and combating increased worker stress around Industry 4.0, but it has also cooperated with firms implementing more Taylorist applications of this paradigm. This partially stems from the UAW historically being more prepared to accept and bargain around Taylorism than their European counterparts—especially German unions, which have long pushed for alternatives to Taylorism (Turner and Auer 1994). The UAW's role then in organizational experimentation is thus far more limited than that involving German and Italian unions, and it has had little or no role in institutional experimentation.

However, when confronting Industry 4.0, union intervention in almost all cases around new technology is largely defensive and late in the adoption process. Since 2000, German unions and works councils have modified codetermination to get greater involvement in technology adoption, but as Bosch and Schmitz-Kießler (2020) show, there remain real difficulties ranging from lack of knowledge of works councilors to firm resistance to sharing powers over technology. This is also a problem for Italian RSUs and even in US UAW plants, where there is a legal obligation for firms to negotiate the employment impacts of technological change; it is still the firm that fundamentally decides what involvement there will be by worker representatives. Thus, while unions have engaged more proactively around new technology and organizational experimentation, and some are now advocating that unions become truly involved in both the codetermined design and implementation of technology, such a scenario remains distant (Gaddi, Garbellini, and Garibaldo 2018).

Yet there are even more significant challenges confronting workers and union participation in wider institutional experimentation. Despite some German and Italian localized institutional experimentation, in all three cases, these take place in a wider context of a neoliberal wage suppression that has limited both productivity increases and technological investment (Francheschi and Mariani 2016; Gordon 2016; Meager and Speckesser 2011; Organisation for Economic Co-operation and Development 2018). Unions themselves have often participated in such suppression to enhance firm and national competitiveness (Kügler, Schönberg, and Schreiner 2018). In the United States, even advocates of labor–management cooperation acknowledge the negative impacts of wage stagnation and the UAW's role in this phenomenon (Cutcher-Gershenfeld, Brooks, and Mulloy 2015). As Moody (2018) stresses, the UAW's agreement to reductions in break times alone has significantly reduced OEM labor costs and hence the wage-push incentives for firms to adopt new technology. As such, some Italian and US observers argue it is vital that any technology-focused organizational experimentation combine both greater workplace participation rights with a wider institutional relinking of wages and productivity (Antonioli and Pini 2014; Madland 2016).

Thus, despite advanced manufacturing workplaces emerging as key sites for union organizational experimentation around Industry 4.0, workplace representatives in all cases rely heavily on national unions for research, training, and other resources to negotiate technological change. Relatedly, strategic firm technological and work-organization decisions are increasingly made at firm or corporate scales, and the ability of German unions to have significant presence on supervisory boards has made a difference in influencing and retaining GPN investment (De Ville 2018). Furthermore, some European and US observers have argued that Industry 4.0 and related new technology and work organization mean that unions should shift toward more collaborationist "enabler of work" strategies

(Cutcher-Gershenfeld, Brooks, and Mulloy 2015; Totterdill 2015). However, for both firms and workers "high road" collaborative initiatives come without guarantees (Osterman 2018). Moreover, the collaborative leverage of unions does not stem simply from its adopting a cooperative stance but also via its credible threat to withdraw labor via strikes (Pohler and Luchak 2015). Indeed, while the Industry 4.0 technological uncertainties that employers are confronting may create "bottom up" spaces for greater worker and union cooperation, firms still jealously guard their managerial prerogatives and power around workplace change. Such positioning does not simply reflect wider structures impinging "from above" but rather how power asymmetries are also constituted within organizations themselves. Thus, if unions want a more proactive involvement in technological change, they cannot assume employers will welcome it. Unions need to foster their associational powers, not simply through strikes but political action around the state, and not only to negotiate workplace and organizational technological change but also to better engage in wider institutional experimentation (Gindin 2019).

Accordingly, even with their relative structural, institutional, and associational advantages, German workplace representatives are confronting organizational scale challenges around Industry 4.0, including a lack of needed technical skills and managerial resistance. Furthermore, in the United States, Italy, and Germany, managerial powers have been augmented by GPN restructuring and neoliberalism—including declining union density and sectoral bargaining derogations. The negative consequences of increased managerial power and wage suppression mean that, in all three cases, union and workplace representative organizational experimentation interventions are often defensive and late in the technological adoption process, while German and Italian unions have achieved only a limited, tenuous "quasi" scaling up of institutional experimentation.

In sum, as presented in this chapter, there is evidence that some US, Italian, and German firms confronted with Industry 4.0–related uncertainties are seeking greater cooperation with trade unions. However, even in Germany, trade unions remain at best junior partners in negotiating with firms whose own powers over technological experimentation have been augmented by GPN restructuring and neoliberalism. As such, questions about worker and union ability to truly codetermine technology are fundamentally political ones that go beyond simply experimentation within an existing status quo. Workers and unions may indeed be able to "negotiate the algorithm," but without a considerable augmenting of their own powers, they risk only a perfunctory role in any Industry 4.0 transition.

ACKNOWLEDGMENTS

I gratefully acknowledge the helpful comments of the research volume editors and two anonymous reviewers. I would also like to acknowledge feedback given on an earlier version of this chapter by participants in the Research Network on Industrial Resilience (RENIR) at the University of Turin and Collegio Alberto, and Chiara Mancini of the CGIL union, Rome, Italy.

REFERENCES

Agostino, Mariarosaria, Anna Guinta, Domenico Scalera, and Francesco Trivieri. 2016. "Italian Firms in Global Value Chains: Updating Our Knowledge." Preprint. https://bit.ly/2KoRewT

Alioti, Gianni. 2018. "FIM-CISL vs. Industry 4.0." *International Union Rights* 25 (3): 18–19. https://bit.ly/3oTLtGq

Antonioli, Daniele, and Paolo Pini. 2014. "Europe and Italy: Expansionary Austerity, Expansionary Precariousness and the Italian Jobs Act." Euro Memorandum Conference, Sep. 25–27, Rome, Italy. https://bit.ly/3iiZHy8

Armaroli, Ilaria, and Silvia Spattini. 2018. "Smart Unions for New Industry: National Report Italy: Case Study on FIM-CISL." Rome, Italy: Associazione per gli studi Internazionali e Comparati sul Diritto del Lavoro e sulle Relazione e sulle Relazioni Industriali (ADAPT). https://bit.ly/3ioAVNe

Avogaro, Matteo. 2018. "Evolution of Trade Unions in Industry 4.0: A German and Italian Debate." In *Working in Digital and Smart Organizations*, edited by Edoardo Ales, Ylenia Curzi, Tomasso Fabbri, Olga Rymkevich, Iacopa Senatori, and Giovanni Solinas, pp. 165–190. London, UK: Palgrave Macmillan.

Bosch, Gerhard, and Jutta Schmitz-Kießler. 2020. "Shaping Industry 4.0—An Experimental Approach Developed by German Trade Unions." *Transfer: European Review of Labour and Research* 26 (2): 189–206.

Brooks, Chris. 2019 (Nov. 11). "Why Did the UAW Agree to Let Ford Expand Its Surveillance Technology for Assembly Workers?" *Jacobin*. https://bit.ly/3svw8xY

Brown, Ronald C. 2018. "Robots, New Technology, and Industry 4.0 in Changing Workplaces. Impacts on Labor and Employment Laws." *American University Business Law Review* 7 (3): 349–382. https://bit.ly/2N2WWoX

Brynjolfsson, Erik, and Andrew McAfee. 2014. *The Second Machine Age: Work, Progress, and Prosperity in a Time of Brilliant Technologies*. New York, NY: Norton.

Byhovskaya, Alena. 2018. "Overview of the National Strategies on Work 4.0: A Coherent Analysis of the Role of the Social Partners." Study. Brussels, Belgium: European Economic and Social Committee. https://bit.ly/39DcBDf

Ciravegna, Luciano. 2006. "Turin's Automotive Cluster: Fiat Crisis and the Threat of Delocalization." Progetto di Ricerca di Interesse Nazionale Working Paper No. 4. https://bit.ly/3sy7QDn

Cirillo, Valeria, Matteo Rinaldi, Jacobo Staccioli, and Maria Virgillato. 2019 (May 20). "Workers Intervention Authority in Italian 4.0 Factories: Autonomy and Discretion." GROWINPRO Working Paper. https://bit.ly/3oVkIkL

Coe, Neil. 2015. "Labour and Global Production Networks: Mapping Variegated Landscapes of Agency." In *Putting Labour in Its Place: Labour Process Analysis and Global Value Chains. Critical Perspectives on Work and Employment*, edited by Kirsty Newsome, Phil Taylor, Jennifer Bair, and Al Rainnie, pp. 171–194. Basingstoke, UK: Palgrave Macmillan.

Cumbers, A. 2015. "Understanding Labour's Agency Under Globalization: Embedding GPNs Within an Open Political Economy." *Putting Labour in Its Place: Labour Process Analysis and Global Value Chains. Critical Perspectives on Work and Employment*, edited by Kirsty

Newsome, Phil Taylor, Jennifer Bair, and Al Rainnie, pp. 131–151. Basingstoke, UK: Palgrave Macmillan.

Cutcher-Gershenfeld, Joel, Dan Brooks, and Martin Mulloy. 2015 (May 6). "The Decline and the Resurgence of the U.S. Auto Industry." Economic Policy Institute Briefing Paper No. 399. Washington, DC: Economic Policy Institute. https://bit.ly/3iugn5W

Dawson, Chester, Keith Naughton, and Gabrielle Coppola. 2019 (Sep. 27). "Auto Workers Fear EVs Will Be Job Killers." *Automotive News.* https://bit.ly/3bMgisX

Deeg, Richard, and Greg Jackson. 2007. "Towards a More Dynamic Theory of Capitalist Variety." *Socio-Economic Review* 5 (1): 149–179.

De Ville, Ferdi. 2018. "Domestic Institutions and Global Value Chains: Offshoring in Germany's Core Industrial Sectors." *Global Policy* 9 (52): 12–20.

Dziczek, Kristin. 2020. "North American Automotive Investment 2009–2019." Zoom Presentation, Aug. 14. Ann Arbor, MI: Center for Automotive Research.

Edwards, Paul, and Paulina Ramirez. 2016. "When Should Workers Embrace or Resist New Technology?" *New Technology, Work and Employment* 31 (2): 99–113.

Francheschi, Francesco, and Vincenzo Mariani. 2016. "Flexible Labor and Innovation in the Italian Industrial Sector." *Industrial and Corporate Change* 25 (4): 633–648.

Frey, Carl, and Ebrahim Rahbari. 2016. "Do Labor-Saving Technologies Spell the Death of Jobs in the Developing World?" Report, Brookings Blum Roundtable. Washington, DC: Brookings Institution. https://brook.gs/38PUgUi

Gaddi, Matteo, Nadia Garbellini, and Francesco Garibaldo. 2018. "Industry 4.0 and Its Consequences for Work and Labour: Field Research Report on the Implementation of Industry 4.0 in a Sample of Italian Companies." Bologna, Italy: Fondazione Sabatini.

Gindin, Sam. 2019 (Nov. 13). "When Militancy Isn't Enough" *Jacobin.* https://bit.ly/3nNp9gg

Gordon, Robert. 2016. *The Rise and Fall of American Growth.* Princeton, NJ: Princeton University Press.

Gramolati, Alesio, and Gaetano Sateriale. 2019. *Contrattare l'innovazione digitale; una cassetta degli attrezzi 4.0.* Rome, Italy: Ediesse.

Groshen, Erica, Susan Helper, John-Paul MacDuffie, and Charles Carson. 2019. (Jan. 1). "Preparing U.S. Workers and Employers for an Autonomous Vehicle Future." Upjohn Institute Technical Report No. 19-036. Kalamazoo, MI: W.E. Upjohn Institute for Employment Research. https://bit.ly/3qyqxVZ

Hall, Peter, and David Soskice. 2001. *The Varieties of Capitalism: The Institutional Foundations of Comparative Advantage.* Oxford, UK: Oxford University Press.

Harbecke, Tim, and Kathrin Filipiak. 2018. "National Report: Germany—Case Study on IG Metall." Smart Unions for New Industry. https://bit.ly/2LHL2Av

Helper, Susan, Raphael Martins, and Robert Seamans. 2019 (May 15). "Who Profits from Industry 4.0? Theory and Evidence from the Automotive Industry." New York, NY: New York University Stern School of Business. https://bit.ly/3qmcjr4

Herod Andrew. 2001. *Labor Geographies: Workers and the Landscapes of Capitalism.* New York, NY: Guilford Press.

Howell, Chris, and Rebecca Kolins Givan. 2011. "Rethinking Institutions and Institutional Change in European Industrial Relations" *British Journal of Industrial Relations* 49 (2): 231–255.

International Labour Organization. 2018. "The Future of Work We Want: A Global Dialogue." Report. Geneva, Switzerland: International Labour Organization. https://bit.ly/3imKFY1

Katz, Harry, and Owen Darbishire. 2000. *Converging Divergencies: Worldwide Changes in Employment Systems*. Ithaca, NY: Cornell University Press.

Kochan, Thomas, Wilma Liebman, and Inez Weitershausen. 2018. "Codetermining the Future of Work: Lessons from Germany." Report. Cambridge, MA: Good Companies, Good Jobs Initiative at MIT Sloan. https://bit.ly/3oVdAF5

Krzywdzinski, Martin. 2017. "Automation, Skill Requirements and Labour-Use Strategies: High Wage and Low-Wage Approaches to High-Tech Manufacturing in the Automotive Industry." *New Technology, Work and Employment* 32 (2): 247–267.

Krzywdzinski, Martin, Ulrich Jürgens, and Sabine Pfeiffer. 2015. "The Fourth Revolution: The Transformation of Manufacturing Work in the Age of Digitalization." *WZB-Mitteilungen* 149: 22–25. https://bit.ly/3iynt9D

Kügler, Alice, Uta Schönberg, and Ragnhild Schreiner. 2018. "Productivity Growth, Wage Growth and Unions." Conference Paper. Frankfurt am Main, Germany: European Central Bank. https://bit.ly/38P0qE1

Leonardi, Salvo, Maria Ambra, and Andrea Ciarini. 2018. "Italian Collective Bargaining at a Turning Point." In *Multi-Employer Bargaining Under Pressure—Decentralisation Trends in Five European Countries*, edited by Salvo Leonardi and Roberto Pedersini, pp. 185–223. Brussels, Belgium: European Trade Union Institute.

Lippert, Inge, Tony Huzzard, Ulrich Jürgens, and William Lazonick. 2014. *Corporate Governance, Employee Voice, and Work Organization: Sustaining High-Road Jobs in the Automotive Supply Industry*. Oxford, UK: Oxford University Press.

Lloyd, Caroline, and Jonathon Payne. 2019. "Rethinking Country Effects: Robotics, AI and Work Futures in Norway and the UK." *New Technology, Work and Employment* 34 (3): 208–225.

Madland, David. 2016 (Oct.). "The Future of Worker Voice and Power." Paper. Washington, DC: Center for American Progress. https://ampr.gs/2N3gt8L

McKinsey & Company. 2019. "Capturing Value at Scale in Discrete Manufacturing with Industry 4.0." Report. Frankfurt, Germany: McKinsey & Company. https://mck.co/3sykL8y

Meager, Nigel, and Stefan Speckesser. 2011 (Sep.). "Wages, Productivity and Employment: A Review of Theory and International Data." European Employment Observatory Thematic Report. Brighton, UK: Institute for Employment Studies, Brighton, UK. https://bit.ly/3qrD39C

Moody, Kim. 2018. "High Tech, Low Growth: Robots and the Future of Work." *Historical Materialism* 26 (4): 3–34.

Müller-Jentsch, Walther. 2008. "Industrial Democracy: Historical Development and Current Challenges." *Management Revue* 19 (4): 260–273.

Müller-Jentsch, Walther. 2018. "Seven Decades of Industrial Relations in Germany: Stability and Change Through Joint Learning Processes." *Employee Relations* 4 (4): 634–653.

Murray, Gregor, Christian Levesque, Glenn Morgan, and Nicholas Roby. 2020. "Disruption and Re-Regulation in Work and Employment: From Organisational to Institutional Experimentation." *Transfer* 26 (2): 135–156.

Noble, Breana. 2019 (Oct. 23). "UAW-GM Deal Adds Tech Committee to Address Industry Changes." *Detroit News*. https://bit.ly/3bMxeQ3

Organisation for Economic Co-operation and Development. 2018. "OECD Economic Survey of Germany (December 20). Report. Paris, France: Organisation for Economic Co-operation and Development. https://bit.ly/3bOoUzi

Osterman, Paul. 2018. "In Search of the High Road: Meaning and Evidence." *ILR Review* 71 (1): 3–34.

Peck, Jamie, and Theodore, Nick. 2007. "Variegated Capitalism." *Progress in Human Geography* 31 (6): 731–772.

Pfeiffer, Sabine. 2017. "Industrie 4.0 in the Making—Discourse Patterns and the Rise of Digital Despotism." In *The New Digital Workplace: How New Technologies Revolutionize Work*, edited by Abigail Marks, Kendra Briken, Shiona Chillas, and Martin Krzywdzinski, pp. 21–42. London, UK: Macmillan Palgrave.

Pohler, Dianne, and Andrew Luchak. 2015. "Are Unions Good or Bad for Organizations? The Moderating Role of Management's Response." *British Journal of Industrial Relations* 53 (3): 423–459.

Pulignano, Valeria, Domenico Carrieri, and Lucio Baccaro. 2018. "Industrial Relations in Italy in the Twenty-First Century." *Employee Relations* 40 (4): 654–673.

Rainnie, Al, and Mark Dean. 2020. "Industry 4.0 and the Future of Quality Work in the Global Digital Economy." *Labour & Industry: A Journal of the Social and Economic Relations of Work* 30 (1): 16–33.

Rutherford, Tod, and John Holmes. 2013. "(Small) Differences That (Still) Matter? Cross-Border Regions and Workplace Governance in the Southern Ontario and US Great Lakes Automotive Industry." *Regional Studies* 47: 116–127.

Schulten, Thorsten, and Reinhold Bispinck. 2018. "Varieties of Decentralisation in German Collective Bargaining." In *Multi-Employer Bargaining Under Pressure—Decentralisation Trends in Five European Countries*, edited by Salvo Leonardi and Roberto Pedersini, pp. 105–148. Brussels, Belgium: European Trade Union Institute.

Seghezzi, Francesco, and Michele Tiraboschi. 2018. "Italy's Industry 4.0 Plan: An Analysis from a Labour Law Perspective." *E-Journal of International and Comparative Labour Studies* 7 (1): 1–32.

Totterdill, Peter. 2015. "Closing the Gap: The Fifth Element and Workplace Innovation." *European Journal of Workplace Innovation* 1 (1): 55–74.

Turner, Lowell, and Peter Auer. 1994. "A Diversity of New Work Organization: Human-Centered, Lean, and In-Between." *Industrielle Beziehungen* 1 (1): 39–61.

United Auto Workers. 2019a. "2019 Proposed Resolution: Special Convention on Collective Bargaining." Mar. 11–13. Detroit, MI: United Auto Workers. https://bit.ly/3qHbdqb

United Auto Workers. 2019b (Oct. 7). "UAW–General Motors Contract Summary: Hourly Workers." Detroit, MI: United Auto Workers. https://bit.ly/3qydMdJ

Vallejo-Peña, Alberto, and Sandro Giachi. 2018. "The Mediterranean Variety of Capitalism, Flexibility of Work Schedules, and Labour Productivity in Southern Europe." *Region* 5 (3): 21–38.

Vanselow, Achim. 2017. "Fear of the World of Robots and How German Trade Unionists Have Been Dealing with This Issue." Presented at "The New Industrial Revolution Is Here. Where Are You?" Apr. 4, Ljubljana, Slovenia. https://bit.ly/3imz0IQ

Wright, Erik Olin. 2000. "Working-Class Power, Capitalist-Class Interests and Class Compromise." *American Journal of Sociology* 105 (4): 957–1002.

Chapter 5

Climate Change and the Future of Workers: Toward a Just Transition

J. Mijin Cha[1]
Occidental College

Todd E. Vachon
Rutgers University

ABSTRACT

The future of work discourse has largely focused on advances in automation, big data, robotics, machine learning, and artificial intelligence. However, the transition away from a growth-oriented fossil fuel–powered economy toward a steady-state sustainable one will also completely reshape existing labor markets, undermine the gains made over generations by workers in historically unionized blue-collar sectors, and further shift employment into sectors where unions have been unable to gain a foothold. The fear these changes elicit makes solutions to the climate crisis tremendously challenging. Alternatively, a just transition for workers and communities could be developed democratically through active participation by a broad base of stakeholders, re-creating "the rules of the game" to ensure shared and sustainable prosperity. This chapter explores three cases of socioecological transitions. In sum, we find that the inclusion of worker and community voice in shaping and implementing transitions is paramount to ensuring the potential for just outcomes.

INTRODUCTION

Since the earliest days, humans have worked. They have used their hands and minds productively to transform natural materials into necessities and luxuries for human consumption, while simultaneously altering the world in which they lived. In any given period and specified geographic or politically bounded space, one can identify the dominant mode of production. Be it subsistence agriculture, feudalism, industrial capitalism, or some other arrangement, humans have organized work and related to the natural world in different ways over time. This rather obvious, but taken-for-granted, fact reveals a simple but fundamental truth about the nature of work—it has been in a constant state of flux since the very beginning. Changing slowly at first over the course of millennia, but then accelerating in recent centuries, especially since the rise of capitalism as the dominant mode of production with fossil fuels as the primary, abundant source of energy throughout the world.

In short, the history of work is the history of socioeconomic change.

This steady process, sometimes driven by technology, other times by shifting social relations or other societal changes, has had significant and differentiated consequences for various social groupings within economies.[2] It is for this reason that periods of transition are invariably accompanied by struggles between those set to lose and those poised to gain. These struggles are shaped by, and in turn can reshape, the existing power relations within societies, which raises several key questions surrounding periods of transition: Who will do what, how, and for whom? What will be the rewards, how much, and who will get them? And perhaps most importantly, who will decide the answers to these and other questions regarding the distribution of work and rewards?

In this chapter, we deploy a labor studies perspective in line with the theoretical thrust of the current volume to explore the broad questions of distribution and governance in the context of one particular case of ongoing socioeconomic change that has been a space of struggle for more than two decades—climate change and efforts to mitigate it. Scientific consensus finds that if greenhouse gas emissions—caused primarily by the burning of fossil fuels—continue at the current rate, the atmosphere will warm by as much as 2.7°F above preindustrial levels by 2040 (Intergovernmental Panel on Climate Change 2018), wreaking havoc on human and animal populations. At the same time, millions of workers employed in the fossil fuel industry and their communities rely on the continuation of this energy system for their livelihoods. For that reason, we focus on the need for a "just transition" from an extractive economy, driven by exploitation of resources, people, and capital, to a regenerative economy that centers the well-being of workers, communities, and the environment.

The field of labor studies, we argue, is uniquely positioned to evaluate questions associated with processes of socioeconomic change. As postulated in Chapter 2 of this volume, the multidisciplinary nature of the field—bringing together theoretical insights from various strands of academic inquiry—combined with its tradition of radical empiricism and commitment to upholding human dignity can help to uncover the means by which a truly democratic and sustainable future can be achieved by and for workers. By uplifting the wisdom of lived experiences, labor studies inquiries actively embrace the power of human agency and the ability for people to remake their social worlds while also recognizing the structural constraints acting on collective efforts to promote change.

In addition to uplifting the wisdom of workers' experiences and ensuring their adequate voice in decision making, centering human dignity also entails ensuring social justice. The words "justice," as in social justice, and "just," as in just transition, share the same Latin root, *ūstitia*, which translates loosely to "equity," "upright," and "righteous." Thus, with equity and voice at its core, we argue that the labor studies field is ideally suited for examining and informing the socioeconomic processes involved in constructing a just transition away from the extractive fossil fuel economy and toward a more sustainable, regenerative economic model.

This chapter is divided into four main sections. First, we establish the relationship between climate change and work by briefly reviewing some recent research on the potential impacts of climate change and climate change mitigation on labor markets and particular industries. Second, we envision the outcome of a just energy transition—where is it that we are going? Next, we explore the ideals and purpose of "just transition" by first discussing the evolution of the idea of just transition and then presenting current examples to highlight worker and community-led just transition in action. Finally, we conclude with an analysis of how, and why, labor studies and the future of work(ers) debate must engage with the climate crisis.

While we focus largely on the reduction in fossil fuel jobs and a transition to more sustainable energy sources and practices, we also use the case of climate change mitigation to consider ways in which socioeconomic transitions in general can be more just for all stakeholders. As we stated at the outset of this chapter, climate change is not the first and will certainly not be the last time humans go through a period of transition. And as history has shown us time and again, periods of transition can either be just or unjust—alleviating or exacerbating existing inequalities (or creating new ones)—depending on the forces at work shaping the transition. In sum, we argue that a just future of work for workers in a constantly changing economy requires a robust and permanent process of democratic decision making with input from all stakeholders in society, not just the powerful individuals and dominant social groups of the given socioeconomic period.

CHANGING CLIMATE, CHANGING ECONOMY

The impact climate change will have on the future of work and workers cannot be overstated. If no further effort is made to reduce climate changing greenhouse gas emissions, the effects of climate change will disrupt every industry. Increased temperatures, sea-level rise, intensified droughts and wildfires, food shortages, armed conflicts, and more frequent extreme weather events mean every segment of the economy and society, regardless of geography or wealth, will be affected in some way by climate change (International Panel on Climate Change 2018). The ability to address the challenges of a changing climate, however, will be dictated by geography and wealth.

The economy-wide reach of climate change means that work, as it now exists, must change. Workers that primarily work outside will need to adjust to increased heat and exposures. Increased intensity of natural disasters mean worksites everywhere must prepare for disruption. And climate-caused displacement will mean workforces will face influxes or contractions of workers, depending on region. A recent report on G20 countries prepared by the International Labour Organization (2018) finds that the increasing frequency and intensity of various environment-related hazards caused or exacerbated by human activity have already reduced labor productivity by 115 million working-life years between 2000 and 2015. Projected temperature increases will also make heat stress more common, reducing the total number of work hours by 1.9% by 2030. Currently, 34% of jobs in the G20 countries rely directly on ecosystem services—jobs in farming, fishing and forestry, soil renewal and fertilization, air and water purification, pest control, pollination, and more. Climate change threatens these systems and the jobs that depend on them (International Labour Organization 2018).

Despite the urgent need to dramatically reduce fossil fuel use to slow the ill effects of climate change, particularly for workers and front-line communities, global energy systems remain largely dependent on burning fossil fuels. In 2018 alone, the world consumed 3.8 trillion metric tons of coal and 36.4 billion barrels of crude oil. According to the US Department of Energy (2018), electric power generation directly employed more than 1.9 million workers in 2016, with 55%, or 1.1 million, of these workers employed in coal, oil, and gas. Millions more are employed in related industries, such as the transportation of fossil fuels, the construction of fossil fuel power plants, and the manufacturing and maintenance of combustion engine vehicles and their components. Table 1 illustrates the total employment and wages for all occupations in six fossil fuel industries in the United States in 2019. Together, these six industries alone account for over 340,000 jobs and $35 billion in annual income (US Bureau of Labor Statistics 2019).

While the employment impacts of climate change itself are estimated to outweigh those of climate mitigation, and many studies even predict a net growth in employment resulting from mitigation efforts (Pollin and Callaci 2016) (owing largely to the labor-intensive nature of renewable energy in the short run), these rosy predictions are of little comfort to the individual fossil fuel worker set to lose their job as a result of government policies deemed necessary to protect the common good. The transition away from a growth-oriented fossil fuel–powered economy toward a regenerative, sustainable economy will completely reshape existing labor markets, erase the gains made over generations by workers in the historically unionized blue-collar energy sector, and further shift employment into sectors where unions have been unable to gain a foothold because of a combination of employer hostility and pro-business labor laws (Vachon 2021a).

The fear these changes elicit among workers and communities makes solutions to the climate crisis tremendously challenging and often leads to "jobs vs. the

Table 1
Total Employment and Wages in Six Fossil Fuel Industries

NAICS Industry Title	Industry Employment, All Occupations	Median Hourly Wage	Average Annual Income	Total Annual Income (billions)
Coal Mining	50,770	$28.38	$61,440	$3.1
Natural Gas Distribution	109,430	$38.27	$85,010	$9.3
Oil and Gas Extraction	141,320	$34.84	$79,330	$11.2
Petroleum and Coal Products Manufacturing	112,200	$33.29	$76,460	$8.6
Pipeline Transportation of Crude Oil	11,800	$35.07	$80,970	$1.0
Pipeline Transportation of Natural Gas	29,830	$33.58	$74,650	$2.2
Total	**343,150**			**$35.4**

Data Source: US Bureau of Labor Statistics (2019). Occupational Employment Statistics.

environment" clashes (Brecher 2014; Sweeney 2015). It is in the interests of capital and corporations that workers and environmentalists are seen at odds with each other. Yet there is no inherent justification for pitting work and economic security against environmental and climate protection. On the contrary, confronting the climate crisis offers a great opportunity to move our society away from the existing cycle of exploiting workers and nature to maximize profits and toward a more democratic, and just, regenerative economy.

FROM EXTRACTION TO REGENERATION

We follow climate justice activists, such as those from the Movement Generation, in calling the current dominant economic model the "extractive economy" and in calling for a shift to a regenerative model (Movement Generation, no date: 17). The extractive economy builds and consolidates wealth through extraction—extraction of resources, extraction of labor, and extraction of capital. Natural resources are extracted for use as fuel and in the production of goods. Resources are extracted at rates that exceed natural replenishment. Wealth is maximized through the extraction and exploitation of labor. Wages are suppressed while productivity is maximized. Systems are structured so that capital is required for basic transactions, and predatory practices arise to extract capital from those without means.

In an extractive economy, the governing system relies on militarism—systemic, state-sanctioned violence and exploitation—to gain control over resources. From destruction and possession of Indigenous lands to global imperialism that controls seed production, violence and instability are needed in order to maintain control.

The impacts on the natural and human worlds of an extractive economy are clear. Resources are rapidly depleting, pollution is pervasive, and the world is on the precipice of climate disaster. Moreover, income inequality is at record levels, and wealth is increasingly concentrated at not just the top 1% of earners, but the top 0.01% (Gold 2017). These disparities are amplified further along the lines of race and gender. With unionization rates declining, workplace democracy is becoming a privilege of the past. As the world recovers from the COVID-19 pandemic, these inequities risk being the defining feature of countries across the world.

From this perspective, a truly just transition requires a move away from an economic model centered on extraction to one centered on regeneration to break these patterns of exploitation. Instead of centering on extraction, the regenerative economy centers on cooperation. Instead of the treadmill of extraction, resources are used sparingly and consumption is reduced. Rather than maximizing production, labor focuses on cooperation and solidarity. In a regenerative economy, the idea of work is expanded beyond what earns capital to an idea that acknowledges all the work individuals do, from raising families to caring for community members. Decision making moves from being concentrated among the elites to small-scale, democratic decision-making processes. And the relationship between natural resources and humans becomes one of cooperation and not dominance. The focus shifts from wealth accumulation to social and ecological equity. This form of transition has come to be called a "transformative" just transition, as it goes far beyond just providing safety-net protections for displaced workers, but rather it envisions an alternative, sustainable, and equitable economy that works for the benefit of all (Vachon 2021b).

A regenerative economy is more than a critique of capitalism; it addresses how to rethink what is valued and how it is valued. Value is often seen as market price—what is one willing to pay for a product? But, as famously argued by Marx, price does not adequately reflect value—the value of the labor that went into producing a good, the value of social reproduction that allows for production, the value of the natural resources that are used for production, and other social costs and benefits are not reflected in the price paid (Marx [1867] 1990). In this regard, the idea of "value" more adequately reflects societal values rather than cost or price. Allowing *values* to drive decisions, rather than *value* as commonly used as a stand-in for price or cost, shifts priorities away from extraction to regeneration.

There is an opportunity now to move from extractive to regenerative by rethinking and revaluing fossil fuel use. The fossil fuel economy is the very definition of an extractive economy. Coal, gas, and oil are extracted to power homes, industries, and economies. Extraction sites are environmentally destructive, and financial benefits from extraction are concentrated among corporations and not workers. Shifting from extraction to regeneration is a transformative process requiring workers and communities to be centered in energy production. Renewable energy must be available to all communities—not just those that can afford solar panels. Displaced workers must be supported through wage replacement, safety-net supports, and access to new work opportunities. Extractive communities must be similarly supported so they are not starved of revenue, and land remediated so that the legacy of fossil fuels does not continue to pollute air and water.

JUST TRANSITION FRAMEWORKS

Given the legacy of inequality and injustice that fossil fuel and extraction have borne and the very real impacts of a changing climate, transitioning to a low-carbon economy is a moral and economic imperative. To stave off the worst impacts of climate change, as discussed above, there must be a transition away from fossil fuels to renewable, clean energy sources. For such a transition to be just, it must center equity and uplift the voices of workers and communities, as was the intention of those who originated the concept of a Superfund for Workers and currently those calling for an inclusive Green New Deal. The extent to which a just transition will incorporate all of these elements is dependent in part on the framework that is adopted by advocates. In what follows, we offer a very brief history of the concept of just transition and broadly outline two just transition frameworks.

A Superfund for Workers

The original name for just transition, the "Superfund for Workers," was developed by late American labor and environmental leader, Tony Mazzocchi of the Oil, Chemical, and Atomic Workers union (now merged with the United Steelworkers of America) and a network of activists, including Mike Merrill and Les Leopold (Leopold 2007; Mazzocchi 1993; Wykle, Morehouse, and Dembo 1991). The superfund name was a play on the federal program initiated in 1980 to fund the cleanup of hazardous wastes at contaminated industrial sites. Alluding to this program, Mazzocchi proclaimed: "There is a Superfund for dirt. There ought to be one for workers" (1993: 41). Summarizing the rationale of Mazzocchi's Superfund for Workers, Brecher says: "It is a basic principle of fairness that the burden of policies that are necessary for society—like protecting the environment—shouldn't be borne by a small minority, who through no fault of their own happen to be victimized by their side effects" (2015: 34). In sum, the underlying goal of the Superfund for Workers was to overcome contrived "jobs vs. the environment" struggles by reconciling social, environmental, and economic concerns.

The term "just transition" is believed to have been first publicly used in 1995 by Les Leopold and Brian Kohler during a presentation to the International Joint Commission on Great Lakes Water Quality (Hampton 2015; Stevis, Krause, and Morena 2019). Describing the proposed just transition fund, they called for full wages and benefits for displaced workers until they retired or found a comparable job; up to four years of tuition for college or vocational training, plus full income while attending school; post-educational stipends or subsidies if no jobs at comparable wages are available after graduation; and assistance with relocation for workers who needed to move for employment (Leopold 1995: 83). Akin to the GI Bill of Rights, which provided various economic and social supports to veterans returning from World War II, a just transition fund could be used to provide economic subsidies and dignity for displaced workers during the transition away from fossil fuels in an effort to prevent the worst impact of climate change.

Programs like those outlined in the Superfund for Workers, which focus predominantly on insurance programs for individual workers and workplaces, are part of what Vachon (2021b) has called the "protective" elements of just transition—the responsive programs needed to protect workers who are displaced as a result of necessary economic shifts, such as environmental or climate policies that promote the common good. Some elements of a protective just transition plan already exist in US policy today—but not for workers displaced by climate change mitigation efforts. For example, the Trade Adjustment Assistance program (TAA) was designed to assist workers negatively impacted by globalization and trade by providing economic support for displaced workers, such as wage supplements, job reallocation allowances, income support for workers in training programs, and skills training and career counseling. While the program is intended to help displaced workers move into equivalent jobs and careers, uneven funding and support, a restricted scope, and fluctuating eligibility requirements have severely limited the its success (Cha et al. 2019).

Beyond the Superfund
In addition to the weaknesses of the existing transition programs described above—which could be drastically improved with proper funding and an expanded scope—a major critique of the protective approach to just transition by climate justice activists and many workers from historically marginalized communities is its relative blindness to the history of racism, discrimination, and exclusion in US labor markets, as well as by many unions. Programs that are designed to protect only workers who initially had access to well-paying, blue-collar jobs in the first place risk further exacerbating existing inequalities along the lines of race, class, and gender as we transition to a more environmentally sustainable economy.

A more proactive, transformative just transition could take a holistic, comprehensive approach that moves beyond just providing protections for displaced fossil fuel workers to addressing issues of healthcare, affordable housing, transportation, and others to ensure all communities and workers can thrive in a low-carbon future. For example, fossil fuel workers will lose their health insurance when they lose their jobs and should be provided with coverage as they transition, but millions of workers in service industries, predominantly women and people of color, don't even have health insurance when they have their jobs. Creating a single-payer healthcare system would not only protect displaced fossil fuel workers, but it would also address inequities in access to healthcare that are the result of past injustices, as well as proactively prepare workers and communities for unforeseen future displacements (such as those caused by the recent COVID-19 pandemic).

Building on Cha et al. (2019), we identify four pillars of a proactive just transition that can be used as a roadmap to an equitable, low-carbon future: (1) strong governmental support, (2) dedicated funding streams, (3) strong, diverse coalitions, and (4) economic diversification. The scale and scope of transition away from fossil fuels is best achieved with consistent, strong governmental support, including short-term policies to provide immediate support to communities and workers negatively impacted by closures, as well as longer-term restructuring of local economies. Both short-term and long-term transition support will need to be fully and consistently funded. As seen in the TAA program example above, inconsistent and uncertain funding streams limit the success of transition programs.

A proactive just transition requires support for workers and communities. Workers and communities have borne the environmental, economic, and health cost of the fossil fuel economy, and both workers and communities must be supported to ensure a just transition to a low-carbon economy. Transition plans that are supported by a diverse coalition and represent different interests are stronger and more likely to identify and address the needs of workers and communities. When these coalitions stay together, the resulting transition addresses workers and communities more holistically and ensures that the solutions to climate change do not exacerbate existing inequalities.

The final pillar of a proactive just transition is diversification of economic bases. Over-reliance on a single industry or sector leaves communities and workers extremely vulnerable when the industry or sector declines. When a community is solely reliant on a power plant for economic security, for example, the consequences of the plant shuttering are far reaching—from the lost wages of displaced workers to reduced tax revenues that impact school funding and essential services to the reduced spending at local businesses. Investing in emerging and growing sectors provides a more diverse economy, and identifying these sectors is an important first step to reimaging new economic bases.

Translating these four pillars into policy can build upon existing programs and also include elements from new initiatives like the Green New Deal, which provides several examples of strong governmental policies, such as a federal job guarantees and investments in renewable energy technologies that proactively address the climate crises while also promoting climate justice and quality job creation (Ocasio-Cortez and Markey 2019). Such a proactive just transition would have a large role for the public sector in addressing the climate crises, a commitment to creating meaningful work for all who want it, a voice for communities in shaping the transition, and a focus on redressing past injustices along the lines of race, class, and gender.

The public sector can be a driver of job creation through public investments. Public projects can include local hiring provisions and prevailing wage standards, which ensure that the jobs created are both good jobs and available to local communities (Madl and Rowell 2017). These projects could include infrastructure upgrades, along with large-scale renewable energy and energy efficiency projects, all of which would meaningfully reduce greenhouse gas emissions and create good, family-sustaining jobs with dignity. These investments should be purposefully targeted to historically marginalized areas to avoid reproducing the existing inequalities embedded in our existing fossil fuel economy.

Targeted investments could, and we argue should, be funded through dedicated funding streams. Transformation into a low-carbon economy is a long-term investment, and programs and initiatives will be most successful if planned on a long horizon with funding predictability. Small business incubators, including community-based renewable energy installers, training and retraining workers, and capacity building among community members, are investments that could help proactively lead the transition to a low-carbon future.

In the following section, we explore three examples of just transition in practice. While none is transformative in nature, each offers insight into the elements of an emerging just transition framework that centers on human dignity. Each incorporates at least one of the four pillars of just transition outlined in this section, and all plant the seeds for what could become a more holistic approach to economic transitioning in general.

JUST TRANSITION IN PRACTICE

Just transition scholars and advocates often uplift the example of the Ruhr region in Germany, which transitioned away from an economy dominated by coal mining and steel manufacturing to a more diverse economy that includes new technical schools, solar development, and cultural institutions (Cha 2017; European Trade Union Institute 2016) . The ability of the Ruhr region to transition into new sectors and away from fossil fuels was dependent on several of the factors discussed above: One, the strong public safety net allowed for immediate assistance for displaced workers, such as unemployment benefits, pension, and healthcare benefits (European Trade Union Institute 2016). Two, the longer-term transformation looked to diversify the industries and sectors in the region, including the courting of high-tech and knowledge-based firms, the expansion of the service sector, and investments in educational infrastructure to create new technical institutions and universities in the region (European Trade Union Institute 2016).

The German government remains committed to transition and recently created the Special Commission on Growth, Structural Economic Change, and Employment to produce just transition plans for two lignite mining areas and to create a time line for completely phasing out coal (UNRISD 2018). The commission comprises multiple stakeholders, including industry, governmental ministries, environmental organizations, and trade unions (UNRISD 2018). The example of the Ruhr region highlights not only that transition is possible, but it also points to the difficulties and challenges that accompany wide-scale transition (Galgóczi 2014). While there are higher rates of unemployment in the Ruhr region than the national average, without the sustained effort and investment over years, the region would suffer from a much higher unemployment rate and the blight of community disinvestment.

Aside from the regional effort in Germany, just transition efforts can also advance on a smaller, plant-by-plant basis. Two examples in the US context are particularly informative—the Huntley coal plant shutdown in New York and the Diablo Canyon nuclear plant phase-out in California. These two cases can be seen as "labor studies in action" because they reveal the importance of workers' voices being central to decision-making processes and workers having a say in decisions affecting their futures.

Owing to the falling cost of natural gas, the Huntley coal-fired power plant in Tonawanda, New York, became economically unviable, and its operator, NRG, began to reduce production as well as its tax payments to the town (Lipsitz and Newberry, no date). The decrease in tax revenue led to three schools in the town closing. In response, the Kenmore Teachers Association, the Western New York Area Labor Federation, the Steelworkers, the IBEW, and the Clean Air Coalition came together to create the Huntley Alliance to organize the town around a transition plan that would save the school system, protect workers, and protect against increased electricity costs for ratepayers (Lipsitz and Newberry, no date).

The alliance succeeded in securing $30 million, which increased to $45 million in 2017, from the New York state legislature to provide gap funding to replace the loss in tax revenue from the closing of the coal plant (McGowan 2017). The town also undertook a visioning and planning process to leverage the state's gap funding to build on existing initiatives and attract new industries to strengthen the tax base and create good, family-sustaining jobs. The resulting document, "Growing the Town's Economic Future," was released in 2017 ("Tonawanda Tomorrow" 2017). The process and resulting plan were advised by a committee comprised of town officials, the Buffalo Center for Arts and Technology, Clean Air Coalition of Western New York, Erie County, and the Western New York Area Labor Federation, AFL-CIO.

The Huntley example highlights how workers beyond those in the energy sector are impacted by an energy transition and how they can work in coalition with community members. Community-led planning is an important tool for ensuring that the voices of workers and communities are centered on the energy transition.

Another case of transition that is instructive is the case of the Diablo Canyon nuclear power plant closing in San Luis Obispo, California. In this case, a diverse coalition was able to secure a transition plan *before* plant closure, allowing for a more proactive, comprehensive plan to be adopted before any worker displacement or tax revenue loss. The operating entity, Pacific Gas and Electric (PG&E), decided to not renew the Diablo Canyon nuclear power plant operating licenses beyond when they were set to expire in 2024 and 2025. This decision meant that advocates had advance notice of the plant closure, and a diverse coalition was able to come together to offer a proactive transition plan to protect workers, the community surrounding Diablo Canyon, and plant workers ("Joint Proposal" 2016). The coalition included the operating utility, PG&E; the two unions representing plant workers, IBEW Local 1245 and the Coalition of California Utility Employees; and three environmental advocacy groups, the Natural Resources Defense Council, Environmental California, and the Alliance for Nuclear Responsibility.

Together, these groups introduced a plan, called the "Joint Proposal," to the California Public Utilities Commission (CPUC), which was the entity responsible for determining the terms of retiring Diablo Canyon. The Joint Proposal focused on three priorities: supporting workers who would be impacted by the plant closure, replacing the power generated by Diablo Canyon by renewable and clean energies, and mitigating the loss of tax revenue to the local community and covering any other costs of the closure ("Joint Proposal," 2016).

The CPUC approved only parts of the Joint Proposal. The proposed package for displaced plant workers was at lower levels than proposed, there was no commitment to replacing the nuclear energy with renewable energy, and there was no funding for a community transition plan (CPUC 2018). The importance of a strong, diverse coalition can be seen in what happened after the CPUC decision. Rejecting the diminished plan, the coalition worked with state legislators to introduce a bill to require the CPUC to accept the original Joint Proposal (SB 1090 2018). The bill passed through the legislature and was signed by then-Governor Brown on September 19, 2018 (St. John 2018).

The Diablo Canyon case highlights the importance of proactive planning and establishing a diverse coalition. Because the plant had not yet closed, the coalition had more leverage to pursue other avenues, such as the legislature, rather than having to immediately deal with the challenges of displaced workers and lost tax revenue. Moreover, the proactive planning allowed the diverse coalition to reject the CPUC plan. In staying together, the coalition won a more just transition that included a full worker transition plan, tax revenue replacement, and a commitment to carbon-free energy.

Table 2 compares the three cases of just transition in practice explored in this chapter—Ruhr, Germany; Tonawanda, New York; and Diablo Canyon, California. As we can see in the third column of the table, the scale of the transition in Ruhr was at the regional level, which was wider reaching than either of the two US cases, which were more geographically limited to particular plants and their surrounding communities. Planning at the regional level allowed for a more holistic approach, drawing from a broader pool of resources and opportunities to create a new economy for the region. The cases of Tonawanda and Diablo Canyon reveal some of the challenges associated with plant closings in economically homogeneous local communities.

The fourth column compares the social actors who were the "protagonists" responsible for driving the transition plans. Given the history of coordinated economic planning in Germany, it should be no surprise that the government

Table 2
Three Cases of Just Transition in Practice

Case	Location	Scale	Protagonists	Mechanisms of Change	Elements of the Transition	Pillars
Ruhr	Germany	Regional	Government, labor, business	Governmental planning; strong worker voice	Transition to renewables; seeded new industries; workforce development	Strong government support; diversification of the economy
Tonawanda	New York	Plant and community	Labor and climate activists	Coalition work; bargaining; legislation	Worker protections; community protections	Strong, diverse coalitions; diversification of the economy; dedicated funding stream
Diablo Canyon	California	Plant and community	Labor and community partners	Coalition work; bargaining; regulatory ruling; legislation	Worker protections; community protections; transition to renewables	Strong, diverse coalitions, which led to strong government support

played a more active role in bringing stakeholders from labor and business together into social dialogue to design the economic transition. In the more liberalized market economy of the United States, labor and community organizations had to organize and fight first for a seat at the table, then for a transition plan that incorporated justice for workers and communities. Relatedly, this created very different mechanisms of change. The process in Germany began with government planning and stakeholder dialogue; in the United States, the process began with coalition building by labor and community groups, followed by organizing for legislation to support a just transition.[3] In Diablo Canyon, the organizing began first at the level of the regulatory agency, and after losing on many of their demands there, moving to the legislative arena.

Looking next at the elements of the transition, the plans in Ruhr and Diablo Canyon included investments in renewable energy sources. In Diablo, this was a major concern of community members wanting a clean source of energy in place after the nuclear plant phases out. Worker and community protections were core to the Tonawanda and Diablo Canyon plans because the United States generally lacks the sort of safety net measures that exist as rights to German citizens, including universal access to healthcare regardless of employment status. Looking at the pillars of just transition represented in each case, we see that strong government support was the starting point in Germany, but it was the end point in the United States, resulting from strong, diverse coalition building. Diversification of the economy was central in Ruhr and Tonawanda.

Despite the variation across these cases, the one common thread is worker voice. While none of these examples rises to the transformative vision of transitioning to a regenerative economy as outlined earlier, they nonetheless underscore the notion that for transitions to be just in any way, workers and communities must have a say in shaping them.

JUST TRANSITION, LABOR STUDIES, AND THE FUTURE OF WORK AND WORKERS

The climate crisis will fundamentally change everything. The labor studies tradition of upholding human dignity, combined with a commitment to radical empiricism, equips the field with the tools and historical perspective needed both to understand the processes driving socioeconomic change and to support justice for workers and communities that are in transition.

Social and economic justice campaigners operate under the simple principle that "nothing about us, without us, is for us." It means decisions that significantly impact people's lives cannot be fair and just without first listening to those people. Ensuring meaningful participation by all stakeholders when designing economic transitions, including workers and members of front-line communities, is in line with the labor studies value of promoting human dignity. After all, what is dignity if not having a say and some degree of control over key aspects of one's life as an individual or in a community?

As the world shifts to a climate safe economy, the experiences and aspirations of workers and communities must be central to defining policies and programs being crafted in city halls; state capitols; Washington, D.C.; and other seats of government around the world. The three examples of just transition in practice described in this chapter highlight the important role of worker voice and participation in shaping transitions to be more just. The AFL-CIO "Commission on the Future of Work and Unions" issued a report in September 2019. Its only mention of climate change was to note that "the battle to combat climate change cannot be waged on a project-by-project basis" and that "the fastest and most equitable way to address climate change is for labor to be at the center of creating solutions" (AFL-CIO 2019: 21).

We agree. And to partially fill this gap, we are working with partners in academia, at the Labor Network for Sustainability, Friends of the Earth, and dozens of local labor and community groups from across the country to facilitate a listening project on the issue of socioeconomic transition. The Just Transition Listening Project, as it is called, captures the experiences and expertise of workers and communities who have experienced previous transitions, who are in the midst of a transition, or who are anticipating job loss and plant closures in their communities. The testimonies will inform policy making, program design, and implementation of transition programs at all levels of government.

Most importantly, the project provides a vehicle for workers and communities to be at the forefront of the conversation about their future. This inclusive process reflects labor studies' commitment to not only uplift and value the experiences of workers and communities but also to engage with the fact that experience is not just a collection of data but is a complex process shaped by meanings and values. This is just one example of the type of publicly engaged scholarship that labor studies scholars can embark on as we not only seek to understand but to shape and support change that re-values work and workers. Or, to paraphrase from the Eleven Theses on Feuerbach: the point is not only to interpret the world but to change it (Marx [1846] 2007).

ENDNOTES

1. The two authors contributed equally to this chapter; names are presented in alphabetic order by surname.

2. For example, when humans transitioned from hunting and gathering to agriculture, a degree of egalitarianism was replaced with new forms of gender inequality. In the 17th and 18th centuries, Europeans who colonized other parts of the world instituted one of the most exploitative labor systems know to humankind—slavery—creating racialized inequalities that still shape the experience of Black lives in America. When mass production and industrial capitalism spread across Europe and North America in the 19th century, skilled artisans became wage laborers, while

factory owners experienced a meteoric rise in wealth and status. At the same time, the discovery of fossil fuels as a powerful energy source brought the number of workers employed in coal mining up from 7,000 in 1840 to 677,000 in 1900, and more than 50,000 miners died on the job between 1870 and 1914.

3. While beyond the scope of this chapter, we note that institutional arrangements matter when considering the role of worker voice in economic transitions, and we encourage further comparative research to evaluate the role of political–economic institutions in shaping transitions like those away from fossil fuels and toward renewable energy.

REFERENCES

AFL-CIO Commission on the Future of Work and Unions. 2019 (Sep.). "Report to the AFL-CIO General Board." Washington, DC: AFL-CIO. https://bit.ly/3a5souv

Brecher, Jeremy. 2014 (Apr. 22). "'Jobs vs. the Environment': How to Counter This Divisive Big Lie." *The Nation*. https://bit.ly/3qOmtAY

Brecher, Jeremy. 2015 (Nov./Dec.). "A Superfund for Workers: How to Promote a Just Transition and Break Out of the Jobs vs. Environment Trap." *Dollars and Sense*. https://bit.ly/3a9czDs

Cha, J. Mijin. 2017. "A Just Transition: Why Transitioning Workers into a New Clean Energy Economy Should Be at the Center of Climate Change Policies." *Fordham Environmental Law Review* 29 (2): 196–220. https://bit.ly/2LVhUGo

Cha, J. Mijin, Manuel Pastor, Rachel Morello-Frosch, James Sadd, and Madeline Wander. 2019. "A Roadmap to an Equitable Low-Carbon Future: Four Pillars for a Just Transition." *Climate Equity Network*. https://bit.ly/2YdeFwf

California Public Utilities Commission (CPUC). 2018 (Jan. 16). "Decision Approving Retirement of Diablo Canyon Nuclear Power Plant." Sacramento, CA: California Public Utilities Commission. https://bit.ly/2Mpj3pv

European Trade Union Institute. 2016 (Feb. 9). "Social Partners and the Collaborative Approach Are Key to the Green Transition of the Ruhr Region. Brussels, Belgium: European Trade Union Institute. https://bit.ly/2YccIjA

Galgóczi, Béla. 2014. "The Long and Winding Road From Black to Green: Decades of Structural Change in the Ruhr Region." *International Journal of Labour Research* 6 (2): 217–240.

Gold, Howard R. 2017. "Never Mind the 1 Percent. Let's Talk about the 0.01 Percent." *Chicago Booth Review*. https://bit.ly/39Y6yJy

Hampton, Paul. 2015. *Workers and Trade Unions for Climate Solidarity: Tackling Climate Change in a Neoliberal World*. New York, NY: Routledge.

"Joint Proposal." 2016 (Jun. 20). "Joint Proposal of Pacific Gas and Electric Company, Friends of the Earth, Natural Resources Defense Council, Environment California, International Brotherhood of Electrical Workers Local 1245, Coalition of California Utility Employees, and Alliance for Nuclear Responsibility to Retire Diablo Canyon Nuclear Power Plant at Expiration of the Current Operating Licenses and Replace It With a Portfolio of GHG Free Resources." https://bit.ly/2M2Xnj4

International Labour Organization. 2018 (Aug. 15). "The Employment Impact of Climate Change Adaptation." Input Document for the G20 Climate Sustainability Working Group. Geneva, Switzerland: International Labour Organization. https://bit.ly/3sVwcqR

Intergovernmental Panel on Climate Change (IPCC). 2018. "Summary for Policymakers of IPCC Special Report on Global Warming of 1.5°C Approved by Governments." Intergovernmental Panel on Climate Change. https://bit.ly/3pdo8Q9

Leopold, Les. 1995. "Our Lakes, Our Health, Our Future. 22–25 September 1995, Duluth, Minnesota." In *Proceedings of the International Joint Commission's 1995 Biennial Meeting on Great Lakes Water Quality*, pp. 80–84. https://bit.ly/3cb5hSf

Leopold, Les. 2007. *The Man Who Hated Work and Loved Labor: The Life and Times of Tony Mazzocchi*. White River Junction, VT: Chelsea Green.

Lipsitz, Richard, and Rebecca Newberry. No date. "Huntley, A Case Study: Building Strategic Alliances for Real Change." *Labor Network for Sustainability*. https://bit.ly/2MrlDel

Madl, David, and Alex Rowell. 2017 (May 2). "How State and Local Governments Can Strengthen Worker Power and Raise Wages." *Center for American Progress Action Fund*. https://bit.ly/3iXFsqd

Marx, Karl. (1846) 2007. "Theses on Feuerbach." In *The German Ideology, Volume I* by Karl Marx and Friedrich Engels, pp. 39–96. New York, NY: International Publishers.

Marx, Karl. (1867) 1990. *Capital: A Critique of Political Economy*. New York, NY: Penguin Books.

Mazzocchi, Tony. 1993. "A Superfund for Workers." *Earth Island Journal* 9 (1): 40–41. https://bit.ly/2Mw45hy

McGowan, Elizabeth. 2017 (Jul. 11). "Rising from the Ashes, a Buffalo Suburb Ends Its Dependence on Coal." *Grist*. https://bit.ly/3okNudF

Movement Generation. No date. "From Banks and Tanks to Cooperation and Caring: A Strategic Framework for a Just Transition." *Movement Generation*. https://bit.ly/3okJie2

Ocasio-Cortez, Alexandria, and Ed Markey. 2019 (Feb. 7). *Resolution Recognizing the Duty of the Federal Government to Create a Green New Deal*. HR 109, 116th Cong., 1st sess.

Pollin, Robert, and Brian Callaci. 2016. "The Economics of Just Transition: A Framework for Supporting Fossil Fuel-Dependent Workers and Communities in the United States." Amherst, MA: Political Economy Research Institute. https://bit.ly/2Yjbp2G

SB-1090. 2018. "SB-1090 Diablo Canyon Nuclear Powerplant." Sacramento, CA: California Legislative Information. https://bit.ly/39lQLFg

St. John, Jeff. 2018 (Aug. 24). "California Passes Bill Requiring Diablo Canyon Plant to Be Replaced With Carbon-Free Resources. *Greentech Media*. https://bit.ly/36df8my

Stevis, Dimitris, Dunja Krause, and Edouard Morena. 2019. "Reclaiming the Role of Labour Environmentalism in Just Transitions." *International Union Rights* 26 (4): 3-4.

Sweeney, Sean. 2015. "Standing Rock Solid with the Frackers: Are the Trades Putting Labor's Head in the Gas Oven?" *New Labor Forum* 26 (1): 94–99. https://bit.ly/36cvyMc

"Tonawanda Tomorrow: Growing the Town's Economic Future." 2017. Buffalo, NY: State University of New York at Buffalo, School of Architecture and Planning. https://bit.ly/3iYRVtx

United Nations Research Institute for Social Development (UNRISD). 2018 (Nov.). "Mapping Just Transition(s) to a Low-Carbon World." Geneva, Switzerland: UNRISD. https://bit.ly/39pwQ8g

US Bureau of Labor Statistics. 2019. "Occupational Employment Statistics." Washington, DC: US Bureau of Labor Statistics. https://www.bls.gov/oes

US Department of Energy. 2018. "2017 U.S. Energy and Employment Report." Washington, DC: US Department of Energy. https://bit.ly/3r0WqGD

Vachon, Todd E. 2021a. "Skin in the Game: The Struggle Over Climate Protection Within the U.S. Labor Movement." In *Anti-Environmental Handbook*, edited by David Tindall, Mark C.J. Stoddart, and Riley E. Dunlap. Cheltenham, UK: Edward Elgar.

Vachon, Todd E. 2021b. "The Green New Deal and Just Transition Frames Within the American Labor Movement." In *Handbook of Environmental-Labour Studies*, edited by Nora Räthzel, Dimitris Stevis, and David Uzzell. New York, NY: Palgrave Macmillan.

Wykle, Lucinda, Ward Morehouse, and David Dembo. 1991. *Worker Empowerment in a Changing Economy: Jobs, Military Production and the Environment.* New York, NY: Apex Press.

PART II
EVOLVING FORMS OF
COLLECTIVE AGENCY

CHAPTER 6

Worker Mobilization and Political Engagement: A Historical Perspective

NAOMI R WILLIAMS
SHERI DAVIS-FAULKNER
Rutgers University

ABSTRACT

This chapter uses a critical race theory and intersectionality lens to examine key historical moments of worker mobilization in the United States. This approach is presented to demonstrate how counternarratives that center workers at the margins broaden our conceptualization of the working class. Using a case study, it offers lessons on building and adapting class solidarity through a broad social justice view. It argues for scholarship that can influence public policy to strengthen the ability of workers to organize and to sharpen worker efforts to counter and reverse the harms of racial capitalism. Scholars need to facilitate worker agency through an intersectional, race-conscious approach to research agendas; support organizing efforts by working people to provide economic security; actively shape the debate around the future of work to advocate for a robust worker movement and the expansion of economic and formal democracy; and build a global base to reshape a political economy that represents most people.

INTRODUCTION

The 2020 murders of Ahmaud Arbery, Breonna Taylor, and George Floyd, coming back to back as they did—just when the pandemic's economic crisis took hold—ushered in a wave of local and national protests. Black, Indigenous, other people of color (BIPOC), and their allies took to the streets to demand a racial reckoning: a confrontation with racial capitalism, Black[1] liberation, and economic justice. BIPOC low-wage workers showcased their "essential" role in the US economy while trying to survive on poverty wages. Local communities demanded yet again to defund the police, for equality before the law, and for safe working conditions. Workers and their allies demanded and continue to call for an end to structural and systemic racism.

These mobilizations, and the people leading them, represent the future of work and workers. They also represent a long history of Black-led, interracial, community-based mobilizations for economic justice and Black liberation in the United States. The spring and summer 2020 mobilizations and protests are often presented as a racial reckoning, but most analyses of the response to the pandemic and ensuing economic crisis fail to understand these mobilizations as worker led and fueled not only by the current crisis but by years of community-based organizing around economic justice and Black liberation.

This most recent wave of mass mobilizations is directly linked to the response to the 2008 economic crisis and corporate-centered recovery efforts that left most working people across the globe struggling to survive. Seen most distinctly in 2011 and 2012 with the Occupy movement, uprisings against attacks on public workers in Wisconsin, and early organizing of the Fight for $15 movement, people increasingly started to talk about and question growing income and wealth inequality. More and more workers, particularly BIPOC low-wage workers in the fast food, hotel, and tourism industries, began demanding a greater share of wealth and profits with renewed organization and momentum.

In the early days of Fight for $15, many voiced skepticism and argued that with a federal minimum wage of just over $7 an hour, $15 was unrealistic and a waste of time and energy. Yet the Fight for $15 (FF15) movement has been the most successful mobilization of working people since the Great Recession. Starting in the fall of 2012, fast food workers and community groups have mobilized low-wage service workers to fight for higher wages and union representation. Worker-to-worker organizing expanded FF15 from fast food workers in New York City to low-wage workers across the nation.

This diverse movement has showcased the result of solidarity across employment sectors, race, gender, nationality, immigration status, and religion as it expanded to part-time faculty at universities, home healthcare workers, and other people employed at less than a living wage. Public pressure through one-day work stoppages, media campaigns dispelling myths of the demographics of fast food employees and highlighting the ways the public subsidizes these workers through social safety net programs, protests at shareholder meetings, and lobbying local and state governments have led to rising minimum wages in local areas across the nation.

When given the chance, most people have voted for increasing the minimum wage across the United States. Even Walmart, the anti-union, global low-road leader among employers, raised wages based on the activism of workers in organizations like Our Walmart and others. Joe Biden included a $15 federal minimum wage proposal in his 2020 presidential campaign messaging.

These recent mobilizations must also be analyzed within the context of the Movement for Black Lives (M4BL). Started in 2012 in response to vigilante and police violence, the M4BL is based within a long tradition of Black radical feminism that is intentionally intersectional and centers the most vulnerable in looking for solutions to state-sponsored violence against people of color in the United States. The 2014 Ferguson, Missouri, mobilizing linked protests over the killing of Michael Brown to systemic abuse of the Black community in the area through over-policing, disfranchisement, and extraction of community resources. BLM protesters linked the battles to more equally distribute economic decision-making power beyond corporate managers and grant Black people equal protection under the law: economic democracy and Black liberation (Ransby 2018; Taylor 2016).

Moreover, the global worker protests on April 15, 2015, highlighted the ways local community members fostered coalitions and worker power around the issues of BLM and economic democracy. These coalitions also helped shape the 2020 protests around COVID-19 response, the economic shutdown, and racial justice (Greenhouse 2019; Orleck 2015; Rosenblum 2017; Taylor 2016). Despite this, these stories are often left out of discussions of the future of work and what economic democracy should look like for an all-inclusive future of workers.

These recent mobilizations, and the organizational efforts of workers surrounding the 2020 US presidential election, illustrate the ways working people are fighting with renewed vigor against runaway inequality, austerity measures, and the attacks on economic democracy that have shaped the growth of neoliberal, global capitalism over the past 40 years. It also shows that workers continue to have the ability to leverage their collective power to influence the political economy of their communities and the nation. Today, when the future of democracy is in question, it is more important than ever that workers mobilize as a united class to ensure more people have access to living wages, safe working conditions, and dignity and respect at work. Labor studies scholars need tools to counter the harms of racial capitalism and help build an inclusive vision of the working class. This chapter argues that by centering the work of Black activists and workers at the margins in the past, we find greater efforts at and benefits of collaboration and a path forward for organizing and supporting worker efforts to empower and mobilize the whole working class in the 21st century.

Yet the neoliberal capitalist agenda is fueled by creating false divisions that trap workers in desperate situations to extract their labor at the lowest possible cost. Too many white workers continue to operate without solidarity for the whole class. The nature of employment has changed so that too many workers fall through the chasms within the employment law apparatus. Politicians do not operate with a genuine understanding of the robust, diverse working class as a constituency unto itself.

As labor studies scholars think about the future of work and workers, they must understand the importance of protecting economic democracy and building solidarity among the whole working class. Using a critical race theory and intersectionality (CRT/I) lens to examine key moments within US history when workers managed to shape the political landscape and expand democracy and economic citizenship reveals the power of interracial worker mobilizations. It offers lessons on building, maintaining, and adapting class solidarity through a broad social justice view. It also provides an impetus within labor studies for scholarship that can influence public policy to strengthen the ability of workers to organize and sharpen their efforts to counter and reverse the harms of racial capitalism. As Cedric Robinson argued so effectively in *Black Marxism*, capitalism was built on principles of racial exclusion and white supremacy (Robinson 2000). False divides along racial lines weaken broad worker mobilizations in the United States because too many white workers continue to be convinced that workers of color are to blame for their inability to maintain economic stability. Furthermore, too many white workers are invested in "whiteness as a form of property," where the primary function of having whiteness is the sole right to exclude others from rights, privileges, and protections (Harris 1993). Racial capitalism has created deep race, gender, and class inequities, while also stripping workers of all races of their collective power to expand economic democracy.

How scholars and pundits think and talk about the working class can help shape an all-inclusive working-class identity and impact better policy-making decisions to expand economic democracy. Most often when scholars refer to the working class, they think in terms of white male workers in industrial settings. However, this narrow view elides the true diversity and robustness of the working class and accentuates the harms of racial capitalism by eroding the collective power of workers. One way labor studies scholars can address this narrow and defeating conceptualization is through using a CRT/I framework in their analyses to add greater complexity to our understanding of 20th-century US labor history. Black workers and immigrant workers (for example) have always been at the forefront of working-class mass mobilizations. Sustained working-class mobilization and political engagement will only come with the full mobilization of a united working class. Labor studies scholars must play a key role in reconceptualizing "working class" to represent all workers.

This chapter outlines the value of bringing a CRT/I approach to labor studies and what that will entail. It then provides a brief counternarrative of the New Deal period, what scholars point to as the heyday of worker mobilization that led to the institutionalization of employment law and collective bargaining rights in the US political economy. The dominant labor narrative misses the ways Black worker mobilizations offered a much broader opportunity for economic citizenship during this period. This counternarrative highlights Black workers and their vital role in building interracial coalitions to use collective power to expand economic democracy for all workers.

Through a case study of the labor community in Racine, Wisconsin, this chapter then provides a close examination of how intersectional mobilizations increased worker power in one local area. This case explores the ways Black labor activists helped build a robust and adaptive working-class identity in the city.

The efforts of Black workers in the civil rights movement paid off in the 1970s and 1980s as the Racine labor community built social justice coalitions to expand economic democracy through supporting welfare reform and fighting for the rights of immigrant workers. Finally, the chapter returns to current mobilizations to uncover historic continuities and offer ways to build worker solidarity despite attempts to shatter alliances with racism, nativism, and xenophobia and to rebuild economic democracy as we contemplate the future of work.

TENETS OF CRITICAL RACE THEORY AND INTERSECTIONALITY

CRT is a scholarly movement that comes out of critical legal studies in the 1980s. It is a framework that scholars use to examine society through the lens of race and power. The concept of "intersectionality" was born of worker and workplace struggles; it is one of the key tenets of the CRT framework used in this essay. Critical race legal scholar Kimberlé Crenshaw (1989) coined the term "intersectionality" to describe what happens when centering the experience of Black women as workers. It reveals how interlocking systems of oppression, racism, and sexism impact the material conditions of Black women's lives and create a unique set of circumstances whereby they have limited or no legal protections. But intersectionality also engages the work of praxis, meaning the purpose for researching the conditions is to organize and struggle for remedies that actually address the injuries *and* transform harmful and exclusionary practices to ensure long-term impact for Black women and other injured groups.

This chapter also functions as a labor counternarrative, which is another key tenet of CRT. This chapter offers a race- and gender-conscious analysis of the dominant labor narrative by employing a "looking to the bottom" approach, which makes visible the stories of marginalized actors that provide guidance for ways to mobilize workers for broader impact (Matsuda 1987). Recognizing that Black women are often at the lowest rung of the economic ladder, when their experiences are made visible, it not only disrupts dominant narratives that center white males as universal subjects who represent a universal worker experience, but oftentimes the remedies created to address the needs of the most marginalized tend to improve conditions for all working people.

In "Whiteness as Property" Cheryl Harris explains that "whiteness has been legally constructed to mean having the absolute right to exclude and the right to own property in the form of human labor (i.e., slaves) and land through the removal of Indigenous peoples" (Davis 2012; Harris 1993). This key tenet also provides a lens for understanding how labor law and labor organizations effectively excluded Black workers and other workers of color from protections, arguing the right to exclude has undergirded challenges to building solidarity across racial groups. The following counternarrative of New Deal worker mobilizations, centering the efforts of Black workers, shows how transforming the way we understand labor struggles, labor history, and the role of labor studies can offer insights for the future of workers and economic democracy.

WORKER MOBILIZATION FROM THE 1930S TO THE CIVIL RIGHTS MOVEMENT

Most scholars look to the period of the 1930s as the heyday of worker mobilization. This focus makes sense because worker activism led to the formalization of our labor law apparatus in the United States. The dominant labor narrative describes the period from 1934 through 1937 with the federal government actively supporting worker mobilization and more workers gaining access to industrial democracy: increased wages, more control over working conditions, and negotiated benefits and job security. It led to a political realignment in the United States; worker participation in Franklin Roosevelt's "New Deal Coalition" helped create the welfare state. Workers, particularly in Congress of Industrial Organizations (CIO) unions, created a culture that inspired people to become engaged citizens and demonstrate worker unity within local unions, across industries, and with other unionized and non-unionized workers in the areas where they operated (Cohen 1990). The New Deal Coalition reshaped the political economy so that an "'American' standard of living was becoming a right of citizenship" (Lichtenstein 2002: 26). Workers took advantage of this shift and organized themselves into unions (union membership increased by five million between 1933 and 1937) and successfully bargained with employers across the nation (Lichtenstein 2002). Workers also used their collective power to support the Democratic Party and expanded their political influence from local to national levels (Cohen 1990; Lichtenstein 2002). By the end of the 1930s, most workers in the United States had a guaranteed minimum wage, retirement safeguards, work and safety laws, and a stronger, though imperfect, social safety net.

However, through the lens of racial consciousness, this (limited) success story is diminished by the pushback from white supremacists, conservatives, and their Republican allies, whose intent was to limit the impact of post-war liberalism and maintain white supremacy (Lichtenstein 2002, 2011; Phillips-Fein 2009). Labor's refusal to pay more than lip service to antiracism, and political attacks such as passage of the 1947 Taft–Hartley Act, placed real limits on the ability of workers to sustain and expand the gains of the 1930s and supports Harris's "Whiteness as Property" thesis (Harris 1993). Yet taking a CRT/I approach can provide a framework for worker liberation using the counternarrative. By centering workers most left out—Black workers, women, workers across the South—we can see what civil rights unionism or social justice unionism did to inspire movement building and expand economic democracy during this period. Also, using Hall's framework of a "long civil rights movement," we can examine post-war worker activism in new ways (Hall 2005). Using intersectionality to link stories often told separately of labor and civil rights, a more nuanced understanding of worker mobilization in the post-war period becomes visible. The work labor activists did in this period expanded citizenship rights by addressing racial and gender inequality in workplaces and in US society more broadly. This activism led to the passage of the 1964 Civil Rights Act and the 1965 Voting Rights Act. Worker mobilization also saw government enforcement of these laws, which expanded and democratized the workforce, politicized another generation of workers, and created the environment for community coalitions to address social and political issues at the local and national levels (Ervin 2017; Sites and Parks 2011). Civil rights activists did not forgo their class analysis as they fought against racial discrimination. The struggle to pass the Civil Rights Act and enforce Title VII had an extraordinary impact on employment opportunities and economic security (Cobble 2004; MacLean 2006).

With far too few exceptions, scholars and policy makers think of the civil rights movement as distinct from workers' movements for economic justice. Yet a reframing of the interconnected history of the civil rights movement sheds light on the ways Black workers at the margins of the labor movement expanded, rejuvenated, and reshaped labor organizations. The social movement that we call the civil rights movement was "sparked by the alchemy of laborites, civil rights activists, progressive New Dealers, and Black and white radicals" (Hall 2005: 1245). The efforts of Black workers inside the house of labor galvanized both the struggle for economic justice and Black liberation.

For example, the Communist Party played a key role in bridging liberation movements by being antiracist in its efforts. Communists made racial justice part of their platform in the 1920s and 1930s, and this effort drew in Black workers, who used the Communist Party and labor activism more broadly to fight for racial equality and justice. Keona K. Ervin details the ways working-class Black women in St. Louis used a strike at local nut factories not only to galvanize the St. Louis working class but also indict the state for failure to protect workers as employers forced down wages after the passage of the 1933 National Industrial Recovery Act (Ervin 2017). Inspired by the Communist Party's unemployed rights movement, the women organized and sought to increase their wages and end the mistreatment they faced at work from racist managers. Workplaces were segregated, and Black women received lower pay than the immigrant Polish women who also worked in the factories. The Black nut workers mobilized other Black women workers in St. Louis who were also confined to the dirtiest jobs in the city and received less pay than other women workers. They used militant mass actions in their strike effort and, as Ervin details, proved themselves central actors in the battle of St. Louis workers for labor rights (Ervin 2017). Robin D.G. Kelley has described the role of Black Communists in Alabama during this same period. They sought to build an antiracist coalition to expand democracy and economic justice against impossible odds. *Hammer and Hoe* examines the ways Black people shaped Communist Party ideologies into their Afrocentric worldview and used the party in creative ways, helping other members to see that Black liberation was intricately tied to labor rights (Kelley 2015). These examples highlight the importance of Black worker strategies against racial capitalism in worker mobilization and political engagement efforts. The organizing efforts and victories in the 1930s laid the foundation for the mobilizations that would come later, particularly in the 1960s.

The 1940s and 1950s are where we see the greatest impact of the worker mobilizations of the early New Deal period for Black workers. By 1953, over one third of workers outside agriculture belonged to unions (Lichtenstein 2002: 54–59). Nationwide, about half a million Black workers joined industrial unions and led the way in addressing racial issues in the workplace. Black workers were galvanized by New Deal legislation and used the rhetoric of economic and political citizenship to gain access to jobs and unions. For example, in Winston-Salem, North Carolina, the members of Local 22 of the Food, Tobacco, Agricultural and Allied Workers of America (FTA) challenged racial capitalism by linking civil rights with labor rights and bridging the divide between home and work. Black workers at the R.J. Reynolds (RJR) Tobacco Company organized in the workplace, and the community and built alliances with the few white workers who recognized the harms of racial capitalism. The women, most of whom were Black, went on strike in 1943 to protest low wages and poor working conditions after having organized during the previous decade to build an interracial labor movement in the city. Their organizing forced RJR to the bargaining table and helped elect the first Black alderman in 1947 (Korstad 2003). In fact, Black workers across the South helped expand unionization in the region, where they took the lead in organizing and cooperating with civil rights activists. For instance, the FTA also built Black-led unions in Memphis. And many left-wing unions that had large minorities of Black workers were able to garner support from white members to advocate for desegregation and political equality of their Black members (Jones 2005).

Black workers also played a key role in addressing gender inequality in the workplace. The role of labor, and antiracist working-class politics more specifically, cannot be overemphasized in the post-war political landscape. As Dorothy Sue Cobble contends, "Class differences remained salient in the New Deal and after, although in newly disguised forms, and [labor] ideologies and institutions had a powerful effect on the formulation and implementation of social and employment policy" (Cobble 2004: 6). "Labor feminists" used the labor movement as the "principal vehicle" to improve the conditions for women in American society. Access to industrial trade unions allowed working-class women to increase women's rights. Notably, in Chicago, members of the United Packinghouse Workers of America (UPWA) built coalitions with community-based groups to address racism in the workplace and in the community. The interracial UPWA leadership made racial justice a high priority because 30% of its membership was

Black. Black men also played a key role in workplace actions because they were segregated in the killing department. If they stopped work, they shut down the whole process. These conditions made organizing support among Black workers critical to the union's success in meatpacking. Like the previous examples, Chicago's Black UPWA members linked economic justice and antiracism and represented Hall's "long civil rights movement" framework. When employers tried to re-segregate women after the war, an interracial coalition fought against downgrading Black women. Black women in UPWA Local 28 organized and won this fight at the Swift plant, and other locals followed their example. While less expansive than the UPWA's program, other left-wing CIO unions also protested against racial discrimination of Black women and fought to integrate workplaces (Cobble 2004).

The political mobilization of the 1960s civil rights movement is only possible because of this long history of Black worker mobilization from the 1930s through the 1960s. As Hall and Jones have detailed, the 1963 March on Washington for Jobs and Freedom was led by Black labor leaders who linked economic justice with racial justice. In the opening speech, Socialist labor leader A. Philip Randolph called for a living wage for all workers so that everyone could afford access to what civil rights advocates were fighting for. Like the period of the early New Deal era, the ability of workers to force the federal government to address social citizenship questions helped shrink the wage gap for all workers and brought a level of pay parity across racial lines. Federal enforcement of the Civil Rights Act of 1964 also expanded the labor movement, helped facilitate public sector unionization, and opened the door to women's expanded leadership within management and labor. The expansion of economic security across that period emphasizes the impact of Black worker intersectional mobilizations, even when met with harsh resistance. An energized workers' movement and strong government support led to greater economic stability in the mid-20th century (Hall 2005; Jones 2013; Sites and Parks 2011). It also created a legacy of race-conscious worker justice movements.

CASE STUDY: BLACK ACTIVISTS BUILD LABOR POWER IN RACINE, WISCONSIN

A micro-view of the Racine, Wisconsin, labor community from the civil rights era to the 1980s examines the impact of civil rights era–Black worker mobilizing efforts at the end of the 20th century. An examination of the ways Black workers successfully made race a key component of labor organizing and the ways the Racine labor community mobilized their collective power in the 1970s and 1980s offers a counternarrative to stories of labor's decline in the 1970s. Many scholars argue that the fight for racial justice split the post-war liberal coalition and pit labor and racial justice advocates against each other (Cowie 2012; Lichtenstein

2002). Yet, as this case demonstrates, the strategic decisions Black workers made in the 1960s to build a multiracial, intersectional working-class identity created a movement that maintained its relevancy and potency into the period of "labor's decline." If scholars center these stories, they can prepare today's labor movement to embrace broad-based mobilizations and counter the harms of racial capitalism.

Racine is a small industrial town that sits between Chicago and Milwaukee on the shores of Lake Michigan. Starting in the late-19th century, Racine developed a diverse industrial economy, fueled by its strategic location between the larger cities and at the point where the Root River flows into Lake Michigan. Production grew around supporting local agriculture, with the manufacture of farm implements and engine parts, tanning facilities, and mills. World War II saw the influx of many Black and Mexican-American workers during the Great Migration. Racine stands out because organized workers managed to stave off the worst effects of deindustrialization that many small rust-belt towns felt until the 1990s. They succeeded against management attacks and political conservatives' attempts at austerity measures because Black worker activism kept the labor movement focused on expansion rather than exclusion (Williams 2021).

For over 40 years, William Jenkins helped shape working-class identity in Racine. The Jenkins family moved to Racine in 1917. After graduation from high school and the death of his father, William Jenkins went to work in local foundries. He eventually found a permanent job at Belle City Malleable and joined United Auto Workers (UAW) Local 553 in the 1940s. Jenkins was also a founding member of the local NAACP, was elected union president in the 1950s, became president of the county labor council in 1962, and was a school board member in the 1970s. Jenkins remembered that most Black people arriving in Racine between the 1930s and the 1950s came straight from the South or just after a stop in Chicago because "this was a good work place, awful good place for work" (Jenkins 1974). The Black population in the city increased to nearly 7,000 by the end of the 1950s, making up around 8% of the total population. Black men moving into Racine mostly found jobs in local foundries, and Black union membership rose during World War II as they filled an increased need for production workers. Most Black women were denied entry in manufacturing jobs and were over-represented in low-wage service work and domestic labor (Williams 2021).

Jenkins's role in the labor community and civil rights movement, along with his collaborators, shaped a form of post-war labor liberalism, which created a multiracial, gender inclusive, multinational group focused on expanding economic democracy in the city. They used their collective power to limit hiring discrimination, fight for welfare reform, and stop attacks on immigrant workers. The efforts of Black workers forced the broader labor community to shift their notions of who belonged in the working class and used this power to improve conditions at work and in the city.

As Black workers came to Racine during World War II, they took advantage of the labor activism in the city and sought out unions as a key path toward economic justice and racial equality. Jenkins remembered that he became more involved in his labor union, UAW Local 553, when he saw the treatment of Black contract workers from the Caribbean during World War II. Management, he said, "misused those guys. What did they know about union contracts? They were really discriminated against. It was bad" (Jenkins 1974).

Jenkins's position as a leader in Local 553 was solidified when he led a sit-down strike over vacation pay in 1945. When bargaining committee members approached Jenkins about leading a work stoppage, he readily agreed. He talked to the workers in his unit and, after several agreed to follow his lead, he sat down in front of his machine in the steel shop. He told the foreman, "So until they make up their mind what they're gonna do, I'm gonna [sit] down here" (Jenkins 1974). In an example of the use of whiteness as property, several foremen attempted to use racial solidarity to get the white workers back to work. Instead, they remained seated, as did others across the foundry, including in the core room. As Jenkins explained, if the core room did not run, the plant could not operate. The work stoppage proved successful, and management reinstated vacation pay. Workers continued to look to Jenkins for advice and guidance, but it was a long time before he was elected to official office. Union leaders used Jenkins's popularity to support their work stoppage efforts but maintained an all-white leadership that failed to address racism among Local 553 membership. Jenkins determined to "keep running for office in the union until I could be of some use to my people" (Jenkins 1974; Pferdehirt 2011). Moreover, workers in the plant, across racial lines, increasingly started to look to him because of his vocal stand for all workers at the foundry. They elected Jenkins union president in 1955 and then president of the county AFL-CIO in 1962. Jenkins then used his position to advocate for all workers and expand labor power in the city.

Jenkins was also deeply involved in the Racine branch of the NAACP, which his father-in-law helped organize in 1947. He became president in the 1950s and recruited many UAW members from surrounding foundries into the racial justice organization. As a union leader in Local 553 and the NAACP branch president, Jenkins used his dual positions to effect change in the community. For example, he actively worked to end racial employment discrimination. In 1962, labor and civil rights activists criticized Mayor Jack Humble's Commission on Human Rights for its failure to make any significant progress in eliminating hiring discrimination in the city. Jenkins issued a statement, asserting, "Mayor Humble must face the fact that when it comes to assisting Negroes gain employment in the white- and blue-collar brackets, his organization is a non-entity" (Williams 2021). Jenkins and others criticized the commission for failing to act on reports that the Racine State Employment Office was administering aptitude tests to Black and Mexican unskilled workers but not to white unskilled applicants. He also charged the commission with ignoring complaints about industry hiring practices in the city. Non-white workers continued to struggle to find placements in most Racine firms—only the foundries and the J.I. Case Company had more than a few non-white employees.

In 1964, the Wisconsin Industrial Commission held statewide hearings on minority hiring. As in other cities, workers in southeast Wisconsin had urged that hearings be held to strengthen campaigns to get a permanent Fair Employment Practices Commission (FEPC) as part of the March on Washington movement. President Roosevelt had issued an executive order outlawing discrimination in national defense contracts in 1941 and established a Fair Employment Practices Committee as an enforcement agency. Black workers, through unions and social justice networks, led the way in creating local pressure to enforce the antidiscrimination efforts of the FEPC (Jones 2013). These are the tactics that helped expand union membership and reinforce linkages between economic and racial justice.

The 19 Racine employers that participated in the hearings testified that minority workers held only 904 out of 15,615 jobs in their firms. Belle City Malleable, where William Jenkins worked, had over 400 Black and Latino workers, while most firms only had two or three, all of them recent hires in the days and weeks before the scheduled hearings. As the largest foundry in the city, Belle City Malleable regularly started hiring Black and Latino workers in the 1940s. These jobs were available because the hot, dangerous working conditions made them the least favorable in the diversified economy of Racine. If workers could find other employment, they did. The hearings confirmed earlier claims of Black working-class activists about the discriminatory hiring practices engaged in by local firms. While there were several Black members like William Jenkins serving in leadership roles in union locals, little concerted effort existed to bring in and train non-white workers across the city's diverse manufacturing industries (Williams 2021). Union leaders and Black worker-activists also sought to create an apparatus inside unions and labor councils to protect against hiring discrimination and in support of a permanent FEPC. Racine's union members across industries—including foundries, publishing, garment making, and teaching—submitted separate but identical resolutions calling for "the immediate appointment by the Executive Board of a new staff position with sole duties confined to working with the Fair Employment Practices program and problems within the State of Wisconsin" at the Wisconsin AFL-CIO convention (Williams 2021). The broad support for this measure illustrates the success of the Black workers' campaign for racial justice within Racine's trade unions.

In addition to fighting within the Wisconsin state AFL-CIO, Black union members joined the Negro American Labor Council (NALC) in 1965. Formed in 1960, NALC sought to push the economic justice issues of racial discrimination within the labor movement, workplaces, and the nation. Local NALC groups recruited members from labor unions to study problems of non-white workers and to look for solutions to those problems (Jones 2013). William Jenkins, Leroy Wooley, Corrine Owens, Keith Mack, and so many others worked within and beyond labor and social justice institutions to reshape race relations in the city. They fought to end discrimination in housing and education as well as jobs. They pushed labor leaders and local politicians to address Black people's concerns. Jenkins, in particular, helped institute a culture of racial justice among union leaders. Despite mixed results, the efforts of Black workers did open the door for expanded social and economic citizenship even after the heyday of the 1960s social movements.

In Racine, Black workers' efforts during the long civil rights movement helped fuel a dynamic and strong labor community that linked economic and racial justice. Three key examples show the results as the Racine labor community adapted to address increasing social and economic demands from workers and community members. The first example involves welfare rights activists and the social workers' union. Their combined efforts created a community coalition that worked to improve urban neighborhoods. In 1969, welfare recipients and unionized social workers rallied together to implement changes in the Racine County welfare office. Momentum started building in August 1968 because of police violence amid building frustration. Black and Latinx residents felt left out of the local job market and trapped in deteriorating neighborhoods. Community groups called on the mayor to move forward on housing code legislation, better policing, and more social services (Williams 2021).

The slow response by city officials fueled a labor–community coalition that brought social workers and welfare activists together. A recent investigation into neighborhood problems had called for public-aid recipients to sit on a community board to make administrative decisions, a consolidation of the county and city public welfare departments, and better training of caseworkers to address recipients' needs. Welfare recipients held a sit-in demanding better treatment and respect from the department and issued a list of demands. Responding to and agreeing with welfare recipients, social workers organized around some of these issues and went on strike (Williams 2021).

International Association of Machinists and Aerospace Workers (IAM) Lodge 437 social workers bargained for pay increases, new training and promotion procedures, and flexibility to deal with clients on a case-by-case basis. Poor working conditions increased turnover in the department and limited the ability of caseworkers to help applicants. Social workers received the support of residents because the strikers' demands included and supported those made by welfare activists. Labor unions, racial justice organizations, and community groups supported this joint effort (Williams 2021).

This community–worker coalition developed as a direct result of labor activists constantly stressing the relationship among the lack of access to jobs, housing discrimination, welfare reform, and neighborhood improvement. After six weeks, the county gave in to the strike demands (Williams 2021). Public debate around the strike emphasized the labor community's continued commitment to the broad-based notion of the post-war liberal idea of economic and social citizenship rights. This labor–community coalition and a housing march added the required political pressure to pass an antidiscrimination housing law through the Racine Common Council.

In the second example from Racine, school employees organized with community members to improve conditions within urban schools. Local 152 of the Service Employees International Union (SEIU), representing the janitors and food service workers for the Racine Unified School District, went on strike in January 1971 mainly over cost-of-living increases. The union linked their complaints to parents' frustration over the closing of a local elementary school. The fire department had ruled the school unsafe during Thanksgiving break and transferred the students to another school, without providing bus service. SEIU Local 152 members pointed to the school board's refusal to put children's safety first. The strike and rhetoric around it brought the school board back to the bargaining table. The public debate and strike paid off for Local 152 in a much-improved labor contract (Williams 2021). It also highlights the continuity with current labor movement initiatives such as Bargaining for the Common Good (McCartin, Sneiderman, and BP-Weeks 2020).

It also paid off in the community, as residents recognized the support of labor activists to help protect minority students. When parents of Howell Elementary School students could not sustain the carpool services to get young students to their new school, county unions paid to provide bus service for the students. These allies worked together to bring the free lunch program to Racine, demand that students impacted by the closing of the elementary school receive hot lunches at their new schools, better integrate schools, and hold the school district to its promise to increase the percentage of non-white teachers and administrators within the school system. It also got William Jenkins elected to the school board, as labor and community activists leveraged their power to remove three members from the school board and replace them with labor-friendly candidates (Williams 2021). These tactics helped expand economic democracy by bringing more stakeholders to the table regarding public financing.

In the final example, union members supported immigrant workers when faced with employer/immigration service attacks in the mid-1980s. In June 1984, the US Immigration and Naturalization Service (INS) started a series of raids at Racine Steel Castings, which was the new name of Belle City Malleable where Jenkins had worked. Over the next several months, INS agents detained 19 workers and charged them with being in the country without proper documentation. This happened during bargaining and leading up to Reagan's re-election campaign (Williams 2021).

Local 553 was ready for the challenge. Union members, across racial lines, pushed back against the "Whiteness as Property" rhetoric in the local media about non-white workers stealing jobs and opportunities from more deserving white workers. The local union understood the ways that Black and Latino industrial workers had faced increased economic hardship during deindustrialization as they lost jobs at faster rates than white workers did. Local 553 President Dick Fought held press conferences to challenge the notion that undocumented workers were stealing jobs from the Racine community. He worked with local Latinx organizations to help families produce their legal documents and argued for the workers' immediate release from detention centers and right to due process. The local Catholic parish raised funds to provide bond for one worker being held in Chicago, and the community came together to help other workers provide the paperwork they needed to stay in the country. Fought also refused to endorse the firing of the 19 workers. The union successfully argued that Racine Steel Castings could not fire the workers until they were deported. In fact, Local 553 successfully got 17 of the 19 union members reinstated to work (Ngai 2004; Williams 2021). These efforts created lasting bonds among Latinx worker organizations, immigration rights groups, and the Racine labor community. Their success also highlights the value of intersectional mobilization efforts to fight against racial capitalism.

As these examples show, the strategies of Black workers during the long civil rights movement opened the door for labor activists to connect racial justice with working-class politics in the following decades. While social discrimination continued to affect non-white residents, the labor community pushed an agenda that embraced racial solidarity and full economic citizenship rights for all Racinians. The efforts of Black workers helped keep the Racine labor movement relevant to the needs of most working people. In Racine, workers continued to rely on their unions as the first path toward economic and social justice and elected union activists to local government. This case is just one example of the power of intersectional organizing at the local level and speaks to the need for additional scholarship to center these stories within labor studies.

MOBILIZING WORKERS FOR THE 21ST CENTURY

So, what happened? Throughout the 20th century, Black workers and their allies fought for economic justice and racial liberation. They mobilized workers across racial lines and pushed lawmakers at every level of government to pass policy that supported full economic citizenship. Why has inequality continued to drag more and more working people into poverty? The answer is racial capitalism and the power of the neoliberal agenda. When white supremacists and powerful business owners saw the collective power of an interracial workers' movement, they went on the attack. Conservatives and Southern oligarchs fought every New Deal program and restricted the expansion of the welfare state. Policy and implementation reinforced racial and gender inequities, such as excluding agriculture and domestic workers and allowing regional differences in pay scales. Federal policy and banking practices increased housing segregation and led to increased educational and employment segregation. Left-led unions that were leading the antiracist charge were purged from the CIO during the Cold War. The Taft–Hartley amendments to the Wagner Act outlawed many of the workers' best tactics against hostile employers: strikes, secondary boycotts, union shops, and political engagement (Hall 2005; Kelley 2021; Lichtenstein 2002; Phillips-Fein 2009).

Liberal policy makers refused to see racial discrimination as tied to employment rights and split enforcement between the NLRB and the Equal Employment Opportunities Commission. This altered the public debate and emphasized the false boundary between race and economic justice (Kelley 2021; MacLean 2006). Failure to properly fund and staff federal and state agencies charged with protecting workers' rights to fair wages, safe working environments, collective bargaining, and freedom from discrimination freed management to ignore labor laws, which have not kept pace with changing employment schemes (Lichtenstein 2002, 2011; Stein 2011). Democrats failed the multiracial labor movement in the 1970s. They offered no solutions for workers as workers, regardless of race. They attempted to mobilize Black people but without connecting economic and racial justice. Failure to pass the 1978 labor law reforms also alienated many white working-class voters, many of whom stopped participating in national electoral politics (Kilpatrick and Stein 2016; Stein 2011).

A. Philip Randolph and other male leaders of the March on Washington movement and large civil rights organizations such as the Southern Christian Leadership Conference failed to fully include Black women leaders and women's organizations in their coalition. This weakened their efforts, and they missed the opportunity to build on the work of radical Black feminists who were also linking economic justice with racial and gender equality (Kelley 2003, 2021; Ransby 2005; Walker-McWilliams 2016). Union leaders at the national level and the AFL-CIO failed to act on their promises of racial justice. As was the case in Racine, only some unions and their leaders fought along with racial justice collaborators in ending discrimination in housing, education, employment, and welfare rights. Too many white workers and union leaders sought to capitalize on racism and nativism and refused to take a race-conscious approach to organizing. Falling into the trap of racial capitalism, they kept their unions exclusionary and lost the ability to use collective power to counter corporate interests and neoliberal policy makers (Battista 2008; Cowie 2012; Kelley 2021; Stein 2011). Yet many workers, and the union organizations that represent them, have learned from the past and are continuing to take an intersectional approach to organizing and mobilizing in their communities.

When workers mobilize, they can often generate enough leverage to reshape local and even national political economies. Workers cannot do it alone. To facilitate worker mobilization and political engagement, scholars, policy makers, and activists must shift the current dominant narrative of "labor." Too often "labor" or "working class" does not represent the true breadth of the labor movement and is narrowly focused on white males in trade unions and excludes workers at the margins: low-wage workers and especially BIPOC women workers. The 21st-century labor movement is more diverse, is (mostly) antiracist, pro-immigrant rights and environmental justice, women led, and based in local communities. When we take a critical lens and shift our focus, we see the leaders of the movement are the low-wage, marginalized workers who are fighting for everyone to have a living wage and dignity at work.

Scholars and political commentators also need to highlight the link between 21st-century social justice movements and a long history of organizing by a diverse group of workers in local communities. The continuities of worker mobilizations from the 1930s until today highlight the ways workers can mobilize and cooperate to leverage their power to move the state to protect economic democracy. Workers from the margins and those left out of legal labor protections continue to design creative ways to fight for dignity at work and economic security for their communities. This is seen in the continued collaboration between FF15 activists and the M4BL. It was put on stark display as the 2020 pandemic crippled the retail, restaurant, and hotel tourism industries. A return to community-level mobilizations like the FF15, Black Lives Matter, and Bargaining for the Common Good movements has also generated remarkable success. The wins in Chicago and Los Angeles have inspired Red for Ed campaigns even in right-to-work areas (Cobble 2001; Fine 2005; Greenhouse 2019; Orleck 2018; Rosenblum 2017). Labor studies scholars must continue "looking to the bottom" for direction on ways to dismantle economic injustices that impact workers more broadly.

By crafting counternarratives that accentuate the diverse groups that have always made up these movements, we can undo the harms of racial capitalism that recreate divisions within the labor movement. We can work to incorporate these narratives into mainstream labor history and reshape the future for workers. By treating labor and racial justice movements as separate constituencies to the Democratic Party, politicians and advocates continue to lose opportunities to mobilize working people. Likewise, the Democratic Party and liberal policy makers more broadly have thwarted working people's power to impact policies that would expand economic and social citizenship rights (Frymer 2008; Lichtenstein 2011; MacLean 2006; Stein 2011). To protect the future for workers, we must put forward public policy initiatives to protect the right of workers to organize and respond to their mobilizations. History has shown that an active, engaged state can expand democracy in workplaces, reduce income and wealth inequality, and engage an informed citizenship. Workers deserve dignity at work, the right to a living wage, access to healthcare, sustainable industries, and a healthy earth with clean water. Those of us engaged in the field of labor studies need to continue to lift up worker agency through an intersectional, race-conscious approach to our research agendas; support organizing efforts by working people to provide economic security; and actively shape the debate around the future of work to advocate for a robust workers' movement and the expansion of economic and formal democracy; and build a global base to reshape a political economy that represents the majority of people.

ENDNOTE

1. Black is a political category, constructed as the negation of white, which has been constructed as the universal subject with a system of exclusive rights, privileges, and protections. We capitalize Black to indicate the difference between them and the work we are doing to disrupt and dismantle those categories and systems.

REFERENCES

Battista, Andrew. 2008. *The Revival of Labor Liberalism*. Champaign, IL: University of Illinois Press.

Cobble, Dorothy Sue. 2001. "Lost Ways of Unionism: Historical Perspectives on Reinventing the Labor Movement." In *Rekindling the Movement: Labor's Quest for Relevance in the Twenty-First Century*, edited by Lowell Turner, Harry C. Katz, and Richard W. Hurd, pp. 82–96. Ithaca, NY: ILR Press.

Cobble, Dorothy Sue. 2004. *The Other Women's Movement: Workplace Justice and Social Rights in Modern America*. Princeton, NJ: Princeton University Press.

Cohen, Lizabeth. 1990. *Making a New Deal: Industrial Workers in Chicago, 1919-1939*. Cambridge, UK: Cambridge University Press.

Cowie, Jefferson. 2012. *Stayin' Alive: The 1970s and the Last Days of the Working Class*. New York, NY: The New Press.

Crenshaw, Kimberlé. 1989. "Demarginalizing the Intersection of Race and Sex: A Black Feminist Critique of Antidiscrimination Doctrine, Feminist Theory and Antiracist Politics." *University of Chicago Legal Forum* 89, Article 8.

Davis, Sheri. 2012. "Precious Opportunities: Black Girl Stories and Resistance Pedagogies as Critical Race Feminist Responses to the Childhood Obesity Epidemic." Doctoral dissertation, pp. 125–126. Emory University. https://bit.ly/2Mhx0pM

Ervin, Keona K. 2017. *Gateway to Equality: Black Women and the Struggle for Economic Justice in St. Louis*. Lexington, KY: University Press of Kentucky.

Fine, Janice. 2005. "Community Unions and the Revival of the American Labor Movement." *Politics & Society* 33 (1): 153–199.

Frymer, Paul. 2008. *African Americans, the Labor Movement, and the Decline of the Democratic Party*. Princeton, NJ: Princeton University Press.

Greenhouse, Steven. 2019. *Beaten Down, Worked Up: The Past, Present, and Future of American Labor*. New York, NY: Alfred A. Knopf.

Hall, Jacquelyn Dowd. 2005. "The Long Civil Rights Movement and the Political Uses of the Past." *Journal of American History* 91 (4): 1233–1263.

Harris, Cheryl I. 1993. "Whiteness as Property." *Harvard Law Review* 106 (8): 1707–1791.

Jenkins, William. 1974. "The Civil Rights History Project: Oral History Interview with William 'Blue' Jenkins." Madison, WI: Wisconsin Historical Society.

Jones, William P. 2005. *The Tribe of Black Ulysses: African American Lumber Workers in the Jim Crow South.* Champaign, IL: University of Illinois Press.

Jones, William P. 2013. *The March on Washington: Jobs, Freedom, and the Forgotten History of Civil Rights.* New York, NY: W.W. Norton.

Kelley, Robin D.G. 2003. *Freedom Dreams: The Black Radical Imagination.* New ed. Boston, MA: Beacon Press.

Kelley, Robin D.G. 2015. *Hammer and Hoe: Alabama Communists During the Great Depression.* 25th Anniversary Ed. Chapel Hill, NC: University of North Carolina Press.

Kelley, Robin D.G. 2021 (Jan./Feb.). "The Freedom Struggle Is a Labor Struggle, Then & Now." *Against the Current*, no. 210.

Kilpatrick, Connor, and Judith Stein. 2016. "Why Did White Workers Leave the Democratic Party?: An Interview with Judith Stein." *Jacobin.* https://bit.ly/2ZE8ceC

Korstad, Robert Rodgers. 2003. *Civil Rights Unionism: Tobacco Workers and the Struggle for Democracy in the Mid-Twentieth-Century South.* Chapel Hill, NC: University of North Carolina Press.

Lichtenstein, Nelson. 2002. *State of the Union: A Century of American Labor.* Princeton, NJ: Princeton University Press.

Lichtenstein, Nelson. 2011. "Labour, Liberalism, and the Democratic Party: A Vexed Alliance." *Industrial Relations* 66 (4): 512–534.

MacLean, Nancy. 2006. *Freedom Is Not Enough: The Opening of the American Workplace.* Cambridge, MA: Harvard University Press.

Matsuda, Mari J. 1987. "Looking at the Bottom: Critical Legal Studies and Reparations." *Harvard Civil Rights–Civil Liberties Law Review* 22: 323–399.

McCartin, Joseph A., Marilyn Sneiderman, and Maurice BP-Weeks. 2020. "Combustible Convergence: Bargaining for the Common Good and the #RedforEd Uprisings of 2018." *Labor Studies Journal* 45 (1): 97–113.

Ngai, Mae. 2004. *Impossible Subjects: Illegal Aliens and the Making of Modern America.* Princeton, NJ: Princeton University Press.

Orleck, Annelise. 2015. "At Home and Abroad, The Labor Movement Comes Roaring Back." *Talk Poverty.* https://bit.ly/3s9j8x4

Orleck, Annelise. 2018. *"We Are All Fast-Food Workers Now": The Global Uprising Against Poverty Wages.* Boston, MA: Beacon Press.

Pferdehirt, Julia. 2011. *Blue Jenkins: Working for Workers.* Madison, WI: Wisconsin Historical Society Press.

Phillips-Fein, Kim. 2009. *Invisible Hands: The Making of the Conservative Movement from the New Deal to Reagan.* New York, NY: W.W. Norton

Ransby, Barbara. 2005. *Ella Baker and the Black Freedom Movement: A Radical Democratic Vision.* Chapel Hill, NC: University of North Carolina Press.

Ransby, Barbara. 2018. *Making All Black Lives Matter: Reimagining Freedom in the 21st Century.* Oakland, CA: University of California Press.

Rosenblum, Jonathan. 2017. *Beyond $15: Immigrant Workers, Faith Activists, and the Revival of the Labor Movement.* Boston, MA: Beacon Press.

Robinson, Cedric. 2000. *Black Marxism: The Making of the Black Radical Tradition.* Chapel Hill, NC: University of North Carolina Press.

Sites, William, and Virginia Parks. 2011. "What Do We Really Know About Racial Inequality? Labor Markets, Politics, and the Historical Basis of Black Economic Fortunes." *Politics & Society* 39 (1): 40–73.

Stein, Judith. 2011. *Pivotal Decade: How the United States Traded Factories for Finance in the Seventies.* New Haven, CT: Yale University Press.

Taylor, Keeanga-Yamahtta. 2016. *From #BlackLivesMatter to Black Liberation.* Chicago, IL: Haymarket Books.

Walker-McWilliams, Marcia. 2016. *Reverend Addie Wyatt: Faith and the Fight for Labor, Gender, and Racial Equality.* Champaign, IL: University of Illinois Press.

Williams, Naomi R. 2021. "Sustaining Labor Politics in Hard Times: Race, Labor, and Coalition Building in Racine, Wisconsin." *LABOR: Studies in Working-Class History* 18 (2): 41–63.

CHAPTER 7

Worker Voice in Technological Change: The Potential of Recrafting

JOEL S. YUDKEN
High Road Strategies

DAVID C. JACOBS
American University

> *Any serious debate about the future of work must begin with the voices of workers and our unions.*
> —AFL-CIO Commission on the Future of Work and Unions

> *The horse is technology. It carries us and we cannot control it. So, we have to begin with intention, asking ourselves, what do we want?*
> —Thich Nhat Hanh, *The Mindfulness Bell*

ABSTRACT

Each new wave of technological change threatens some industries and downgrades the position of their workers, while generating new jobs in other areas. We obviously cannot reverse the historical processes that have diminished the skills of workers and subordinated their actions to the dictates of automated systems. Instead, we introduce a recrafting framework that reconceptualizes the organization and practices of work based on a modern application of craft elements and values. In this strategy, workers regain control over their livelihoods and expand their voice in decisions over emerging technologies. Toward this end, we propose measures that increase the craft content of work and promote worker interests in the deployment of technology, such as technology bargaining, shared economic gains, expanded worker involvement in technology development and deployment, promotion of skill-based automation, and robust transition assistance.

INTRODUCTION

That workers should "check their brains at the door" has been the view of employers since the Industrial Revolution. In the 20th century, this view was embedded into industrial systems by the widespread adoption of scientific management and the assembly line. As Robert Kanigel writes, "After [Henry] Ford and [Frederick] Taylor got through with them, most jobs needed less of everything—less brains, less muscle, less independence" (Kanigel 1997: 498). We cannot reverse the processes that over the past two centuries have diminished workers' skills and subordinated their actions to the dictates of machines. Looking toward the future, we propose a strategy for strengthening workers' voice to regain and reshape control over their work and livelihoods by applying the defining elements of craft to modern industrial work environments. We especially are interested in expanding workers' voice in decisions over emerging technologies. Toward that end, we introduce what we call a *recrafting* framework that reconceptualizes the organization and practices of work based on a modern application of craft elements and values.

Recrafting entails undoing three central characteristics of modern industrial work: the minimization of workers' skills, the separation of conception and execution, and managerial monopoly over knowledge and control of the labor process. Getting there requires embracing the insight of an Aspen Institute report that "technology is not destiny" (McKay, Pollack, and Fitzpayne 2019: 3). It is a matter of choice whether new technologies enhance and expand or diminish and replace the capabilities of workers. Technological change is ultimately the product of human agency and authority, not an autonomous force whose direction we cannot control.

In this chapter, we explore how we can expand worker voice in the development and deployment of technologies that support the retention and creation of skilled, high-paying jobs while promoting a broadly shared economic prosperity. In the first section, we trace the evolution of labor's response to technological change to highlight the continual challenge of establishing effective worker voice. We next propose a contemporary model of craftwork to guide labor's strategy on technology. In the third section, we demonstrate that technological development is not deterministic. Finally, we propose a robust program of how to restore worker voice with workplace-level and broader institutional reforms that honor workers' skills and empower them across nodes of decision making.

THE WORKER VOICE CHALLENGE

There were strong worker responses to the impact of technological change at the start of the Industrial Revolution. Early in the 19th century, artisanal worker movements, such as the Luddites and Chartists in England, challenged the new industrial machines and factory modes of production threatening their livelihoods, communities, and way of life. There have since been several periods of rapid technological and industrial change, accompanied by transformations in the nature of work and employment. By the last half of the 19th century, worker movements had shifted from protesting craft-destroying mechanization to forming labor unions to fight for decent wages and working conditions in new manufacturing industries. In the 20th century, increasing use of automated machinery and production processes sparked worries about how technological change could create unemployment. These concerns subsided during World War II but emerged again as electronic computers found wide use in government and commerce in the post-war decades (Herzenberg and Alic 2019: 13).

The American writer Kurt Vonnegut's prescient 1952 classic, *Player Piano*, describes a dystopian world dominated by a supercomputer where most workers have been displaced by machines. The novel expresses fear about an emerging industrial "revolution" brought about by computer automation that would deskill and displace large numbers of workers in the real world (Jacobs and Yudken 2003). The 1960s and 1970s saw expanding use of new technologies—transistors, integrated circuits, and microprocessors, followed by ubiquitous applications—and the seeds of the future Information Age, such as the Internet and advanced telecommunications technologies (satellites and GPS), which fully took root in the 1990s. Military programs drove most of the initial technological development, leading to its diffusion into the economy, often disruptive of economic, social, and cultural life in the decades that followed.

Steve Herzenberg and John Alic note that the "digital disruption of the U.S. labor market" was already under way in the 1960s, with "factories increasing levels of automation making products designed and reconceived for lower labor content and in offices everywhere because of computerization and IT" (Herzenberg and Alic 2019: 2). Concerns about automation led President Lyndon B. Johnson to establish a national commission to examine the extent of technology impacts on the economy and employment. The new and evolving digital technologies diffused throughout modern economies in subsequent decades, especially the 1970s through the first decades of the new millennium. This precipitated new debates about their effects on goods and services production and accompanying impacts on jobs (McKinsey Global Institute 2017).

A landmark event in worker responses to these challenges was the 1972 strike at the General Motors plant in Lordstown, Ohio, where the Chevrolet Vega was introduced to compete with Japanese imports. The plant was the auto industry's most advanced automated factory, with a highly mechanized assembly line, computerized quality control, and 26 robots. It was part of GM's strategy to drive up output while slashing costs. In late winter 1972, Lordstown Assembly's over 8,000 assemblers, represented by the United Auto Workers (UAW), walked off the job after the company sped up the assembly line to excessive levels—a jump in the production rate from 60 to 100 cars an hour (Guilford 2018).

As Gwynn Guilford reports in *Quartz*, the Lordstown "uprising" sparked by the speedup became "a national symbol of blue-collar disaffection" with the degrading and mind-numbing nature of modern industrial work itself. The media dubbed it the "Lordstown syndrome," referring to modern workers' experiences of on-the-job alienation in increasingly automated workplaces. The workers, Guilford writes, had "rebelled against GM's experiment with a bold new management style that put a premium on automation while treating assemblers as though they were little whirring parts of one giant machine" (Guilford 2018). Although the Lordstown strike ended the speedup, there was little progress securing humanized working conditions. Job security, wages and benefits, and work rules remained important. But the strike largely was motivated by the goal of giving workers greater say over factory operations along the lines of successful European management models (Bunch 2018).

American labor unions historically have not embraced the "radical" position of the Lordstown activists and have responded in a more moderate fashion to the introduction of new technology into workplaces. More often, unions have not directly resisted automation but called for managing its implementation through collective bargaining and political actions. Many union leaders, such as UAW president Walter Reuther, understood the deskilling and job displacement impacts of unchecked adoption of new technologies in modern production. However, labor leaders also recognized that automation, properly applied, can increase productivity and enterprise competitiveness, potentially creating new and upskilling some existing jobs, even as others are lost. After all, UAW's "Treaty of Detroit" with GM in 1950 largely ceded union control over production to management, to win good wages, benefits, and pension (De Gier 2010).

In the 1960s, A. Philip Randolph of the International Brotherhood of Sleeping Car Porters voiced a similar position in response to concerns that automation in the railroad industry would displace Black workers. He cautioned that it would be foolish to "resist technology's progress," maintaining that "you cannot destroy the machine. You cannot stifle the invention of various geniuses in the world." He argued that "the community and government have a responsibility" to see that technology produces public goods, and he proposed principles "that should govern technology's design and use." Technology isn't "just the domain of technical experts or privileged classes," he declared; it is the "collective creation of the people," who should share in its fruits (McIlwain 2020).

The qualified success of the International Longshore and Warehouse Union's (ILWU) response to containerization through collective bargaining is likewise instructive. Containerization was considered a "revolutionary new technology," an entirely new way of working ships in the 1950s that permanently transformed longshoremen's work (Cole 2013: 203). Led by Harry Bridges, the ILWU, in representing West Coast longshoremen, fought for and won a major agreement with the shipping companies. It was an early union effort to influence the introduction of a transformative technology with major job impacts into an industry sector—"to get a share of the machine." Overcoming internal opposition, the union argued that new technology cannot always be resisted. It accepted heavy job losses to preserve union power in a strategic industry in the global economy. The union in San Francisco and other West Coast ports survived the introduction of a major new technology, and it remains strong, engaged, and influential (Cole 2013: 203).

Globalization, Technology, and the Future of Work

These historical examples aside, choices about investing in and diffusing advanced technologies that affect the nation's workforce should be evaluated in the light of public policy goals such as industrial competitiveness. Over the past half century, the labor community has tried to address not only the impacts of technological change on workers' jobs and livelihoods but also the challenges of globalization. Beginning in the 1980s, rising international competition and domestic imports, driven by problematic trade, tax, and currency policies— amplified by advances in technology—led to massive economic dislocations in America's industrial regions. These negative impacts reached a peak over the first decade of the 21st century, with losses of over 50,000 manufacturing plants and nearly 6 million manufacturing jobs.

Recognizing this, the AFL-CIO Industrial Union Department (IUD) in 1991 and 1992 held conferences on labor and technology development, triggered by fears of rapid computerization and automation leading to deskilling and job loss. As reported in their proceedings, *Software and Hardhats, Technology and Workers in the 21st Century*, the conferences focused as much on the United States losing its technological edge in key industries and the loss of manufacturing jobs as it did on technology as a workplace issue (Work and Technology Institute 1992).

By the late 1990s, the rise of the Internet and its ubiquitous applications brought renewed concerns about job impacts. Labor interest in this issue grew in the early 2000s, as several unions worried about how the Internet and online commerce were going to affect their members' jobs. In our 2003 book, *The Internet, Organizational Change and Labor*, we argued that we may be in the "throes of a new industrial revolution" driven by "continuous, complementary advances, and convergence, in microelectronics, computing, telecommunications, and related technologies," which could substitute "computing for mental labor on a significant scale" (Jacobs and Yudken 2003: 11). In retrospect, we were on the cusp of a broader and more rapid expansion of the Internet and its impacts on our economy and society than we could have anticipated.

These themes have a renewed resonance, as modern societies feel the effects of yet another wave of more powerful, intelligent, and versatile digital automation and information technologies. Collectively referred to as Industry 4.0, these technologies include robotics, artificial intelligence (AI), machine learning, 3D manufacturing, and the Internet of Things (IoT), among others. As before, there has been vociferous debate about the consequences of these technologies for

America's workforce, as well as for US global competitiveness. Again, the fear is that new, advanced digital automation technologies will create massive unemployment and fissured workplaces.

Predictions about the extent of these impacts vary greatly. A McKinsey Global Institute study estimates that nearly a third of workers may need to transition to entirely different occupations by 2030 as a result of automation (McKinsey Global Institute 2017; McKay, Pollack, and Fitzpayne 2019: 6). Herzenberg and Alic predict that AI will penetrate our workplaces to a greater extent than previous IT systems, in part because of machine learning, processes in which computers incrementally improve their performance in specific narrow domains by absorbing massive amounts of data" (Herzenberg and Alic 2019: 2). At the same time, they discount fears that robots will soon replace humans, noting that AI-enabled automation will likely remain behind human capabilities for the foreseeable future in work requiring judgment, tacit skills and common sense—tasks that infuse many parts of most jobs." In short, while disruptions in the US labor market are likely, these impacts continue earlier trends and may represent less of a disjuncture than what has occurred over previous decades (Herzenberg and Alic 2019: 2).

Similarly, data show that automation historically has created more jobs than it has displaced, largely because of higher labor productivity (McKay, Pollack, and Fitzpayne 2019: 5). Many workers will still be displaced, many jobs and tasks altered, and certain occupations may become obsolete (McKay, Pollack, and Fitzpayne 2019: 6) even as new jobs are created. The most vulnerable jobs involve cognitive and manual tasks that are repetitive and involve predictable actions like operating machinery, preparing fast food, and collecting and processing data, while nonroutine cognitive and manual jobs may grow. While wages and living standards for some workers may grow, those of other workers might fall, or at best remain stagnant. Moreover, if trends from the mid-1970s continue, many if not most workers may not share equitably in the rewards of productivity gains generated by new technologies (Bivens and Mishel 2015).

These are just projections into an unknown future, with many possible trajectories. It is clear, though, that what actually happens will greatly depend on those whose voices are most empowered to guide the investment in and implementation of new technologies, for what ends, and under what conditions. Recent studies have attempted to get a handle on not just the impacts on work but also on the strategies and policies for responding to them.

For example, MIT professor Thomas Kochan, writing for the Task Force on the Future of Work, calls for workers to have a voice in decisions concerning the impact of emerging technologies, "to ensure their interests are addressed and to contribute their knowledge about how these advancing technologies can be integrated with organizational practices and work systems to achieve maximum production, augment how they work, and build high-quality jobs" (Kochan 2020: 5). Kochan also is correct that achieving those gains will require "significant innovations in the institutions and public policies governing work," reflecting the considerable obstacles workers face to obtain and exercise their voice in modern industrial workplaces (Kochan 2020: 5). This is a very apt formulation of the issue that our chapter explores.

THE RECRAFTING FRAMEWORK

Like Kochan, we focus on the roles, capabilities, and power of working people and their representatives to address the workplace challenges from emergent technological change. However, we attempt to go beyond the industrial relations precedent, rooted in modern industrial organization and managerial prerogatives. We propose a recrafting framework to reconceive workplace organization and practices to expand workers' control over their work (and associated technologies). In doing so, we align ourselves with the fundamental assumptions of the labor studies discipline, as have some others in this volume, with its normative focus on the emancipation of workers.

This framework takes as its baseline a modernized conception of craft production, craftwork, and craftsmanship. The displacement of crafts as the once dominant mode of human material production and work was not a minor feature of the Industrial Revolution. It was the central theme. Early in the Industrial Revolution, the new factory system allowed employers greater control over workers' pace than was possible in the old system of contracting out, forming the basis for the detailed division of labor in production. In addition, craft tools were replaced by more sophisticated technologies that subordinated workers to the dictates of the machine. The wide application of scientific management principles and "Fordism" during the first half the 20th century eroded craft production further.

Scientific management, pioneered by Frederick Taylor, imposed a system of labor discipline and workplace organization based on time and motion studies of human efficiency and incentive systems. Henry Ford revolutionized manufacturing with the introduction of mass production, involving the application of moving assembly lines and standardization, to make affordable automobiles for mass markets. As noted earlier, the principles guiding these changes were the deskilling of workers, separation of conception and execution, and management control over the labor process. The end goal was to render the worker's knowledge and practices independent of craft tradition, subordinating the skills and abilities of workers to management control (Yudken 1987: 42). And that situation prevails in most workplaces today.

By recrafting, our intention is not to resurrect traditional crafts in the modern world (though there remain thriving pockets of historically based crafts today). Nevertheless, we believe craft embodies widely valued dimensions, such as productive excellence, innovation, and quality, which can be applied to modern production and products. In work with high craft content, workers do not "check their brains at the door" but are well trained and skilled and have a high degree of autonomy to exercise judgment and control in their jobs. In short, *recrafting can be defined as applying the essential elements and values of the craft labor process as a benchmark for redesigning the organization of work and production in the future.*

Elements of Craft

The word *craft* comes from the Old English *craeft*, connoting power, physical strength, and skill. Although the historical notion of craft referred mainly to the production of material goods, it also applied to other vital human activities in pre-industrial societies, such as farming, hunting, warfighting, and healing. In the modern era, craft similarly refers to any productive activity involving the creative application of skills based on the mastery of specialized knowledge of media, means, and methods (Yudken 1987: 156). The principal elements of the craft labor process, which in its idealized form can be applied to all productive activities (producing goods and services), include the following (Yudken 1987: 13):

- The integration of conception and execution
- Control over the production process, including media, means, and methods
- Emphasis on skills, knowledge, and expertise
- Control over the pace of work
- Autonomy and independence
- Customization of the processes and products of production
- A high value on craftsmanship and quality
- A more direct relationship between producers and customers
- A strong self-identification with the productive activity itself

Craftwork encompasses the mastery of skills, exercise of judgment, and active participation in the creative processes of design. It embodies the attributes of excellence, quality, distinctiveness, usability, and affordability. Craftwork is not just about producing high-quality products and services, but it also is fundamentally an economic activity, providing workers their livelihoods. A related characteristic is the close interrelationship of workers engaged in productive activities to the outcome of that process, reflecting a more "intimate" relationship between the producer and final consumer of the product or service in the marketplace. Craft workers care whether their customers are satisfied that they were delivered high-quality, useful, and affordable products and services (Yudken 1987: 162–163).

The attributes of craft and craftsmanship are almost universally appreciated. Long craft traditions have contributed to the modern industrial successes of US trade competitors, such as Japan, Germany, and Italy. Craft norms are rooted in these nations' economic histories, informing their modern cultures of excellence, quality, service, and the valuing of workers, which also contribute to their global competitiveness. Indeed, it can be argued that they have adopted collective forms of craft applied to their industrial systems (Pringle, no date).

America's rich craft tradition dating back to its colonial days fueled the inventiveness and industrial growth of the early republic that helped make it the manufacturing powerhouse it was to become. The Arts and Crafts movement in America in the early 1900s emerged from criticism of the mechanized, impersonal way of life being created by the Industrial Revolution (Clericuzio 2017; Wiggins 2019). An artisanal handicrafts movement, it was very influential in the decorative arts, particularly in the design of manufactured home décor (such as furniture) and other products, as well as in architecture. Craft qualities remain highly revered in modern industrial design.

Craftwork is not normally associated with modern industrial and "postindustrial" workplaces and occupations. Nevertheless, there are many occupations today that retain a degree of craft content, such as building and construction trades (carpenters, electricians, ironworkers, pipefitters) that overlap with industrial trades (machinists, mechanics, welders), many of which had roots in pre-industrial crafts. All these occupations involve a fairly high level of skill, requiring workers to obtain specialty training (community and technical colleges, apprenticeships) and certifications to do their jobs. Numerous other skilled professions and occupations (engineers, scientists, doctors, lawyers, academics, artists, musicians) also have strong craft elements. These jobs require considerable skills, education, and training, and their practitioners often go through their own form of apprenticeship (bachelor's degree), journeyman (master's degree), and master craftsman (Ph.D., M.D., or other professional degree) certification, in order to practice their "craft."

We do not seek to idealize craftwork. The historical crafts world in most cultures and times was far from ideal; it was very hierarchical, with huge inequities. Nevertheless, the essential elements and values identified above were inherent in the historical craft production and market worlds. Our conceptualization of craft argues that these remain relevant and may even take on new importance in advanced industrial societies.

Several scholars have attempted to unhinge the craft notion from its historical mooring, conceiving it as a progressive concept for organizing future work and production in advanced high-technology societies. For example, C. Wright Mills wrote about the ideal of craft, which he contrasts with the alienation of modern work—white-collar work in particular (Mills 1951; Yudken 1987: 115). Harry Braverman promoted a vision "for an age that has not yet come into being" in which craft satisfaction will be united with modern science and engineering to produce an "age in which everyone will be able to benefit, in some degree from this combination" (Braverman 1974; Yudken 1987: 11). Michael Piore and Charles Sabel present craft as a progressive paradigm for industrial-economic change rather than an ideal of a bygone era (Piore 1984; Piore and Sabel 1984; Yudken 1987: 11). However, these visions do not provide us with a roadmap to an advanced technological world where craft values characterize most work and production.

The connection between worker voice, worker power, and craft is central to understanding and responding to the impacts of new technologies and processes introduced into workplaces. This, in turn, is key to forging a strategy for recrafting worker voice in the modern era—in which workers' agency influences the trajectory of technological development in production activities and their consequences for workers and their livelihoods. Our task is to determine the best strategies, policies, and actions for applying the essential elements and values of craft to restructure work organizations and expand worker voice in modern industrial settings.

Similarly, recrafting is about elevating workers' power to promote their interests in the processes of technological and organizational change. This is not solely about advancing the interests of workers (and sharing the benefits of advanced technology) but about building "a new social contract at work capable of meeting the needs of all stakeholders—workers, employers and their investors, and the overall economy and society" (Kochan 2020: 2).

TECHNOLOGY IS NOT DESTINY

A common view, central to mainstream economics, is that technological advance is inexorable, the product of forces external to business operations and markets. It assumes workers, consumers, and businesses are capable only of adapting to— but not shaping—new technology, either for intermediate use in production or for end-use products. In contrast, we view technological change as the product of human preferences, choices, and actions, now overdetermined by hierarchical structures rooted in economic and political power.

Technology is the application of individual and group knowledge to make tools by which humans have achieved social reproduction and material production and distribution since the beginning of human culture. Technological innovation is one of the most creative and important human endeavors, vital to our species' physical, material, and cultural well-being. This has not been a simple linear trajectory. Technology has emerged in patterns mediated by class, power, race, and gender. Looking closely at how technology has been developed and applied in economic activities, we clearly see the role of human agency and authority.

Throughout most human history, technology inventions—tools for hunting, food production, clothing, heating and cooking, housing, warfare, and the like— were mainly the product of trial and error and accidental discoveries. The inventors were undoubtedly involved in, and intimately familiar with, the processes that applied those innovations, driven by the needs of their families, tribes, communities, and societies. Many, if not most, innovations in products, processes, techniques, and design in the pre-industrial age originated with artisans tinkering in their workshops. Many of the inventors of technologies that launched the Industrial Revolution were craft workers. James Hargraves, inventor of the spinning jenny, central to the industrialization of weaving, was a weaver and carpenter. John Kay, inventor of the spinning frame, a key textile manufacturing innovation, was a clockmaker. Machine tools, steam engines, and steel making, among the most important technologies of the first and second Industrial Revolutions, stemmed from discoveries early in the pre-industrial era. Several great American inventors who paved the way for 20th-century industrial development came from humble backgrounds and started in the industrial trades. Henry Ford grew up on a farm and apprenticed as a machinist. Orville and Wilbur Wright were self-educated mechanics and engineers who worked as printers, bicycle repairers, and manufacturers before inventing the first successful motor-operated airplane.

Nevertheless, scientific knowledge based on the research of early scientific pioneers, starting in the Enlightenment, and continuing into the 19th and 20th centuries, informed the inventive processes that led to the Industrial Revolution. By the late 1800s, the wave of technological innovations that fueled industrialization, replacing crafts production in industry after industry, was primarily the products of engineers, scientists, entrepreneurs, and inventors from the more educated and wealthier classes. However, widescale application of scientific knowledge underlying the development of revolutionary new technologies did not arise until the mid-20th century, and systematic application to engineering design processes underlying modern innovations in the United States mainly emerged out of World War II.

Building on the precedent of wartime mobilization, new federal programs supported large-scale investments in research and development (R&D) and education to train a new generation of scientists and engineers. Billions of taxpayer dollars were poured into industrial and university laboratories across the country, often working with government laboratories to support critical national missions (defense, space, health, energy) and economic growth. America's science and technology infrastructure, based on this broad and powerful public–private partnership, became the envy of the world.

Many innovations and products invented under federal R&D programs "spun off" into civilian markets, helping to shape modern economies for the past 80 years. This was facilitated not just by R&D but by government purchases of new, critical technologies (such as integrated circuits used in military systems in the 1960s) that helped US manufacturers reduce production learning curves until they became commercially competitive. The Internet, which has become a transformative force in our society, emerged out of R&D support by the Defense Advanced Research Projects Agency (DARPA). Other commercially significant spin-offs include the jet engine, GPS, lasers, computers, AI, and robots. Many companies also invested in R&D, often encouraged or supported by government programs. These efforts generated technologies, products, and processes that not only have met the needs of consumers and supported national goals but shaped and reshaped industrial processes and workplaces over the years.

As this brief walk through science and technology history illustrates, the products and tools that we use every day are not the outcome of mysterious forces beyond our understanding and control. All technological innovations have been created in response to human goals, needs, aspirations, and desires. They are the product of human ingenuity and agency, usually enabled by collective resources to meet market demands and public needs. This is particularly true of the material bases of our work and productive activities. However, we also need to understand who has been instrumental in driving the evolution of technologies—and that there have been both winners and losers. Unfortunately, all too often in economic history, the manifestations of technology development have followed the golden rule—that is, those who have the gold make the rules (see Lester and Piore 2006)!

In advanced industrial economies, the wealth and power to make those rules have increasingly fallen into the hands of financial and corporate elites. The enormous technological advances over the past four decades have contributed to and enhanced the crisis of economic inequality in our nation, if not the world. While bringing great wealth and power, the fruits of these advances have not been equitably shared and have been skewed increasingly along class, racial, and gendered divisions of labor—and their applications have magnified this disparity.

As we enter the third decade of the 21st century, our civilization has reached an inflection point regarding the use of technologies applied to our modes of manufacturing, transportation, energy generation and use, healthcare, housing, food production, and national security. Aside from the impacts on jobs and livelihoods, these technologies raise concerns on a larger scale about the dangers of climate change and threats to our survival from ever more lethal weapons (all problems further compounded by the COVID-19 pandemic). Interwoven with these challenges is that of expanding worker voice to effectively address the consequences for working people and their communities.

One must acknowledge, however, inherent obstacles to changing the direction of new technologies once they are introduced and receive major investments. Technological solutions can get "locked in" when incorporated into production processes or products sold into markets, constraining the ability to change how technologies evolve. Innovations develop along specific trajectories, with new advances building on, reinforcing, and extending existing technology pathways (e.g., fossil fuel energy systems). This increases barriers to alternative technologies, even if they may be economically, environmentally, and socially better for our society (e.g., renewable energy). The challenge is altering the economic and political power relations that guide investments in new technologies, which help to overcome this lock-in.

In any case, we don't need to accept that the technological advances that fuel and drive us in a direction are inevitable. As the Vietnamese Zen master Thich Nhat Hanh implies in his metaphor in the epigraph to this chapter, while technology is a collective activity that "carries us," we can't completely control it. However, we can give it direction. But we first need to ask, "What do we want?" (Nhat Hanh 2014).

RESTORING WORKER VOICE

Lordstown laid down a marker, foreshadowing that future generations of workers might not be content to accept agreements limited to wages, benefits, work rules, working conditions, and job security. Although these bargaining objectives continue to be critical, Lordstown workers were primarily motivated by strong dissatisfaction with the quality of their jobs.

Whether working on assembly lines or in high-tech, professional, or service occupations, workers want decent incomes and economic security and to share in the gains from technological advances. Protection of worker respect and dignity has long been a provision in bargaining agreements. Most workers also want work that is satisfying, meaningful, interesting, and useful. And they desire work that is safe, healthy, and free from surveillance threats to their privacy and freedom posed by the new generation of smart technologies. Finally, workers deskilled or displaced because of technological and organizational change want—indeed, need—help transitioning to good new jobs and income security.

Having a voice in the quality and the content of jobs as the craft model demands is relevant to all of these questions. Control over conception and execution traditionally has been the prerogative of management and business owners. Recrafting contemporary work and occupations would allow workers a greater influence throughout the processes of design, development, and production. Worker input into how workplaces are organized would include selecting, introducing, and integrating new technologies, tools, and equipment into work systems.

In short, in a recrafted work environment, workers are invited to share their knowledge, skills, and experience in introducing changes in their workplaces that affect not only the quality of their work but also their productivity. This also translates into workers placing a high value on—indeed, taking pride in—craftsmanship and the quality of the products or services they are involved in producing. Many of these values can be found in occupations such as the professions;

building, construction and industrial trades; high-tech (e.g., software designers); and others with work processes that have high craft content—that is, there is a strong self-identification with the product (and service) they produce. This often coincides with appreciation of the needs and concerns of the customers they serve, which in turn can improve employers' bottom lines. This approach, synonymous with high-performance work organizations (discussed below), requires a more engaged workforce in implementing new technologies and processes into productive activities, which can yield successful outcomes and productivity gains.

Another craft element that workers value—but remains constrained in many work environments—is control over their use of time, physical movement (including the pace and rhythm of work), and mental activities. The Lordstown "rebellion" was triggered by GM's attempt to increase control over employees' pace and movements by speeding up its assembly lines. Finally, a hallmark of occupations and workplaces with strong craft values is that workers have resources and time to obtain the knowledge, expertise, and skills (mental, manual, and interpersonal) needed for doing their jobs. Critics point to employers' inadequate investment in employee training to support pipelines for new workers or help incumbent workers upgrade their skills, despite complaints about a "skills gap" for certain occupations. This is a failure of public policy as much as it is of employer behavior (Alden and Taylor-Kale 2018).

Although aspirational for American workers, the achievement of craft-oriented goals has been uneven across the workforce. Many professional, skilled-trades, and high-end technical occupations contain a high degree of craft content. However, the amount of this content reflects how much control a worker has over his or her job and work environment, constrained by the inherent flexibility in the organizational structure and rules that govern an employer's operations (Yudken 1987: 15, 164). Lower-skilled jobs, such as retail clerks, restaurant servers, and cleaners, have a much lower level of craft content, though there may be greater knowledge and skills required to do such jobs (physical dexterity, face-to-face communication, visual recognition, and situational adaptability) than is often attributed to such work (Giamo 2020). Raising the level of craft content of these jobs and increasing equity across the workforce will depend on representation, advocacy, and policy.

New Opportunities

Although the new wave of smart technologies entering workplaces represents a genuine challenge to the security and quality of many jobs today, it also may offer new opportunities. We could see the generation of new jobs and occupations tied to the new technologies, though not all are necessarily skilled or contain much craft content. The challenge is to realistically apply a recrafting strategy to increase worker voice and craft content in todays—and tomorrows—workforce. That strategy, encompassing policies, practices, and actions for transforming work and workplaces, is meant to be applied across a wide spectrum of productive activities and workplaces in modern economies.

As noted earlier, the approach is to apply the craft labor process as a benchmark for redesigning the organization of work and production in the future. Every stage of this process requires measures that enable and extend worker voice to influence how new technologies are introduced into workplaces, and to protect and extend worker interests. In short, the goal is to shift the impacts of technological and organizational change away from displacing and deskilling jobs, toward skills upgrading, job enrichment, and job creation.

The AFL-CIO has picked up where the IUD left off 30 years ago but is using a wider lens. In 2017, it established the AFL-CIO Commission on the Future of Work and Unions, bringing together labor leaders and economic, technical, and workforce experts from a number of industry sectors. Its purpose is to study and recommend ways to bring "workers' voices into the future of work debate" and rebuild worker bargaining power in an economy that is "leaving too many people behind." A central concern is to understand and address the impacts of technological change on work. Its broader purpose is to strengthen and grow "worker bargaining power," which is the "surest path to an economy that works for all of us, not just wealthy elites" (AFL-CIO 2019: 1–2).

The report further stresses the strategic importance of strengthening individual and collective bargaining power to ensure technology is used to help working people achieve broadly shared prosperity. It also supports working people demanding a seat at the table in technology design, development, and deployment. Workers not only should have a say in shaping technological change in their workplaces but also "in the halls of power, to ensure new digital tools and management by algorithms are not used to weaken worker bargaining power, reinforce systemic inequality and discrimination, diminish job quality; or infringe on human dignity and privacy" (AFL-CIO 2019).

A Recrafting Agenda

Many of the AFL-CIO's measures are key elements of a recrafting agenda for expanding worker voice to shape the trajectories of technological advance and promote worker interests. The AFL-CIOs initiative itself is a hopeful step in engaging the labor community and leadership in a strategy to greatly expand the involvement and representation of working people in shaping a positive future of work with broadly shared economic gains and meaningful, satisfying jobs. Drawing on these ideas, Kochan's complementary analysis and recommendations (Kochan 2020), and other work, we outline below initiatives, policies, and actions that strengthen worker voice in the deployment of technology in productive activities, which expand the craft content of their work and support the needs of workers.

Broadening Collective Bargaining

Strengthening worker bargaining power must be a top labor and public policy priority. Individually and through expanded collective representation, workers need to take legal and political actions that address the economic and technological challenges to theirworkplaces and livelihoods. Without increasing union membership and expanding collective bargaining, it will be very hard to carry out the recrafting agenda.

Collective bargaining must extend beyond the traditional terms and conditions of employment. Technology bargaining agreements give workers a say on decisions, usually considered management prerogatives, regarding the design and choice of products or services, the introduction of new technologies, and control over work organization. A study by Lisa Kresge at the UC Berkeley Labor Center shows that unions have leveraged collective bargaining agreements to address technological change for many decades, even as early as the 1940s (Kresge 2020). The International Association of Machinists and Aerospace Workers'(IAM) proposed a Technology Bill of Rights in the early 1980s that affirmed the absolute right of workers, through their trade unions and bargaining units ... to participate in all phases of management deliberations and decisions that lead or could lead to the introduction of new technology or the changing workplace system design, work processes and procedures for doing work, including the shutdown or transfer of work, capital, plant and equipment" (IAM 1982: 196–197).

Sharing the Gains

The economic gains from introducing new technologies into workplaces should be broadly shared (AFL-CIO 2019; Kochan 2020). A common view is that, while the introduction of new technologies will cause job deskilling and losses, the economic gains from the associated productivity growth will "trickle" down to workers. After World War II until the mid-1970s, worker wages and labor productivity trends were highly correlated, both growing at respectable rates. Since then, worker incomes have largely stagnated, as productivity rates continued to grow (Bivens and Mishel 2015). Although this trend tracks with increasing income inequality in the United States, it raises concerns about how new smart technologies could further these inequities, especially among demographic groups left behind in terms of household incomes and wealth. The most important strategy in securing greater shared gains is to strengthen the individual and collective bargaining power of working people (AFL-CIO 2019; Kochan 2020: 6). Also, public policies that support investments in new technologies should be designed to ensure that benefits are distributed fairly and broadly and that working people capture their fair share, even as worker voice helps determine the course of technological change itself (AFL-CIO 2019: 17).

A Seat at the Table

Workers or their representatives need "a seat at the table" to shape the direction of technology R&D, investment, and implementation programs sponsored by government, business, academia, and other institutions. Labor representatives or designated experts have served as advisors to government programs, as members on technical boards and committees, and in policy making and legislative positions in government. In the late 1990s, the AFL-CIO IUD designated labor-friendly experts to serve as full-time advisors at the National Institute of Standards and Technology (NIST) and the NIST Manufacturing Extension Partnership (MEP), a federal program that provides assistance to small manufacturers. There also were designated labor specialists" at MEP Centers (e.g., Michigan, Pennsylvania). Labor-friendly representatives have served in positions inside executive branch departments, such as the Departments of Energy, Labor, and Commerce, among others, and on major science and technology advisory bodies, such as National Academies of Sciences boards and panels. In his first term, President Obama designated Ron Bloom, a policy expert from the United Steelworkers to serve as his first manufacturing czar." Bloom helped spearhead the creation of the Manufacturing USA program, which includes 14 advanced technology R&D centers located around the country, operated by partnerships among government, industry, and research institutions (Scheiber 2009).

The AFL-CIO commission calls for engagement with technology leaders early in the R&D process, providing R&D funding to support technologies that benefit working people and maximize broad societal benefit (AFL-CIO 2019: 19). Of particular interest is its recommendation for a technology institute "to develop expertise and gain access to critical information concerning new technologies that may transform work and displace workers, but also help unions more effectively represent working people." To implement this goal, the AFL-CIO and affiliated unions will forge partnerships with universities and research institutions (AFL-CIO 2019: 33).

Kochan also calls for a wider array of options for giving workers a voice, going beyond existing labor law, to play more robust roles in advising and sharing of decision making with their employers (Kochan 2020). Several bills have been introduced in Congress to establish codetermination in the United States (McGaughey 2019). Codetermination requires employee representatives to sit on corporate boards of directors and have a voice equal to those of shareholder representatives (Tyler 2019). Along with works councils closer to the shop floor, this action would facilitate corporate investments in new technologies, equipment, and processes to support skill upgrades for existing workers and adjustment assistance to workers displaced by new technologies (Tyler 2019).

Expanding Worker Involvement

Worker involvement initiatives are especially important for recrafting modern industrial practices. They give workers an opportunity to guide the implementation of new technology in the immediate workplace. They can range from employee suggestion systems to employee–management working groups, such as quality circles, problem-solving groups, and task forces (Manufacturing Extension Partnership 1998).

Rooted in the "American human resource" model of the 1950s, these reforms evolved to foster job enrichment, better communication, and employee engagement to enhance job satisfaction and improve job performance (Appelbaum and Batt 1994: 18–19). Largely applied piecemeal in the United States, these practices drew on foreign models of workplace reorganization, such as Swedish sociotechnical systems, Japanese lean production, and German diversified quality production (DPQ), which to varying degrees include employee participation in production decision making (Appelbaum and Batt 1994: 29–42). DPQ, for example, was developed to customize high-volume quality-competitive products by combining the craft skills of a highly trained workforce with digitally enabled technologies (Appelbaum and Batt 1994: 39–42). The model's ability to adjust to new technology and changing market conditions is enhanced by works councils and other labor–management institutions (Sorge and Streeck 2018: 16).

In the United States, unions, especially the IAM, have led efforts to establish high-performance work organizations (HPWOs). HPWOs enlist the intelligence, commitment, knowledge, and creativity of front-line workers throughout production and design processes, often through self-directed work teams (Jarboe and Yudken 1996; Kaminski, Bertelli, Moye, and Yudken 1996). Although employee involvement has mainly been initiated by management or through labor–management agreements, collective bargaining can strengthen worker involvement in addressing technological change, giving unions input into technology decisions that enable them to better manage concerns such as job loss, skill enhancement, training, and health and safety (Richardson 1992: 171).

Skill-Based Automation

Bargaining over technology can be especially effective in helping unions push for innovative agreements to enable worker say in the design, procurement, and adoption of new technologies, to limit job deskilling and encourage the adoption of skill-based automation. For example, a 2019 agreement between the UAW and GM affirmed that the introduction of new technology will not move work out of the bargaining unit and ensured that UAW members would retain the higher-skilled work associated with new technology. It also established a joint union–management National Committee on Advanced Technology to discuss the impact of future technologies on UAW members (United Auto Workers 2019).

Skill-based automation and worker-centered design applies worker knowledge, skill, and creativity to establish highly productive, high value–added systems. The goal is to develop production systems and their technologies that incorporate workforce needs, respect workers' intellectual capabilities, and pursue flexibility and innovation (Richardson 1992). Many European countries have had skill-based technology development programs (Richardson 1992). In the United States, a study of the food processing industry explored structures for skill-based design within unions (i.e., technology committees), which supports participatory design processes and presses companies to form local joint worker–management design processes (Cherkasky and Scannell 1999). Another study identified examples where workers and firms have explored collaborative ways to redesign work and influence technology design (Emspak 1995: 566). Such an effort in the custom woodworking industry assessed the industry's technological needs, encouraged the design and use of new technologies, and integrated them into apprenticeship programs. The report concluded that worker organizations understand that "technology can be designed and implemented in ways that might preserve or embrace skill while at the same time meeting more traditional business needs" (Emspak 1995: 568).

Transition Assistance

America needs a more robust, comprehensive system to help workers dislocated by technological change and other economic shocks (e.g., defense downsizing, trade agreements, climate change mitigation). Proposed legislation based on the Trade Adjustment Assistance (TAA) program would help workers dislocated by new technology and other causes (Stettner 2019a, 2019b). TAA has helped workers, businesses, and communities adjust to losses associated with trade policies. The proposed bill would extend TAA-type benefits to help technology-displaced workers obtain new skills, qualify for new jobs, or comfortably retire through measures such as early warning, education and training, income supports, job search assistance, retirement bridges, and more. Unions already engage in training partnerships with employers (apprenticeships, sectoral partnerships, skill standards certification) to help incumbent workers qualify for higher-skilled, better-paying positions (Yudken, Croft, and Stettner 2017). Also needed are programs to give youth and workers from underserved populations (people of color, women) opportunities to be educated and trained for new high-tech jobs. However, retraining is not sufficient if there are no new jobs available. Federal and state economic adjustment programs to aid businesses and communities affected by economic dislocation also need to be enhanced (Alden and Taylor-Kale 2018). The necessary reforms include business technical assistance services, economic development planning, innovation investment programs, and labor-friendly capital stewardship initiatives (Yudken, Croft, and Stettner 2017).

RECRAFTING AMERICA'S FUTURE OF WORK

The recrafting agenda has new salience, as we face the challenge of yet another tidal wave of new digital technologies. Robots will not take over all work. However, technological advances once again threaten to undermine many middle-class jobs, contribute to inequality, and reduce social mobility. To address these dangers, workers must build worker voice and increase their power. Many strategies to shape the future of work are available as we outlined, but none of them will be possible without a rebound in the fortunes of the labor movement and the proliferation of alternative forms of worker representation.

REFERENCES

AFL-CIO Commission on the Future of Work and Unions. 2019 (Sep.). "Report to the AFL-CIO General Board." Washington, DC: AFL-CIO. https://bit.ly/2UtEd7l

Alden, Edward, and Laura Taylor-Kale. 2018. "The Work Ahead: Machines, Skills, and U.S. Leadership in the Twenty-First Century." Independent Task Force Report No. 76. New York, NY: Council on Foreign Relations. https://on.cfr.org/2YBa8nC

Appelbaum, Eileen, and Rosemary Batt. 1994. *The New American Workplace: Transforming Work Systems in the United States.* Ithaca, NY: ILR Press.

Bivens, Josh, and Lawrence Mishel. 2015 (Sep. 2). "Understanding the Historic Divergence Between Productivity and a Typical Worker's Pay: Why It Matters and Why It's Real." Briefing Paper #406. Washington, DC: Economic Policy Institute. http://bit.ly/2JezAGI

Braverman, Harry. 1974. *Labor and Monopoly Capital.* New York, NY: Monthly Review Press.

Bunch, Will. 2018 (Nov. 29). "In 1970s, Workers at This GM Plant Helped to Reinvent the American Dream. Instead, They Watched It Fade Away." *The Philadelphia Inquirer.* https://bit.ly/3arbMhg

Cherkasky, Todd, and Ray Scannell. 1999. "Making Technology Work for Workers." *WorkingUSA* 2 (6): 28–46.

Clericuzio, Peter. 2017 (Feb. 25). "The Arts & Crafts Movement: Overview and Analysis." *The Art Story.* https://bit.ly/3ax82ed

Cole, Peter. 2013. "The Tip of the Spear: How Longshore Workers in the San Francisco Bay Area Survived the Containerization Revolution." *Employee Responsibilities and Rights Journal* 25: 201–216. https://bit.ly/2YFx1q8

De Gier, Erik. 2010. "Paradise Lost Revisited: GM and the UAW in Historical Perspective." Nijmegen, Netherlands: Nijmegen School of Management, Institute for Management Research, Radboud University. https://bit.ly/3pI01ct

Emspak, Frank. 1995. "Integrating the Work Force Into the Design of Production Systems." *IFAC Proceedings Volumes* 28 (15): 565–569. https://bit.ly/39HAuuE

Giamo, Cara. 2020 (Feb. 26). "Power to the People: MIT's Work of the Future Report Wants to Prepare Us for the Automation Revolution." *MIT Technology Review.* https://bit.ly/3pHAiRG

Guilford, Gwynn. 2018 (Dec. 30). "GM's Decline Truly Began With Its Quest to Turn People Into Machines." *Quartz.* https://bit.ly/3oK0mKm

Herzenberg, Steve, and John Alic. 2019 (Feb.). "Towards an AI Economy That Works for All." A Report of the Keystone Research Center Future of Work Project, Harrisburg, PA. https://bit.ly/3oKmILX

International Association of Machinists and Aerospace Workers (IAM). 1982. *Let's Build America.* Upper Marlborough, MD: IAM.

Jacobs, David C., and Joel Samuel Yudken. 2003. *The Internet, Organizational Change, and Labor: The Challenge of Virtualization.* New York, NY: Routledge.

Jarboe, Kenan Patrick, and Joel Yudken. 1996. *Smart Workers, Smart Machines: A Technology Policy for the 21st Century.* Washington, DC: Work and Technology Institute.

Kaminski, Michelle, Dominick Bertelli, Melissa Moye, and Joel Yudken. 1996. *Making Change Happen: Six Cases of Unions and Companies Transforming Their Workplaces.* Washington, DC: Work and Technology Institute.

Kanigel, Robert. 1997. *The One Best Way: Frederick Winslow Taylor and the Enigma of Efficiency.* New York, NY: Viking.

Kochan, Thomas A. 2020 (May 14). "Worker Voice, Representation, and Implications for Public Policies." Briefing Paper. MIT Task Force on the Work of the Future, Cambridge, MA. https://bit.ly/3toECY0

Kresge, Lisa. 2020 (Dec. 3). "Union Collective Bargaining Agreement Strategies in Response to Technology." Working Paper. UC Berkeley Labor Center, Berkeley, CA. https://bit.ly/2LdaVrT

Lester, Richard K., and Michael J. Piore. 2006. *Innovation: The Missing Dimension.* Cambridge, MA: Harvard University Press.

Manufacturing Extension Partnership. 1998 (Sep.). "Workforce Case Studies." MEP Successes: Case Study Series. Gaithersburg, MD: National Institute of Standards and Technology.

McGaughey, Ewan. 2019. "Democracy in America at Work: The History of Labor's Vote in Corporate Governance." *Seattle Law Review* 42: 697–753. https://bit.ly/3tlLc1D

McIlwain, Charlton. 2020 (Jan 30). "The Three Civil Rights–Era Leaders Who Warned of Computers and Racism." *Slate.* https://bit.ly/36CR7Wb

McKay, Conor, Ethan Pollack, and Alastair Fitzpayne. 2019 (Apr. 2). "Automation and a Changing Economy, Part I: The Case for Action." Aspen Institute Future of Work Initiative, Washington, DC. https://bit.ly/3alJW5K

McKinsey Global Institute. 2017 (Jan.). "A Future That Works: Automation, Employment and Productivity." McKinsey & Company. https://mck.co/3sntURp

Mills, C. Wright. 1951. *White Collar: The American Middle Classes.* Oxford, UK: Oxford University Press.

Nhat Hanh, Thich. 2014. "The Horse Is Technology." *The Mindfulness Bell* 66 (Summer): 4–9.

Piore, Michael. 1984. "The End of Mass Production? Implications for Work and Social Structure." Presentation. Conference on Technology and Meaningful Work, April 4–7. Kutztown, PA: Institute for Policy Studies.

Piore, Michael, and Charles F. Sabel. 1984. *The Second Industrial Divide.* New York, NY: Basic Books.

Pringle, Patricia. No date. "Monozukuri—Another Key Look at a Key Japanese Principle." Japan Intercultural Consulting. https://bit.ly/3cNyuD9

Richardson, Charley. 1992. "Progress for Whom? New Technology, Unions and Collective Bargaining." In *Software & Hardhats: Technology and Workers in the 21st Century. A Report of Two Conferences*, pp. 151–174. Washington, DC: Labor Policy Institute.

Scheiber, Nelson. 2009 (Dec. 6). "Manufacturing Bloom." *The New Republic.* https://bit.ly/3avBlNV

Sorge, Arndt, and Wolfgang Streeck. 2018. "Diversified Quality Production Revisited: Its Contribution to German Socio-Economic Performance Over Time." *Socio-Economic Review* 16 (3): 587–612. https://bit.ly/3rf9tEx

Stettner, Andrew. 2019a (Sep. 12). "Should Workers Facing Technological Change Have a Right to Training?" The Century Foundation, New York, NY, and Washington, DC. https://bit.ly/3asbV3Y

Stettner, Andrew. 2019b (Oct. 1). "How to Respond to Job Losses From Technology, Trade, and Policy Choices." The Century Foundation, New York, NY, and Washington, DC. https://bit.ly/2Mk7al5

Tyler, George. 2019 (Jan. 10). "The Codetermination Difference." *The American Prospect.* https://bit.ly/3cBrYiE

United Auto Workers. 2019 (Oct. 17). "UAW–GM Contract Summary: Hourly Workers." https://bit.ly/3tksB60

Wiggins, Pamela. 2019 (May 26). "The History of the Arts and Crafts Movement." *The SpruceCrafts.* https://bit.ly/3cNAiMr

Work and Technology Institute. 1992. *Software & Hardhats: Technology and Workers in the 21st Century. A Report of Two Conferences.* Washington, DC: Labor Policy Institute.

Yudken, Joel Samuel. 1987 (Jun.). "The Viability of Craft in Advanced Industrial Society: Case Study of the Contemporary Crafts Movement in the United States (Volumes I and II)." Ph.D. Dissertation, Stanford University, Stanford, CA.

Yudken, Joel S., Thomas Croft, and Andrew Stettner. 2017 (Oct. 16). "Revitalizing America's Manufacturing Communities." The Century Foundation, New York, NY, and Washington, DC. https://bit.ly/36BBE8K

CHAPTER 8

Both Broadening and Deepening: Toward Sectoral Bargaining for the Common Good

JOSEPH A. McCARTIN
Georgetown University

ERICA SMILEY
Jobs With Justice

MARILYN SNEIDERMAN
Rutgers University

ABSTRACT

In recent years, worker advocates have advanced two approaches to expanding collective bargaining and reviving worker power. One approach is sectoral bargaining, whose proponents argue for resurrecting tantalizing precedents and passing new laws that would empower workers to bargain wages and working conditions with multiple employers across an entire sector. The second approach is Bargaining for the Common Good (BCG), which seeks to transform bargaining by bringing community voices to the bargaining table, centering racial justice, and dramatically expanding the scope and content of bargaining. This chapter argues that we must fuse these approaches. If workers are to realize the promise of democracy in the context of the globalized, racialized, and financialized capitalism of the 21st century, the chapter argues, such a fusion is necessary.

INTRODUCTION

In a 2019 essay in *The American Prospect*, keen observer of US labor politics Harold Meyerson cited two exciting new departures emerging among labor and its allies. Both were "expanded forms of bargaining" that he believes point the way forward toward the renewal of the labor movement in response to the challenges of 21st century capitalism: sectoral bargaining and Bargaining for the Common Good, or BCG (Meyerson 2019). In this chapter, we want to emphasize our need to merge these two developments and to begin thinking about *sectoral Bargaining for the Common Good*. Our need to do this, we believe, is all the more urgent because support for sectoral bargaining is growing quickly, and efforts to pass laws promoting sectoral bargaining might soon become possible. If this happens, we must ensure that the *kind* of sectoral bargaining that emerges is up to the needs of workers today. The fusion of sectoral bargaining and BCG, we argue, offers community members and union members an opportunity to partner around a long-term vision for the structural changes they want to see in their communities and at work, recharging democracy in the process.

That there is growing support for sectoral bargaining as a tool to empower US workers is increasingly evident. In recent years, a growing number of labor activists and their allies have called for reforms to make it easier to bargain on a sectoral basis (Madland 2019; Shelton 2019). With the release in January 2020 of "Clean Slate for Worker Power: Building a Just Economy and Democracy," the final report of the Clean Slate Project chaired by Ben Sachs and Sharon Block of Harvard Law School, the call for sectoral bargaining gained renewed momentum. If we are to redress the forces that weaken workers' voice on the job, the report argued, "we need to enable collective bargaining between unions and multinational industries, not just unions and firms" ("Clean Slate for Worker Power" 2020: 3).

We applaud these calls for sectoral bargaining. We see the coalescing of support around this idea as part of a welcome shift away from the narrow focus solely on eliminating barriers to workplace organizing through card-check certification, as the failed Employee Free Choice Act would have done had labor's allies managed to enact it during the Obama presidency. Eliminating barriers that make it difficult to form unions simply will not be enough to empower workers unless we also reinvent collective bargaining to deal with the ways in which the economy has changed over the past half-century. Sectoral bargaining would be an important step toward remaking bargaining in the ways workers need.

But we also believe that sectoral bargaining will be an insufficient step if it does not also dramatically expand the *content, participants, and purposes* of bargaining in the way that BCG aspires to do. If workers win sectoral bargaining rights while retaining the narrow structure of the collective bargaining process as it came to be defined over the course of the 20th century, they will not have won the power that they must have if they are to address their needs and attain their aspirations in the 21st century. Therefore, we urge that sectoral bargaining be integrated with an approach to deepening and broadening the bargaining process that has been pioneered by unions and community groups under the rubric of Bargaining for the Common Good.

Of course, winning sectoral bargaining in any form would constitute an important step forward. Workers in nations that allow sectoral bargaining, such as Germany, have greater bargaining leverage than their US counterparts (OECD

2017).[1] And Americans need not look only to other nations for a model for how to institute sectoral bargaining. As labor law scholar Kate Andrias has shown, the Fair Labor Standards Act (FLSA) of 1938 allowed for the formation of tripartite union–employer–government committees that provided the scaffolding for sectoral bargaining in some industries—that is, until that provision of the law was repealed in 1949 (Andrias 2019b). There have been recent efforts to reclaim that FLSA precedent and to develop new departures in labor law that allow for a broadening of bargaining (Andrias 2016). In 2015, New York State convened a wage board of the sort that the FLSA had once facilitated in order to research and make recommendations on phasing in a $15 minimum wage for fast food workers over a period of years.

Thus far, however, most discussions of the need for sectoral bargaining have viewed the scope of bargaining workers might win under it in narrow terms. The New York fast food wage board, for example, confined its recommendations to the question of wages only. The Clean Slate Project is only slightly more expansive in its view, stressing that "sectoral agreements can help take *wages and working conditions* out of competition for all the firms in the sector" (italics ours) ("Clean Slate for Worker Power" 2020: 14).

We believe that sectoral bargaining must reach broader and go deeper than that. Winning the ability to set wage standards and address basic working conditions in a sector will leave too much power in the hands of unaccountable corporate leaders. It will also fail to give workers the ability to attack the dynamics of racialized inequality that have been flourishing under 21st-century capitalism beyond the worksite in their neighborhoods. We must expand the horizons of bargaining even as we extend it on a sectoral basis if we are to give workers the tools they will need in the years ahead not only to fight for what they deserve from their direct employers but to reconstruct our endangered democracy on a footing appropriate to the demands of this age.

In what follows, we will begin by reviewing the lessons of collective bargaining's recent history to show that the narrowing of bargaining's content contributed to the narrowing of the scope of its coverage. This history, we believe, suggests that we think expansively about the purposes of bargaining if we hope to widen its scope of coverage sectorally. Then we will discuss the ways in which initiatives undertaken by unions and community allies through BCG help us imagine the sort of regime we need to create.

LESSONS LEARNED FROM COLLECTIVE BARGAINING'S CONTESTED HISTORY

At its inception in the United States, collective bargaining was an expansive concept, and workers conceived of its *potential content* in broad terms. Consider the Black washerwomen of Atlanta, who outnumbered Atlanta's male laborers and organized in extremely precarious conditions in the 1880s. These women worked long hours, interacted with dangerous chemicals, and suffered the abuse of employers who still saw them as property. Even when they were paid, they earned less than $10 a month. They joined together to form the Washing Society, a union of laundry workers seeking better pay and conditions. And without any kind of handbook, they (and others like them throughout the South) started organizing. Given that each of them had several employers, all private and individual families, they targeted the city itself—going on strike to seek more citywide standards for their industry, not unlike the standards demanded in the domestic workers' bill of rights movements of today. When collective bargaining finally emerged in 20th-century America, workers like these were excluded from its benefits. Their exclusion in turn helped ensure that the form of collective bargaining that did take shape would be uneven, insufficiently ambitious, and unable to adapt to changing political and economic conditions (Hunter 1998: 74–97).

When industrial workers fought for collective bargaining during the World War I era and again in the Great Depression, the term that best captured what they desired was *industrial democracy*. Indeed, they embraced that term with more enthusiasm than "collective bargaining" itself because it better articulated their broader aims—to win a voice both in the workplace and in politics (Derber 1970; McCartin 1997). The expansiveness of private sector workers' vision was revealed in their occupation of factories in the sit-down strikes of the 1930s; in the militant spirit of the industrial union movement, which continued to articulate demands for industrial democracy; and in unions' demands that industrial conversion for World War II be guided by workers' interests and voices, as the plan put forth by Walter Reuther of the United Auto Workers (UAW) proposed (Lewis 1937; Lichtenstein 1995).

And yet while industrial unionism was driven by an expansive vision, that vision consistently subordinated the aspirations of workers of color, who were minorities in most unions, to the concerns of the majorities of white members whose votes determined union leadership. The passage of the Wagner Act and the Railway Labor Act, both of which extended collective bargaining rights to workers, and the formation of the Congress of Industrial Organizations also led to the displacement of Black workers' unions and tended to push issues of racial justice down in the hierarchy of union demands (Arnesen 2002; Lee 2014).

The aspirations and concerns of workers of color began to receive more attention in collective bargaining as public sector workers began organizing in the 1950s and 1960s, in many cases inspired by the emerging civil rights movement. Shortly after the passage of the Voting Rights Act of 1965, Jerry Wurf, the fiery leader of the American Federation of State, County and Municipal Employees (AFSCME), proclaimed that the "democracy of our political life deserves full extension into the labor relations of our public life" ("Government Employee

Relations Report" 1967: B3). As Wurf's words suggest, public sector workers were seeking not only better wages and a union but a say over the policies they carried out on their jobs. Illustrating this impulse, the 1965 strike of the Social Service Employees Union in New York City saw social workers advocate on behalf of the community they served by demanding a series of significant reforms in the city's welfare system (Moisano 2020).

Over time, however, the content of collective bargaining was narrowed in both the private and the public sectors by employer opposition, changes in law, and shifts in politics. The narrowing began in the private sector as World War II came to a close and labor conflict suppressed by the war erupted with renewed fury. After reluctantly enduring union expansion for a decade, employers were determined to dig in against further encroachments by the union movement on managerial prerogatives. A fateful battle took place between the UAW and General Motors in 1945–46, when autoworkers struck—demanding not only a hefty wage increase to make up for wartime restrictions on wage increases but a voice in key management decisions such as the pricing of GM's automobiles. The union contended that GM could easily meet its wage demands without passing on the increase to consumers in the form of higher prices for GM's fleet of cars, and they demanded that the company open its books to prove it. The company adamantly refused to allow the union any voice over its sales strategy and refused to open its books. After a months-long stalemate, the union capitulated, accepting a wage increase but withdrawing its broader demands (Lichtenstein 1995: 220–247). A year later, the Taft–Hartley Act empowered employers to block similar encroachments on managerial prerogatives in future labor conflicts. Private sector unions were soon funneled into a firm-centered bargaining that focused narrowly on wages and working conditions.

A similar story of constriction unfolded in the public sector. After the 1965 strike in New York City, city officials developed rules imposing a structure on collective bargaining that it had lacked to that point. The codification of public sector collective bargaining that followed had a dual effect: it stabilized public sector unions as entities whose future was assured; at the same time, however, it limited what unions could bargain over, denying them the right to bargain over their agencies' policies, an arrangement the unions quickly accepted (Goulden 1982: 132–133).

As the content of collective bargaining was narrowed during the post-war era, so too was the *scope* of its coverage, which in the late 1930s threatened to be broad indeed, thanks to the passage of the FLSA in 1938. As Kate Andrias has shown, the architects of the FLSA hoped that the act would work in tandem with the Wagner Act to strengthen and spread worker bargaining power. The FLSA provided for the creation of a system of tripartite industry committees that had the power to negotiate minimum wages on an industry-by-industry basis. This system, its designers hoped, would do more than guarantee minimal subsistence wages. As Andrias argues, they sought nothing less than to "empower unions to negotiate for all workers, to build a more egalitarian political economy, and to remake the very structure of American democracy" (Andrias 2019a: 32).

After passage of the FLSA, the director of the Department of Labor's Wage and Hour Division convened tripartite committees in 70 industries. Between 1938 and 1941, these committees negotiated wage scales that covered 21 million workers. As Andrias shows, these committees "took seriously their responsibility to represent non-union workers, viewing the process as a way to undertake a form of collective bargaining for unrepresented workplaces" (Andrias 2019a). Unions would attempt to organize the unorganized in the wake of these wage agreements, pointing out that a strong union could help enforce the new standard, a tactic that proved quite successful. The creation of the National War Labor Board (NWLB) in 1942 set up conditions for further expansion of this system, as the NWLB favored the tripartite approach begun under the rubric of the FLSA.

Yet the promising developments set in motion by the passage of the FLSA and continued during the war by the NLWB did not survive long in peacetime. By 1945, the American Federation of Labor (AFL) had concluded that tripartism favored the rival Congress of Industrial Organizations (CIO) and grew increasingly opposed to its continuation. As post-war labor conflict escalated, national politics shifted against unions with the Republican takeover of the both houses of Congress in 1946 and the passage of the Taft–Hartley Act over Truman's veto in the following year. The grand visions of the FLSA's architects crumbled. Lacking a strong coalition that could protect it, the FLSA's experiment with sectoral bargaining was terminated in 1949 in a deal for a minimum wage increase. After the termination of the tripartite committees, collective bargaining became increasingly firm centered, and unions lacked leverage to extend their gains to unorganized workers as effectively as they had done under the FLSA (Andrias 2019b: 684–688).

Nonetheless, some unions successfully resisted the relentless narrowing of collective bargaining's coverage. As Lynn Rhinehart and Celine McNicholas have reminded us, despite a national labor relations act that "establishes a single worksite, and at most a single employer, as the default unit for bargaining" and prevents unions from insisting that employers bargain together on a multi-employer basis with the union or a group of unions, a number of unions were able to win and maintain models of bargaining that extended beyond individual workplaces (Rhinehart and McNicholas 2020: 3).

Unions used a variety of approaches to try to expand the scope of their agreements. The most time-honored was, no doubt, the effort to construct *national agreements*. This approach dated at least to the turn of the 20th century, when the United Mine Workers of America (UMWA) reached an agreement in 1898 with coal operators in the Central Competitive Field (CCF) that included bituminous regions of Illinois, Indiana, Ohio, and Pennsylvania and when the

International Association of Machinists (IAM) negotiated the Murray Hill Accords with the National Metal Trades Association two years later. Neither effort was a true national success, for the UMWA proved unable to extend the standards it had won in the CCF to Alabama, West Virginia, and other regions where operators took an anti-union approach (Baratz 1955), and the IAM's agreement, which was theoretically national, broke down within a year over enforcement disputes (Montgomery 1987: 261–269). In the post–New Deal era, unions experienced more success in achieving national agreements. By 1950, the UMWA was negotiating national agreements with the Bituminous Coal Operators Association (Dubofsky and Van Tine 1986: 352–354). And in 1964, the most ambitious and significant national agreement was won when the Teamsters union negotiated the first National Master Freight Agreement with Trucking Employers, Inc., an employers' association that spoke for the nation's trucking employers. At its height, the NMFA covered 450,000 drivers and hundreds of employers.

Another innovation was *coordinated national bargaining* undertaken by multiple unions with a single employer. This was the approach developed by unions that negotiated with General Electric (GE) in the post-war era. Jointly bargained GE contracts covered about 50,000 workers at their height in the 1980s. In the auto industry, the UAW developed *pattern bargaining* with the Big Three US automakers (General Motors, Ford, and Chrysler), singling out a single employer for a possible strike and then demanding that the other employers accept the basic terms of that first agreement. In the garment industry, needle trades unions created what were called *jobbers agreements*, which bound both contractors and their suppliers (Rhinehart and McNicholas 2020).

Yet all of these examples of multi-employer or multiple-worksite bargaining that attempted to extend the scope of agreements suffered over time. While each of the innovations proved empowering to workers at the outset, the degree of empowerment they provided was limited, short lived, or both. The Teamsters' NMFA began to unravel once trucking was deregulated in 1980 and trucking companies began withdrawing from the agreement to take advantage of the newly competitive environment. Today, the NMFA covers fewer than 30,000 drivers (Goldsmith 2014). The coordinated bargaining by unions at GE was undercut by the company's offshoring and subcontracting of jobs to the point that it now covers fewer than 7,000 (Brown 2011). The UAW's pattern bargaining ceased functioning as an offensive strategy during Owen Bieber's leadership of the union in the 1980s as plant closings and the failure to organize Honda and Nissan threw the union on the defensive (Rothstein 2016: 135–142). Meanwhile, the garment trades' jobbers agreements did not survive the globalization of textile and apparel manufacturing (Anner, Bair, and Blasi 2013). With private sector unionization dipping under 10% by 2000, the ability of unions to extend coverage beyond individual employers simply evaporated.

This history suggests a relationship between the narrowing of the content of collective bargaining and the shrinking of its scope of coverage. The narrow forms of collective bargaining that prevailed in both the private and public sector by the 1970s were simply not up to the challenges faced by workers and their communities in subsequent decades. Private sector collective bargaining was devised in an era when subcontracting and the "fissured" workplace were not yet realities, when the concept of "maximizing shareholder value" had not yet been articulated, before hedge funds and private equity firms appeared. Public sector bargaining emerged in an era of moderately progressive taxation and before the term "privatization" had yet been coined. As neoliberalism and financialization refashioned the economy after 1980, traditional collective bargaining proved unable to restrain growing and increasingly racialized inequality. The narrow content of collective bargaining as it existed in the last quarter of the 20th century did not give unions leverage to challenge the forces that were unraveling the political and economic conditions that made their bargaining possible in the first place.

Worker organizations have attempted to adapt to these changes, nonetheless, and some of their adaptations are promising. One such adaptation has emerged in the garment industry in which globalization undermined the jobbers' agreements that unions once utilized to lift labor standards. The Asia Floor Wage Alliance (AFWA), a network of garment sector unions and other worker organizations from countries throughout Asia, seeded with the support of Jobs With Justice in the United States and India's New Trade Union Initiative, has innovated in this area. This transnational collaborative effort among unions and worker-based organizations in Asia allows working people to negotiate with their direct employer in textile and apparel factories and undermines the ability of multinational corporations to pit one country's workers against another's in search of the lowest price.

Across Asia, the minimum wage varies as governments try to compete for business. Suppliers are loath to pay more than the minimum, given the pressures from the large multinational brands such as H&M, The Gap, and Walmart to keep costs low. So, in 2005, AFWA assessed what a living wage would be across Asia—considering the costs of food and basic necessities in each country to establish a universal formula for calculating the livable wage. This calculation establishes a shared, cross-border floor wage, allowing working people in the garment sector to make consistent wage demands and negotiate with large garment suppliers.

Recognizing the suppliers' position within the overall apparel economy, the unions within AFWA push the garment suppliers to pay the minimum wage—fighting to increase it at the state level when possible—while negotiating other local conditions that they have control over. But they now simultaneously push the multinational brands to pay suppliers enough to pay more—a wage that matches the floor wage calculated for that country.

This approach gets to the heart of 21st-century bargaining in supply chains. It is a tripartite approach allowing garment workers to negotiate with their governments in setting the minimum wage, their direct employers in the factories, and the profiteers—the multinational corporations controlling industry wages—all in a transnational collaboration among unions. Since the real power and money does not lie with the individual garment production companies but with the multinational retailers such as Adidas, H&M, The Gap, and Walmart who determine the product price from each country based on the national minimum wage, the unions that form the Asia Brand Bargaining Group of AFWA seek to bargain with those retailers as well as with the garment companies with whom they work, and they seek compensation directly from those retailers. So, if the garment suppliers pay the country's minimum wage, AFWA calls on the multinational brands to make an additional wage contribution to make up the difference between the minimum wage and the floor wage that AFWA has calculated for the relevant country.

Recognizing that garment workers in any one country do not exist on an island, the AFWA seeks to have an equal role in governing the industry as a whole. Rather than allowing suppliers and the ultimate retailer to pit the working people from one country against those of other countries, which would lead to lower wages for workers in all of the countries, working people can therefore negotiate across national boundaries for fair wages. Furthermore, by targeting the large retailers, working people in the global South can expand the social consciousness of consumers and leverage their greater access to United States and European public opinion to highlight the unethical conduct on the supply chains and pressure the US and European multinational brands to come to the bargaining table (Clean Clothes Campaign 2014; Global Labor Justice 2019).

Although the AFWA is still a work in progress, it points to two ways we must transform collective bargaining: expanding the range of those who are at the bargaining table and crafting agreements that transcend national boundaries.

Such adaptations will not be sufficient, however, if we do not also adapt collective bargaining to the realities created by the resurgence of monopoly and the impact of financialization. To date, most proponents of sectoral bargaining have had little to say about the impact of these phenomena on corporate behavior in relation to the prospects of creating a 21st-century collective bargaining regime.[2] This is a potentially dangerous oversight, for we are clearly living through an era when economic and political life are increasingly defined by monopolization and financialization (Stoller 2019; Wu 2018). Between 2000 and 2017, the Herfindahl–Hirschman Index, which measures the degree of concentration in a given market, increased in three quarters of US industries, and behemoths such as Amazon, Apple, AT&T, Facebook, Google, Microsoft, and Verizon now dominate their respective industries and exert a degree of corporate power over Americans' lives not seen since the days of the robber barons (Abdela and

Steinbaum 2018; Leonhardt 2018; Stewart 2018, 2020). Meanwhile, the financialization of our economy has dramatically altered the balance of power between workers and their employers. Private equity firms and hedge funds have played a major role in reorganizing enterprises in ways that have extracted value by saddling them with debt and outsourcing their jobs (Appelbaum and Batt 2014).

The need to adapt collective bargaining to a world economy that has been reshaped by financialization becomes clear when we examine the experience of nations that already practice forms of sectoral bargaining. Consider the case of Germany, a country with one of the most advanced systems of sectoral bargaining and worker voice in corporate decision making (the German system of codetermination). Even there, the ability of unions to bargain effectively on a sectoral basis has been fast eroding. As Tobias Schulze-Cleven reminds us, between 1996 and 2016, the share of German workers covered by sectoral collective bargaining fell from 70% to 51% in the nation's west, and from 56% to 36% in its east, while the shares of private sector workers covered by collective bargaining above the company level have dropped to 46% in the west and 29% in the east (Schulze-Cleven 2017: 55).

As the German case suggests, simply extending to unions the right to bargain sectorally and giving them a seat on corporate boards is unlikely to do much to expand workers' true bargaining power. Unless workers can win a form of sectoral bargaining that empowers them to directly challenge growing monopoly power and economic concentration, we can count on these forces undoing whatever gains workers make in the short run, as they are already in the process of doing in Germany. This is not an argument to abandon the idea of sectoral bargaining. Rather, it is an argument for *deepening the content* of bargaining even as we strive to expand the *scope* of its coverage. If we seek to create an effective form of sectoral bargaining, then we need to deepen its content in ways that empower workers to address both the problems of subcontracting, franchising, temping, and supply-chaining that have led to the "fissuring" of the labor market at the bottom of the economy and the increasing financialization and growing monopoly that are restructuring the economy from above—bargaining needs to be broad and deep enough that it empowers workers also to deal with the ways in which their work and their community intersect. Broadening the content of bargaining in this way, we argue, also necessitates that we expand the *participants* in bargaining. Bargaining must become a vehicle to win power not only for workers but for communities, consumers, renters, homeowners, student loan holders, and others whose interests are impacted by the entities with which workers seek to bargain.

How can we adapt sectoral bargaining to the demands of the economy we face in the 21st century? We believe that the experience of BCG can help us imagine what those adaptations might look like.

TOWARD SECTORAL BARGAINING FOR THE COMMON GOOD

BCG emerged following the Great Recession as public sector unions came under attack from opponents such as Wisconsin's governor Scott Walker and as already underserved working-class communities—especially communities of color—saw austerity plans devastate public services. Beginning among teachers in St. Paul and Chicago, unions began reaching out to community allies, including them in the shaping of bargaining demands and using their contract campaigns as vehicles to raise and advance demands that spoke to their communities' needs—not only to the immediate concerns of the workers they represented, such as the demand that the schools cease doing business with banks that would foreclose on students' families during the school year. Unions and community allies who adopted this model came together in 2014 in a conference in Washington, D.C., to found a network, and in the years since they have expanded that network, training others in how to pursue BCG campaigns (McCartin and Sneiderman 2018).

BCG campaigns have self-consciously attempted to transform the participants, processes, and purposes of collective bargaining in ways that could be applied in sectoral bargaining. Whereas traditional collective bargaining was a binary undertaking between labor and management, BCG campaigns have fought to win a seat at the table for the community and its concerns. They advanced demands that reach over the heads of the public officials with whom they usually negotiate in an effort to pull the financial interests and corporate titans that generally shape government priorities into the bargain, and they have urged government agencies to claw back unjustified tax breaks and renegotiate their relationships with Wall Street. By doing so, they have changed the process of collective bargaining by ignoring the parameters of the mandatory, permissible, and impermissible bargaining issues, opening up the bargaining process to greater public scrutiny and accountability. Whereas traditional collective bargaining stresses the codification of wages and working conditions, BCG campaigns have aspired to broaden bargaining to address issues of structural inequality and systemic racism and to build an enduring alliance of power between unions and their community-based allies.

BCG campaigns have been evolving rapidly in creative new directions. Strikes by teachers in Los Angeles and Chicago in 2019 are indicative of this learning process. In January, the United Teachers of Los Angeles staged a week-long strike against the Los Angeles Unified School District. Wages were a secondary concern in the strike (McAlevey 2019). The union conducted mass picketing in the rain not to win a greater salary increase—it settled for the 6% raise that the schools had offered at the outset—but rather to advance the demands that were most important to its community allies. These included smaller class sizes, nurses in every school, a legal help line for immigrant families, and an end to random searches. They won on these issues (Kohli 2019; United Teachers of Los Angeles 2019).

In October 2019, the Chicago Teachers Union (CTU) walked out in conjunction with Local 73 of the Service Employees International Union, which represents school support staff. Prior to the walkout, the CTU had advanced what was, in some ways, the most ambitious set of demands yet brought forth during a BCG campaign, including a demand that Chicago take action on the growing housing crisis that was causing rising homelessness and school-emptying patterns of gentrification, and was pricing teachers themselves (who by law must live in Chicago) out of affordable housing. The union demanded that Chicago provide housing assistance for new teachers, hire staff members whose jobs would be to assist students and families who were in danger of losing their housing, and take other steps to advocate for more affordable housing overall in the city (Burns 2019). Chicago Mayor Lori Lightfoot called the CTU's housing demands a distraction, and the *Chicago Sun-Times* said they "had no place at the bargaining table," but the union stuck to its guns, won a program aimed at serving homeless students, and put the issue of housing unaffordability on the agenda for future action ("Reality Check to Teachers Union" 2019).

We are now seeing indications of how BCG can be translated into the private sector. One such indication is the Committee for Better Banks (CBB), a coalition of bank workers, community organizations, consumer advocacy groups, and unions such as the Communications Workers of America coming together to improve conditions in the bank industry. The CBB has drafted a bank workers' bill of rights in which its members call for the elimination of unreasonable sales goals and performance metrics that reward them for pushing unwanted or predatory products on customers. Its organizers hope to create a union of bank workers that bargains not only on its members' behalf but also on behalf of the customers they serve.

Campaigns like those discussed above represent an effort to revive the sort of expansive vision that had drawn workers to fight for collective bargaining in the first place during the first half of the 20th century. At that time, workers were more apt to characterize their aspirations as a desire for *industrial democracy* than they were to confine them to the particulars of a union contract (McCartin 1997). As it evolved between the 1940s and the 1970s, however, collective bargaining was increasingly confined to the narrow issues of wages, hours, and working conditions (Derber 1970; Lichtenstein and Harris 1993). BCG campaigns seek to reimagine bargaining as a tool that can address problems beyond the individual workplace—and indeed beyond an individual sector.

It is precisely such an expansive vision that we believe must inform sectoral bargaining if it is to deliver any real and lasting power for workers. For what good will it ultimately do if workers win the power to negotiate wage standards across a sector if their income gains are immediately wiped out by increased housing costs or their neighborhoods lost to gentrification? What good will it do workers to win the ability to bargain across a sector if the dominant corporate actors in that sector hold a monopoly power that allows them to simply pass off any gains by workers in the form of increased prices for consumers. What good will it do workers to bargain sectorally if private equity firms buy companies in that sector, burden them with unpayable debts, and shrink their workforces before off-loading their husks?

Workers cannot win the power they need vis-à-vis 21st-century capitalism unless they can begin to bargain broadly about a broad range of issues that extend far beyond wages, hours, and working conditions. Meaningful representation on corporate boards, as advocated by the Clean Slate Project and embodied in bills introduced by Democratic US senators Elizabeth Warren and Tammy Baldwin, would constitute an important step in the right direction. But unless workers can also raise demands that infringe on a range of subjects that are currently left to management's unilateral determination, such representation is unlikely to be enough to protect workers' interests and to ensure that when they bargain, their demands advance the common good.

The recent upheavals in reaction to the murders of George Floyd, Breonna Taylor, and Ahmaud Arbery, and other acts of racialized police brutality, we believe, are likely to provide further impetus to the rethinking of the nature and scope of collective bargaining. As police unions come under attack for using their collective bargaining agreements to shield patterns of abusive misbehavior, the nature of the bargaining process is coming under closer scrutiny and debate (DiSalvo 2020; Saunders 2020). In many ways, the police union problem is highlighting the defects of a collective bargaining system, binary in its structure and narrow in its focus, that evolved in the 20th century. Again, Harold Meyerson (2020) has proven to be an astute analyst of the significance of this problem. He writes that "until they can bargain for the common good, enlisting as allies and embracing the demands of the people they police," police unions "should not be part of the broader labor movement." As Bill Fletcher Jr. (2020) rightly notes, even if bargaining was entirely ended, police "would just find other ways to wield political power, and elected officials would find other excuses to hide behind." Yet bargaining reform in the context of a defund/refund movement might make a huge difference in pointing us toward a new and better way of ensuring community safety. As the labor movement wrestles with the problem of police unions, it will again be forced to reckon with the need to widen its thinking on what bargaining must become if it is to adequately deal with the problems of workers in the 21st century.

Make no mistake—we are currently witnessing a broader rethinking of bargaining than has occurred since the early 20th century. It is important that the fruits of this rethinking be embedded within the vision of sectoral bargaining that many are now mobilizing to win. We cannot afford to win a form of sectoral bargaining that focuses narrowly on wages and workplace standards. We need sectoral Bargaining for the Common Good.

ENDNOTES

1. The Organisation for Economic Co-operation and Development (OECD) finds: "Overall, collective bargaining coverage is high and stable only in countries where multi-employer agreements (i.e., at sector or national level) are negotiated and where either the share of firms which are members of an employer association is high or where agreements are extended also to workers working in firms which are not members of a signatory employer association. In countries where collective agreements are signed mainly at firm level, coverage tends to go hand-in-hand with trade union density. Workers in small firms are generally less likely to be covered as these firms often do not have the capacity to negotiate a firm-level agreement, or a union or another form of worker representation is absent at the workplace." See Chapter 4, "Collective Bargaining in a Changing World of Work," *OECD Employment Outlook 2017* (OECD 2017; https://bit.ly/2MKBDc7)

2. For example, financialization is mentioned once in passing (p. 56) and monopoly is unmentioned in "Clean Slate for Worker Power" (2020); neither term is mentioned in David Madland's "How to Promote Sectoral Bargaining" (2019).

REFERENCES

Abdela, Adil, and Marshall Steinbaum. 2018 (Sep.). "The United States Has a Market Concentration Problem: Reviewing Concentration Estimates in Antitrust Markets, 2000–Present." New York, NY: The Roosevelt Institute. https://bit.ly/39XtLNh

Andrias, Kate. 2016. "The New Labor Law." *Yale Law Journal* 126 (1): 2–100. https://bit.ly/2YTvEEh

Andrias, Kate. 2019a (Spring). "A Seat at the Table: Sectoral Bargaining for the Common Good." *Dissent.* https://bit.ly/2YVjCdu

Andrias, Kate. 2019b. "An American Approach to Social Democracy: The Forgotten Promise of the Fair Labor Standards Act." *Yale Law Journal* 128 (3): 616–709. https://bit.ly/3cKdE7w

Anner, Mark, Jennifer Bair, and Jeremy Blasi. 2013. "Toward Joint Liability in Global Supply Chains: Addressing the Root Causes of Labor Violations in International Subcontracting Networks." *Comparative Labor Law & Policy Journal* 35 (1): 1–43.

Appelbaum, Eileen, and Rosemary Batt. 2014. *Private Equity at Work: When Wall Street Manages Main Street.* New York, NY: Russell Sage Foundation.

Arnesen, Eric. 2002. *Brotherhoods of Color: Black Railroad Workers and the Struggle for Equality.* Cambridge, MA: Harvard University Press.

Baratz, Morton S. 1955. *The Union and the Coal Industry.* New Haven, CT: Yale University Press.

Brown, Alexandra. 2011 (May 24). "G.E. to Unions: Drop Dead." *Labor Notes.* https://bit.ly/3rAsW2X

Burns, Rebecca. 2019 (Oct. 14). "What's at Stake in Chicago Teachers' Strike: Whether Unions Can Bargain for the Entire Working Class." *In These Times.* https://bit.ly/3rwRv0q

Clean Clothes Campaign. 2014. "Living Wage in Asia: 2014 Report." https://bit.ly/3cU0959

"Clean Slate for Worker Power: Building a Just Economy and Democracy." 2020. Labor and Worklife Program, Harvard Law School. https://bit.ly/36Tnq3n

Derber, Milton. 1970. *The American Idea of Industrial Democracy, 1865–1965.* Champaign, IL: University of Illinois Press.

DiSalvo, Daniel. 2020 (Jun. 8). "Not Public Spirited: Government–Employee Unions—Including Those for Police—Put the Power and Interests of Their Workers Above the Public Interest." *City Journal.* https://bit.ly/3pUG2HI

Dubofsky, Melvyn, and Warren Van Tine. 1986. *John L. Lewis: A Biography*. Champaign, IL: University of Illinois Press.

Fletcher, Bill Jr. 2020 (Jun 12). "The Central Issue Is Police Repression, Not Police Unions," *In These Times*. https://bit.ly/2OfsbxQ

Global Labor Justice and the Asia Floor Wage Alliance. 2019. "End Gender-Based Violence and Harassment." https://bit.ly/3rwXe6s

Goldsmith, Jack. 2014 (Jan. 15). "Sad Coda to the 50th Anniversary of the Teamsters National Master Freight Agreement." *On Labor*. https://bit.ly/3tLHGxQ

Goulden, Joseph C. 1982. *Jerry Wurf: Labor's Last Angry Man*. New York, NY: Atheneum.

Government Employee Relations Report. 1967 (Jun. 26). 198: B-3.

Hunter, Tera. 1998. *To 'Joy My Freedom: Southern Black Women's Lives and Labor After the Civil War*. Cambridge, MA: Harvard University Press.

Kohli, Sonali. 2019 (Jun. 18). "L.A. Unified Board Votes to End Random Student Searches." *Los Angeles Times*. https://lat.ms/3tDTGRE

Lee, Sophia Z. 2014. *The Workplace Constitution from the New Deal to the New Right*. New York, NY: Cambridge University Press.

Leonhardt, David. 2018 (Nov. 25). "The Monopolization of America." *New York Times*. https://nyti.ms/3aMdPwe

Lewis, John L. 1937. *Industrial Democracy*. Washington, DC: Committee for Industrial Organization.

Lichtenstein, Nelson. 1995. *The Most Dangerous Man in Detroit: Walter Reuther and the Fate of American Labor*. New York, NY: Basic Books.

Lichtenstein, Nelson, and Howell John Harris, eds. 1993. *Industrial Democracy in America: The Ambiguous Promise*. New York, NY: Cambridge University Press.

Madland, David. 2019 (Jul. 10). "How to Promote Sectoral Bargaining in the United States." Center for American Progress Action Fund. https://bit.ly/2MHTdxm

McAlevey, Jane. 2019 (Feb. 28). "'There Are So Many Things That We Can Learn From This Strike': An Interview with Alex Caputo-Pearl." *Jacobin*. https://bit.ly/3cQShBy

McCartin, Joseph A. 1997. *Labor's Great War: The Struggle for Industrial Democracy and the Origins of Modern American Labor Relations*. Chapel Hill, NC: University of North Carolina Press.

McCartin, Joseph A., and Marilyn Sneiderman. 2018. "Bargaining for the Common Good: An Emerging Tool for Re-Building Worker Power." In *No One Size Fits All: Worker Organization, Policy, and Movement for a New Economic Age*, edited by Janice Fine, Linda Burnham, Kati Griffith, Minsun Ji, Victor Narro, and Steven Pitts, pp. 189–203. Champaign, IL: Labor and Employment Relations Association.

Meyerson, Harold. 2019 (Sep. 2). "Bargaining for More: Can Unions Change Labor Law So That They Can Reach a Deal with All Employers?" *The American Prospect*. https://bit.ly/3aCXmdW

Meyerson, Harold. 2020 (Jun. 10). "Bargaining Against the Common Good: On the Problem of Police Unions." *The American Prospect*. https://bit.ly/3tzFfyf

Moisano, Chris. 2020 (Jun. 18). "The Social Service Employees Union Was a Model of Public-Sector Unionism." *Jacobin*. https://bit.ly/3tAAILL

Montgomery, David. 1987. *The Fall of the House of Labor: The Workplace, the State, and American Labor Activism, 1865–1925*. New York, NY: Cambridge University Press.

Organisation for Economic Co-operation and Development (OECD). 2017. "Employment Outlook 2017." Paris, France: Organisation for Economic Co-operation and Development. https://bit.ly/36RzTEK

"Reality Check to Teachers Union: Affordable Housing Has No Place at the Bargaining Table." 2019 (Oct. 9). *Chicago Sun-Times*. https://bit.ly/3rsulsf

Rhinehart, Lynn, and Celine McNicholas. 2020 (May 4). "Collective Bargaining Beyond the Worksite: How Workers and Their Unions Build Power and Set Standards for Their Industries." Economic Policy Institute. https://bit.ly/3p1Rz6O

Rothstein, Jeffrey S. 2016. *When Good Jobs Go Bad: Globalization, De-Unionization, and Declining Job Quality in the North American Auto Industry.* New Brunswick, NJ: Rutgers University Press.

Saunders, Lee. 2020 (Jun. 9). "No Union Contract Is a Shield for Police Brutality." *USA Today*. https://bit.ly/3ty2iJI

Schulze-Cleven, Tobias. 2017. "German Labor Relations in International Perspective: A Model Reconsidered." *German Politics and Society* 35 (4): 46–76.

Shelton, Chris. 2019. "Sectoral Bargaining: America's Past, Present, and Future." Conference Session. Future of American Labor: Initiatives for a New Era Conference, Georgetown University Law Center, Washington, DC, Feb. 8, 2019. https://bit.ly/3tDg2mo

Stewart, Emily. 2018 (Nov. 26). "America's Monopoly Problem, in One Chart." *Vox*. https://bit.ly/3tJul9l

Stewart, Emily. 2020 (Feb. 18). "America's Monopoly Problem, Explained by Your Internet Bill." *Vox*. https://bit.ly/3cNjViM

Stoller, Matt. 2019. *Goliath: The 100-Year War Between Monopoly Power and Democracy.* New York, NY: Simon & Schuster.

United Teachers of Los Angeles. 2019. "What We Won and How It Builds Our Future." https://bit.ly/3aMdZE7

Wu, Tim. 2018. *The Curse of Bigness: Anti-Trust in the New Gilded Age.* New York, NY: Columbia Global Reports.

Chapter 9

The Role of Labor Education in Revaluing Workers: Historical, Current, and Future

Victor G. Devinatz
Illinois State University

Robert Bruno
University of Illinois Urbana-Champaign

ABSTRACT

Through analyzing the past, present, and future of US labor education and worker education, we argue that prior to collective bargaining's institutionalization circa 1945, US worker education was focused on providing trade unionists and workers with classes emphasizing *both* societal transformation and the "tool" courses for labor relations through independent labor colleges such as Brookwood Labor College, Highlander Folk School, and Commonwealth College. Upon the institutionalization of collective bargaining, US labor education primarily stressed "tool" courses through university-based labor education programs. However, we argue that in the 21st century with union density's sharp decline, US labor education must return to its roots of emphasizing *more* societal transformation coursework while retaining "tool" courses in educating groups of workers numerically expanding in the labor force, including immigrants, women, youth, and people of color.

INTRODUCTION

University-based labor education extension and labor studies degree programs emerged in the United States in the post–World War II period. These programs developed during US labor's Golden Age (1948–1980) when much of US manufacturing's heavy industries (e.g., auto, steel, and rubber) were heavily unionized, with US manufacturing employment reaching 19,553,000 jobs in June 1979 (Jeffrey 2019). Additionally, from 1960 to 1980, US public sector union membership expanded rapidly, with government workers engaging in militant collective actions to achieve collective bargaining rights and individual states passing laws allowing public employees to organize unions and to negotiate contracts with their employers.

Nevertheless, labor education and labor studies emerged in the 20th century to provide working-class people with the necessary knowledge for understanding their workplace roles and in developing their skills in organizing unions, participating in collective actions, and administering labor organizations (Dwyer 1977: 180). Labor education and labor studies can still play that role in the early 21st century. The purpose of this chapter is to investigate US labor education and worker education's function in examining "the future of work" during the 21st century's third decade. We argue that prior to the institutionalization of collective bargaining circa 1945, US worker education was geared toward providing trade unionists and workers with classes focused on *both* societal transformation and the "tool" courses for labor relations through independent labor colleges. Upon collective bargaining's institutionalization, US labor education emphasized primarily "tool" courses through university-based labor education programs. However, we contend that in the 21st century with union density's dramatic decline, US labor education must return to its roots of stressing *more* societal transformation coursework while retaining "tool" courses in educating groups of workers numerically expanding in the labor force, including immigrants, women, youth, and people of color.

The chapter proceeds first with an exploration of US labor education and worker education's early years (1900s–1940s), focusing on 20th-century labor education institutions, including Brookwood Labor College, Highlander Folk School, and Commonwealth College, and their contributions to the established American Federation of Labor (AFL) and the embryonic Congress of Industrial Organizations (CIO) unions. The second section appraises US labor education, labor studies, and worker education's role during labor's Golden Age and into the 1990s when declining union density led to an AFL-CIO leadership change, resulting in a rethinking of labor education. The third section discusses what US labor education and worker education can provide in shaping the future of work through investigating the new reality confronting 21st-century US trade unionism. The chapter concludes with final thoughts on US labor education's role in the future of work.

THE EARLY YEARS OF US WORKER EDUCATION

US worker education, which emerged in the early 20th century, was strongly influenced by the British worker education movement, with British and US labor colleges sharing "common roots during the social ferment of the 19th century." British worker education came to reflect the British trade union movement's socialist orientation with promoting "education for changing the social order" (Nash 1981: 65). Compared with its more politically oriented British counterpart,

US labor education was heavily influenced by business unionism, especially after World War II. Despite its more conservative orientation, US labor education possessed a modicum of the ideology of social reform that permeated British worker education. Two Americans, Walter Vrooman and Charles Beard, established Ruskin College at Oxford in 1898 to educate and prepare working-class students to serve the British labor movement. Two years later, they founded the US Ruskin College in 1900 (Barrow 1990: 396). British developments in worker education influenced the formation of US labor colleges. At the peak of the US labor college movement in the mid-1920s, at least 60 labor colleges existed across the country. Throughout the 1920s, one scholar has estimated that more than 300 labor colleges were created, with each institution offering between one and 75 classes per academic term and enrollments varying from a handful of students to thousands in metropolitan areas such as New York City. One approximation from 1923 considered the total number of students who had matriculated at such colleges to be nearly 30,000 (Barrow 1991: 6). For example, in 1918, at the Socialist Party of America's (SPA) membership peak, attendance at the Rand School of Social Science in New York City, which was established by SPA adherents, numbered some 5,000 students (Recchiuti 1995: 156). In the late 1940s, New York City's Jefferson School of Social Science, organized by the Communist Party USA (CPUSA), enrolled 8,000 to 10,000 students annually in all its branches, with a large percentage being trade unionists (Gettleman 2002: 341–342).

These labor colleges adopted one of two structures: they were either residential colleges located at a college campus, often in a rural, idyllic setting; or nonresidential colleges in urban areas that conducted evening and weekend classes. Examples of these latter institutions include the Seattle Labor College, Trade Union College (Boston), and the Milwaukee Workers College (Peters and McCarrick 1976: 114–116).

Most labor colleges were founded in large metropolitan areas either by university professors, teachers, trade unionists, and other community activists, or separately by trade union federations or radical political parties (e.g., the SPA, the CPUSA). The labor colleges possessed two educational goals. One objective was to deliver information to rank-and-file workers and to teach them organizational skills so that they could effectively mobilize as trade unionists at worksites as well as become informed citizens in their communities. A second goal was to provide advanced and specialized education in the social sciences and the professions to adult workers who it was presumed would return to the trade union movement to utilize their skills in the service of the working class (Barrow 1991: 6–7).

To provide a better understanding of the missions, purpose, and activities of these early labor education programs, we will look more closely at the three most prominent labor colleges of the era—Brookwood Labor College, Commonwealth College, and the Highlander Folk School—in their drive to help the AFL and the CIO achieve their primary objective of educating trade unionists. While differences existed, these three institutions shared a similar overarching educational philosophy and practices.

Brookwood Labor College, 1921–1937

Brookwood Labor College, established in 1919 as the Brookwood School in Katonah, New York, was considered the most important US residential labor college when it was established in June 1921. Providing "pragmatic techniques with visionary goals" (Howlett 1981: 166), the purpose of Brookwood's curriculum was to educate students to return to trade unions as active organizers and rank-and-file union leaders as opposed to becoming part of the union bureaucracy (Altenbaugh 1990: 93).

Brookwood's coursework was designed to further the objectives of the AFL's craft unionism—to encourage the organization of unions while fighting for better wages and working conditions and a reduction in work hours by developing "a technically trained leadership and an intelligent membership." Courses offered to help achieve these practical goals included trade union organization; structure, government, and administration of trade unions; labor journalism; labor legislation and administration; the strategy of the labor movement; public speaking; and training in speaking and writing (Howlett 1993: 58–59).

Brookwood's two-year curriculum was based on the social sciences, with first-year courses including the mechanics of studying, history, English, social psychology, social problems, the function of worker education, and writing and performing labor drama. History of the US trade union movement, international labor movements, advanced economics, social literature, labor journalism, methods of trade union organization, and trade union bookkeeping as well as speech and rhetoric were second-year course offerings (Howlett 1993: 62; Barrow 1990: 401). Topics covered in economics courses included social problems, child labor, credit control, and unemployment, while history courses examined the emergence of social and political institutions, trade unions, and international trade union movements. Exceptional students were urged to matriculate for a third year to focus on a professional area of graduate study (Barrow 1990: 401–402).

Brookwood class sizes rarely exceeded 20 students, with professors teaching two classes (with two sections per class) each semester in their areas of expertise. Lectures constituted the major mode of pedagogical practice, with group discussion fostered after the lectures. Students were expected to read widely and to critically analyze their readings in group discussions (Howlett 1981: 169–170). Certainly, one problem was that not all students possessed the necessary academic preparation. For example, in 1927, more than half of Brookwood's students had acquired only a grade school education, which meant that many had to enroll in basic reading and writing classes before tackling more advanced classes (Altenbaugh 1990: 97). Despite these difficulties, Brookwood students possessed a surprising degree of motivation. Helen Norton Starr, a labor journalism instructor from 1925 to 1935, remarked that she enjoyed teaching at the school immensely because "she had to nudge students to leave the library late in the evening." Although Brookwood's academic program was lengthy and rigorous, few students failed to complete their studies (Bloom 1990a: 75).

Besides taking coursework at the college, students were encouraged to contribute through discussion, analysis, and participation in extramural reform causes including the fights for social justice and against economic inequality. Examples of such external activities during the 1920s and 1930s included the institution's faculty members and students participating in the 1924 Conference for Progressive Political Action that backed Senator Robert M. La Follette's bid for the US presidency, the 1926 campaign designed to unseat Massachusetts Senator William Butler in that year's election, the 1927 demonstrations and efforts to stop the execution of anarchists Nicola Sacco and Bartolomeo Vanzetti, the unemployed movement, the Free Tom Mooney campaign, and the Continental Congress of Workers and Farmers (Howlett 1993: 62–63). They were also encouraged to engage in socialist activities more generally and contribute to the formation of a labor party.

Brookwood started with just 15 students in its first year, but 50 to 75 students attended Brookwood annually in the years following its first graduation in 1924, although enrollment plummeted during the Great Depression (Robinson 1968: 65). More women than men attended, with most coming from the clothing and mining industries, ranging in age from 21 to 35 years old (the average age was 29). Trade unionists comprised nearly 85% of the students, with their unions choosing them for attendance and providing at least some scholarship funds (Howlett 1981: 168). For students not receiving scholarships, the minimal average annual cost was $200, and many students performed domestic work at Brookwood to reduce their attendance expenses (Robinson 1968: 65). Brookwood graduated over 400 throughout its life span before shuttering in 1937.

Although the AFL's trade union leadership attacked Brookwood at its 1928 convention for its "strongly communistic sympathies and, presumably, affiliations" and for fomenting the students' "disloyalty to the American Federation of Labor" (Grabiner 1979: 195), this was not the cause for its closure in 1937. Besides suffering from severe financial problems, the school's staff and board of directors had constant turnover, and the school failed to adequately recruit from the CIO's newly organized mass production industries. Further, the institution was unable to obtain sufficient financial and organizational assistance from unions, such as the United Auto Workers and the International Ladies' Garment Workers' Union, that supported Brookwood's mission. The school's SPA ties initially greatly helped Brookwood, although its continuing relationship to the SPA contributed to the school's "isolation and decline" (Bloom 1990b: 26).

Commonwealth College, 1922–1940

Commonwealth College's origins date to December 1917, when a workers' co-operative colony, a self-governing entity in which workers produce for their own sustenance, moved to Vernon Parish, Louisiana, from California. Kate Richards O'Hare, a well-known socialist who had experience with the first US residential labor college, Ruskin College (Florida) in 1916–1917, met William Edward Zeuch, a University of Illinois economics instructor, and they moved together with her family to the colony in late spring 1923. Although O'Hare and Zeuch desired to establish a residential labor college, the colony was unwilling to pro-vide sufficient financing for the college, leading to O'Hare's departure in late summer 1924 with Commonwealth College relocating to Mena, Arkansas, in late December 1924 before ultimately finding a permanent home 13 miles west of Mena in Arkansas' Polk County in 1925 (Cobb 1964).

In its first few years, Commonwealth College lacked a clearly structured academic program; students took courses based on their interests and needs. The college focused on offering "tool" and background courses, each taught three hours per week over a 15-week semester. Classes included "economics, English, history and government, law, mathematics, music, psychology, sociology, ste-nography and modern languages" (Altenbaugh 1990: 100). US labor history was taught under economics in an approach similar to the University of Wisconsin's economist–historians as represented by John R. Commons (Altenbaugh 1990: 101). Unlike at degree-granting institutions, these courses emphasized "economic, social and labor problems as they affected the discipline" (Cobb 2000: 119). Besides engaging in academic coursework, students (and faculty members) de-voted 20 hours of work per week to the college's operation, which included farm-ing, cooking, canning, printing, and more (Sandler 1985: 47).

In 1926, a systematic review of the school's curriculum resulted in Commonwealth College offering more traditional courses with an academically oriented faculty. Two years later, the college's academic program became more formal, with the implementation of the quarter system. At that time, the reme-dial program, known as the preparatory school, provided to non–high school graduates, was replaced with an orientation year consisting of tutorials prepared for individual students. One more curriculum restructuring occurred in 1930, with courses divided into four major specializations—worker education, labor economics, labor journalism, and labor law. Each track required study across nine quarters, or three academic years. Regardless of specialization, the first year of study included "American history, American government, effective writing, history of civilization, [and] economics." Classic and public speaking were man-datory for three of the four tracks. Once students began their "major" courses during the second and third years, the only required classes were general psy-chology and the history of unionism. Students were compelled to take labor history for all specializations except labor law. The orientation year became shortened to one quarter. Since most Commonwealth students could devote only a few quarters to study, a one-year labor course was developed to meet students' needs (Cobb 2000: 120).

Upon the utopian socialist Zeuch's expulsion as Commonwealth College director and his 1931 replacement with Lucien Koch, a former student expressing more militant views, the institution moved from delivering theoretical worker education combined with communal living to one of radical labor movement activism. Examples include a Commonwealth staff member and three students traveling to Harlan County, Kentucky, with food and other resources to aid the organization of coal miners in April 1932. In August 1932, four Commoners journeyed to the Illinois coal fields, encouraging the formation of a progressive miners' union as an alternative to the United Mine Workers of America, which had recently negotiated a wage cut. Moreover, the college also sent a labor organizer to help unionize the Weaver Pants Company in Corinth, Mississippi, at the request of the Amalgamated Clothing Workers of America (Cobb 1973: 139–141).

Additionally, Commonwealth College faculty and staff from both the Socialist and Communist factions became active in helping to organize the Southern Tenant Farmers' Union (STFU). Altenbaugh (1990: 234–235) argues that scholars dispute Commonwealth's role in the STFU; Cobb and Grubbs (1966) maintain the relationship was problematic, while Koch and Koch (1972) contend that the Commoners' STFU work was a college highpoint. Although Commonwealth's connection with the STFU remained complicated (Cobb 2000: 161–186), seven union members were sent to the college, and by the spring quarter of 1936, eight additional tenant farmers attended (Cobb and Grubbs 1966: 299).

Although the STFU merged into the United Cannery, Agricultural, Packing and Allied Workers of America in September 1937, the STFU seceded in March 1939, changing its name to the National Farm Labor Union after World War II. With the STFU and other unions no longer supporting the school, Commonwealth College lost its *raison d'être* as its ties to the southern trade unions disintegrated. Experiencing financial, curriculum, leadership, and legal problems (owing to its ideology), Commonwealth College folded in 1940 (Altenbaugh 1990: 242–244).

The Highlander Folk School

The Highlander Folk School (HFS) was founded in Monteagle, Tennessee, in 1932 by Myles Horton and Don West as a meeting and training ground for social change, which eventually focused on CIO organizer education and training in the 1930s and 1940s (Preskill 1991). As the school took shape, its philosophy was to connect academic education to practical activities. Early in 1933, Horton felt that Highlander education should result in Southern workers engaging in "conscious class action" leading to some form of socialist society (Glen 1996: 28).

Highlander emphasized basic "tool" courses, the social sciences, and labor-oriented topics. For example, during the 1932–1933 first and second resident sessions, courses were offered on the history of social change and social survey techniques, as well as classes in psychology, cultural geography, social and economic problems, and social literature. For the spring 1934 academic resident term, students took five courses—industrial problems, public speaking, English grammar, labor history, and literature. During the 1934 summer resident program, labor history, psychology, labor journalism, labor drama, and public speaking were course offerings (Horton 1989: 80, 87, 90–92).

From 1938 to 1942, the HFS residential worker education program was geared toward aiding the CIO industrial unions and their unionization campaigns. As such, most students were CIO union members, although other attendees included farmworkers, the unemployed, and members of relief worker unions. While Highlander was concerned with achieving the CIO's pressing needs, it still focused on constructing a politically involved and socially responsible interracial trade union movement that would include industrial workers and farmworkers, employed and unemployed workers, and native-born and immigrant workers, with courses including parliamentary law, labor journalism, union problems, labor history, and economics (Horton 1989: 114–117, 122).

Additionally, Highlander engaged in CIO union extension work in New Orleans in 1941–1942, focusing on educating local union leaders on basic union activities such as handling grievances, dues collection, scheduling and organizing department and committee meetings, and carrying out wage surveys. HFS also held monthlong (May to June) Southern CIO Schools in 1944, 1945, and 1946 for local union leaders. Besides including classes on subjects such as shop steward training, labor law, parliamentary law, labor history, economics, and public speaking, classes were offered on how to develop good relationships with civic groups, fighting against racial discrimination, farmer–labor unity, and job creation after World War II's conclusion (Glen 1996: 95–120).

As early as the summer of 1934, HFS faculty members and students were helping both local labor unions and the Monteagle community (Glen 1996: 37). One example of HFS building industrial unionism was its involvement in the Textile Workers Organizing Committee's 1937 organizing drive, the South's first CIO unionization campaign, in which the school devoted all its resources and experienced much success (Horton 1989: 102–103). During 1939, winter-term students ran a soup kitchen, collected money, and delivered speeches in backing a stay-in of Grundy County Works Progress Administration employees (Glen 1996: 65).

Highlander's trade union work decreased in 1949, although the institution still taught 1,000 students that year in extension and residential programs. Although the school's union education continued from 1950 to 1953, the CIO's division between CPUSA-led unions and non-Communist industrial unions that resulted in the CPUSA-led unions' 1949–1950 expulsion from the industrial federation led to the CIO dissolving its relationship with the school in August 1953 (Glen 1996: 117–126). During the remainder of the 1950s and throughout the 1960s, Highlander trained civil rights leaders, such as the legendary Rosa Parks, and during the 1970s through the 1990s, the institution educated Appalachian activists.

The three independent labor colleges described in this section demonstrated the value and effectiveness of combining "tool" coursework with societal transformation programming in helping to build the CIO unions. With Brookwood and Commonwealth having folded by World War II, labor education shifted to primarily large public universities and was taught in extension divisions or services after the war. For example, the University of Minnesota's Industrial Relations Center was established in 1945, the University of Illinois' Institute of Labor and Industrial Relations in 1946, and the New York State School of Labor and Industrial Relations at Cornell University in 1945. We turn to a closer examination of these post-war, university-based programs in the next section.

UNIVERSITY AND COLLEGE LABOR EDUCATION AND LABOR STUDIES

Labor Education in the 1950s–1980s

With the change in venue following the close of World War II, the purpose for labor education was contested. Did labor education primarily serve a missionary purpose, akin to the ideological inspirations of Brookwood, Commonwealth, and Highlander? Or should it embrace more pragmatic technical skills training that raised the efficiency of union officers? Adherents could be found on both sides of the debate. Resolving the differences was critical to how university-based labor education would be appropriated and defined.

As taught within the academy, two ideal types of education were proffered. First, a "nuts and bolts" or "bread and butter" approach focused on classes like labor history (largely devoid of a societal transformation orientation), communications, grievance handling, organizing, health and safety, collective bargaining, and labor law. The goal was leadership development, problem solving, organizational proficiency, and institution building. Union members would understand the cause of labor, appreciate its historical role, and be better equipped to participate in the organization's work. Education would be done exclusively through labor organizations and not delivered directly to individual workers. Labor education was for "unionists" and not for individual workers because worker rights were derived from labor agreements and unionization. Labor educators would endeavor to meet "worker educational needs as they arise from their participation in unions" (Schmidman, Marrone, and Remington 1990: 292, as cited in MacKenzie 1984). If done effectively, individual workers would be properly indoctrinated, and education would fulfill Walter Reuther's charge to "organize the organized." The purpose was for labor education to "build greater loyalty to the labor movement."[1]

Alternatively, an ideal type focused on the individual union member's ideological and philosophical development would mean offering courses on political theory, economics (including Keynesianism and Marxism), cultural identity, and teaching that addressed race, gender, and class. The objective from this standpoint was to raise workers' class consciousness to help them become "active, self-determined members of society" (Schachhuber 1979: 151). Here the attention was less on skills development and organizational behavior—and more on personal transformation that contributed to a more equitable and just society. Labor education would be fundamentally political, and the workplace understood as a political space where power is asserted and class relations formed.

Consensus largely settled on the former approach and tracked the labor movement's evolution with large capital firms. Providing classes to union officers and paid staff on how to better do their jobs representing millions of union workers was consistent with the organizational development of an institution impacting thousands of workplaces. Educating members about what their unions do and trying to establish the loyalty of those workers to their unions was essential to developing the labor movement as a countervailing power to big capital. Labor education would be first and foremost about union building. Two concurrent developments shaped this emergent labor educational paradigm.

First, influenced by the field of industrial relations pioneered decades earlier by John R. Commons, university-based labor education programs proliferated in the late 1940s.[2] Second, following the AFL-CIO merger in 1955, business unionism and compromise between labor and capital dominated industrial relations practice. The industrial relations model accepted institutional parties committed to workplace harmony. Consequently, the industrial relations educational curriculum prioritized the common interests of labor and management.

After World War II, labor unions were powerful institutions influencing the growth of the economy and shaping political outcomes. They were part of the "social contract." Labor education, therefore, needed to reflect the growing legitimacy of labor as a pillar of America's post-war leadership. The goal was to help union officers become community leaders who would achieve and preserve industrial peace. As university industrial relations programs expanded and recognized labor's institutional prominence, in 1962 the labor movement and academic labor educators drafted the first statement "defining their respective roles in developing educational services" (cited in "Joint Statement" 1977).[1] The resulting agreement centered on labor extension, noncredit university teaching that developed basic skills by offering "tool" courses, and de-emphasizing broader political, economic and social questions.

In 1977, labor educators and their union patrons reaffirmed their educational commitments. "The purpose of labor education is to prepare labor leaders, potential leaders, and interested members for more effective participation in their organizations and, as citizens, in a democratic society" ("Joint Statement" 1977). In 1985, the AFL-CIO's Committee on the Evolution of Work urged unions to "devote greater resources to train officers, stewards, and rank-and-file members" (Gray and Kornbluh 1991: 569).

To some, it was an unfortunate overconcentration on basic skills training influenced by conservative union leaders. In truth, the early years of worker education never rested comfortably with many national labor leaders, especially those affiliated with the AFL. As noted earlier, the AFL condemned Brookwood College as "radical" in 1928. By the 1950s, the popular education trainings developed at Highlander and Brookwood were viewed by most union leaders as subversive and in need of excising. In their place was a fixation on solving union-specific problems and an abandonment of larger ideological and political projects. It was arguably a "taming of worker education" that de-emphasized labor as a societal force for "social reconstruction" and political change in America (Tarlau 2011: 364). Instead of training workers for "conscious class action," labor education would function primarily to socialize workers toward meeting union organizational needs.

Labor Studies After World War II

After World War II, industrial relations developed as an academic field. A couple of decades later, universities and colleges also began incrementally to offer degrees in labor studies to union members (Dwyer 1977). Labor studies possesses a different academic orientation than industrial relations. Whereas industrial relations concentrates on labor–management relations, the mission of labor studies is to explore the multidimensional aspects of a worker's life experience and the role that unions play in society. In 1968, Rutgers offered the first labor studies degree. By the late 1970s, there were roughly 50 institutions of higher education offering majors or credit classes in labor studies. The majority were community colleges that used an open admission system (waived the need for test scores) to enroll students. The AFL-CIO sponsored its own credit program initially in partnership with Antioch College and through the George Meany National Labor College until its closing in 2014.

Unlike labor education, labor studies was either a two- or four-year academic course of study leading to an associate's or baccalaureate degree. The curricula varied widely but most consisted of a combination of traditional leadership courses (e.g., collective bargaining, labor history, union administration, and labor law) and liberal arts subjects (e.g., philosophy, political science, sociology, economics, literature). Labor studies courses took the individual worker as the subject of personal development through an examination of ideas pertinent to work, workplaces, worker organizations, and the social contexts in which they were embedded. Unlike a class designed to teach a specific union-related task, these courses were meant to inspire a critique of society. With a labor studies background or degree, union members would be better able to advocate for societal transformation on behalf of workers. This course of study was open both to union members and traditional college students interested in working for a labor union or in the labor relations field.

Labor educators and union officials did not greet the introduction of university labor studies degree programs uniformly. At the annual meeting of the University and College Labor Education Association (precursor to United Association for Labor Education, UALE), the issue of "credentialism" was constantly debated. Some educators argued that credit classes were a "distortion and even a corruption of traditional labor values" (Gray 1977: 19). Labor educators were warned that the "academization of labor education" would impair labor education's commitment to meet the needs of union members to strengthen the role of unions as a countervailing power to business (Lieberthal 1977).

Whatever the pros and cons of credentialing are, union member enrollments in labor studies degree programs have never been extensive. Most instructional hours for workers are in noncredit, extension settings. The critical question is not whether certificate or degree programs should coexist. There is need and intellectual justification for both. In fact, the extensive levels of income inequality and concentration of wealth in America have underscored the urgency of adopting degree programs that focus on the role of work in society. Nonetheless, many union members will continue to be reached in noncredit settings. Therefore, to continue being relevant, university programs have had to seriously consider the substance of their labor education offerings. Relevancy, however, was dependent on the purpose for labor education.

Labor Education in the 1990s

While fundamental to union behavior, the reliance on organizational efficiency proved to be too narrow a basis for building a relevant theory of worker education from the 1950s through the 1980s. Massive changes to labor markets forced international flows of human migration, disruptive technologies, deep erosion of the social contract, fierce corporate defense of unregulated capitalism, political assaults on organized labor, fissured work relations, and the creation of a class of workers who are not employees diminished the value of basic skills training. Unions still needed to file grievances and bargain contracts. Organizational competency mattered more than ever. But neoliberal economic hegemony was destroying the political foundation upon which workers were entitled to representation. The results were devastating. Unions continued to bring unfair labor cases before regulatory boards, file arbitration cases, sign new collective bargaining agreements, fund political campaigns, mobilize members to vote, and for a while, with the growth in public sector workers, organize new members. They also saw their density in the private sector fall precipitously. The question persevered, "Labor education, for what?"

University labor educators could train union leaders and raise worker awareness of labor's origin story, but while labor's house was being fortified, the ground underneath was disappearing. Something was missing. It was certainly good to know how to move a grievance to step two or negotiate contract language. Contracts and the law had to be enforced. However, if labor's ability to influence larger economic and political outcomes was eroding, at what point would nothing meaningful be left to enforce? John Sweeney's win in the first contested AFL-CIO presidential election, in 1995, ignited a flowering of nontraditional educational ideas. Sweeney encouraged academics to develop classes to deepen the critical thinking of union members. Classes on economics, which in some cases compared the thinking of Ricardo, Keynes, Marx, and Friedman, were developed. Additionally, instead of simply "get out the vote" training, classes on the rise of the New Right and class-based political theory were taught. The core theme was organize or die. The emphasis shifted from "servicing" (i.e., contract enforcement) to consciousness raising and membership activism.

New curricula also poured out of the AFL-CIO's Organizing Institute and Education Department. Among others, they stressed internal organizing, organizational transformation ("change to organize"), economic (or "pocketbook") literacy, and raising a worker's understanding of post-Reagan political shifts. University labor educators affiliated with the UALE were invited to participate in professional development and to recommend curriculum ideas. Many higher education instructors faithfully complied. Most were subsequently trained and enthusiastically offered classes to the unions and central labor bodies within their jurisdictions. Some found takers, but others saw little change in the composition of their trainings, and everyone accumulated thick, three-holed instructor curriculum guides. But labor's membership trajectory continued declining, and union identity as a predictor of political behavior further receded. Globalization, neoliberalism, and bipartisan political retreat from Joe Hill's notion of an "all for one and one for all" union challenged labor educators to reconceptualize labor education, which had become less focused on societal transformation over the last half century (Hill 1910). This outcome may have been different if labor studies degree programs had been more strongly supported after their formation.

LABOR EDUCATION FOR THE 21ST CENTURY

As labor educators retool their programs for the remainder of the 21st century, one theme has been paramount. Programming should align with the internal changes that labor unions must make to increase their ability to represent and lift up *all* workers. Educators, as well as a number of unions, have cited falling union density, rapidly spreading anti-union state laws, reduced union political potency, lack of member activism, tensions within the membership over hot-button issues, inability to organize nontraditional workers, race and gender inequities in representation and leadership, union structure, and the lack of worker rights literacy as areas subject to reassessment. Programs have subsequently introduced trainings to address all of those concerns. They have done so with one purpose in mind: to improve the capacity of organized labor to bring justice for *all* workers. Labor education continues to recognize the essentialism of organized labor to advancing societal justice and has adopted a curriculum that is essential to responding to the ambiguities of a changing work landscape.

Under any imagined future scenario, workers (by any name) will continue to be subject to exploitation. No matter the evolution of work itself—be it done directly or by operating drones—the folks who do the labor will create the value. Whether it is exchanged on an app or through an employment office, labor power will be exercised for profit. Even the most benign "future of work" will necessitate vibrant worker organizations. The labor movement recognized that work and employment relations were changing and has sought to bring attention to the subject. For example, in 2017, the AFL-CIO authorized the formation of its Commission on the Future of Work and Unions. A year later, it held a public conference of the commission, called "The Future of Work in a Digital Age." In both cases, the labor movement's continued relevance to workers was associated with an ability to appeal to new workers and adapt to novel forms of work.

In turn, labor educators recognized that for a workers' movement to grow, classes would need to address labor market changes, opportunities to expand unionization, and strategies to nourish an activist base. While it is not the objective of this chapter to provide a summary of every creative university labor education program, there are six areas of contemporary study that deserve mention and encouragement. These subjects are and will continue to be particularly impactful, no matter the shifting contours of work.

The first area of study is immigration. People will, much as they always have, immigrate to the United States for work. Unfortunately, organized labor has had a vacillating relationship with immigration policy and immigrant workers. While the AFL-CIO reversed its historic opposition to immigration in 2000, the willingness of unions to expose leadership and membership to immigration education has been tepid at best. Retired labor educator Bruce Nissen notes in a published case study of a university training focused on immigrant workers that unions "unable or unwilling to incorporate immigrants or to develop leadership from their ranks will inevitably fail to grow" (2002: 110). In 2018, staff at the University of Illinois' Labor Education Program took part in a weeklong AFL-CIO train-the-trainer course on immigration. The training was designed so that university labor education programs and individual unions could conduct their own immigration workshops.

The second area of study is young workers. Any structural changes in how work is done will logically be inherited by workers entering the labor force. Consequently, education for and with young workers is considered "key to [labor's] renewal strategies" (Larouche and Dufour-Poirier 2017: 101). In 2009, the AFL-CIO signaled the importance of youth-focused education programs with the publication of its "Young Workers: A Lost Decade" report. The federation followed up by forming its Next Up Young Worker Program and Young Worker Advisory Council. Labor education classes on developing members under 30 years of age into future union leaders proliferated and coincided with young worker groups formed within several unions. AFL-CIO president Richard Trumka acknowledged the linkage between unionism and a changing work landscape: "We need a unionism that makes sense to the next generation" (Shuler and Marschall 2014: 6). The future of work and the American labor movement are dependent on young workers. Labor education that helps unions reposition themselves to be "truly relevant to contemporary youth" will be itself relevant (Shuler and Marschall 2014).

In addition, matching labor education to the importance of union transformation included programs on investing in women union leaders. Since 1976, UALE's Midwest School for Women Workers has brought "working women together to develop leadership skills, understand the challenges and issues facing the labor movement, and learn from one another" (University of Illinois School of Labor and Employment Relations, no date). The labor school at the University of Illinois, for example, has run an annual women's labor leadership program for nearly 40 years.[3] In the past few years, the Illinois program has added an advanced leadership component.

Fourth, labor education that supports the strengthening of a broad-based labor movement includes addressing the economic status of people of color generally and racism directly. Classes that provide space for trade union members to confront the perpetuation of racial inequities and discrimination in society, the workplace, and the labor movement are critical to labor's survival and offered in diverse formats. Some training exclusively focuses, for example, on Black and Latinx workers' labor history and leadership development. Others encompass a racial lens in discussing politics or union governance. They all embody a recognition that once "black workers construct a dialectical relationship with the labor movement, organized labor will develop the means to drive social transformation in the United States" (Wood 2019: 397).

A fifth subject is how labor educators treat teaching about politics. The self-defeating occurrence since 1972 of a substantial percentage of union members voting for anti-labor public officials and on the basis of noneconomic issues (e.g., gun rights, gender and sexual liberation, religious identity, abortion, nationalism, crime, drug use) inspired programs to tackle political ideology more directly.

Classes on "Gays, Guns, Government, and God" or others similarly titled were designed to reveal the origins, growth, and machinations of right-wing conservatism.[4] The learning objective included helping workers to understand that antagonistic business and civic forces were endeavoring to tear workers from their class affinities. In response, labor educators developed trainings with a sharper-pointed political critique. Classes emphasized the importance of labor leaders acting on an expansive political terrain that spoke to the tribulations of a broader working class. For some educators, it was a "radical-lite" pedagogy; for others it was "social-movement unionism," and there were others still who insisted that an anti-capitalistic framing be taught that would change the world through class struggle (Dolgon and Roth 2016).

Finally, labor education really needs to encompass *worker education*. Falling union density has meant that a burgeoning labor force is either working "at will" or without statutory protections and rights. In response, labor educators have turned increasingly to doing something contrary to the legacy of labor education: they are educating non-union workers. Nonrepresented workers, including many who do not speak English as their primary language, are employed in hourly low-wage sectors, misclassified gig jobs, and part-time positions and are the most vulnerable in society. Most are legally documented, but some are not. With union density in the private sector at approximately 6%, there is a substantial and growing non-union labor force in need of education. Paralleling the expansion of worker centers and partnering with community advocacy groups and worker development organizations, labor educators have developed "worker rights literacy" trainings.[5] Classes are taught directly to workers and to organizational leaders in a train-the-trainer format. When conducted with government and community organizations, the classes include a detailed "how to" trainer's manual. Worker education designed for non-union–represented workers is a new terrain for university labor education programs. Nonetheless, it is hard to imagine how labor unions will persevere and prosper without the unorganized being educated about their employment rights.

CONCLUSION

In this chapter, we have endeavored to chronicle the evolution of labor education in the United States. With a focus on historical and contemporary examples, we identified two periods of labor education. The first, occurring in the first half of the 20th century, was delivered by independent labor colleges that provided trade unionists and workers with classes focused on societal transformation and basic courses in labor relations. The second unfolded after World War II, when collective bargaining was institutionalized in the country. Labor education now primarily emphasizes "tool" courses for union officers and members, along with credit classes in industrial relations for traditional students through university-based labor education and labor studies programs.

Although early US worker education and labor colleges from the early 1900s to the mid-20th century did not lead to societal transformation as hoped, there were, nonetheless, significant achievements registered. One common denominator of these labor colleges was that they combined both rigorous academic coursework with student and faculty participation in the US trade union movement and related activities where they practiced the principles, concepts, and ideas learned in the classroom. Moreover, surveys of Brookwood graduates from 1926 and 1931 indicated that alumni had significantly contributed to the trade union movement in becoming union organizers, grievance committee representatives, business agents, labor journalists, and teachers and administrators at other labor colleges, as well as Socialist and Communist party officers (Barrow 1990: 402). While Commonwealth College and Highlander also trained US labor movement participants (Altenbaugh 1990: 253; Horton 1989: 103), Brookwood numerically outstripped those other colleges in developing CIO activists (Altenbaugh 1990: 256–265).

Early US worker education and the US labor colleges provided workers with knowledge that work and workplaces could be organized differently and that those workers could be societal transformation agents. Moreover, early labor education helped to build the industrial unions so that, today, societal transformation programming can aid in the revitalization of the union movement. If labor education engages with broader working-class issues such as climate change, affordable housing, and progressive taxation, for example, and trains unions to employ Bargaining for the Common Good, the labor movement repositions itself to grow and to speak for unorganized workers as well.

With collective bargaining's institutionalization after the CIO's stabilization upon World War II's conclusion, university-based labor education became the leading mode of delivery from the 1950s to the present. From the 1950s to the 1980s, the institutionalist model dominated industrial relations as it did labor education, which emphasized pursuit of the "social contract" between labor and capital. As such, labor education focused on presenting "tool" courses for unions (and their members) in fulfilling their roles in obtaining the objectives of business unionism. By the 1990s, it had become clear that labor was in trouble, with massive deindustrialization, advancing neoliberalism, and plummeting union density. When John Sweeney was elected AFL-CIO president in 1995, labor education was at least temporarily reinvigorated with the inclusion of courses emphasizing the increasing consciousness and member activism of trade unionists. Despite these innovative developments in labor education, unions (as well as non-union workers) remained under heavy assault.

As labor education enters the 21st century's third decade, labor educators must instruct unionists and workers on controversial issues such as immigration, reach out to young workers who represent the future of any labor movement, continue to develop women trade union leaders, teach about racism and the economic inequality experienced by people of color, emphasize the increasing importance of politics while devising strategies to combat the extant right-wing populism, and reintroduce worker education to workers not in the traditional labor movement but involved in worker centers and community organizations.

Labor educators must also take advantage of opportunities for increased worker engagement as current events rapidly unfold. The COVID-19 pandemic beginning in the spring of 2020 has demonstrated capitalism's extreme vulnerabilities in generating societal inequality. It has further demonstrated how many workers are taking extreme risks to their well-being while delivering crucial goods and services (e.g., grocery store workers, truck drivers, warehouse workers, healthcare workers). In addition, as tens of millions of unemployed workers struggle to survive in an economy both dependent on their labor and unwilling to secure it, their vulnerability has never been more obvious. While "being" never completely determines consciousness, labor and worker educators have been presented with a radically transformed terrain for conducting future education. If, to modify a point that Marx made about philosophy, the purpose of labor education is not simply to help workers better understand the world but to change it, then educators may now have an opening to reach workers who have been forever impacted by their current experiences.

ENDNOTES

1. The statement was drafted by the University and College Labor Education Association, the American Association of Junior and Community Colleges, the AFL-CIO, and international unions at the Joint Labor Education Conference held at the Walter and May Reuther UAW Family Education Center in November 1976.

2. The University of Wisconsin School of Workers was formed in 1924, and by the late 1970s, 37 programs existed in 25 states. For example, the University of Illinois' Institute (later upgraded to School) of Labor and Employment Relations opened in 1947.

3. The Regina V. Polk Women's Labor Leadership Conference is a four-day residential conference made possible through the generosity of the Regina V. Polk Fund for Labor Leadership (https://bit.ly/39SILMa).

4. Professor Robert Bruno (University of Illinois) and Lisa Jordan (currently the Education Director of the United Steelworkers Union) developed and taught a multiple-unit class on political economy that used the four G's made infamous by Richard Nixon and Ronald Reagan to win support from rank-and-file workers.

5. Alison Dickson is a senior instructor in the Labor Education Program in the School of Labor and Employment Relations at the University of Illinois. In addition to teaching employment rights, she developed, with the assistance of colleagues, a curriculum manual on teaching worker rights. The manual is in its third edition.

REFERENCES

Altenbaugh, Richard J. 1990. *Education for Struggle: The American Labor Colleges of the 1920s and 1930s*. Philadelphia, PA: Temple University Press.

Barrow, Clyde W. 1990. "Counter-Movement Within the Labor Movement: Workers' Education and the American Federation of Labor, 1900–1937." *Social Science Journal* 27 (4): 395–418.

Barrow, Clyde W. 1991. "Playing Workers: Proletarian Drama in the Curriculum of American Labor Colleges, 1921–1937." *Journal of Arts Management and Law* 20 (4): 5–29.

Bloom, Jonathan D. 1990a. "Brookwood Labor College." In *The Re-education of the American Working Class*, edited by Steven H. London, Elvira R. Tarr, and Joseph F. Wilson, eds., pp. 71–83. Westport, CT: Greenwood Press.

Bloom, Jonathan D. 1990b. "Brookwood Labor College: The Final Years, 1933–1937." *Labor's Heritage* 2 (2): 24–43.

Cobb, William H. 1964. "Commonwealth College Comes to Arkansas, 1923–1925." *The Arkansas Historical Quarterly* 23 (2): 99–122.

Cobb, William H. 1973. "From Utopian Isolation to Radical Activism: Commonwealth College, 1925–1935." *The Arkansas Historical Quarterly* 32 (2): 132–147.

Cobb, William H. 2000. *Radical Education in the Rural South: Commonwealth College, 1922–1940*. Detroit, MI: Wayne State University Press.

Cobb, William H., and Donald H. Grubbs. 1966. "Arkansas' Commonwealth College and the Southern Tenant Farmers' Union." *The Arkansas Historical Quarterly* 25 (4): 293–311.

Dolgon, Corey, and Reuben Roth. 2016. "Twenty-First-Century Workers' Education in North America: The Defeat of the Left or a Revitalized Class Pedagogy?" *Labor Studies Journal* 41 (1): 89–113.

Dwyer, Richard. 1977. "Workers' Education, Labor Education, Labor Studies: An Historical Delineation." *Review of Educational Research* 47 (1): 179–207.

Gettleman, Marvin E. 2002. "No Varsity Teams: New York's Jefferson School of Social Science, 1943–1956." *Science & Society* 66 (3): 336–359.

Glen, John M. 1996. *Highlander: No Ordinary School*. Knoxville, TN: University of Tennessee Press.

Grabiner, Gene. 1979. "Conservative Labor Leaders Clean House: The Case of Brookwood Labor College." *Educational Theory* 29 (3): 195–209.

Gray, Lois S. 1977. "Academic Degrees for Labor Studies—A New Goal for Unions." *Monthly Labor Review* 100 (6): 15–20.

Gray, Lois, and Joyce Kornbluh. 1991. "New Directions in Labor Education." *Proceedings of the Spring Meetings*, Chicago, IL, Apr. 25–27, 1991, pp. 569–574. Madison, WI: Industrial Relations Research Association.

Hill, Joe. 1910. "'Workers of the World, Awaken!' by Joe Hill." Songs and Poems. *Zinn Education Project*. https://bit.ly/36Okvck

Horton, Aimee Isgrig. 1989. *The Highlander Folk School: A History of its Major Programs, 1932–1961*. Brooklyn, NY: Carlson.

Howlett, Charles F. 1981. "Organizing the Unorganized: Brookwood Labor College, 1921–1937." *Labor Studies Journal* 6 (2): 165–179.

Howlett, Charles F. 1993. *Brookwood Labor College and the Struggle for Peace and Social Justice in America*. Lewiston, NY: Edwin Mellen.

Jeffrey, Terence P. 2019 (Jun. 7). "12,839,000: Manufacturing Jobs at Highest Level Since 2008," June 7. *CSN News*. https://bit.ly/3ruNfi5

"Joint Statement on Effective Cooperation Between Organized Labor and Higher Education." 1977. *Labor Studies Journal* 1 (3): 291–295.

Koch, Raymond, and Charlotte Koch. 1972. *Educational Commune: The Story of Commonwealth College*. New York, NY: Schocken Books.

Larouche, Melanie, and Melanie Dufour-Poirier. 2017. "Revitalizing Union Representation Through Labor Education Initiatives: An Examination of Two Trade Unions in Quebec." *Labor Studies Journal* 42 (2): 99–123.

Lieberthal, Mil. 1977. "On the Academization of Labor Education." *Labor Studies Journal* 1 (3): 235–245.

MacKenzie, Robert. 1984. *Organized Labor Education and Training Programs*. Columbus, OH: National Center for Research in Adult, Career and Vocational Education, Ohio State University.

Nash, Al. 1981. *Ruskin College: A Challenge to Adult and Labor Education*. Ithaca, NY: New York State School of Industrial and Labor Relations.

Nissen, Bruce. 2002. "The Role of Labor Education in Transforming a Union Toward Organizing Immigrants: A Case Study." *Labor Studies Journal* 27 (1): 109–127.

Peters, Ronald J., and Jeanne M. McCarrick. 1976. "Roots of Public Support for Labor Education 1900–1945." *Labor Studies Journal* 1 (2): 109–129.

Preskill, Stephen. 1991. "'We Can Live Freedom:' The Highlander Folk School as a Model for Civic Education." *Social Science Record* 28 (2): 11–21.

Recchiuti, John L. 1995. "The Rand School of Social Science During the Progressive Era: Will to Power of a Stratum of the American Intellectual Class." *Journal of the History of the Behavioral Sciences* 31 (2): 149–161.

Robinson, James W. 1968. "The Expulsion of Brookwood Labor College from the Workers' Education Bureau." *Labour History* 15 (Nov.): 64–69.

Sandler, Mark. 1985. "Workers Must Read: The Commonwealth College Library, 1925–1940." *The Journal of Library History (1974–1987)* 20 (1): 46–69.

Schachhuber, Dieter. 1979. "The Missing Link in Labor Education." *Labor Studies Journal* 4 (2): 148–156.

Schmidman, John, John Marrone, and John Remington. 1990. "Labor Education as a Method of Enhancing Employee Rights and Responsibilities." *Employee Responsibilities and Rights Journal* 3 (4): 291–305.

Shuler, Elizabeth, and Daniel Marschall. 2014. "AFL-CIO Initiative Mobilizes Young Workers." *Perspectives on Work* 18 (1): 6–9, 103.

Tarlau, Rebecca. 2011. "Education and Labor in Tension: Contemporary Debates about Education in the US Labor Movement." *Labor Studies Journal* 36 (3): 363–387.

University of Illinois, School of Labor and Employment Relations. No date. "Midwest School for Women Workers." https://bit.ly/3oRKG8d

Wood, Augustus. 2019. "The Crisis of the Black Worker, the U.S. Labor Movement, and Democracy for All." *Labor Studies Journal* 44 (4): 396–402.

PART III
REPRODUCTIVE WORK AS A
CRUCIBLE OF INNOVATION

The Future of Work for Domestic Workers in the United States: Innovations in Technology, Organizing, and Laws

ELAINE ZUNDL
Harvard Kennedy School

YANA VAN DER MEULEN RODGERS
Rutgers University

ABSTRACT

This study explores how domestic worker organizations are innovating in the context of the future of work. These organizations and the workers they represent are using innovations not only in organizing domestic worker bill of rights campaigns but also in creating new digital platforms with portable benefits, strengthening efforts to prevent wage theft, and reconceptualizing collective bargaining strategies to address the poor working conditions experienced by domestic workers. We use a qualitative approach focusing on interviews with New Jersey advocates and other stakeholders involved with domestic workers to provide a novel depiction of how they are engaged in different kinds of collective action in pursuit of greater domestic worker rights. The interview results provide insight into how the innovations improve the terms of employment for domestic workers and ensure that their remuneration matches the value of their work.

INTRODUCTION

Paid care workers in private households across the United States face significant challenges because of the low value attached to care work and the difficulty of regulating work that occurs in private homes. Labor law violations, lack of social protections, and precarious terms of employment are endemic among domestic workers. Low wages and poor working conditions are problematic not only for domestic workers but also the people they care for because the quality of care may be compromised. These concerns have gained increasing attention as the aging US population outsources more of its caring labor to paid workers, especially women of color and women migrants from lower-income countries. The COVID-19 pandemic has further highlighted the plight of paid care workers. Many lost their jobs as a result of the necessary measures taken to slow the spread, while those who remained employed were deemed as essential healthcare workers but were generally not provided adequate personal protective equipment to keep safe.

Most domestic workers in the United States are women (92%), and about one third are immigrants—a much higher ratio than other occupations. In the global chain of care, domestic workers are doing the care work that makes other women's paid employment possible. This substitution of paid for unpaid care work typically performed by women applies not only to childcare, but also to the care of elderly, sick, and disabled family members, as well as performing household tasks such as housecleaning. Domestic workers earn some of the lowest wages among all occupations and chronically experience wage theft, including receiving wages below the minimum, having wages withheld arbitrarily and without recourse, or not being paid overtime. The lack of formal contracts and predictable work schedules are also common problems. The growing use of Internet-based technology to hire care workers and housekeepers in the "gig economy" has contributed to the insecure nature of domestic work, and workers without access to the Internet have been placed at a disadvantage in access to jobs. Sexual harassment, sexual abuse, and other forms of physical abuse also plague domestic workers, problems compounded by the fact that their work takes place in the private sphere. This issue has gained increasing attention in the wake of the global #MeToo movement, but the problem persists. In response to poor working conditions, nine states and two municipalities have passed some version of a domestic worker bill of rights (DWBOR) in which workers are guaranteed the minimum wage, overtime, rest periods, paid vacation time, disability benefits, and/or protection from sexual harassment and discrimination.

This study explores how domestic worker organizations such as unions, nonprofit organizations, co-ops, and immigrant rights groups are innovating in the context of the future of work. These organizations and the workers they represent are using innovations not only in organizing DWBOR campaigns but also in creating new digital platforms with portable benefits, strengthening efforts to prevent wage theft, and reconceptualizing collective bargaining strategies to address the poor working conditions experienced by domestic workers. We use a qualitative approach focusing on interviews with New Jersey advocates and other stakeholders involved with domestic workers to provide a novel depiction of how they are engaged in different kinds of collective action in the pursuit of greater domestic worker rights. The interviews provide insight into these four types of innovations that are designed to improve the terms of employment for domestic workers and ensure that their remuneration matches the value of their work. This chapter will proceed in three sections. First, we explain the industry context of domestic work and the recent trends in this workforce. Then, we explain our interviews with domestic worker advocates. The main part of the paper provides an analysis of the four types of innovations that are aimed at improving conditions for domestic workers. We conclude with implications of the findings for post-pandemic approaches to domestic worker rights.

DOMESTIC WORK: INDUSTRY BACKGROUND

Collective action in pursuit of better working conditions and higher pay for domestic workers has a long history in the United States. Often considered one of the earliest catalysts of this movement, in 1881, close to 3,000 predominantly African American women in Atlanta went on strike to protest their low pay as washerwomen. Atlanta's washerwomen's strike led to higher pay and more autonomy for the city's domestics, and it encouraged women in other low-pay caregiving occupations to use similar tactics to obtain better wages and working conditions. Over the years, despite preconceptions that housekeepers, nannies, and personal assistants were unable to organize, various groups formed and mobilized together to push for higher pay and better working conditions (Boris and Nadasen 2008). Frustration over the exemption of domestic workers from federal and state-level labor codes helped to fuel these efforts to engage in collective action, as did numerous high-profile stories of worker rights violations (Hondagneu-Sotelo 2007).

Historically, domestic workers in the United States have been excluded from major pieces of legislation to protect workers, including the 1935 Social Security Act (which gave workers the right to a pension and unemployment insurance), the 1935 National Labor Relations Act (which gave workers the right to organize into trade unions and bargain collectively), and the 1938 Fair Labor Standards Act (FLSA), which granted workers the right to a minimum wage and overtime pay for hours beyond a 40-hour work week. It took more than 30 years of pressure from various stakeholders for Congress to amend the FLSA in 1974 and grant most domestic workers the right to earn the minimum wage and overtime pay, including undocumented immigrants. However, certain categories of domestic workers continued to be exempted from the minimum wage and overtime regulations, including casual babysitters and workers who provided "companionship services" to the elderly and to disabled, sick, or injured individuals. Live-in domestic workers were also exempted from the right to overtime pay, although they were entitled to earn the federal minimum wage for all hours worked. The US Department of Labor further amended the FLSA in 2015 to expand coverage to more types of direct care givers, including home health aides, personal care assistants, nursing aides, and other professional caregivers (US Department of Labor 2018). Moreover, in 2016, Congress proposed an amendment to prevent wage theft and to increase employer liability in lawsuits filed by workers to recover stolen wages (the Wage Theft Prevention and Wage Recovery Act), but the legislation did not move past the committee stage. Thus, while there has been progress in increasing protections, it has been slow and incomplete.

As shown in Figure 1, the absolute number of domestic workers in the United States has risen steadily, from 1.7 million in 2003 to almost 2.5 million by 2019.[1] Growth in the number of home health aides, especially those who are employed by an agency, accounts for all of this increase.[2] Both the share and the absolute number of nannies, housecleaners, and home-based daycare providers have fallen over time. By 2019, agency-based home health aides comprised 58% of all domestic workers, up from just 35% in 2003. In contrast, the proportion of domestic workers employed as home-based daycare providers dropped from about one quarter to 11% during the period, reflecting both the decline in the absolute number of home daycare providers and the large increase in the number of home health aides.

Domestic workers are predominantly women. As shown in Table 1, 92% of all domestic workers in the years 2017 through 2019 were women, with an even higher percentage for housecleaners, nannies, and home daycare providers. About one third of domestic workers are immigrants, either naturalized or not naturalized. This share is higher than for nondomestic workers. Also of interest is the relatively high representation of non-naturalized immigrants among housecleaners (51%) relative to the other job categories (18% or less). Cleaning work is generally the least valued and most invisible, and it employs a disproportionate number of non-naturalized immigrants.

The invisible nature of domestic work is problematic because it reproduces a paradigm where disadvantaged and marginalized populations are forced to perform the labor of social reproduction. With a limited government infrastructure

Figure 1
Number of Domestic Workers in the U.S. by Category, 2003–2019

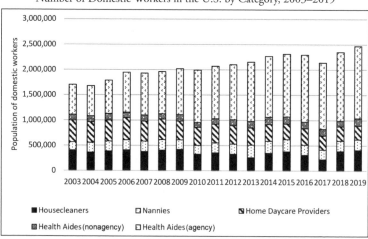

Source: Constructed using Current Population Survey Outgoing Rotation Group microdata for 2003–2019.

Table 1
Domestic Workers in the United States by Gender,
Citizenship Status, and Race, 2017–2019 (percentages)

	Nondomestic Workers	Domestic Workers	House-cleaners	Nannies	Home Daycare Providers	Health Aides (Nonagency)	Health Aides (Agency)
Gender							
Women	46.2	91.6	96.0	98.1	97.4	85.8	88.9
Men	53.8	8.4	4.0	1.9	2.6	14.2	11.1
Nativity							
US born	82.8	64.5	30.6	71.6	69.9	74.1	69.9
US naturalized	8.5	15.0	18.4	10.9	12.6	10.9	15.6
Immigrant not naturalized	8.8	20.5	51.0	17.6	17.6	14.9	14.5
Race/ethnicity							
White	63.0	40.8	28.0	63.7	52.9	49.8	37.3
Black	11.3	21.5	6.3	7.5	13.1	19.7	29.3
Hispanic	17.1	29.1	61.7	24.1	29.5	20.2	22.5
Asian	6.2	5.9	2.0	2.9	3.1	5.5	7.8
Other	2.4	2.7	2.0	1.9	1.4	4.8	3.1

Source: Constructed using Current Population Survey Outgoing Rotation Group pooled microdata for 2017–2019.

to support care work, families have turned to the market to obtain these services. Low-wage and time-intensive reproductive work is disproportionately performed by women of color and enabled by legal, political, and economic exclusions that have prevented people of color from organizing and competing for better paying jobs. The legacy of these exclusions helps to explain why migrant women of color make up a substantial proportion of workers in these jobs. Undocumented women are frequently tracked into domestic work because of constraints they face from immigration policies combined with the lack of public regulation of private homes (Rodríguez 2007). Lingering fear of deportation creates a situation of constant vigilance that makes forming political alliances very difficult.

While the domestic work industry provides essential services to families, the critical care work that domestic workers provide remains one of the most unregulated in the United States (Bernhardt, DeFilippis, and McGrath 2007). Wages and working conditions are often negotiated individually between household employers and domestic worker, making regulation and enforcement weak. Even when domestic workers are employed by an agency, wages are still low and enforcement of labor laws is still problematic. The burden of ensuring compliance with regulations and negotiating for fair working conditions falls largely on the shoulders of the workers themselves, the majority of whom are women. As a result, compensation and working conditions can vary greatly. Domestic workers also face various classification issues, including misclassification. In the case of domestic workers employed by an agency, if they are dispatched to work with different client households, they are often classified as independent contractors. This misclassification deprives the workers of important workplace protections such as the minimum wage, overtime, workers compensation, and health and safety regulations. Domestic workers who work for multiple families are often referred to as "live out" workers, in direct contrast to "live in" workers who reside full-time in the family's home and often provide overlapping responsibilities including childcare, cooking, and cleaning.[3] Most housecleaners work as live-outs and work for multiple households per week, thus piecing together jobs to create full-time employment. Housecleaners and other day laborers are often not protected under paid sick time or workers compensation mandates— not because the law expressly excludes them but owing to the nature of their employment relationships. When domestic workers work for multiple employers, they are unable to accrue the required working-hour thresholds to qualify for such protections. Workers who are employed full-time with a single employer are subject to greater protection.

What data there are on the working conditions faced by domestic workers in the United States paint a rather bleak picture of low pay, labor law violations, and poor conditions. A benchmark 2012 report, which sampled 2,086 domestic workers across 14 cities, found high rates of wage theft through various forms of underpayment and nonpayment of wages and overtime pay that workers were legally owed (Burnham and Theodore 2012). As shown in Figure 2, about one quarter of respondents earned less than the minimum wage, although that rate was higher for live-in domestic workers who had the value of room and board deducted from their cash wages. Almost 90% of domestic workers were not guaranteed overtime. Domestic workers also reported pressure from employers to engage in extra work. Lack of respect and no recognition for the value of their work are also common issues reported by domestic workers. Deeply intertwined with these problems are common perceptions that care work should be provided out of altruism and generosity rather than a desire for financial compensation.

Inadequate coverage for domestic workers in the FLSA and in state legislation, as well as poor enforcement of labor standards that do cover domestic workers, has contributed to a surge in collective action in pursuit of innovations to how domestic workers are paid and how their work is valued. The next section describes our methodology for exploring these innovations among domestic worker organizations.

PARTICIPANT INTERVIEWS

We conducted a set of semi-structured interviews with ten leaders from ten non-profit organizations that advocate for domestic workers, low-wage workers, and immigrants in New Jersey.[4] Our interviews, conducted in the fall of 2018,

Figure 2
Labor Standard Violations Among Domestic Workers in the United States

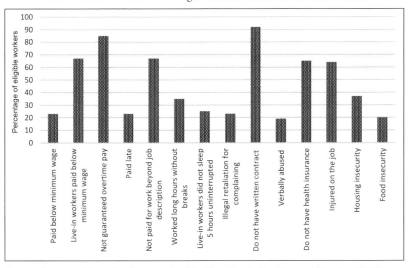

Source: Constructed from data for a sample of 2,086 workers in Burnham and Theodore (2012).

focused on the experiences of the domestic workers they represent, along with the actions they took to support their workers, including any possible engagement they had in organizing a DWBOR campaign. We first identified organizations for our sample by reaching out to those with a reputation for working with domestic workers and identified additional organizations through snowball sampling. We then conducted a set of additional interviews with representatives from two organizations outside of New Jersey that have developed worker-centered digital platforms for organizing domestic workers. The first organization, Up & Go, is a worker co-op for housecleaning and maid services in New York City. It is a second-generation co-op because it not only matches housecleaners with potential clients, but it also provides services that support the scaling up and development of new co-ops. Worker co-ops are considered a fairer way to organize low-wage workers such as domestic workers because the groups are self-governing, and they set standards. Such co-ops could leverage platforms to further benefit the workers who participate (Scholz and Schneider 2017). Funding and support for developing Up & Go came from a local nonprofit agency specializing in co-ops, a philanthropic organization, and the municipal government.

The second organization, Carina, is a partnership between the state of Washington and Service Employees International Union (SEIU) Local 775. Carina is a platform that connects home healthcare workers represented by SEIU with potential clients who use Medicare or Medicaid to pay for services. Either the home care worker or the potential client can use the platform to place an advertisement and to set up a meeting. A state caseworker is involved in the matching process to ensure that both parties meet eligibility requirements.

These interviews informed our study of innovations in digital platforms for domestic workers.

DOMESTIC WORKER INNOVATIONS

The interviews provide a better understanding of how worker rights advocates have engaged in collective action to pursue innovations in how domestic workers are paid, protected, and valued. These innovations, which are further explored in the remainder of this chapter, include (1) DWBOR legislation in various states, (2) new digital platforms, (3) wage theft recovery, and (4) reinforcement of collective bargaining efforts. Key stakeholders in these efforts include community-based groups (also known as worker centers) that aim to organize domestic workers and provide support along a number of dimensions, including education, training, occupational health, and legal assistance (Fine 2006; Milkman and Ott 2014). Several of these worker centers along with other advocacy groups and community organizations came together in 2007 to form the National Domestic Workers Alliance (NDWA), which has proven instrumental in pushing for more inclusive labor laws and stronger enforcement at the state level to protect domestic workers.

Domestic Worker Bill of Rights

As of October 2020, DWBOR legislation exists in ten states and two municipalities, with active campaigns under way in multiple states, including New Jersey. DWBOR legislation has included protection against discrimination and harassment, paid time off, meal and rest breaks, notice of termination, protection against retaliation, the right to written employment agreements, mandatory days off, support for workers to prepare their own meals, overtime, and family leave. The NDWA and affiliated organizations have used lessons learned from prior campaigns to improve on existing bills and address the core challenges that workers face. These efforts are often referred to as DWBOR 2.0 legislation.

In our interviews with New Jersey advocates, there was a sense that early DWBOR legislation was not inclusive of many of the issues that their workers were experiencing. Nonprofit leaders were generally familiar with a DWBOR because they collaborate with national organizations or advocates from other states who have worked on these campaigns. One of the organizers shared that they had luck passing legislation locally because the conditions in the area were particularly bad for domestic workers. This person's organization helped to pass a municipal resolution to support a bill of rights mandating that workers receive regular breaks while cleaning houses. When asked if this might lead to a statewide bill of rights, the interviewee stated that workers were skeptical that a DWBOR would address their needs: "The bill of rights was geared to nannies and people working in one home. It wasn't really applicable to their reality."

When asked about New York's DWBOR, some of our key informants distinguished between the needs of domestic workers in New York versus those in New Jersey. In their eyes, New York (especially New York City) appears to have a larger proportion of live-in domestic workers employed directly by private households. This relatively higher concentration of live-in workers makes the DWBOR—with its focus on days off, breaks, and overtime pay—appear more relevant in New York than in New Jersey. This view was not universal, however, as some of our key informants did have experience with live-in domestic workers. These findings suggest our informants were innovating based on the local context of their workers. One key informant stated, "I think part of the issue is that there isn't a union or an entity pushing a bill of rights or organizing, combined with the fact that in New York there is a greater density of people working in that industry."

The NDWA has shifted attention to addressing the limitations that the interviewees mentioned. More recent campaigns continue to fight for rights established in prior bills but also target the omission of private homes from Occupational Safety and Health Act (OSHA) regulations and the lack of collective bargaining rights to raise industry standards. Other important features of DWBOR 2.0 legislation include an increased focus on enforcing legislation against wage theft, especially by including models for co-enforcement between state and city agencies that facilitate a partnership with domestic worker centers and community organizations to do outreach and education to both workers and employers. These same centers and organizations would also be formalized into wage or worker standards boards that work as a tool to raise industry standards.

Legislation passed by the city of Seattle in 2018 represents a major innovation on prior DWBOR laws. This bill established new labor standards and protections for domestic workers, including a Domestic Workers Standards Board, which is charged with creating and implementing higher standards for workers, including higher wages, written contracts, and a portable benefits system. In 2019, in large part a result of pressure from the NDWA, Philadelphia passed a city-level bill of rights (Bill No. 190607), which included a portable benefits system for paid time off made available through an app. The legislation is innovative because it provides a stand-alone legal right to paid time off that will accrue and aggregate the hours worked by domestic workers from multiple employers, thereby ensuring that a greater number of domestic workers benefit from paid time off. This app, called Alia, allows employers and workers to opt into a benefit program. The program allows workers to accept contributions from multiple employers (or clients), and the benefits are attached to the worker.

New Digital Platforms

The new portable benefits systems in the Seattle and Philadelphia reforms are excellent examples of innovations in digital platforms used to connect workers with employers. Stakeholders who are pursuing innovations in how domestic workers are paid and valued are developing worker-centered digital platforms that facilitate access to benefits as well as new ways of organizing. The worker-centered platforms improve on earlier platforms such as Care.com that focus mostly on worker flexibility and responsiveness. Critics have objected to the way in which digital platforms have framed platform work as part of the sharing economy or as a vehicle for entrepreneurship. They argue that these narratives are partially responsible for the ability of digital-platform companies to exploit workers in the gig economy and capitalize on the lack of regulation in some industries like domestic work (Calo and Rosenblat 2017; Rosenblat, Levy, Barocas, and Hwang 2017; Sundararajan 2016). Although platforms like Care.com require the user to submit data on pay and documentation, workers complain that employers fail to comply with the rules. For example, pay rates in advertisements on a particular platform were not observed on the platform's private messaging feature, and actual weekly wages often fell below the minimum wage (Ticona and Mateescu 2018). For some, platforms such as Care.com are used more as an initial means of connecting the employer with the worker, and subsequent conversations are taken offline, thus limiting the accountability of household employers to adhere to the advertised pay rates.

Relatively more men than women are employed by platform-based companies as an additional source of income to supplement their day jobs; women tend to do platform work as their sole source of income (Forde et al. 2017). Bias against protected characteristics such as gender, race, and disability can negatively impact employment and earnings. This phenomenon is also known as "algorithmic discrimination" because of the ways in which automated technologies reinforce inequality (Rosenblat, Levy, Barocas, and Hwang 2017). Others argue that gender identity and sexual orientation are manipulated by different platforms in order to appeal to clients' gender-specific demands for workers (Schoenbaum 2016). Workers operating on digital platforms invest unpaid labor in advertising their services or cultivating a social media identity. This additional online work can be difficult for older workers who are less familiar with how to promote themselves online, and it can also disadvantage women who are more likely to be targets of online harassment. Moreover, gender pay gaps persist regardless of feedback scores, experience, occupational category, working hours, and educational attainment, which suggests that gender inequality is embedded in the operation of platforms (Barzilay and Ben-David 2016).

We used our interviews to explore the extent to which domestic workers and organizations that represent them have made innovations to better utilize digital platforms for finding employment and improving working conditions. In the two organizations we studied (Up & Go and Carina), workers were vocal partners in how these platforms were developed. In response to co-op workers' concerns about privacy, Up & Go decided against allowing potential clients to view workers' profiles, while Carina opted for abbreviated profiles focused only on care-related skills and experience. While workers at Carina are responsible for updating their profiles, they do not have the ability to customize their profile, thus reducing the potential for competition and bias.

These worker-centered platforms establish trust in a different way than large private platforms do. Large, traditional platforms rely on recruiting an oversupply of workers to the site, forcing workers to compete against each other for clients. This system leads not only to an influx of workers and downward pressure on wages but also to little quality control or consistency in work standards. To address this quality issue, large platforms use rating systems and algorithms to filter out workers who do not measure up. In contrast, Up & Go establishes trust through early human interaction when contacting clients by allowing users to take the conversation offline. Carina matches clients only with unionized workers who are vetted and trained through the state system. Funding for this training is provided by the state because it has a vested interest in saving money by reducing employee turnover. A state caseworker checks that the match is appropriate.

Leaders from the domestic worker organizations we interviewed agreed that traditional platforms complicate potential legal recourse when workers encounter offline issues like wage theft and harassment. One interviewee said that domestic workers are frequently blacklisted from platforms if they make complaints about unpaid wages or poor working conditions. Domestic workers are often burdened with the responsibility of trying to get reinstated on the sites so that they can continue to access new opportunities. Our respondent said that domestic workers do not have the time or ability to protest their conditions: "Many of our clients find their work through Internet platforms, and we have unscrupulous employers, and bad practices are widespread.... It increases the complexity of their legal case, which might be a barrier." Our interviewees also said that domestic workers cannot turn to platforms to help them with issues of fraud or unpaid hours. They suggested that platforms collect a great deal of data on workers but fail to assist workers when clients do not hold up their part of the bargain. For example, platforms can obscure the identity of "bad actors" who may then simply create a new profile and continue to offer substandard terms of employment. This ability to create new profiles increases the complexity of filing a claim with the state or appearing in court.

Traditional platforms that target domestic workers often recast cleaning and maintenance work as side work for supplemental income. They also target younger workers and college students, promoting intermittent cleaning work as entrepreneurial. These younger workers are less likely to see themselves as a "domestic worker" than the immigrant female workers who have traditionally taken on this kind of work. In fact, one respondent from Up & Go suggested that the big platforms are not interested in the more traditional kinds of domestic workers who form the core membership of co-ops:

> We've asked co-op members if they've heard of some of the plat-
> forms and they hadn't even heard of them. They might not have
> had the capacity to download or navigate the app. I think the
> biggest barrier is a language barrier ... and the app is entirely in
> English.

Both Up & Go's and Carina's workers are less comfortable with technology and email than the target audience of other platforms. Large platforms place the burden on workers to learn how to use the technology effectively. In contrast, worker-centered platforms focus on understanding and mitigating these barriers to accessing their platforms. To make sure that the platforms are appropriate for their target populations, both Up & Go and Carina perform continual user testing. They refine the design of their platforms not only to benefit their workers economically but also to ensure that workers can use them. Carina has invested substantial resources to ensure that their platform is not overly cumbersome while at the same time protecting the sensitive medical information of their clients.

The representatives we interviewed emphasized that successful partnerships between government agencies and community organizations were essential for making their platforms successful. They relied on state and local institutions for support for various needs, including data sharing, platform development, feasibility studies, and user testing. A representative from Carina emphasized the importance of these relationships because they ensured the platform was integrated into existing state and local structures:

> The union and the state are both aligned in their interest in
> keeping workers working in their jobs, which helps clients get
> care, not get institutionalized, and aligns with their preferences.
> This is a cost savings for the state and for the union. It helps
> stabilize their membership.

In the case of Up & Go, New York City's interest in the platform was to grow the number of co-ops, while in the case of Carina, the state of Washington was looking to save money on turnover and training of home health workers. The state of Washington also benefited from the platform's data, which can be used to address gaps in access to providers. In this way, government partners perceived their role as long-term investors, and they were active stakeholders in advancing the economic standing of domestic workers in the local economy.

Wage Theft Recovery and Enforcement

Our interviews made clear that worker organizations believed that wage theft was a central issue and prioritized this work over pursuing a DWBOR, largely because they want to promote legislation that most effectively targets the needs of the greatest number of their constituents. Wage theft legislation impacts not only domestic workers but also landscapers, day laborers, and other immigrant workers. For example, one of our key informants stated, "There are a lot of informal arrangements out there, and all those workers are only getting eight hours of the minimum wage when they should be getting overtime." This emphasis on wage theft is consistent with results from a survey of low-wage workers that one of the nonprofits conducted in 2018. Of the 90 workers who responded, 70% reported that they were not paid enough (Solis 2018).

Precariously employed immigrant workers experience even greater risk for wage theft violations, and undocumented immigrant women are the most likely to experience minimum wage violations. Undocumented workers who typically have limited access to emergency assistance and government subsidy programs because of their immigration status—and who may avoid leveraging law enforcement and other government agencies for fear of arrest or deportation—are often left with limited recourse to mitigate the impact of wage theft on their households. Wage theft can lead to a number of negative outcomes for individuals and households, including financial hardship, depression, food insecurity, and lack of adequate healthcare.

Another useful source for information on wage theft among domestic workers is Bernhardt, Spiller, and Polson (2013), a study based on a survey of 4,387 low-wage workers across 16 job categories conducted in 2008 in three US cities (Chicago, Los Angeles, and New York). This sample represents a population of about 1.6 million low-wage workers, and home-based childcare, healthcare, and personal service providers constituted about 15% of the sample. Overall, two thirds of eligible low-wage workers experienced some sort of a pay violation in the week prior to the survey. Workers also reported a number of other violations related to breaks for rest and meals, illegal retaliation from employers for complaining or organizing, and obstacles to receiving workers compensation for workplace injuries. Certain workers are statistically significantly more likely to experience a violation of their right to get paid the minimum wage: women, Hispanics, undocumented immigrants, and high school dropouts. Of all the occupations examined, childcare and healthcare providers in private households had the highest odds of experiencing minimum wage violations.

Wage theft contributes to the overall low pay of domestic workers compared with other paid employees. Tabulations based on microdata for the United States indicate that nominal wages for domestic workers are roughly $3 to $4 per hour lower than for nondomestic workers (Figure 3).[5] In addition, hourly wages for domestic workers still show more instability compared with nondomestic workers, whose nominal wages have risen fairly steadily since 2003–2005. In terms of real wages, on average, most hourly wage workers have seen no increase in take-home pay since 2003–2005.

Hence, there is a clear need for innovation to address these kinds of pay inequities. Efforts are under way to enforce wage and hour standards by including

Figure 3
Median Hourly Wages, 2003–2005 Through 2017–2019

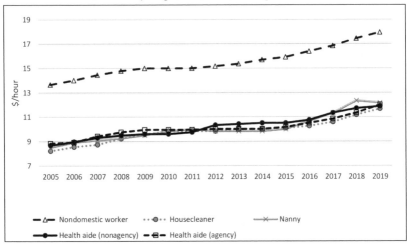

Note: Each data point represents the median hourly wage of three years of pooled microdata from the CPS (so 2005 is constructed with 2003–05 data, 2006 is constructed with 2004–06 data, and so on). Wage data were unavailable for home daycare providers.

worker organizations in labor standards boards associated with DWBOR 2.0 legislation. Another innovation is the addition of funding to support education and outreach, thereby advancing what is known as strategic enforcement (Fine 2015). Normative models of enforcement are predicated on traditional firm-to-employee relationships in which workers have sufficient power and voice to protest violations (Weil 2014). Worker organizations play an important role in helping to educate workers and employers about workplace regulation. They can also provide critical information to regulatory agencies about where violations are prevalent and mechanisms that create poor conditions for workers. The nonprofit leaders we interviewed agreed that domestic workers employed by agencies or informal brokers sometimes experienced violations that differed from those employed directly by the household. However, they believed these two types of domestic workers were equally vulnerable to abuse because of their immigration status, the intimate nature of the work, and the obstacles to taking legal action.

Some of the organizations that provide legal services believe wage theft is a focal point among domestic worker advocates because it can be addressed by legal means. Workers may be more interested in gaining respect or dignity despite the low-wage work they do, but in most cases, they can receive legal recognition only through the enforcement of wage and hour laws. One informant stated, "Wage theft is the thing that people have a remedy for. … People can get some kind of relief through filing a claim."

Collective Bargaining

Collective bargaining is a long-standing issue for domestic workers who are employed in a context where traditional collective bargaining is not practicable. Although some domestic workers have successfully managed to unionize, most have not due to resource and networking constraints. For example, home health aides in Washington and in-home childcare workers in California have successfully unionized by capitalizing on their funding from state agencies. In our case study, sectoral bargaining supports the work of the Carina Care platform because it serves workers and families receiving Medicaid and Medicare funding. For workers paid by private household employers, the path to collective bargaining is unclear.

In 2010, as part of New York's DWBOR, a feasibility study was ordered to determine how domestic workers could be included in the New York State Employment Relations Act. The study outlined how this act could be amended to include domestic workers, with the caveat that employees and employers would need to voluntarily submit to the process. Worker organizations have admitted that it is difficult to conceptualize a typical collective bargaining arrangement for domestic workers. Yet they have proposed bargaining units organized by geography and type of domestic worker.

While collective bargaining remains an unsettled issue, stakeholders involved in working on DWBOR 2.0 legislation have emphasized sectoral bargaining, which would create a wage and standards board to replace the reliance on a model of firm-level bargaining. Legislation put forward in July 2019 by Senator Kamala Harris and Representative Pramila Jayapal to enact a federal DWBOR included provisions for a board comprised of equal numbers of domestic worker representatives and employer representatives. The board would make recommendations on wages and standards to the Secretary of Labor, who would either implement, recommend legislation, or report why the board's recommendations could not be implemented. Worker organizations representing domestic workers, especially the NDWA and its affiliates, have argued that they should have a presence on this board because they can represent the voice of more workers. To be effective, sectoral bargaining legislation needs to protect worker rights to organize because domestic workers currently do not have protection from retaliation if they participate in organizing activities.

Several of our interviewees spoke to the difficulty of organizing domestic workers for state campaigns. Some organizers are able to locate workers by offering other services like health and safety training or classes in English as a second language. However, the nature of domestic work poses several difficulties for organizers, such as the spread of single workers across different households and their relative isolation:

> This is not something that we can do on our own. We have reached out to national organizations to learn more about their

> experiences, but we need the support of other organizations
> around the state. ... There also seems to be little information
> about domestic workers in New Jersey. ... Instead of organizing
> one workplace or workers in one workplace, people are employed
> by individual households.

Collective bargaining can be a powerful remedy to the disrespect and harassment that domestic workers experience. One of our interviewees said that domestic workers in the municipality covered by their organization were regularly asked to scrub the floor on their hands and knees, a practice that workers believed to be extremely demeaning. "You have to get people to focus on their rights. The biggest issue historically, when you went to work as a Latino, they required you to get on your knees and scrub the floors, and they refuse to do the work on their knees." Our key informants consistently emphasized that the low-wage workers they represent are concerned not only with wage theft but also with formally gaining dignity and respect. Closely linked with this problem was a desire among workers to have stronger enforcement of labor laws and explicit assurances of the ways in which labor laws will be enforced. Domestic workers view labor law enforcement as a means toward commanding more respect for their work.

CONCLUSION

Data from interviews with leaders from nonprofit organizations that represent domestic workers indicate that domestic workers are mobilizing in the development of new methods to improve workplace conditions and the terms of employment for domestic workers. These new methods include domestic worker bills of rights, digital platforms, wage theft recovery efforts, and sectoral bargaining strategies. Such innovations in pursuit of benefits and protections for domestic workers could also benefit other low-wage workers struggling with precarious and nontraditional work arrangements. For example, housecleaners who are represented by Up & Go's platform exemplify the struggles of many other gig workers. Moreover, DWBOR 2.0 campaigns highlight how the current infrastructure and systems for enforcing labor standards are simply not suited to the unique context of private homes and household employers. Crucial for the success of a campaign for legislation to protect domestic workers is a strong organizing capacity to help advocates and workers navigate the political climate to push new legislation and stronger enforcement.

Interviews we conducted with representatives from worker-centered platforms indicate that large traditional digital platforms that match domestic workers with household employers either ignore or further alienate the older immigrant workforce. In the discourse on digital-platform work, there are concerns that big platforms promote themselves as working toward the social good through the sharing economy, while at the same time they erode worker protections (Scholz and Schneider 2017). In contrast, worker-centered platforms that are buttressed by strong non-profit groups can work with state and local governments to develop feasible alternatives. These platforms can meet the needs of worker organizations, governments, and community organizations while leveraging existing systems. Some warn that, while the platforms developed by worker-centered platforms such as Carina and Up & Go might seem like a universal solution for marginalized workers, interventions need to be carefully rooted in local communities and specific contexts (van Doorn 2017). Our research suggests that these worker-centered platforms have succeeded in promoting well-being because they promote compliance with labor standards, they partner with government agencies and community organizations for funding and key services, and they are true to the values of the unions and coops that developed them.

These innovations in the ways that domestic worker organizations and the individuals they represent have acted collectively to improve the terms of employment are needed now more than ever. The United States has over 2 million domestic workers, many of whom have experienced acute labor market setbacks and income insecurity during the COVID-19 pandemic. Since the start of the pandemic, domestic worker organizations have reported growing concerns about violations of worker rights. The risks and violations are particularly severe in the case of international migrant domestic workers because their rights are further circumscribed by immigration law and practice (Kabeer, Razavi, and Rodgers 2021). During the lockdowns, migrant domestic workers have often been caught between different degrees of lockdown in the United States and their home countries, leaving many without jobs and in legal limbo. They have not been able to access unemployment benefits and were unable to qualify for emergency response measures (such as healthcare or cash), nor could they look for alternative employment or return home because of travel restrictions. Not only has the pandemic exposed deep chasms in the United States by gender, race, and class, it has also exposed the urgent need for intensified collective action to protect the economic security and well-being of the domestic workers who clean, cook, and care for families across the country.

ENDNOTES

1. Figure 1 is constructed with microdata from the Current Population Survey Merged Outgoing Rotation Group (Flood et al. 2018). This subsample of the CPS is restricted to adults who are engaged in paid employment and were interviewed in the fourth and eighth month of the CPS survey rotation. Our employment sample retains all workers ages 18 and above, and we compare individuals who are employed in private households (labeled "Domestic Workers") with all other workers who are employed outside of households (labeled "Nondomestic Workers").

2. Domestic workers are divided into five categories using the definitions in Shierholz (2013): housecleaners, nannies, home-based daycare providers, nonagency-based home health aides, and agency-based home health aides. Our estimates are likely to underestimate the true number of

domestic workers given the inherent difficulties in the CPS in surveying domestic workers, especially undocumented immigrants.

3. Au pairs are an additional live-in category under the J-1 exchange visitor visa program. The program is intended as a cultural exchange, but emerging research has shown that the host families treat au pairs like workers. For more, see https://cdmigrante.org/shortchanged.

4. The interviews were approved by the Rutgers University Institutional Review Board and included the provision that interview subjects would remain anonymous (Protocol # 2018001923).

5. The wage sample is the same as the sample described in note 1 but further restricted to all employed individuals with positive reported hourly wages or weekly earnings. Home-based daycare providers are excluded from the wage sample because they are self-employed and do not report hourly wages or weekly earnings. Similar to the precedent set by Shierholz (2013), we constructed an hourly wage measure by taking weekly earnings, which included overtime and tips, and dividing it by usual hours worked per week. If this measure was less than a respondent's reported hourly wage, then we used their reported hourly wage.

REFERENCES

Barzilay, Arianne, and Anat Ben-David. 2016. "Platform Inequality: Gender in the Gig-Economy." *Seton Hall Law Review* 47: 393–431.

Bernhardt, Annette, James DeFilippis, and Siobhan McGrath. 2007. "Unregulated Work in the Global City." Brennan Center for Justice at New York University of Law. https://bit.ly/3rT2BgF

Bernhardt, Annette, Michael Spiller, and Diana Polson. 2013. "All Work and No Pay: Violations of Employment and Labor Laws in Chicago, Los Angeles and New York City." *Social Forces* 91 (3): 725–746.

Boris, Eileen, and Premilla Nadasen. 2008. "Domestic Workers Organize!" *WorkingUSA: The Journal of Labor and Society* 11 (4): 413–437.

Burnham, Linda, and Nik Theodore. 2012. *Home Economics: The Invisible and Unregulated World of a Domestic Worker.* New York, NY: National Domestic Workers Alliance.

Calo, Ryan, and Alex Rosenblat. 2017. "The Taking Economy: Uber, Information, and Power." *Columbia Law Review* 117 (6): 1623–1690.

Fine, Janice Ruth. 2006. *Worker Centers: Organizing Communities at the Edge of the Dream.* Ithaca, NY: Cornell University Press.

Fine, Janice Ruth. 2015. "Co-Production: Bringing Together the Unique Capabilities of Government and Society for Stronger Labor Standards Enforcement." Report. New York, NY: LIFT Fund.

Flood, Sarah, Miriam King, Renae Rodgers, Steven Ruggles, and Robert Warren. 2018. Integrated Public Use Microdata Series, Current Population Survey: Version 6.0 [dataset]. Minneapolis, MN: IPUMS.

Forde, Chris, Mark Stuart, Simon Joyce, Liz Oliver, Danat Valizade, Gabriella Alberti, Kate Hardy, Vera Trappmann, Charles Umney, and Calum Carson. 2017. *The Social Protection of Workers in the Platform Economy.* Brussels, Belgium: Policy Department A of the European Parliament.

Hondagneu-Sotelo, Pierrette. 2007. *Doméstica: Immigrant Workers Cleaning and Caring in the Shadows of Affluence,* 2nd ed. Berkeley, CA: University of California Press.

Kabeer, Naila, Shahra Razavi, and Yana Rodgers. 2021. "Feminist Economic Perspectives on the COVID-19 Pandemic." *Feminist Economics* 27 (1): 1–28.

Milkman, Ruth, and Ed Ott, eds. 2014. *New Labor in New York: Precarious Workers and the Future of the Labor Movement*. Ithaca, NY: Cornell University Press.

Rodríguez, Encarnación Gutiérrez. 2007. "The 'Hidden Side' of the New Economy: On Transnational Migration, Domestic Work, and Unprecedented Intimacy." *Frontiers: A Journal of Women Studies* 28 (3): 60–83.

Rosenblat, Alex, Karen Levy, Solon Barocas, and Tim Hwang. 2017. "Discriminating Tastes: Uber's Customer Ratings as Vehicles for Workplace Discrimination." *Policy & Internet* 9 (3): 256–279.

Schoenbaum, Naomi. 2016. "Gender and the Sharing Economy." *Fordham Urban Law Journal* 43: 1023–1070.

Scholz, Trevor, and Nathan Schneider. 2017. *Ours to Hack and to Own: The Rise of Platform Cooperativism, A New Vision for the Future of Work and a Fairer Internet*. New York, NY: OR Books.

Shierholz, Heidi. 2013. "Low Wages and Scant Benefits Leave Many In-Home Workers Unable to Make Ends Meet." Washington, DC: Economic Policy Institute.

Solis, Steve. 2018 (May 19). "Lakewood Cleaners Still Scrub on Their Knees, Forgo Lunch Breaks, Survey Says." *Asbury Park Press*.

Sundararajan, Arun. 2016. *The Sharing Economy: The End of Employment and the Rise of Crowd-Based Capitalism*. Cambridge, MA: MIT Press.

Ticona, Julia, and Alexandra Mateescu. 2018. "Trusted Strangers: Carework Platforms' Cultural Entrepreneurship in the On-Demand Economy." *New Media & Society* 20 (11): 4384–4404.

US Department of Labor, Wage and Hour Division. 2018. "Home Care: Domestic Service Final Rule Frequently Asked Questions." Washington, DC: US Department of Labor.

van Doorn, Niels. 2017. "Platform Labor: On the Gendered and Racialized Exploitation of Low-Income Service Work in the 'On-Demand' Economy." *Information, Communication & Society* 20 (6): 898–914.

Weil, D. 2014. *The Fissured Workplace: Why Work Became So Bad for So Many and What Can Be Done to Improve It*. Cambridge, MA: Harvard University Press.

CHAPTER 11

Graduate Student Employee Unionization in the Second Gilded Age

WILLIAM A. HERBERT

Hunter College, City University of New York

JOSEPH VAN DER NAALD

Graduate School and University Center, City University of New York

ABSTRACT

In debates on the future of work, a common theme has been how work became less secure through the denial of employee status. Though much of the attention has focused on other industries, precarity has also affected those working in higher education, including graduate student employees, contributing to what is now called the "gig academy." While universities have reassigned teaching and research to graduate assistants, they have also refused to recognize them as employees. Nevertheless, unionization has grown considerably since 2012, most significantly at private institutions. Utilizing a unique dataset, this chapter demonstrates that between 2012 and 2019, graduate student employees voted overwhelmingly for representation. The chapter contextualizes this growth within the history of their unionization movement. We argue that legal rights have been a predominant factor, with graduate assistants confronting, and frequently overcoming, their misclassification. Those experiences provide lessons for workers in other industries facing similar obstacles.

INTRODUCTION

Changes in the organization of work have major ramifications for the approximately four million people working in American higher education (Ginder, Kelly-Reid, and Mann 2019: 4), a sector that is a central realm of social reproduction in the information economy. Conscious economic decisions by universities and colleges have led to certain workers being denied legal employee status and labor rights. Those decisions are not recent phenomena, but they are emblematic of today's Second Gilded Age, and their cumulative effect is profound.

The growth of low-wage and precarious labor in higher education has prompted scholars to refer to the birth of a "gig academy" (Kezar, DePaola, and Scott 2019). Among the changes in higher education has been the increased reliance on graduate student employees (GSEs) to perform academic work, with institutions refusing to recognize them as employees and opposing their right to unionize. The classification issue stems from GSEs playing a dual role at universities. On the one hand, they teach and conduct research for compensation. At the same time, they are doctoral students mentored and supervised by faculty. While their financial situation is often insecure, many of them come to this dual role with high social capital as children of parents with advanced degrees (Mullen, Goyette, and Soares 2003; Posselt and Grodsky 2017).

This chapter analyzes data demonstrating remarkable GSE unionization growth since 2012, when union density was last examined (Berry and Savarese 2012). The data include election results, final outcomes, voting determinants, and national union affiliations during the period. We apply a sectoral approach—separating public and private institutions—to our analysis because, until the period under study, GSE representation was almost exclusively at public universities.

The recent growth is contextualized within the half-century history of campus organizing. We demonstrate that economic, structural, and social issues have been central factors driving patterns of unionization. A fourth factor, labor rights, has been a predominant obstacle facing GSE unionization. We describe GSE strategies and tactics to challenge their misclassification and demonstrate how organizing and positive legal changes are intertwined. The chapter shows that militant and sustained organizing led to positive legal changes, with even unsuccessful efforts inspiring sustained cultures of resistance (Hatton 2020: 141). GSE successes in challenging misclassification and attaining representation provide important lessons for workers in other industries seeking to challenge misclassification. The chapter concludes with a discussion of the road ahead, including the likelihood of additional growth in GSE union density following the withdrawal of a proposed administrative rule aimed at denying employee status to student workers.

A BRIEF HISTORY OF GSE UNIONIZATION

The earliest GSE unionization efforts coincided with renewed faculty demands for collective bargaining following a hiatus resulting from Cold War domestic repression (Herbert 2017). The causal factors underlying GSE unionization are like those attributed to faculty unionization: economic, structural, legal, and the impact of social movements (Ladd and Lipset 1973: 4). Those who are younger, ideologically motivated, nontenured, marginalized, and without a sense of a future in academia are more likely to support collective action on campus (Ladd and Lipset 1973: 25–26).

The original GSE organizing campaigns at the University of California at Berkeley and the University of Wisconsin at Madison faced a fundamental structural constraint: the lack of collective labor rights. At Berkeley, the American Federation of Teachers (AFT)-chartered union organized around working conditions and larger social issues. The union was never formally recognized, and it eventually disbanded (Cain 2018: 58–59). In 1969, the Teaching Assistants' Association (TAA) at Madison became the first voluntarily recognized union, leading to a historic 1970 contract. Like its predecessor at Berkeley, the TAA raised and fought for issues beyond GSE working conditions (Christenson 1971; Feinsinger and Roe 1971).

From the beginning, GSE organizing has challenged shifts in higher education that increasingly assign teaching and research responsibilities to low-paid graduate assistants, postdoctoral employees, and contingent faculty, while future prospects for secure academic employment have diminished (Johnson and Entin 2000; Julius and Gumport 2003; Kezar, DePaola, and Scott 2019). The primary drivers of GSE unionization are wages, health benefits, and other working conditions (Cain 2017: 125–126). Another goal has been to alter the hierarchical power dynamics within academic labor, thereby decreasing the potential for abuses (Hatton 2020: 198–200).

The shift in institutional employment practices has been characterized as corporatization with graduate assistants exploited as "cheap labor" (Hatton 2020: 42; Julius and Gumport 2003; Lafer 2003; Rhoads and Rhoades 2005). In the ten-year period from 2005 to 2015, GSE employment growth was triple the rate of growth of tenure-track faculty (Kezar, DePaola, and Scott 2019: 60). By 2017, graduate assistants and contingent faculty made up 73.2% of the entire academic workforce, yet GSE compensation had fallen below the average cost of living in most major cities (Kroeger, McNicholas, von Wiplert, and Wolfe 2018; McNicholas, Poydock, and Wolfe 2019: 9).

GSE unionization has often been imbued with militant resistance and social movement unionism (Kitchen 2014). Strikes reflect that militancy, with GSE strikes making up 17% of all higher education strikes between 2012 and 2018 (Herbert and Apkarian 2019). The collective resistance has helped maintain organizing campaigns despite the relatively short-term nature of employment and the regular turnover of bargaining unit members (Kitchen 2014). This provides an important organizing lesson for current campaigns among precarious workers in other industries (Covert 2020).

Major surges in GSE union activity have often coincided with other social movements taking place on and off campus. The campaigns at Berkeley and Madison emerged from the free speech and anti–Vietnam War movements, respectively. At the University of Missouri, a GSE union formed to oppose proposed health insurance cuts, to improve compensation, and to support the Black Lives Matter movement (Eligon and Pérez-Peña 2015; Korn, Peters, and Belkin 2015).

Other recent campaigns have aligned with the Occupy Wall Street, the Fight for $15, and the #MeToo movements and have been inspired by labor organizing on other campuses (Buchanan, Misse, and Weatherford 2016; Crow and Greene 2019: 193, 203; Douglas-Gabriel 2018; Kezar, DePaola, and Scott 2019: 133–135; McCarthy 2012).

Support from national unions has also been critical in campus organizing by providing essential resources and labor allies (Dixon, Tope, and Van Dyke 2008). Nevertheless, while faculty, labor, and community support have played important roles in GSE campaigns, this support has not always guaranteed success (Dixon, Tope, and Van Dyke 2008; Julius and Gumport 2003).

Campaigns have frequently occurred at elite universities, where there are long histories of student protest (Dixon, Tope, and Van Dyke 2008: 389). At the same time, some faculty, including self-described progressives, have joined administrators to oppose GSE unionization because it challenges their privileges, prerogatives, and authority (Harvey 2006: 141–142; Robin and Stephens 1996: 46–47).

What is unique is that GSE campaigns have often received extensive support from unions known for private sector representation rather than from traditional educational organizations (Julius and Gumport 2003; Kezar, DePaola, and Scott 2019: 131–132). For example, Columbia University's staff union provided crucial assistance in the rebirth of the GSE union on that campus (Crow and Greene 2019: 200).

Of all the factors concerning GSE unionization, however, labor law has been predominant, playing two critical but contradictory roles. It has been a notorious obstacle, particularly at private universities and at public institutions in states without collective bargaining laws (Dixon, Tope, and Van Dyke 2008). Once labor rights have been recognized, however, the law sets the framework for unionization growth and negotiations (Herbert and van der Naald 2020; Julius and Gumport 2003). The importance of legal rights is consistent with early findings about the key role legal changes played in the rise of faculty unionization at public institutions (Garbarino 1975: 62–64; Ladd and Lipset 1973: 5).

UNION CERTIFICATION OR VOLUNTARY RECOGNITION

Over its history, the GSE union movement has employed two procedural means for overcoming misclassification and attaining unionization: certification by a labor relations agency or voluntary recognition by the university.

Certification is the more secure method. If an employer does not object to a representation petition or its objections are resolved, a union can be certified relatively quickly after an election or a card check in states that allow it (Herbert 2011). However, certification can be delayed or forestalled when an institution chooses to litigate GSE employee status or bargaining unit composition issues.

To avoid the costs of litigation, voluntary recognition agreements are reached that can lead to representation. By agreement, the parties can decide that an election or card check will be administered by a third party, mandate employer neutrality, set rules regarding union access, and define the scope of negotiations following recognition (Eagen 2016; Herzfeld 2016; New York University–GSOC/ UAW 2013).

The decision to enter into an agreement can reflect an institution's respect for the right of campus workers to self-organization (Herbert 2017: 3). For example, the University of Michigan has a formal voluntary recognition and neutrality policy that accepts the fundamental right of collective representation (University of Michigan Board of Regents 2020). Frequently, sustained organizing campaigns supported by politicians, community members, and alumni are necessary to persuade recalcitrant universities to reach a voluntary recognition agreement.

At the University of Connecticut, elected officials played an instrumental role in persuading the university to enter into an agreement (Eagen 2016; Herzfeld 2016). United Auto Workers (UAW) representative Ken Lang described the campaign as "an organizer's dream" (Herzfeld 2016: 2), with voluntary recognition being granted only a few months after organizers started collecting union cards. Similar agreements have been reached at New York University (NYU), Cornell, Georgetown, and Brown (Table 1, beginning on page 232). A major limitation of this procedure is that a university has the prerogative to withdraw recognition following the expiration of a contract, which happened at Madison in 1980 (Craig 1987) and NYU in 2005 (Herbert and van der Naald 2020).

Labor's pursuit of certification or voluntary recognition has been in response to differences in legal precedent in the private and public sectors, as well as existing political and organizing environments. We, therefore, present below the distinct histories of GSE unionization in the private and public sectors before turning to developments since 2012.

IN THE FACE OF OBSTACLES: GSE UNIONIZATION PRIOR TO 2012

Private Sector Law and GSE Unionization Prior to 2012

National Labor Relations Board (NLRB) precedent has been a perennial obstacle to GSE unionization on private university campuses. In the two periods when that barrier was toppled, a flood of formal unionization efforts followed, strongly supported by national unions.

The NLRB began classifying graduate assistants as primarily students in the early 1970s (*Adelphi University* 1972). In 1974, the NLRB ruled that Stanford University physics department research assistants did not have the right to unionize because they were primarily doctoral students and not employees (*Leland Stanford Junior University* 1974). For the next two decades, federal precedent remained unchanged, treating paid GSE labor as not subject to the National Labor Relations Act (NLRA). Despite that barrier, organizing efforts continued, primarily at private institutions including Yale, Brown, Columbia, and Brandeis (Dixon,

Tope, and Van Dyke 2008). Perhaps the most well-remembered campaign took place at Yale, where organizing began in 1989 (Hayden 2001). Early strikes at Yale led to increased GSE compensation and training (Dixon, Tope, and Van Dyke 2008). In 1995, approximately 250 Yale teaching assistants participated in a grade strike in an unsuccessful effort to compel voluntary recognition (Robin and Stephens 1996).

At the turn of the 21st century, the legal landscape began to change (Herbert and van der Naald 2020). In 2000, an NLRB Board majority of Clinton-appointed members ruled that NYU graduate assistants had the right to organize (*New York University* 2000). The reversal led to the first contract at a private university (Herbert and van der Naald 2020). The legal change was a catalyst for the filing of representation petitions at Brown, Cornell, Pratt, Tufts, Columbia, and Yale (Pollack and Johns 2015; *Pratt Institute* 2003). An election at Yale resulted in a GSE vote against representation (Dixon, Tope, and Van Dyke 2008: 377). At Cornell, graduate assistants voted to reject unionization by a 2–1 margin (Dullea 2003).

A subsequent certification election was held at Brown, but the ballots were impounded after the university again challenged GSE employee classification (*Brown University* 2004). Other pending petitions and elections met similar procedural fates (Pollack and Johns 2015; *Pratt Institute* 2003).

Following the election of President George W. Bush, a change in NLRB Board composition led to the overturning of the *New York University* decision and a return to classifying graduate assistants as primarily students (*Brown University* 2004). Following the decision, NYU refused to negotiate a new agreement after the first contract expired (Herbert and van der Naald 2020). The restored legal obstacle led to a decline in formal representation efforts (Dixon, Tope, and Van Dyke 2008: 378). Between January 1, 2006, and December 31, 2013, there were only two GSE representation petitions filed with the NLRB. During the same period, over two dozen petitions were filed to represent contingent faculty, resulting in new bargaining units at private universities including American, Georgetown, and Tufts (NLRB FOIA LR-2017-0964 and 2020-0423).

Public Sector Law and GSE Unionization Prior to 2012

Since 1969, administrative agencies and courts in various states have recognized GSE rights to unionize and engage in collective bargaining or have certified a union to represent them (Herbert and van der Naald 2020). This precedent did not come easy and often required lengthy campaigns, lobbying, and litigation. For example, State University of New York (SUNY) graduate assistants organized for over two decades before a union was certified to represent them (Barba 1994). It took years of litigation before SUNY's legal challenge to GSE employee status was finally rejected [*State of New York (State University of New York)* 1991].

Early determinations in some states, such as Oregon and California, denying GSE bargaining rights were later reversed (*Oregon University System* 2013; *Regents of the University of California* 1989, 1998; *University of Oregon* 1977). Laws in some states, such as Minnesota, Illinois, and Washington, were amended to explicitly grant collective bargaining rights, while laws in a few other states continue to exclude them. In Missouri and Florida, appellate courts have ruled that graduate assistants have a state constitutional right to union representation (Herbert and van der Naald 2020).

SIGNIFICANT GROWTH IN UNION REPRESENTATION 2012–2019

From 2012 to 2019, there were 39 formal representation efforts—27 at private universities, including 10 at Yale and 12 at public institutions. These figures do not include campaigns that did not lead to a representation petition or a voluntary recognition agreement. Our analysis draws on a unique data set of formal representation matters involving academic labor, including faculty and graduate assistants, over the past eight years (see Herbert, Apkarian, and van der Naald 2020) The data were gathered from representation petitions, voluntary recognition agreements, ballot tallies, certifications, administrative and court decisions, and other available documents.[1]

Private Sector Formal Representation Efforts: 2012–2019

Since 2012, the greatest number of formal representation efforts was at private universities. Many were on the same campuses where graduate assistants began organizing in the 1990s and 2000s (Dixon, Tope, and Van Dyke 2008). The first successful private sector effort occurred at NYU. Following a multi-year union campaign, the UAW and NYU entered into a voluntary recognition agreement in 2013 for a non-NLRB election (New York University–GSOC/UAW 2013). This agreement was reached only after the UAW dropped pending NLRB representation petitions (*New York University* 2010; *Polytechnic Institute of New York University* 2011). It defined the bargaining unit to exclude research assistants in science and mathematics departments, and it committed NYU to remain neutral prior to the election (New York University–GSOC/UAW 2013). After an overwhelming vote in favor of representation, NYU voluntarily recognized the UAW, and they negotiated a new contract (Herbert and van der Naald 2020).

In 2014, the UAW filed petitions on behalf of graduate and undergraduate assistants at Columbia and at the New School seeking to overturn the *Brown University* decision. While those cases were pending, Cornell and an AFT-affiliated union reached a voluntary recognition agreement (Cornell University–CGSU–NYSUT/AFT 2016). The agreement created guidelines restricting administrative communications about unionization but, unlike the NYU–UAW agreement, did not mandate university neutrality.

A new NLRB Board majority, appointed by President Obama, issued a decision in 2016 reversing the *Brown* decision, thereby restoring GSE employee status (*Columbia University* 2016). The *Columbia University* decision ushered in another historic chapter in student worker unionization. The decision was applied to the New School organizing effort (*The New School* 2017), and it triggered a non-NLRB election at Cornell. Subsequent NLRB representation elections at Columbia and the New School resulted in the UAW being certified to represent combined units of graduate and undergraduate assistants. Only after a seven-day strike at Columbia did the institution finally agree to negotiate; however, the agreement also included a no-strike pledge (Columbia University–GWOC/UAW 2018).

Over the next two years, GSE representation petitions were filed at 11 other private universities including American, Brandeis, Harvard, Tufts, and Yale (Table 1). Unlike earlier periods, the concerted power of organizing drives led some private institutions to agree to the scheduling of representation elections without legal objections. At Brown and Georgetown, the AFT negotiated agreements that led to voluntary recognition after non-NLRB elections. Other major universities continued to resist by trying to overturn the *Columbia University* decision and litigate other issues. Yale challenged the effort by UNITE HERE to represent departmental bargaining units rather than a university-wide unit.

Despite university legal challenges, the NLRB held elections, resulting in the certification of unions at Boston College, Loyola University Chicago, University of Chicago, and Yale. At Duke University and Washington University, the graduate assistants voted against representation, leading to the withdrawal of those petitions.

Following the 2016 presidential election, the majority composition of the NLRB Board changed again, leading unions to re-examine their organizing strategies. The filing of new NLRB petitions slowed, and unions began withdrawing representation petitions at institutions actively relitigating the GSE employee status issue. While the unions did not articulate a reason for the withdrawals, media reports indicated that the withdrawals were due to growing concerns that the new NLRB majority would use one of the pending cases to overturn the *Columbia University* decision (Flaherty 2018). This strategic labor retreat underscores again the centrality of labor law and politics as factors in GSE unionization.

Consistent with labor's fears, the new NLRB Board majority in 2019 took regulatory action to reverse *Columbia University*. Rather than wait for a litigated case, the agency announced a proposed rule to exclude all student employees in higher education from federal labor law protections (Herbert and van der Naald 2020). The proposed rule, however, was withdrawn in March 2021 following the appointment of NLRB Chairman Lauren McFerran and the termination of NLRB General Counsel Peter Robb by President Biden (National Labor Relations Board 2021).

Public Sector Formal Representation Efforts: 2012–2019

Since 2012, growth of new bargaining units in the public sector has continued but at a slower rate than before. Representation petitions and one voluntary recognition agreement led to six new GSE bargaining units at public institutions, along with the expansion of a unit at Oregon State University. The majority (four) of the new bargaining units resulted from card checks rather than elections.

Union representation was rejected at the University of Minnesota and the Pennsylvania State University, despite decades of organizing and a clear legal right to collectively bargain (Ross 2012; Schackner 2001, 2018). Representation efforts at the University of Missouri and the University of Pittsburgh remain unresolved, and at the University of Michigan–Ann Arbor, a representation petition was dismissed on jurisdictional grounds.

AN ANALYSIS OF THE DATA: 2012–2019

This section begins with an analysis of 31 private and public sector representation election results in the period 2012–2019 that includes those situations where petitions were later dismissed or withdrawn. We then examine the total growth in unionization, including sectoral differences, a comparison with earlier periodic upsurges, and the correlation between the *Columbia University* decision and successful private sector unionization.

Election Ballot Results

The election ballot tallies in 2012–2019 demonstrate a strong preference for union representation. In 84% of the 25 private sector certification elections, a majority voted in favor of unionization. Favorable election results in ten of those efforts did not result in final positive outcomes because the petitions were later withdrawn for strategic reasons (Table 1). In the public sector, six elections were held. Three elections resulted in favorable ballot results. A majority in two elections voted against representation, and the election in a sixth was overturned as the result of union objections. In addition, unions were certified or recognized on three other campuses following card checks that demonstrated majority support for representation in those bargaining units (Table 1).

When graduate assistants voted in favor of representation, it was on average by wide margins: nearly three to one in the private sector and more than four to one in the public sector. Further, in elections where the majority voted against representation, the ballot counts were closer (43.2% to 56.8%). Similar wide margins are visible when we compare voting patterns across procedural type. In non-NLRB elections where the majority voted in favor of unionization, the average margins in favor to those against was greater than in agency-conducted elections (Table 2, page 237). Greater success in negotiated third-party elections is unsurprising because the parties' agreements limited the ability of universities to influence voters on the question of representation.

Despite an overall preference for representation, the period from 2012 also witnessed rejection of union representation in elections at five large research institutions and one university department. Unionization was rejected at the University of Minnesota, with approximately 62% voting against representation, the fourth rejection at that university over the decades (Ross 2012). At Penn State, the ballot tally showed that 60% rejected representation. In the private sector, Cornell graduate assistants voted against representation in an election conducted under a voluntary recognition agreement. At Duke, 63.5% voted against unionization, while at Washington University, 55.4% voted to reject representation. There was also a negative election result in one of nine Yale departmental elections.

Determinants in Election Results

Scholars have identified social pressure favoring unionization, dissatisfaction with working conditions, and perspectives on organized labor as primary variables impacting voter behavior in representation elections (Cain 2017; Davy and Shipper 1993). Related to those variables are two other factors: employer anti-union campaigns and union organizing strategies and tactics (Bronfenbrenner 1997, 2009; Lafer 2003).

The lopsided election results in favor of representation during the period under study, along with the history of the GSE labor movement, strongly suggest that voter support was affected by job dissatisfaction, an understanding that union representation would improve their status and workplace conditions, and that a favorable vote would be a statement of resistance and solidarity. The neutral stance taken by some campus administrators on the question of GSE representation might also explain the strong votes in favor. Owing to the nature of our data set, however, correlating those variables with each election outcome would be speculative because we lack sufficient campus-specific information. Voter survey results and interviews with graduate assistants, union organizers, faculty, and administrators are necessary to reach fully informed conclusions.

Employer Anti-Union Conduct

The purpose of anti-union campaigns is to counteract union support and challenge the value of union instrumentality. One common tactic is to portray a GSE union as a "third party" and describe collective bargaining as not in the best interests of the university or the graduate assistants (Dullea 2003).

Despite fierce legal resistance by many institutions against unionization and application of other union avoidance strategies in 2012–2019, a substantial percentage of the election results were pro labor. Those results include elections held at institutions that took a more neutral approach to the question of representation. Both findings are somewhat surprising because increased employer opposition has been central to the general decline in union success (Bronfenbrenner 2009).

This does not mean, of course, that union avoidance strategies have not impacted voter behavior. The vote against representation at the University of Pittsburgh was set aside because of employer misconduct (*Employes of University of Pittsburgh* 2019). In contrast, neutral decision makers found insufficient evidence of misconduct to order new elections at the University of Minnesota and at Cornell (*University of Minnesota, Unit 10* 2012; *Cornell University and Cornell University Students United* 2018). Those findings underscore the weak legal regulations over employer efforts to influence GSE vote outcome.

There is also evidence that administrators at institutions tried to instill fear among international students about their immigration status (Bittle 2017; Reyes 2018; Schackner 2018). While that conduct might have led to negative election outcomes at Penn State and Washington University, Columbia graduate assistants voted overwhelmingly in favor of union representation despite the targeting of international students.

Bargaining Unit Size

Prior scholarship has established that bargaining unit size plays a key role in certification election outcomes, with workers in smaller units more likely to vote in favor of unionization (Farber 2001; Heneman and Sandver 1983). The data from the 2012–2019 GSE elections lend support to those findings. Nearly 90% of bargaining units with fewer than 1,000 voted in favor of representation. Among units with a size larger than 1,000, however, approximately 58% voted to unionize.

Departmental Differences

Another potential electoral determinant is the relative level of support for unionization by academic department. It has been argued that union support differs between teaching assistants in the humanities and social sciences, and research assistants in the sciences (Dixon, Tope, and Van Dyke 2008: 379; Lafer 2003). While all share common experiences and similar aspirations, stratifications across departments have the potential to yield different levels of support. Research assistants are paid more on average than teaching assistants, but they face more abusive and coercive working conditions (Hatton 2020: 6–7; National Education Association 2019: 11).

The expectation of weaker support among research assistants might explain why some campaigns have focused on organizing teaching assistants only (Dixon, Tope, and Van Dyke 2008: 379). At NYU, science and mathematics research assistants were excluded by agreement from the bargaining unit (New York University–GSOC/UAW 2013). Research assistants at the University of Iowa were also excluded through a stipulation (*University of Iowa/State Board of Regents* 1994).

Table 1
Formal GSE Representation Efforts, 2012–2019

Year	Institution (Department)	Sector	Affiliate	Vote Count	Unit Size	Outcome	Pre–Election Agreement	Existing Nontenure Track Faculty Union
2012	Univ. of Minnesota	Public	UAW	1142–1857	4395	Dismissal After Election	No	Yes
2012	Montana State Univ.	Public	AFT–NEA	195–67	587	Recognition After Election	No	Yes
2013	Oregon State Univ.	Public	AFT	287–32	1505	Unit Clarification Added 767 to Existing GSE Unit	No	No
2013	New York Univ.	Private	UAW	630–10	1257	Recognition After AAA Election	Yes	Yes
2014	Univ. of Connecticut	Public	UAW		2165	Recognition After Card Check	Yes	Yes
2014	Univ. of Michigan–Ann Arbor	Public	AFT		2128	Jurisdictional Dismissal	No	Yes
2016	Portland State Univ.	Public	AAUP–AFT		793	Certification After Card Check	No	Yes

Year	Institution (Department)	Sector	Affiliate	Vote Count	Unit Size	Outcome	Pre–Election Agreement	Existing Nontenure Track Faculty Union
2016	Yale Univ. (Comparative Literature)	Private	UNITE HERE		22	Withdrawal Before Election	No	No
2017	Loyola Univ. Chicago	Private	SEIU	71–49	210	Certification After Election	No	Yes
2017	Yale Univ. (Physics)	Private	UNITE HERE	26–30	63	Dismissal After Adverse Election	No	No
2017	Duke Univ.	Private	SEIU	398–691	2298	Withdrawal After Adverse Election	No	Yes
2017	American Univ.	Private	SEIU	212–40	761	Certification After Election	No	Yes
2017	Brandeis Univ.	Private	SEIU	88–34	219	Certification After Election	No	Yes
2017	Tufts Univ.	Private	SEIU	129–84	281	Certification After Election	No	Yes
2017	The New School	Private	UAW	502–2	1052	Certification After Election	No	Yes
2017	Washington Univ.	Private	SEIU	174–216	494	Withdrawal After Adverse Election	No	Yes

Year	Institution (Department)	Sector	Affiliate	Vote Count	Unit Size	Outcome	Pre–Election Agreement	Existing Nontenure Track Faculty Union
2017	Columbia Univ.	Private	UAW	1602–623	4256	Certification After Election	No	No
2018	Boston College	Private	UAW	270–224	778	Withdrawal After Election and Certification	No	No
2018	Yale Univ. (East Asian Languages)	Private	UNITE HERE	5–1	27	Withdrawal After Election and Certification	No	No
2018	Yale Univ. (English)	Private	UNITE HERE	22–4	35	Withdrawal After Election and Certification	No	No
2018	Yale Univ. (History of Art)	Private	UNITE HERE	17–2	22	Withdrawal After Election and Certification	No	No
2018	Yale Univ. (Mathematics)	Private	UNITE HERE	8–3	12	Withdrawal After Election and Certification	No	No
2018	Yale Univ. (Geology and Geophysics)	Private	UNITE HERE	9–7	16	Withdrawal After Election and Certification	No	No

Year	Institution (Department)	Sector	Affiliate	Vote Count	Unit Size	Outcome	Pre–Election Agreement	Existing Nontenure Track Faculty Union
2018	Yale Univ. (Political Science)	Private	UNITE HERE	19–14	72	Withdrawal After Election and Certification	No	No
2018	Yale Univ. (Sociology)	Private	UNITE HERE	12–3	19	Withdrawal After Election and Certification	No	No
2018	Yale Univ. (History)	Private	UNITE HERE	39–7	56	Withdrawal After Election and Certification	No	No
2018	Univ. of Chicago*	Private	AAUP–AFT	1103–479	2457	Withdrawal After Election and Certification	No	Yes
2018	Univ. of Pennsylvania	Private	AFT		2300	Withdrawal Before Election	No	No
2018	Harvard Univ.⁺	Private	UAW	1931–1523	5050	Certification After Election	Yes	No
2018	Pennsylvania State Univ.	Public	NEA	950–1438	3799	Dismissal After Adverse Election	No	No
2018	Cornell Univ.	Private	AFT	856–919	2500	Dismissal After AAA Election	Yes	Yes

Year	Institution (Department)	Sector	Affiliate	Vote Count	Unit Size	Outcome	Pre–Election Agreement	Existing Nontenure Track Faculty Union
2018	Univ. of Chicago*	Private	IBT	67–13	199	Certification After Election	No	Yes
2018	Illinois State Univ.	Public	SEIU	160–36	475	Certification After Election	No	Yes
2018	Georgetown Univ.	Private	AFT	555–108	1059	Recognition After AAA Election	Yes	Yes
2018	Brown Univ.	Private	AFT	576–394	1258	Recognition After AAA Election	Yes	No
2019	Oregon Health and Sciences Univ.	Public	AFSCME		251	Certification After Card Check	No	No
2019	Southern Illinois Univ.–Edwardsville	Public	SEIU		341	Certification After Card Check	No	Yes
2019	Univ. of Pittsburgh	Public	USW	675–712	2534	New Election Ordered	No	No
2019	Univ. of Missouri	Public	NEA		2600	Pending Election or Card Check	No	No

Note: Year represents the year of union certification, union recognition, or the withdrawal of a representation petition following an election or certification.

†In the first election in December 2016 at Harvard University, GSEs voted against UAW representation. After the election was set aside by an NLRB Regional Director, the unit voted in favor of representation.

*This University of Chicago unit includes graduate and undergraduate students working in the libraries.

Table 2
Voting Patterns by Procedures and Sector, 2012–2019

	Majority Votes in Favor	Majority Votes Against
Private Sector	84% (21)	16% (4)
Public Sector	50% (3)	50% (3)*

	Majority Votes in Favor		Majority Votes Against	
	Proportion of Votes in Favor	Proportion of Votes Against	Proportion of Votes in Favor	Proportion of Votes Against
Total	75.3%	24.7%	43.2%	56.8%
Private	74.4%	25.6%	44%	56%
Public	82%	18%	42.2%	57.8%
Agency Election	74.6%	25.4%	42.4%	57.6%
AAA Election	80.5%	19.5%	48.2%	51.8%

Note: Proportion of votes calculated as the average of all ratios of votes in favor to votes against (or vice versa) for each election effort. These proportions include 25 election efforts by units at private sector institutions and six by units at public sector institutions. Twenty-one agency elections and three AAA were conducted where the majority voted in favor. Six agency elections and one AAA were conducted where the majority voted against.

*Included is the election at the University of Pittsburgh, but the results were set aside by the Pennsylvania Labor Relations Board.

The UNITE HERE strategy of seeking to represent graduate assistants at Yale on a departmental basis provides rare but limited data to test the disciplinary divide argument concerning support for unionization. While the data address election results by department, they do not identify the respective percentages of teaching and graduate assistants in each department.

The Yale ballot tallies listed in Table 1 reveal that the highest level of support for unionization was in the humanities and social sciences. At the same time, there was greater support in mathematics than in political science and a clear split in the physical sciences, with geology and geophysics supporting unionization and physics voting against representation (Herbert and Apkarian 2017: 33). These electoral results suggest that while academic discipline can impact voter behavior, it is not a determinative factor in ballot outcomes.

Contingent Faculty Bargaining and Organizing

It is common for scholars to link graduate assistants and contingent faculty when discussing low-wage precarious academic work (Kezar, DePaola, and Scott 2019). At institutions that rely extensively on contingent faculty, graduate assistants are more likely to seek union representation (Dixon, Tope, and Van Dyke 2008: 389).

Despite substantial growth in contingent faculty unionization since 2012 (Herbert, Apkarian, and van der Naald 2020), GSE votes in favor of representation do not appear to have been affected by the existence of a contingent faculty bargaining unit. In elections where GSEs voted in an election to unionize, just 45.8% of the cases had an existing contingent faculty bargaining unit. When GSE units voted against unionization, 57.1% of the institutions had a contingent faculty unit.

On the basis of their similar working conditions, it would be reasonable to anticipate that graduate assistants and contingent faculty would seek to unionize and negotiate together in one bargaining unit. This is particularly true based on literature suggesting that GSEs are more successful when they are in combined units with faculty (Julius and Gumport 2003: 199). Between 2012 and 2019, however, graduate assistants and contingent faculty did not seek representation in one bargaining unit. This is true even on campuses where both groups unionized within a year or two of each other. At NYU, American, Brandeis, and Tufts, the same unions represent distinct units of contingent faculty and graduate assistants. In contrast, there are now new bargaining units with graduates and undergraduates at Columbia, Harvard, and the New School. The lack of joint representation efforts may reflect tensions between the two groups over wages, benefits, and status (Berry 2005: 137).

Alternatively, the lack of new combined contingent faculty/GSE organizing might be a consequence of legal considerations. The *Columbia* decision was issued only after many new contingent faculty units had been certified. In addition, there might have been concerns that precedent against combined units with tenure-track faculty would be extended to a unit with contingent faculty [*Adelphi University* 1972; *State of New York (State University of New York)* 1991]. Lastly, unions might not have sought combined units out of fear that it would internalize potential conflict of interests between the groups of employees (Garbarino 1975: 116).

Total Unionization Growth: 2012–2019

Between 2012 and 2019, total GSE unionization grew precipitously. We estimate that 62,656[2] graduate assistants were in certified or recognized bargaining units in the United States in 2012 (Herbert, Apkarian, and van der Naald 2020). By 2019, the number grew by more than 20,000 to 83,050, a more than 32.5% increase (Figure 1).[3] The growth during that period was substantially greater than between 2006 and 2011 (7,379) and outpaced similar upsurges during the two preceding five-year periods: 2000–2005 (18,012) and 1995–1999 (17,700) (Berry and Savarese 2012: xiv).

Sectoral Distinctions

The most striking aspect of the recent growth is its sectoral character. In 2012, GSE bargaining units were exclusively located at 30 public institutions and two

Figure 1
GSE Representation Growth 2012–2019

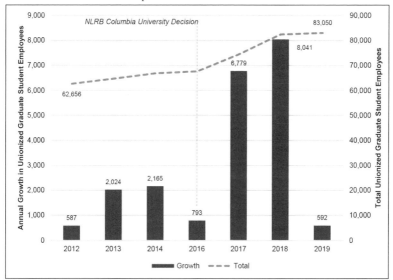

research foundations with SUNY and CUNY (Berry and Savarese 2012: 50–54; Herbert, Apkarian, and van der Naald 2020: 20–21).

Between 2012 and 2019, there were 17 newly certified or recognized bargaining units, with 11 at private institutions containing the overwhelming majority (15,602, or 74.3%) of newly represented graduate assistants. In contrast, the total increase in public sector bargaining units was 5,379 (Table 1). Much of the private sector increase is attributable to large units at Columbia (4,256) and Harvard (5,050), constituting more than half of the total growth. New private sector units tended to exceed new public sector units in size, as the median new unit at private universities (1,052) is nearly double that of a new unit in the public sector (531). The largest and smallest units in 2012–2019 were in the private sector: 5,050 and 199 (Table 1).

National Union Affiliations

The dominant role played by nontraditional educational unions in GSE unionization has continued since 2012 (Julius and Gumport 2003: 188). Affiliations with unions without long histories of representing tenure-track faculty may reflect a reaction by graduate assistants to feeling proletarianized on campus despite their familial and class origins (Mullen, Goyette and Soares 2003; Posselt and Grodsky 2017).

In 2012, slightly more than 50% of graduate assistants were represented by the UAW and two other private sector unions (Berry and Savarese 2012: xiii). In the following seven years, 68% of newly unionized graduate assistants were in bargaining units represented by the UAW (Figure 2). This is due, in part, to large units that include undergraduate assistants.

The recent period has seen the Service Employees International Union (SEIU), which has been successfully organizing contingent faculty, begin to organize graduate assistants as well. The union now represents over 2,200 graduate assistants in four private sector bargaining units (American, Brandeis, Loyola, and Tufts Universities) and two in the public sector (Illinois State University and Southern Illinois University–Edwardsville). AFT has also continued to increase its GSE representation, with new bargaining units at Brown, Georgetown, and Portland State.

LESSONS LEARNED AND THE ROAD AHEAD

The GSE union movement exemplifies the intertwined relationship of organizing, legal change, and unionization. From the start, GSE organizing campaigns have challenged academic capitalism, including the exploitation of precarious labor. Resistance to the restructuring of higher education, along with close alliances with other social movements, have been core elements of campus organizing. The application of social unionism has helped sustain the campaigns despite constant changes in leadership and membership.

Figure 2
New Graduate Student Union Membership by Affiliate, 2012–2019

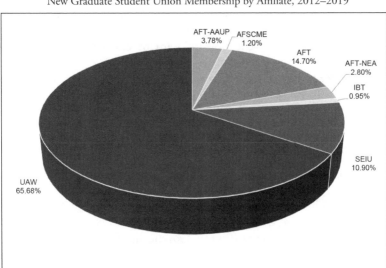

Through organizing, litigation, and lobbying, graduate assistants have often broken through the legal barrier of misclassification. In many situations, the campaigns have been decades long. To effect change, graduate assistants have fought for voluntary recognition agreements, consent elections or card checks, reversal of adverse legal precedent, changes to state laws, and recognition of a state constitutional right to organize. Each time legal obstacles and institutional opposition have fallen, unionization has grown rapidly, as the surge during the period of 2013–2019 demonstrates.

By far the most difficult campaigns have been at large private universities. This is the result of well-financed institutional opposition, which has applied classic union avoidance strategies and adverse legal precedent. The data presented for the period before and after the *Columbia* decision reaffirm that when given a choice, graduate assistants vote overwhelming in favor of representation, with the margin of victory greater in third party–conducted elections than in NLRB elections.

While anti-union efforts by institutions have had some negative impact on electoral outcomes, it has not been a final determinative factor. Despite extensive litigation to deny graduate assistants the vote, 84% of private sector elections resulted in votes in favor of unionization. Nevertheless, university efforts to have graduate assistants reclassified as primarily students by a Trump-appointed NLRB Board majority led to a strategic labor organizing retreat on some campuses, even after favorable elections.

The NLRB's 2019 proposed rule to strip student workers of the right to unionize had placed a dark cloud over the future value of NLRB certification procedures for unionization. If the proposed rule had been adopted, graduate and undergraduate assistants at private institutions would have had to resume collective action outside the law to improve their working conditions and attain voluntary recognition. The March 2021 withdrawal of the proposed rule and the upcoming appointments by President Biden to the NLRB Board will result in a greater degree of legal stability over the classification of graduate assistants as employees under the NLRA. The stability gained by those changes will set the stage for another surge in formal GSE representation efforts on private university campuses.

Future survey research, followed by structured interviews, is warranted to examine GSE perspectives, motivations, and priorities in all or some of the 39 formal representation efforts we discussed in this chapter. These methods can help examine more closely the determinants of voter behavior in specific representation elections and test the scope of GSE unity with contingent faculty and with other low-paid campus workers. Another avenue of research should be targeted at administrators and faculty members to understand their perspectives and motivations in accepting or opposing GSE unionization in 2012–2019. Such surveys would be particularly useful in understanding divisions on campus among academic labor groups and how those differences have impacted the growth in unionization.

Inherent in our research methodology are certain limitations. We relied on eligible voters to determine the size of the bargaining units, although the unit size might have changed, particularly because of the COVID-19 pandemic. In focusing on formal representation efforts, we did not examine organizing and advocacy efforts on other campuses that did not lead to a representation petition or a voluntary recognition agreement. Future research should update our data and expand the scope of our inquiry.

The GSE unionization movement has a great deal to teach misclassified and precarious workers in other industries who have begun organizing in today's gig economy. Many of those workers are confronting a familiar legal obstacle faced by graduate assistants: the claim that they are not employees and are thus without the right to collectively bargain. The successes of graduate assistants in winning battles over misclassification and attaining workplace protections through union representation in the face of employer opposition and legal limitations offer important lessons for other precarious and misclassified workers in the Second Gilded Age.

ENDNOTES

1. For a more detailed methodological description, see Herbert, Apkarian, and van der Naald 2020: 10.

2. In 2012, the National Center for the Study of Collective Bargaining in Higher Education and the Professions recorded 64,424 graduate assistants in certified or recognized bargaining units in the United States (Berry and Savarese 2012). This figure included teaching assistants at the University of Wisconsin at Madison (3,131), despite the union's decision in the year prior to not seek recertification under Wisconsin's restrictive collective bargaining law (Verburg 2011). The figure excluded existing GSE bargaining units at Montana State University and at the CUNY and SUNY research foundations. In calculating our total of 62,656, we subtracted the Madison unit size and added the unit sizes from Montana State (778) and the research foundations at CUNY and SUNY.

3. This figure includes undergraduate student employees in four of the new bargaining units at Columbia University, the New School, Harvard University, and the University of Chicago.

REFERENCES

Barba, William C. 1994. "The Graduate Student Employee Union in SUNY: A History." *Journal for Higher Education Management* 10 (1): 39-48.

Berry, Joe. 2005. *Reclaiming the Ivory Tower: Organizing Adjuncts to Change Higher Education.* New York, NY: Monthly Review Press.

Berry, Joe, and Michelle Savarese. 2012. *Directory of U.S. Faculty Contracts and Bargaining Agents in Institutions of Higher Education.* Series II, No. 2. New York, NY: National Center for the Study of Collective Bargaining in Higher Education and the Professions, Hunter College, City University of New York.

Bittle, Jake. 2017 (Oct. 5). "This University Suggested International Students Could Be Reported to ICE If They Unionized." *The Nation*. https://bit.ly/3u38SrL

Bronfenbrenner, Kate. 1997. "The Role of Union Strategies in NLRB Certification Elections." *ILR Review* 50 (2): 95–212.

Bronfenbrenner, Kate. 2009. "No Holds Barred—The Intensification of Employer Opposition to Organizing." Briefing Paper No. 235. Washington, DC: Economic Policy Institute. https://bit.ly/2ZnEYk8

Buchanan, B.B., Blanca Misse, and Alan-Michael Weatherford. 2016 (Aug. 16). "Resolution on Taking an Active Anti-Racist Stand in Our Unions and Support the Movement for Black Lives." *Thecgeu.org*. <http://www.thecgeu.org/past-cgeu-annual-meetings/2016-conference-resolutions/resolution-on-taking-an-active-anti-racist-stand-in-our-unions-and-support-the-movement-for-black-lives/>.

Cain, Timothy R. 2017. *Campus Unions: Organized Faculty and Graduate Students in U.S. Higher Education*. ASHE Higher Education Report Series, Vol. 43, No. 3. San Francisco, CA: Jossey-Bass.

Cain, Timothy R. 2018. "A Long History of Activism and Organizing: Contingent Faculty, Graduate Students, and Unionization." In *Professors in the Gig Economy*, edited by Kim Tolley. Baltimore, MD: Johns Hopkins University Press.

Christenson, Arlen. 1971. "Collective Bargaining in a University: The University of Wisconsin and the Teaching Assistants Association." *Wisconsin Law Review* 1971 (1): 210–228.

Columbia University–Graduate Workers of Columbia/UAW. 2018 (Nov. 19). "Framework Agreement." https://bit.ly/2ZjxqyP

Cornell University–Cornell Graduate Students United–NYSUT/AFT. 2016 (May 16). "University Conduct Rules and Recognition Election Agreement." https://bit.ly/3jU1hHq

Covert, Bryce. 2020 (Mar. 30). "Like Uber, but for Gig Worker Organizing." *The American Prospect*. https://bit.ly/3jU1qKY

Craig, Judith S. 1987. "Teaching Assistant Collective Bargaining at the University of Wisconsin–Madison: Part 1. An Administrator's Perspective." In *Institutional Responsibilities and Responses in the Employment and Education of Teaching Assistants: Readings from a National Conference*, edited by Nancy Van Note Chism, pp. 53–59. Columbus, OH: Center for Teaching Excellence.

Crow, Andrea, and Alyssa Greene. 2019. "Mobilizing Academic Labor: The Graduate Workers of Columbia Unionization Campaign." In *Women Mobilizing Memory*, edited by Ayşe Gül Altınay, María José Contreras, Marianne Hirsch, Jean Howard, Banu Karaca, and Alisa Solomon, pp. 192–205. New York, NY: Columbia University Press.

Davy, Jeanette A., and Frank Shipper. 1993. "Voter Behavior in Union Certification Elections: A Longitudinal Study." *Academy of Management Journal* 36 (1): 187–199.

Dixon, Marc, Daniel Tope, and Nella Van Dyke. 2008 "The University Works Because We Do: On the Determinants of Campus Labor Organizing in the 1990s." *Sociological Perspectives* 51 (2): 375–396.

Douglas-Gabriel, Danielle. 2018 (Apr. 12). "Harvard's Graduate Student Union Demands Better Sexual Harassment Protections." *Washington Post*. https://wapo.st/3apyXK1

Dullea, Henrick N. 2003 (Jan. 17). "How Cornell Beat a Union by Letting TA's Vote." *Chronicle of Higher Education*. https://bit.ly/2Z.srTFX

Eagen, Michael. 2016. "Graduate Assistants, Unionization, and Negotiations—The UConn Perspective." *National Center Proceedings 2016: Our Future is Now in Higher Education, Special Issue, Journal of Collective Bargaining in the Academy*, Article 19.

Eligon, John, and Richard Pérez-Peña. 2015 (Nov. 9). "University of Missouri Protests Spur a Day of Change." *New York Times.* https://nyti.ms/2ZoaPBg

Farber, Henry S. 2001. "Union Success in Representation Elections: Why Does Unit Size Matter?" *ILR Review* 54 (2): 329–348.

Feinsinger, Nathan P., and Eleanore J. Roe. 1971. "The University of Wisconsin, Madison Campus— TAA Dispute of 1969–70: A Case Study." *Wisconsin Law Review* 1971 (1): 229–274.

Flaherty, Colleen. 2018 (Feb. 15). "Realities of Trump-Era NLRB." *Inside Higher Ed.* https://bit.ly/3jTHR5o

Garbarino, Joseph W. 1975. *Faculty Bargaining: Change and Conflict: A Report Prepared for the Carnegie Commission on Higher Education and the Ford Foundation.* New York, NY: McGraw-Hill.

Ginder, Scott A., Janice E. Kelly-Reid, and Farrah B. Mann. 2019. "Enrollment and Employees in Postsecondary Institutions, Fall 2017; and Financial Statistics and Academic Libraries, Fiscal Year 2017." Washington, DC: National Center for Education Statistics. https://bit.ly/3arvZVs

Harvey, Marcus. 2006. "Graduate Employee Organizing and Representation." In *Academic Collective Bargaining,* edited by Ernst Benjamin and Michael Mauer, pp. 134–158. Washington, DC, and New York, NY: American Association of University Professors and Modern Language Association,

Hatton, Erin. 2020. *Coerced: Work Under Threat of Punishment.* Berkeley, CA: University of California Press.

Hayden, Grant M. 2001. "The University Works Because We Do: Collective Bargaining Rights for Graduate Assistants." *Fordham Law Review* 69 (4): 1233–1264.

Heneman, Herbert G. and Marcus H. Sandver. 1983. "Predicting the Outcome of Union Certification Elections: A Review of the Literature." *ILR Review,* Vol. 36, No. 4, pp. 537–559.

Herbert, William A. 2011. "Card Check Labor Certification: Lessons from New York." *Albany Law Review* 74 (1): 93–173.

Herbert, William A. 2017. "The History Books Tell It? Collective Bargaining in the 1940s." *Journal of Collective Bargaining in the Academy* 9 (1): 1–40.

Herbert, William A., and Jacob Apkarian. 2017. "Everything Passes, Everything Changes: Unionization and Collective Bargaining in Higher Education." *Perspectives on Work* 21: 30–35.

Herbert, William A., and Jacob Apkarian. 2019. "You've Been with the Professors: An Examination of Higher Education Work Stoppage Data, Past and Present." *Employee Rights and Employment Policy Journal* 23 (2): 249–277.

Herbert, William A., Jacob Apkarian, and Joseph van der Naald. 2020. *Supplementary Directory of New Bargaining Agents and Contracts in Institutions of Higher Education, 2013–2019.* New York, NY: National Center for the Study of Collective Bargaining in Higher Education and the Professions, Hunter College, City University of New York.

Herbert, William A., and Joseph van der Naald. 2020. "A Different Set of Rules? NLRB Proposed Rule Making and Student Worker Unionization Rights." *Journal of Collective Bargaining in the Academy* 11 (1): 1–36.

Herzfeld, John. 2016 (Apr. 6). "Speakers Show Split Views on Impact of NLRB Case on Graduate Assistants." *Bloomberg BNA Daily Labor Report,* No. 66. https://bit.ly/3qsuTy3

Johnson, Kimberly Quinn, and Joseph Entin. 2000. "Graduate Employee Organizing and the Corporate University." *New Labor Forum* 6 (Spring–Summer): 99–107.

Julius, Daniel J., and Patricia J. Gumport. 2003. "Graduate Student Unionization: Catalysts and Consequences." *The Review of Higher Education* 26 (2): 187–216.

Kezar, Adrianna, Tom DePaola, and Daniel T. Scott. 2019. *The Gig Academy: Mapping Labor in the Neoliberal University.* Baltimore, MD: Johns Hopkins University Press.

Kitchen, Deeb-Paul. 2014. "Can Graduate Students Re-Energize the Labor Movement?" *Thought & Action* (Fall): 47–61.

Korn, Melissa, Mark Peters, and Douglas Belkin. 2015 (Nov. 10). "Race Wasn't the Only Issue at University of Missouri." *Wall Street Journal.* https://on.wsj.com/2ZjYQ7t

Kroeger, Teresa, Celine McNicholas, Marni von Wiplert, and Julia Wolfe. 2018 (Jan. 11). "The State of Graduate Student Employee Unions: Momentum to Organize Among Graduate Student Workers is Growing Despite Opposition." Washington, DC: Economic Policy Institute. https://bit.ly/3pqpdDw

Ladd, Everett Carll Jr., and Seymour Martin Lipset. 1973. *Professors, Unions, and American Higher Education.* Washington, DC: The American Enterprise Institute for Public Policy Research.

Lafer, Gordon. 2003. "Graduate Student Unions: Organizing in a Changed Academic Economy." *Labor Studies Journal* 28 (2): 25–34.

McCarthy, Michael. 2012. "Occupying Higher Education: The Revival of the Student Movement." *New Labor Forum* 21 (2): 50–55.

McNicholas, Celine, Margaret Poydock, and Julia Wolfe. 2019 (Dec. 19). "Graduate Student Workers' Rights to Unionize are Threatened by Trump Administration Proposal." Washington, DC: Economic Policy Institute. https://bit.ly/3jTL9Wi

Mullen, Ann L., Kimberly A. Goyette, and Joseph A. Soares. 2003. "Who Goes to Graduate School? Social and Academic Correlates of Educational Continuation after College." *Sociology of Education* 76 (2): 143–169.

National Labor Relations Board Freedom of Information Act (NLRB FOIA) Responses. NLRB Case Nos. LR-2017-0964 and -2020-000423 (in authors' possession).

National Labor Relations Board. 2021 (Mar. 15). "Jurisdiction—Nonemployee Status of University and College Students Working in Connection with Their Studies." *Federal Register* 86 (48): 14297. https://bit.ly/3amXTBh

National Education Association. 2019. "Faculty Pay: The Special Salary Issue 2019." *NEA Higher Education Advocate* 37 (1): 1–39.

New York University–Graduate Student Organizing Committee/UAW. 2013 (Nov. 26). "Neutrality and Election Agreement." https://bit.ly/2N9snOM

Pollack, Sheldon D., and Daniel V. Johns. 2015. "Northwestern Football Players Throw a 'Flail Mary' but the National Labor Relations Board Punts: Struggling to Apply Federal Labor Law in the Academy." *Virginia Sports & Entertainment Law Journal* 15 (1): 77–109.

Posselt, Julie R., and Eric Grodsky. 2017. "Graduate Education and Social Stratification." *Annual Review of Sociology* 43: 353–378.

Reyes, Juliana Feliciano. 2018 (Apr. 13). "Union Organizers Say Penn State Is Trying to Scare Foreign Grad Students with ICE—and It's Working." *Philadelphia Inquirer.* https://bit.ly/3aqV3f4

Rhoads, Robert A., and Gary Rhoades. 2005. "Graduate Employee Unionization as Symbol of and Challenge to the Corporatization of US Research Universities." *The Journal of Higher Education* 76 (3): 243–275.

Robin, Corey, and Michelle Stephens. 1996. "Against the Grain: Organizing TAs at Yale." *Social Text* 49 (Winter): 43–73.

Ross, Jenna. 2012 (Mar. 26). "Grad Student Workers at U Reject Union Again." *Star Tribune.* http://strib.mn/3aqBzra

Schackner, Bill. 2001 (Feb. 4). "PSU Grad Students Push to Unionize." *Pittsburgh Post-Gazette.* https://bit.ly/2ZkxbmS

Schackner, Bill. 2018 (Apr. 24). "Penn State Graduate Assistants Vote Down Union Attempt." *Pittsburgh Post-Gazette.* https://bit.ly/3ps6A1Q

University of Michigan Board of Regents. 2020 (Jun. 25). "Board Resolution Regarding Employer Neutrality, Cooperative Determination and Recognition of Bargaining Units, and Notification of Agreements." https://bit.ly/3qqgWRb

Verburg, Steven. 2011 (Aug. 20). "TA Union Bows Out Under New Law." *Wisconsin State Journal,* p. A1.

Court and Administrative Decisions

Adelphi University, 195 NLRB 639 (National Labor Relations Board 1972).

Brown University, 342 NLRB 483 (National Labor Relations Board 2004).

The Trustees of Columbia University, 364 NLRB No. 90 (National Labor Relations Board 2016).

Cornell University and Cornell University Students United, Re: Election Objections, May 16, 2018. Howard C. Edelman, Arbitrator. https://bit.ly/2Zm5KsZ

Employes of the University of Pittsburgh, 51 PPER §24 (Pennsylvania Labor Relations Board 2019).

Leland Stanford Junior University, 214 NLRB 621 (National Labor Relations Board 1974).

The New School, NLRB Case No. 02-RC-143009 (National Labor Relations Board 2017).

New York University, 332 NLRB 1205 (National Labor Relations Board 2000).

New York University, NLRB Case No. 02-RC-023481 (National Labor Relations Board 2010).

Oregon University System, OERB Case No. UC-04-12 (Oregon Employment Relations Board 2013).

Polytechnic Institute of New York University, NLRB Case No. 29-RC-12054 (National Labor Relations Board 2011).

Pratt Institute, 339 NLRB 971 (National Labor Relations Board 2003).

Regents of the University of California, 22 PERC §29084 (California Public Employee Relations Board 1998).

Regents of the University of California, 13 PERC §20087 (California Public Employee Relations Board 1989), 8 Cal. Rptr. 2d 275 (Cal. Ct. App. 1992).

State of New York (State University of New York), 24 NYPERB 3035 (New York Public Employee Relations Board 1991), conf'd, *State of New York (State University of New York) v. New York State Public Employment Relations Board,* 586 N.Y.S.2d 662 (N.Y. App. Div. 1992).

University of Iowa/State Board of Regents, PERB Case Nos. 4959 and 5463 (Iowa Public Employment Relations Board 1994).

University of Minnesota, Unit 10, BMS Case No. 12-PCE-7h3 (Minnesota Bureau of Mediation Services 2012).

University of Oregon, Case No. C-207-75, 2 PECBR 1039 (Oregon Employment Relations Board 1977).

CHAPTER 12

The Future of US Public School Reform: Elevating Teacher Voice

Saul A. Rubinstein
Rutgers University

John E. McCarthy
Cornell University

ABSTRACT

This chapter traces the history of neoliberal public school reform in the United States and explores how these approaches have not produced the results promised. It then presents national research on how reforms based on union–management partnerships and the resultant collaborative systems in public schools have improved outcomes for student performance, teacher turnover, innovation, and knowledge sharing, particularly in lower-income schools. We also explore the changing roles of local unions and their leaders who are engaged in these partnership arrangements. Of particular interest for this volume is the impact of elevating union leader and teacher voice. The chapter concludes by moving from research to practice by reporting on promising approaches to scaling the model at a state level, thus establishing collaborative school reform as a research-based, proven alternative to past neoliberal education policies.

INTRODUCTION

For decades, motivated by comparisons of United States public school student performance against international benchmarks, a debate has raged across the country regarding the best way to reform and improve K–12 public education in the United States. Yet surprisingly, Democrats and Republicans have been mainly on the same side in this debate, even while they have been able to agree on little in other policy areas. Furthermore, common policies supported by Democrats and Republicans over six administrations have repeatedly failed to produce the promised outcomes, even as both parties have continued to adhere to essentially the same neoliberal education reforms.

This chapter begins with a review of education reform policies in the United States, starting with the influence of mass production management philosophies on the relationships of administrators and teachers. We then examine and critique the specific neoliberal reforms advanced by both Republican and Democratic administrations over the past 40 years. This is followed by the introduction of an alternative approach to public school reform rooted in new institutional relationships (partnerships) between teachers unions and school administration that elevates the voice of teachers as professionals in school planning, decision making, and problem solving. We describe the results of our national research on the impact of these more collaborative and professional relationships on student achievement, teacher retention, and sharing of innovation. We conclude with an examination of efforts by key state-level educational stakeholders in New Jersey to apply this research in creating policies that promote union–management partnerships and greater educator collaboration as a model for school improvement.

THE INFLUENCE OF SCIENTIFIC MANAGEMENT

Public schools in the United States today continue to carry the legacy of organizational and management principles developed a century ago by Frederick Taylor. Taylor clearly differentiated the work of management (planning and thinking) from that of labor (implementing management's plans). His *Principles of Scientific Management*, published in 1911, was heralded by many scholars and education leaders as an objective, scientifically grounded means by which to ensure that teachers and teaching methods were efficient and that the materials students were taught complied with standards (Brooks and Miles 2008; Callahan 1962; Emery 2007; Nelson and Watras 1981). Some drew explicit analogues between schooling and factory work, viewing children as the raw materials to be molded by teachers to meet the needs of society, as if progressing along an assembly line (see Rogoff, Matusov, and White 1998).

Just as scientific management in manufacturing attempted to separate labor from decisions regarding the appropriate method of work, scientific management in schools attempted to remove or minimize teachers' influence over important matters regarding children's schooling (Callahan 1962; Emery 2007; Nelson and Watras 1981). This is because matters of curriculum development were believed to be too complex to be left to teachers or laypeople who were unfamiliar with popular managerial theory: "Only those who had studied the textbooks, read the research, taken the courses and mastered the theories could be permitted to decide what children should learn," as well as how they should learn it (Ravitch 2001: 164). The model envisioned by proponents of scientific management in education was one in which administrators worked to develop the best curriculum, learning materials, instructional plans, and metrics for evaluation, and then passed these guidelines on to teachers, who were expected to faithfully carry them out. This policy of applying industrial "efficiency" techniques to education spread quickly. Principals took on the role of middle managers. Superintendents assumed an executive role, establishing curriculum, instructional practices, and standardized metrics for evaluating performance throughout the district as a whole.

Throughout the 20th century, the efficiency movement attempted to transition teachers from philosophers of education, actively engaged in determining what should be taught and how to teach it, to passive instruments for fulfilling whatever pedagogical techniques were laid down from up high (Callahan 1962; Oakes 1986). Knowledge became divided into ever-smaller areas, sequestered by classrooms and deemed valuable only insofar as it bore association with defined, measurable outcomes (Oakes 1986). Unsurprisingly, teacher opposition bubbled to the surface (Callahan 1962; Oakes 1986). Teachers objected to the Tayloristic standardization of their craft not just because it undermined their agency as professional educators but because it miscalculated what was of value, emphasizing cost per student and a quantifiable gain at the expense of what was less tangible but nonetheless important.

THE NEOLIBERAL NARRATIVE IN THE PAST 40 YEARS OF US PUBLIC SCHOOL REFORM

In the late 20th century, school reform became driven not only by Taylorist views of assembly line teachers but also by the free-market theories of neoliberalism. Schools were no longer thought of as just factories but also like businesses subject to market forces. Specifically, neoliberalism is a worldview that holds that everyone is better off when individual freedom and property rights are protected through free markets so that people can pursue their own self-interest unfettered by government regulations. Neoliberals believe in minimizing the state's role, except where government is necessary to protect free markets.

The past 40 years of school reform policy refined over six administrations, both Republican and Democrat, clearly adopted this neoliberal ideology about the importance of free markets in public education through expanding the use of charter schools, vouchers, and privatization. These market-based approaches to education reforms have been connected to a set of managerial principles rooted in the legacy of mass production and characterized by a rigid hierarchy that separated thinkers (management) from doers (labor), and a horizontal division of labor that reduces the discretion exercised by employees by setting explicit standards for each task and job and then ensuring adherence with those standards through supervisors.

With roots in Taylor's efficiency movement of the early 20th century, this neoliberal approach operates under the "assumption that if [educators] adhere to the rules—teaching the prescribed curriculum, maintaining the correct class sizes, using the appropriate textbooks, and accumulating the right number of course credits—students will learn what they need to know" (DuFour and Eaker 1998: 22). Decision making about core issues under this model is removed from those who carry out the task of teaching, while student learning and teacher effectiveness are viewed as something distillable to a set of core criteria that can be precisely measured and used for evaluation and comparison. In seeking to expose public schools to the forces of the competitive marketplace, the neoliberal approach assumes that the problem with US public education is the withheld discretionary effort by teachers that results from a lack of accountability, incentives, and pressure (Darling-Hammond and Montgomery 2008). With greater competition through charter schools, vouchers, and privatization, neoliberals hope to provide less job security for teachers and therefore assume they will be motivated to work harder and more effectively. Public schools that lag behind must improve or risk closure. Charter schools are seen to hold special promise because they operate outside the restrictive policies of the district bureaucracy and accompanying union rules (Carpenter and Noller 2010).

In public school reform, this shift to standards and outcomes (test results) and away from a focus on ensuring adequate resources, particularly for high-poverty schools, underemphasizes the impact of poverty on student achievement. Teachers are held accountable through monitoring their compliance with standards and measuring outcomes, thereby reducing their professional voice and agency.

This legacy of top-down reform that limited teacher voice as professional educators can be found in the reforms put forward by both Republican and Democratic administrations over the past four decades. During Ronald Reagan's first term in office, his administration created a National Commission on Excellence in Education that produced the famous 1983 report, "A Nation at Risk: The Imperative for Educational Reform." This report claimed underachievement by US students on comparative international standardized tests and warned that American education had been "eroded by a rising tide of mediocrity that threatens our very future as a Nation and a people (US National Commission on Excellence in Education 1983). Reagan then leveraged this claim to enact legislation that expanded the collection and use of comparative student test data from the National Assessment of Educational Progress (NAEP). It argued that substandard student achievement was a global risk to the United States both economically and socially. While questions have been raised about the validity of the research behind the report, the Reagan administration nonetheless used it to set the stage for a new national education reform agenda by pushing for higher standards in US K–12 education, for expanded use of tests nationwide to measure achievement, and for greater use of private sector business and free-market approaches through more parental choice in their children's schools (Ravitch 2020; Rhodes 2012).

Since the publication of "A Nation at Risk," the growing perception in the United States has been that the country's education system has fallen sharply off course and that decisive involvement by the federal government was necessary to help gain its competitive bearings. Active federal involvement in school reform increased momentum in the late 1980s under the presidency of George H.W. Bush, who continued support for these educational policies in concert with state leaders across the country, including then-Governor Bill Clinton, first through the "National Educational Goals" of 1989 including school readiness, graduation goals, and subject-matter proficiency. Pushed further by private sector business advocates, the Bush administration argued in 1991, in its "America 2000" proposal, for increased voluntary standards and testing, and private school choice through vouchers. The proposal failed to gain congressional approval over several issues, including school choice; however, it further shaped the framing of US public school reform around the issues of standards, testing, accountability, and choice.

The Clinton administration continued this trajectory through the Goals 2000: Educate America Act and the Improving America's Schools Act that established national standards, pressured states through funding to adopt aligned standards and tests, and required school and district accountability through report cards analyzed by states to determine progress for all students, as well as disadvantaged students, against these standards. These policy initiatives also shifted the question of educational equity away from differences in access to resources and toward providing equitable standards and curriculum. An important alliance for this reform strategy emerged between the entrepreneurs within the business community and other advocates of free-market approaches and civil rights leaders and liberals concerned with equity issues. Charters, in particular, were seen as a way to give children in underserved communities a higher-quality education.

This public school reform agenda intensified under the administration of George W. Bush. His No Child Left Behind (NCLB) law passed the House and Senate with overwhelming bipartisan support in 2001. This legislation called for testing every child in grades 3 through 8 in both math and reading and again in high school. By 2007, science testing was to be introduced. States could develop their own standards and choose their own tests, but schools had to show "Adequate Yearly Progress" with 100% grade-level proficiency in reading and math by 2014. As a first step for forcing accountability, students could transfer to another school if schools did not meet yearly goals. If a school continued to "fail," corrective action would be taken by changing curriculum, increasing teaching hours, and/or firing faculty and administration. As a final punitive step if schools did not improve sufficiently, they could be closed, turned into a "charter school" with private management, or taken over by the state.

Charter schools receive public funding but are run independently of the public school district by private management organizations or community-based groups. They typically have no publicly elected school boards and operate for the most part without teachers unions. Charters are also exempt from many of the state regulations and laws that cover public schools. Management companies that run charters can be for profit or nonprofit. Thus, market reform advocates believed that the choice parents could make to move their children out of public schools and into charters would discipline the public schools to improve. They also believed that turning over public education to private management organizations would improve education through privatization—managing schools privately with public dollars.

Bush was also a proponent of another market-based reform—vouchers. Vouchers are publicly funded scholarships that parents can use to send their children to private or parochial schools. It was believed this choice by parents would again create a market by which public schools would be in competition with private schools, forcing public schools to improve or face the prospect of having no students. NCLB rested on the reform logic that the problem with education was inadequate expectations and accountability. Thus, setting high standards and well-articulated goals, along with greater monitoring through standardized tests and private sector competition, would improve student outcomes across the board. Bush expanded the federal role in education by pushing this standards, testing, accountability, and choice reform agenda. The testing regime introduced by NCLB became law across the country.

Barack Obama's secretary of education, Arne Duncan, put Bush's NCLB reforms on steroids. The Obama administration's Race to the Top (RTTT) program created an intense competition for $4.35 billion in post-recession 2009 stimulus funding. To compete for these funds, states had to change their laws and education policies to improve standards, expand the use of student testing and use those results to evaluate teachers and hold them accountable for student performance (value-added assessments), as well as increase competition through the use of charter schools. Thirty-four states, the District of Columbia, and Puerto Rico had to modify their education laws and policies in order to be eligible to submit reform plans and receive funding under RTTT. Forty-six states and the District of Columbia put together RTTT reform plans, but only 18 received funding. Thus, Duncan used the leverage of this funding (less than 1% of total US school spending) to change education policies and laws across the country to increase the use of common standards and high-stakes testing for students and to introduce punitive accountability measures through the use of these tests in teacher evaluations and in the decisions to close schools, as well as the expansion of charter schools and vouchers.

Continuing to promote these policies, Donald Trump's secretary of education, Betsy DeVos, worked hard to expand school choice and privatization, especially through the use of vouchers.

So the reforms outlined above, from Reagan through Trump but pursued most aggressively by the Bush administration (NCLB) and its better-funded cousin (RTTT), are all neoliberal approaches to education reform combining free-market policies (charters and vouchers) with an increased managerial emphasis on standards, testing, control, and bureaucratic accountability measures.

Neither NCLB nor RTTT was research based—there were no studies or evidence that these approaches would work. Instead these reforms were pushed because of ideology—that markets would produce better results than the public sector and that student achievement would improve if schools were privately managed (not necessarily by educators) and rooted in more corporate business-like practices. This also meant less democratic governance because charter, private, and for-profit schools operate without publicly elected school boards and typically do not have teachers unions.

A Lack of Results

Despite their popularity with policy makers, these neoliberal approaches to school reform have not only had a negative impact on school climate by undervaluing teachers—dismissing their professional input and attacking their unions—they have also failed to produce the promised results. They have not raised test scores; for example, NAEP scores have been flat over this 40-year period (National Assessment of Educational Progress 2019; Ravitch 2020). Overall, a variety of studies have shown that charter schools on average have not performed any better than public schools (Center for Research on Education Outcomes 2009, 2013, 2015, 2019). Further, evaluation of charter performance also suffers from a selection bias—compared to their public counterparts, charters often have more-involved families and more-motivated students, they enroll proportionately fewer students with learning disabilities or who are English Language Learners (ELL), and they have fewer students with discipline issues. Concluding that charters were not producing equity by closing the achievement gap, the NAACP in 2016 abandoned its support for charters and called for a moratorium on their further expansion. The research on voucher programs has demonstrated that they actually produced worse results for students (Ravitch 2020).

A 2016 evaluation of RTTT by the US Department of Education itself could not determine whether the reforms it promoted had any impact on student test scores despite the multibillion-dollar investment (US Department of Education 2016). In 2018, the RAND Corporation and the American Institutes of Research studied the value-added assessment program that the Department of Education, the Gates Foundation, and others had promoted to evaluate teachers based on student test scores. The research found that this costly reform had no impact on teaching quality or student achievement (RAND 2018). By then, nearly all states that had adopted the two national common core standards tests pushed by Duncan (Partnership for Assessment of Readiness for College and Careers (PARCC) and Smarter Balanced Assessment Consortium) had reversed course and dropped them.

On the other hand, the punitive accountability measures adopted by NCLB and even more intensively by RTTT had exacted a huge cost. Billions of dollars had been spent on testing, the creation of new standards and related curriculum, the purchase of new educational materials, new systems of teacher evaluation, and school closures. Further, since only reading and math were tested, other subjects were cut, de-emphasized, or received reduced instruction time. Yet educators had been vilified by NCLB and RTTT and demoralized by the reform movement's value-added testing regime that wasted teaching time on extensive testing and test preparation. Teachers began leaving the profession at the fastest rate on record (Hackman and Morath 2018), and as teacher shortages increased, this assault made it even more difficult to attract young people to the teaching profession. And worse, the legacy of the neoliberal reforms of RTTT—increased testing, accountability through evaluation and school closures, and attempts at instituting market discipline through charters and vouchers—were now written into law in a majority of states thanks to the leverage exercised by Duncan.

Further, neoliberal reform policies—dominated by market-driven approaches coupled with top-down bureaucratic mandates for teacher accountability practices that rely heavily on high-stakes standardized testing—have created friction between teachers unions, administrators, school boards, parents, policy makers, and other stakeholders in public education and have fueled disagreements over how to improve the quality of teaching and learning for children. While many factors make consensus elusive when it comes to school reform, a key obstacle to finding agreement around educational improvements and bringing such improvements to fruition has been division among the key stakeholders, particularly teachers unions and administration.

AN ALTERNATIVE NARRATIVE: A COLLABORATIVE APPROACH TO PUBLIC SCHOOL IMPROVEMENT

Scholars suggest that the most sought-after outcome for education moving forward should be systems that promote commitment, continued learning, and informed experimentation among highly trained professionals (DuFour and Eaker 1998; DuFour, Eaker, and DuFour 2008; Fullan 1993, 2007, 2010). The argument is that educational change, like organizational change, is an inherently human and social endeavor. Reform by mandate neglects the human side of organizations under the assumption that what is designed and forcefully implemented from the top will be faithfully carried out by those in the classroom. However, research shows that successful, sustained reform requires that educators be committed to the goals and strategies that will be collectively undertaken (Evans 2001). This means that teachers should have voice in decisions regarding how standards will be used, which instructional practices and learning materials will be incorporated, and how assessment will be implemented so as to encourage shared goals and decisions that educators are committed to carrying out (see Stoll et al. 2006 for a review).

An area of school reform that has gone particularly unexplored is the potential for collaboration between teachers unions and administration directed at school improvement. Yet, within some districts and schools in the United States, union leaders and school administrators have found an alternate path to improving student performance not rooted in neoliberal market solutions or in test-based teacher accountability policies but instead centered on building strong relationships and collaboration among educators and focused on teaching quality and educational improvement for students. When applying these ideas to public education, we define union–management partnerships to be institutional arrangements that provide opportunities for union leaders, administrators, school board members, and teachers to work together, identifying and solving problems, planning, and making decisions.

Researchers have recognized that a quality partnership between district management and the local union may help to create an environment conducive to teamwork and professional community (DuFour, Eaker, and DuFour 2008; Fullan 2007). The underlying assumption is that reform will be more sustainable when both labor and management share the same vision and agree on the appropriate course for carrying it out. The role of the union in directly promoting district innovations has also been recognized—but to a very limited degree and without much elaboration. Providing an exception, Koppich (2005) has studied a small number of "reform bargaining" school districts, including Minneapolis, Denver, and Montgomery County, Maryland, in which collective bargaining contracts extend well beyond wages and working conditions into education policy and the quality of teaching and learning.

To date, with few exceptions, there are very limited cases in the literature that deal with collaborative reform efforts that have a broad focus on the improvement of the overall operations of school districts from the school board to the classroom, including teaching and student performance. Our work attempts to fill that gap through exploring the impact of extensive collaboration between teachers and administrators, sustained over decades by union–management institutional partnerships. Our research is also unique in analyzing how these partnerships emerged, were structured, contributed to school quality, and endured over long periods of time.

There is a long history in the United States of private sector joint union–management collaboration to improve organizational performance; for example, dating back to the 1920s in the textile, apparel, and railway industries (Slichter 1941). Slichter concluded that these collaborative arrangements could resolve contradictions between industrial jurisprudence that protects worker rights through a system of rules, and the productivity that can be restricted by those rules. These efforts expanded during the organizing drives after the New Deal and were extensive in the armaments industries during the early and mid-1940s (Golden and Parker 1949; Golden and Ruttenberg 1942; Slichter, Healy, and Livernash 1960). During the crisis of World War II, more than 600 organizations had labor–management joint committees working together to solve quality and production problems in support of the war effort. Most of these arrangements vanished in the 1950s because the urgent need to bolster wartime production disappeared, and management reasserted its claim to managerial prerogatives.

A more recent body of literature on labor–management partnerships has studied these arrangements over the past 40 years as US industries have restructured their work organizations, human resource management, and labor relations systems in the face of global competition (AFL-CIO 1994; Eaton, Rubinstein, and McKersie 2004; Eaton and Voos 1994; Freeman and Rogers 1999; Heckscher 1988; Kochan, Katz, and McKersie 1986; Levine and Tyson 1990; Osterman 2000; Piore and Sabel 1984; Wilkinson, Gollan, Marchington, and Lewin 2010). These arrangements have been used in a number of US industries including automotive (Adler 1995; MacDuffie 1995; Rubinstein 2000; Rubinstein and Kochan 2001), computer and business equipment (Cutcher-Gershenfeld 1987), steel (Frost 1998; Hoerr 1988; Ichniowski and Shaw 1999; Rubinstein 2003), healthcare (Kochan, Eaton, McKersie and Adler 2009), communications (Heckscher, Maccoby, Ramirez, and Tixier 2003), and pharmaceuticals (Rubinstein and Eaton 2009). Research has shown that increased participation in decision making and problem solving, and the use of collaborative team-based work organization, results in substantial improvements to quality and productivity (Appelbaum, Bailey, Berg, and Kalleberg 2000; Ichniowski et al. 1996).

Organizational networks are increasingly important when change is rapid, and flexibility, responsiveness, and problem solving are critical for success. Union–management collaboration facilitates the creation of such networks, linking people across organizations who have the knowledge and resources necessary for rapid coordination, effective decision making, and problem solving. When unions use their infrastructure to help create these networks, high levels of trust can result, and this adds tremendous value to organizational innovation, responsiveness, and effectiveness (Kaufman and Levine 2000; Rubinstein 2000, 2001; Rubinstein and Kochan 2001).

Over the past few decades, unions have typically not been characterized as being at the forefront of public school reform. In fact, while some scholars have suggested that the presence of unions is associated improved student performance (Vachon and Ma 2015), others have argued that unions reduce student performance (Hoxby 1996).

RESEARCH RESULTS: THE IMPACT OF UNION–MANAGEMENT PARTNERSHIPS AND EDUCATOR COLLABORATION

In earlier research, we examined cases of successful school reform that resulted from collaborative partnerships between teachers unions and administrators working together in innovative ways to improve teaching quality and student performance, a stark contract to the neoliberalist approaches. We analyzed these cases to identify the common elements that all school districts with long-term union–management partnerships shared (Rubinstein and McCarthy 2012).

We then looked more deeply into these partnerships to examine the collaboration that occurs within schools between teachers and administrators. Specifically, we studied the way partnerships have impacted student achievement by fostering more productive collaboration within schools. We also explored the mechanisms by which union–management partnerships can facilitate teacher collaboration and improve student performance (Rubinstein and McCarthy 2014, 2016). In what follows, we review some of these findings as they pertain to student achievement, teacher turnover, poverty, and knowledge sharing.

Since 2016, we have expanded this research through a nationwide study of the impact of union–management partnerships and educator collaboration on educational outcomes in public schools across the country. As of this writing, our database includes over 450 schools in 25 school districts in six states: California, Illinois, Maine, Massachusetts, Minnesota, and New Jersey. We focus on school and district decision making and problem solving, particularly as they apply to the relationship among administrators, teachers, and their unions. We are interested in how collaborative processes at the school level—specifically, shared decision making; goal alignment; and teacher discretion, voice, and psychological safety[1]—impact student performance, teacher turnover and engagement, sharing of innovation, and the ways teachers view their principals and union leaders as resources. In addition, we study how union–management partnerships in school districts shape school culture.

Educator Collaboration and Student Achievement

In our earlier published research (Rubinstein and McCarthy 2014, 2016) on 30 schools in one district, we found a relationship between school-level collaboration and student achievement. In our national study, we were able to match math and language arts performance data to 162 schools surveyed in the 2015–2016 academic year. Figure 1 shows school-level collaboration predicting the percentage of students performing at or above standards in English language arts, after we controlled for poverty (percentage of students on free or reduced-price lunch), teacher experience, and school type (elementary, middle, high school). The reported positive association is statistically significant and suggests that the highest level of collaboration corresponds to roughly 12.5% more students performing

Figure 1
Collaboration and English Language Arts Performance

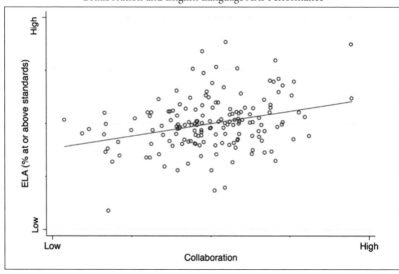

at or above standards, compared to the lowest level of collaboration. We found similar results when we examined the effect of collaboration on math scores, although not quite at the same magnitude. The impact of collaboration on math scores was statistically significant, as the highest level of collaboration corresponded to an additional 4.5% of students performing at or above standards, compared with the lowest level of collaboration.

Collaboration, Teacher Turnover, and School Commitment

Our earlier research also found a strong association between educator collaboration and reduced teacher turnover, and this effect was particularly pronounced in high-poverty schools (Rubinstein and McCarthy, forthcoming). Specifically, our work found that turnover in high-poverty schools was 3.5 times the rate of that in low-poverty schools when school-level educator collaboration was low. However, when collaboration was high, there was no statistical difference between turnover in high-poverty and low-poverty schools (Figure 2).

In our more recent national study, we examined teachers' self-reported commitment to their current school and found similar patterns to our earlier research. For example, we found that collaborative schools improved educators' commitment, particularly in schools serving low-income communities. As depicted in Figure 3, the association between school collaboration and the attachment of educators to their school is generally positive, but this positive effect is stronger in schools where student poverty is high. At the highest level of collaboration, there was no statistical difference between teacher commitment in high-poverty and wealthier schools.

Figure 2
Collaboration, Poverty, and Turnover

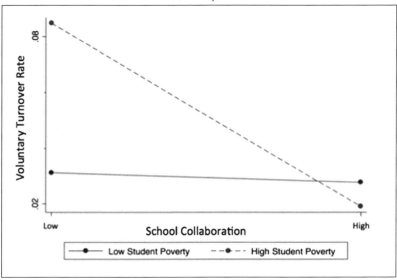

Figure 3
Collaboration, Poverty, and Commitment

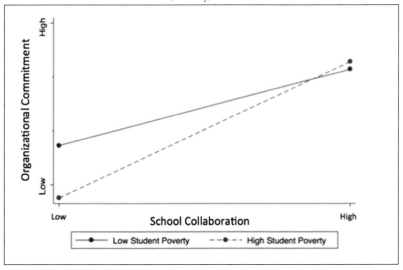

Union Leaders, Networks, and Partnerships

As mentioned earlier, union–management partnership is defined by the extent to which union leaders and district administration work together to improve teaching and learning. One of our primary research interests is whether formal union–management partnerships can foster school-level processes that improve teaching quality and student learning. In a study of 30 schools in one district with a strong, long-standing partnership, we found that many school-level union leaders took on unique roles and responsibilities to improve teaching and learning. Specifically, we found that these union leaders helped to foster more extensive, more productive school collaboration, as shown in Figure 4 (Rubinstein and McCarthy 2016). We also found that teachers in schools with stronger collaboration are more likely to know about and implement innovations from other schools, and that union representatives who have more ties to other union representatives facilitate this knowledge sharing (McCarthy 2019; McCarthy, forthcoming). So the network of union leaders added value to knowledge sharing across the district.

District-Level Union–Management Partnerships as a Catalyst for School-Level Collaboration

In our national study, we also investigated the impact of formal union–management partnerships at the district level on educator collaboration at the school level. We

Figure 4
Union Leader Ties and Knowledge Sharing

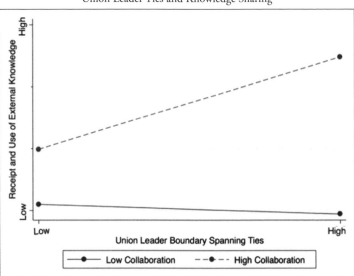

found that district-level partnerships were a significant predictor of school-level educator collaboration. As Figure 5 depicts, school districts with strong partnerships tended to have more collaborative schools, and this result is statistically significant. Our data also suggested that school-level union representatives viewed their responsibilities differently in high-partnership than in low-partnership school districts: in high-partnership school districts, school representatives were more likely to view collaboration building as central to their responsibilities as union leaders. We conclude that formal district-level union–management partnerships can be an important antecedent of school-level collaboration.

Summary of the Findings from Our Research

- School-level collaboration improves student performance (English language arts and math), even after we control for poverty.
- School-level collaboration reduces voluntary turnover and increases school commitment. These effects are particularly strong for high-poverty schools.
- Highly collaborative schools and strong union-leader networks increase cross-school knowledge sharing.
- Formal union–management partnerships at the district level seem to be a catalyst for building highly collaborative schools, as we find that district partnerships are positively associated with school collaboration.

Figure 5
District Partnership and School Collaboration

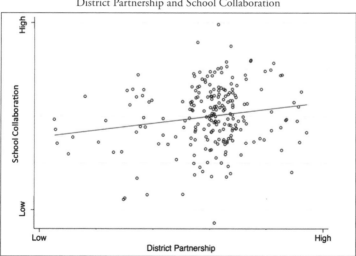

- School representatives in high-partnership districts are more likely to view collaboration building as central to their union roles and responsibilities.
- We also found that collaboration, including shared decision making, goal alignment, teacher discretion, voice, and psychological safety, are all positively associated with teachers' perceptions of individual teacher and collective faculty effectiveness.

Tests can reveal deficiencies in student knowledge but can offer little more beyond alerting parents and teachers to a problem. Union–management partnerships and collaborative efforts, because they are problem focused, can take the critical next steps and help drive thinking about ways to increase student learning. These types of partnerships are designed to use collaboration among educators to find solutions to gaps in student achievement and then effectively implement those solutions because those closest to the problem—with tacit knowledge of it—are key stakeholders in the improvement process.

PUTTING RESEARCH INTO PRACTICE: A LABORATORY OF DEMOCRACY

In May 2013, leaders from the New Jersey School Boards Association (NJSBA), the New Jersey Education Association (NJEA), the American Federation of Teachers New Jersey (AFTNJ), the New Jersey Association of School Administrators (NJASA), and the New Jersey Principals and Supervisors Association (NJPSA) met to review the early research described above linking collaboration and student achievement. They also explored ways to introduce collaborative approaches in New Jersey to enhance the quality of public education. As a result, these state level organizations joined together to form the NJ Public School Labor–Management Collaborative to encourage and facilitate greater collaboration among unions and management at the state and district levels to strengthen and improve teaching and learning across New Jersey. The state leaders of the Collaborative meet regularly and have been working together to create formal union–management partnerships across districts and within schools to foster greater collaboration among educators to improve schools in a wide variety of ways.

As of this writing, 23 districts covering 128 schools have attended workshops organized by the Collaborative to build capacity for collaborative work, priority setting, joint decision making and problem solving, strategic planning, and organizational change. Based on the success with these districts, the Collaborative has been trying to build an infrastructure in the state to expand capacity and offer follow-up facilitation in order to reach a critical mass of districts statewide.

This infrastructure includes organizing all districts involved into an "Interdistrict Learning Network" that meets twice a year so that leaders from all districts (superintendents, union leaders, principals, school board members, and teachers) can come together to share experiences and help each other deepen their collaboration around teaching and learning. The Collaborative has also trained facilitators from the early adopting districts (superintendents, union presidents and other leaders, school board members, principals, and teachers). These facilitators help to build capacity in new districts.

In this way, New Jersey has become what former Supreme Court Justice Louis Brandeis called a "laboratory of democracy," experimenting with new social and economic policies at the state level to determine results before expanding them across the country. The state is trying to play a role in a national movement for collaborative school reform—demonstrating that teachers, administrators, parents, and communities working together can make dramatic improvements in the quality of education.

This approach offers a clear contrast to the neoliberal reforms of the past 40 years offered by both Democratic and Republican administrations. First, it is based on an institutional or pluralist perspective valuing the legitimacy of multiple stakeholders in our public school systems—school boards, administrators, teachers unions, faculty and staff, parents and students. In particular, it elevates the voice of teachers and their unions. The approach values input, dialog, and improvement through joint problem solving, decision making, and implementation. This is in stark contrast to the neoliberal approach of top-down managerial decision making.

This approach is also problem focused, bringing all resources to bear on finding solutions instead of trying to use market forces to compete with and "discipline" public schools into improvement. Resources are devoted to bringing professionals together to find new and better ways to educate instead of spending on more and higher stakes testing. Unlike the neoliberal policies, there are actual data that show that union–management partnerships and the resulting educator collaboration produce improved outcomes: higher student achievement, cross-district innovation and learning, and greater teacher retention and commitment to remaining in the teaching profession. This is especially true in high-poverty schools.

There is also a shift in the drivers of education reform (Figure 6): From markets to multiple stakeholders; from testing to teaching and learning; from policy makers in Washington, D.C., to local and state educators; from a command-and-control perspective to one based on partnership and collaboration; from a top-down approach to believing the answers are in the room or in the school.

Figure 6
Shift in the Drivers and Focus of Education Reform

	From	To
What?	Markets	Multiple Stakeholders
	Testing	Teaching & Learning
Who?	Policy Makers/DC	Educators/ States
How?	Command/Control	Partnership/ Collaboration
	Top-Down	Answer in the Room

CONCLUSION

Our research into this institutional multi-stakeholder collaborative approach to school reform suggests it is a viable alternative to the neoliberal policies of the past. While neoliberalism has its roots in the ideology of free-market managerialism, collaborative school reform is rooted in multi-stakeholder institutional pluralism. Its democratic values are combined with 21st-century organizational and employment relations practices. As state-level unions, school boards, and administrator associations work together to scale this approach, they are building on the US tradition of states as laboratories of democracy.

In this work, we have taken an institutional and organizational perspective, looking at schools as systems and examining employment relations practices as antecedents to systematic change. The focus is not simply the presence of unions but the organizational systems and industrial relations in school districts—the mechanisms that encourage trust and collaboration and build strong networks among teachers and create strong partnerships with administrators. Indeed, numerous education researchers have encouraged greater levels of professional collaboration among teachers as a means of improving student achievement (DuFour and Eaker 1998; DuFour, Eaker, and DuFour 2008). While several studies have shown that greater levels of social capital (Leana and Pil 2006; Pil and Leana 2009) and collaboration (Goddard, Goddard, and Tschannen-Moran 2007) can have positive implications for student performance, there is little known about the institutional antecedents to professional collaboration, particularly in the context of public schools.

We attempt to fill this gap in the literature by examining union–management partnerships as catalysts for professional collaboration in public schools— specifically, the value that they can bring to organizational performance by creating a culture of collaboration elevating the voice of teachers as professionals and an infrastructure for shared problem solving and decision making with management. The industrial relations literature has a long tradition of exploring the impact of labor relations and union–management collaborative efforts on organizational performance. With a few exceptions (Johnson 1984; Kerchner, Koppich, and Weeres 1997), these arrangements have not been extensively studied in public education. Further, there has been little exploration of the causal mechanisms by which labor–management partnerships affect student performance. Our work not only offers strong evidence that union–management partnership relations have important implications for education quality and student achievement, but it also suggests that these performance gains are attributable to greater workforce collaboration.

ENDNOTE

1. Psychological safety is the extent to which one perceives that he or she can be open and question policies or decisions without fear of reprisal.

REFERENCES

Adler, P.S. 1995. "'Democratic Taylorism': The Toyota Production System at NUMMI." In *Lean Work: Empowerment and Exploitation in the Global Auto Industry*, edited by S. Babson, pp. 207–219. Detroit, MI: Wayne State University Press.

AFL-CIO. 1994 (Feb.). "The New American Workplace: A Labor Perspective." Report by the AFL-CIO Committee on the Evolution of Work. Washington, DC: AFL-CIO.

Appelbaum, Eileen, Thomas Bailey, Peter Berg, and Arne Kalleberg. 2000. *Manufacturing Advantage: Why High-Performance Work Systems Pay Off*. Ithaca, NY: Cornell University Press.

Brooks, Jeffrey, and Mark Miles. 2008. "From Scientific Management to Social Justice … and Back Again? Pedagogical Shifts in the Study and Practice of Educational Leadership." In *Leadership for Social Justice: Promoting Equity and Excellence Through Inquiry and Reflective Practice*, edited by Anthony H. Normore. Charlotte, NC: Information Age.

Callahan, Raymond E. 1962. *Education and the Cult of Efficiency: A Study of the Social Forces That Have Shaped the Administration of the Public Schools*. Chicago, IL: University of Chicago Press.

Carpenter, Dick II, and Scott Noller. 2010. "Measuring Charter School Efficiency: An Early Appraisal." *Journal of Education Finance* 35 (4): 397–415.

Center for Research on Education Outcomes. 2009. "2009 Report Summary." Stanford, CA: Stanford University. https://stanford.io/3gv1hxT

Center for Research on Education Outcomes. 2013. "National Charter School Study 2013." Stanford, CA: Stanford University. https://stanford.io/38Idn2d

Center for Research on Education Outcomes. 2015. "2015 Report Summary." Stanford, CA: Stanford University. https://stanford.io/3vaWKF8

Center for Research on Education Outcomes . 2019. "Charter School Performance in the State of Washington." Stanford, CA: Stanford University. https://stanford.io/3awpRKS

Cutcher-Gershenfeld, Joel. 1987. "Xerox and the ACTWU: Tracing a Transformation in Industrial Relations." In *Human Resources Management*, 2nd ed., edited by Fred K. Foulkes and E. Robert Livernash. Englewood Cliffs, NJ: Prentice Hall.

Darling-Hammond, Linda, and Kenneth Montgomery. 2008. "Keeping the Promise. The Role of Policy in Reform." In *Keeping the Promise? The Debate Over Charter Schools*, edited by Leigh Dingerson, Barbara Miner, Bob Peterson, and Stephanie Walters. Washington, DC: Rethinking Schools.

DuFour, Richard, and Robert Eaker. 1998. *Professional Learning Communities at Work: Best Practices for Enhancing Student Achievement*. Bloomington, IN: Solution Tree Press.

DuFour, Richard, Robert Eaker, and Rebecca DuFour. 2008. *Revisiting Professional Learning Communities at Work: New Insights for Improving Schools*. Bloomington, IN: Solution Tree Press.

Eaton, Susan, Saul A. Rubinstein, and Robert McKersie. 2004. "Building and Sustaining Labor–Management Partnerships: Recent Experiences in the U.S." *Advances in Industrial & Labor Relations* 13: 139–156.

Eaton, Adrienne, and Paula Voos. 1994. "Productivity Enhancing Innovations in Work Organization, Compensation, and Employee Participation in the Union vs. Non-Union Sectors." *Advances in Industrial & Labor Relations* 6: 63–109.

Emery, Kathy. 2007. "Corporate Control of Public School Goals: High-Stakes Testing in Its Historical Perspective." *Teacher Education Quarterly* 34 (2): 25–44.

Evans, Robert. 2001. *The Human Side of School Change: Reform, Resistance, and the Real-Life Problems of Innovation*. San Francisco, CA: Jossey-Bass.

Freeman, Richard B., and Joel Rogers. 1999. *What Workers Want*. Ithaca, NY: Cornell University Press.

Frost, Ann. 1998. "Variation in Labor–Management Collaboration Over the Redesign of Work: Impacts on Work Organization and Outcomes." *Advances in Industrial & Labor Relations* 8: 89–117.

Fullan, Michael. 1993. *Change Forces: Probing the Depths of Educational Reform*. Levittown, PA: Psychology Press.

Fullan, Michael. 2007. *Leading in a Culture of Change*. Fulshear, TX: Somerset House.

Fullan, Michael. 2010. *All Systems Go: The Change Imperative for Whole System Reform*. Thousand Oaks, CA: Corwin Press.

Goddard, Yvonne, Roger Goddard, and Meghan Tschannen-Moran. 2007. "A Theoretical and Empirical Investigation of Teacher Collaboration for School Improvement and Student Achievement in Public Elementary Schools." *Teachers College Record* 109 (4): 877–896.

Golden, Clinton S., and Virginia Parker. 1949. *Causes of Industrial Peace Under Collective Bargaining*. New York, NY: Harper & Bros.

Golden, Clinton S., and Harold Ruttenberg. 1942. *Dynamics of Industrial Democracy*. New York, NY: Harper & Bros.

Hackman, Michelle, and Eric Morath. 2018 (Dec. 28). "Teachers Quit Jobs at Highest Rate on Record." *Wall Street Journal*. https://on.wsj.com/2P0y7Le

Heckscher, Charles. 1988. *The New Unionism: Employee Involvement in the Changing Corporation*, New York, NY: Basic Books.

Heckscher, Charles, Michael Maccoby, Rafael Ramirez, and Pierre-Eric Tixier. 2003. *Agents of Change: Crossing the Post-Industrial Divide*. Oxford, UK: Oxford University Press.

Hoerr, J.P. 1988. *And the Wolf Finally Came: The Decline of the American Steel Industry*. Pittsburgh, PA: University of Pittsburgh Press.

Hoxby, Caroline M. 1996. "How Teachers' Unions Affect Education Production." *Quarterly Journal of Economics* 111 (3): 671–718.

Ichniowski, Casey, and Kathryn Shaw. 1999. "The Effects of Human Resource Management Systems on Productivity: An International Comparison of U.S. and Japanese Plants." *Management Science* 45 (5): 621–769.

Ichniowski, Casey, Thomas Kochan, David Levine, Craig Olson, and George Strauss. 1996. "What Works at Work: Overview and Assessment." *Industrial Relations* 35 (3): 299–333.

Johnson, Susan Moore. 1984. *Teacher Unions in Schools*. Philadelphia, PA: Temple University Press.

Kaufman, Bruce E., and David I. Levine. 2000. "An Economic Analysis of Employee Representation." In *Nonunion Employee Representation: History, Contemporary Practice, and Policy*, edited by Bruce Kaufman and Daphne Gottlieb Taras, pp. 149–175. Armonk, NY: M.E. Sharpe.

Kochan, Thomas, Adrienne Eaton, Robert McKersie, and Paul Adler. 2009. *Healing Together: The Labor–Management Partnership at Kaiser Permanente*. Ithaca, NY: Cornell University Press.

Kochan, Thomas, Harry Katz, and Robert McKersie. 1986. *The Transformation of American Industrial Relations*. New York, NY: Basic Books.

Kerchner, Charles Taylor, Julia E. Koppich, and Joseph G. Weeres. 1997. *United Mind Workers: Unions and Teaching in the Knowledge Society*. San Francisco, CA: Jossey-Bass.

Koppich, Julia. 2005. "Addressing Teacher Quality Through Induction, Professional Compensation, and Evaluation: The Effects on Labor–Management Relations." *Educational Policy* 19 (1): 90–111.

Leana, Carrie R., and Frits K. Pil. 2006. "Social Capital and Organizational Performance: Evidence from Urban Public Schools." *Organization Science* 17 (3): 353–366.

Levine, David, and Laura D'Andrea Tyson. 1990. "Participation, Productivity, and the Firm's Environment." In *Paying for Productivity*, edited by Alan S. Blinder. Washington, DC: Brookings Institution.

MacDuffie, John Paul. 1995. "Human Resource Bundles and Manufacturing Performance: Organizational Logic and Flexible Production Systems in the World Auto Industry." *Industrial and Labor Relations Review* 48 (2): 197–221.

McCarthy, J.E. Forthcoming. "Labor–Management Partnerships' Effects on Unionists' Interaction Networks: Evidence from US Public Schools." *Industrial Relations*.

McCarthy, J.E. "Collaboration, Student Poverty and Teacher Turnover." Working Paper.

McCarthy, J.E. 2019. "Catching Fire: Institutional Interdependencies in Union-Facilitated Knowledge Diffusion." *British Journal of Industrial Relations* 57 (1): 182–201.

National Assessment of Educational Progress (NAEP). 2019. "The Nation's Report Card." Washington, DC: National Assessment of Educational Progress. http://nces.ed.gov/nationsreportcard/

Nelson, Richard, and Joseph Watras. 1981. "The Scientific Movement: American Education and the Emergence of the Technological Society." *Journal of Thought* 16 (1): 49–71.

Oakes, Jeannie. 1986. "Keeping Track, Part 1: The Policy and Practice of Curriculum Inequality." *Phi Delta Kappan* 68 (1): 12–17.

Osterman, Paul. 2000. "Work Reorganization in an Era of Restructuring: Trends in Diffusion and Effects on Employee Welfare." *Industrial and Labor Relations Review* 53 (2): 179–196.

Pil, Frits K., and Carrie Leana. 2009. "Applying Organizational Research to Public School Reform: The Effects of Teacher Human and Social Capital on Student Performance." *Academy of Management Journal* 52 (6): 1101–1124.

Piore, Michael J., and Charles F. Sabel. 1984. *The Second Industrial Divide.* New York, NY: Basic Books.

RAND Corporation. 2018. "Improving Teaching Effectiveness. Final Report: The Intensive Partnerships for Effective Teaching Through 2015–2016." Santa Monica, CA: RAND Corporation. https://bit.ly/3qLsa2h

Ravitch, Diane. 2001. *Left Back: A Century of Battles Over School Reform.* New York, NY: Simon & Schuster.

Ravitch, Diane. 2020. *Slaying Goliath.* New York, NY: Knopf.

Rhodes, Jesse. 2012. *An Education in Politics: The Origin and Evolution of No Child Left Behind.* Ithaca, NY: Cornell University Press.

Rogoff, Barbara, Eugene Matusov, and Cynthia White. 1998. "Models of Teaching and Learning: Participation in a Community of Learners." In *Handbook of Education and Human Development,* edited by David R. Olson and Nancy Torrance, pp. 373–398. Oxford, UK: Blackwell.

Rubinstein, Saul A. 2000. "The Impact of Co-Management on Quality Performance: The Case of the Saturn Corporation." *Industrial and Labor Relations Review* 53 (2): 197–218.

Rubinstein, Saul A. 2001. "Unions as Value-Adding Networks: Possibilities for the Future of U.S. Unionism." *Journal of Labor Research* 22 (3): 581–598.

Rubinstein, Saul A. 2003. "Partnerships of Steel—Forging High Involvement Work Systems in the US Steel Industry: A View from the Local Unions." *Advances in Industrial & Labor Relations* 12: 115–144.

Rubinstein, Saul, and Adrienne Eaton. 2009. "The Effects of High Involvement Work Systems on Employee and Union-Management Communications Networks." *Advances in Industrial & Labor Relations* 16: 109–135.

Rubinstein, Saul A., and Thomas Kochan. 2001. *Learning From Saturn: Possibilities for Corporate Governance and Employee Relations.* Ithaca, NY: Cornell University Press.

Rubinstein, Saul, and John E. McCarthy. 2011. "Reforming Public School Systems Through Sustained Union–Management Collaboration." Report. Washington, DC: Center for American Progress. https://ampr.gs/3vsjiBY

Rubinstein, Saul, and John E. McCarthy. 2012. "Public School Reform Through Union—Management Collaboration." *Advances in Industrial & Labor Relations* 20: 1–50.

Rubinstein, Saul, and John E. McCarthy. 2014. "Teachers Unions and Management Partnerships: How Working Together Improves Student Achievement." Report. Washington, DC: Center for American Progress. https://ampr.gs/3czq0xA

Rubinstein, Saul, and John E. McCarthy. 2016. "Union–Management Partnerships, Teacher Collaboration, and Student Performance." *Industrial and Labor Relations Review* 69 (5): 1114–1132.

Rubinstein, Saul A., and John E. McCarthy. Forthcoming. *A Challenge To School Reform Policy: Positive Evidence From Within U.S. Public Schools.*

Slichter, Sumner. 1941. *Union Policies and Industrial Management*. Washington, DC: Brookings Institution.

Slichter, Sumner, James J. Healy, and E. Robert Livernash. 1960. *The Impact of Collective Bargaining on Management*. Washington, DC: Brookings Institution.

Stoll, Louise, Ray Bolam, Agnes McMahon, Mike Wallace, and Sally Thomas. 2006. "Professional Learning Communities: A Review of the Literature." *Journal of Educational Change* 7: 221–258.

Taylor, Frederick. 1911. *The Principles of Scientific Management*. New York, NY: Harper and Brothers.

US Department of Education. 2016. "Race to the Top: Implementation and Relationship to Student Outcomes, Executive Summary." Report. Washington, DC: US Department of Education.

US National Commission on Excellence in Education. 1983. "A Nation at Risk: The Imperative for Educational Reform." Report. Washington, DC: Government Printing Office. https://bit.ly/2OZNsM5

Vachon, Todd, and Josef Ma. 2015. "Bargaining for Success: Examining the Relationship Between Teacher Unions and Student Achievement." *Sociological Forum* 30 (2): 391–414.

Wilkinson, Adrian, Paul J. Gollan, Mick Marchington, and David Lewin. 2010. *The Oxford Handbook of Participation in Organizations*. Oxford, UK: Oxford University Press.

Chapter 13

Empowering Workers: Education and Training in the Changing Labor Market

Alysa Hannon
Heather McKay
Michelle Van Noy
Rutgers University

ABSTRACT

When the unemployment rate goes up in the United States, familiar calls for skills development ring out from the media, policy makers, and business. Yet skills development in the United States is complicated, as any change to workforce education involves myriad systems, institutions, government agencies, and policies that are all heavily influenced by employers functioning within the American liberal market economy. Skills development policies and practices designed under these conditions are not always structured in ways that strengthen the power and position of workers. In this chapter, we review the conceptual parameters of skilling in the United States and highlight key strategies that can promote worker interests within the country's existing systems and empower workers to better buffer against the existent challenges of the labor market, particularly those of a liberal market economy.

INTRODUCTION

When the unemployment rate goes up in the United States, familiar calls for skills development ring out from the media, policy makers, and business. Yet skills development in the United States is complicated, as any change to workforce education involves myriad systems, institutions, government agencies, and policies that are all heavily influenced by employers functioning within the liberal market economy. Skills development policies and practices designed under these conditions are not always structured in ways that strengthen the power and position of workers. For example, policies and narratives around workforce training in the United States often blame workers for their unemployment or low wages and place the burden—cost and otherwise—on them for improving the quality of their employment through training. There are practitioners and policy makers on the ground, however, who are developing models for workforce development policy and practice with the goal of promoting worker interests. In this chapter, we review the conceptual parameters of skilling in the United States and highlight key strategies that can promote worker interests.

THE LIMITS AND PROMISES OF SKILLS DEVELOPMENT IN THE UNITED STATES

Skills development in the United States is commonly viewed as a core strategy to address societal economic woes. When the economy is troubled, as it was during the Great Recession and more recently as a result of the COVID-19 pandemic, calls for skills development abound (Baker 2020). During the Great Recession, there was strong bipartisan support for investment in skills training through nearly $2 billion grants for Trade Adjustment Assistance and Community College Career Training (TAACCCT). In the throes of the pandemic, reports on skills shortages and the need for skills development were strewn across newspapers, magazines, and the Internet.

Skills development is not just a topic of interest during economic downturns. Discussions about the future of work and the need for workers to continually acquire new skills to operate within the changing labor market are ever present. Nongovernmental agencies, consulting firms, and academics have contributed to the conversation about the coming wave of automation and technology that could drastically change how work is done and what work is (Autor, Mindell, and Reynolds 2019; Manyika et al. 2017; Organisation for Economic Co-operation and Development 2019). Some jobs may disappear entirely, new jobs will be created, and new skills will be prioritized. Projections vary on the degree to which jobs will be eliminated because of technology, but most suggest there will be some significant changes to what it means to work. Not everyone agrees that these changes will negatively affect workers, however. Some argue that automation creates new opportunities. James Bessen (2020) provides some evidence that when major industries automate, employment often rises rather than falls. Bessen's work suggests that technology will likely have varied impacts in different industries over time, meaning that some industries will grow at the same time others decline. This vision of the future, while not as dire as many others, still impacts workers in that it requires that they adapt to transition to new occupations. This often involves acquiring new skills and sometimes even relocating.

Some scholars remind us that the implementation of technology and automation and the changes to work that result are not inevitable. They argue instead that such shifts should be viewed as choices made by people (Brown, Lloyd, and Souto-Otero 2018). This argument centers on the idea that people and institutions have some power as to how, why, and whether work changes and in what ways. Still, there is little doubt that, in the United States, the people and institutions making those choices are influenced more by employers than workers whose lives are perhaps most profoundly affected by them. Ultimately, shifts in the labor market create a need for ongoing skills development as workers face employment instability and must adapt to changing job requirements. The economy has shifted from one in which skills development could be primarily completed early in the life course to one in which lifelong learning is necessary.

If workers do not adapt to the changing labor market, there are real consequences. Case and Deaton (2015) observe that "deaths of despair" are plaguing middle-aged, working-class, White Americans whose life expectancy has been declining over recent years because of increases in suicide and drug overdoses. They argue that this public health crisis results from the disappearance of decently paid manufacturing jobs that once gave meaning and purpose to working-class life in America. This reality is often cited as the reason for the rise of the current manifestations of the populist movement in American politics. This dynamic is not new to Black Americans, who have faced economic discrimination and inequities in access and opportunity in skills development throughout American history. Social, political, and institutional forces outside of Black workers' control and the realities of systemic racism have led to fewer educational opportunities and significant barriers to success. The results of skilling efforts often have less fruitful results for Black workers in terms of both employment opportunities and wages (Card, Devicienti, and Maida 2011; Gould and Wilson 2020).

Even given the clear challenges for Black workers that must be addressed, skills development can be good for workers, businesses, and the economy. When done well, high-quality education and workforce training can produce benefits for all: workers can get good jobs, businesses can improve efficiency, and economic productivity can receive a boost (Holzer, Davis, Miller-Adams, and Singleton 2020). For workers, research shows that higher levels of education correspond, on average, to higher levels of employment, higher wages, and a lower likelihood of job loss (Baum 2014). Those with more education—particularly college degrees—are also typically healthier, more engaged citizens and have more opportunities available to them than adults with no post-secondary education.

However, in the United States, skills training is not always done well. Institutions are not well established to create a coherent system with pathways that lead workers to economic opportunity. Workers are increasingly responsible for developing their skills and navigating their educational and career pathways on their own. They are also asked to bear the financial, time, and risk burdens of skilling and education with few supports. Workers must navigate the many training options and figure out how to absorb training into their already complex lives as members of families and communities. These economic realities are not typically recognized in policy, practice, and rhetoric around skills development.

While skilling is important for workers, and having an educated workforce is good for the economy, skilling is not the silver bullet that it is sometimes made out to be. Even when workers have skills, the demand for their labor may not exist, or their labor may not be adequately compensated. Wages have been stagnant, and work is increasingly becoming precarious and contingent. These economic challenges are often not the result of skills deficiencies but rather are reflections of larger systemic issues in the labor market. There is a danger that the notion of a skills mismatch can be "a convenient—and perhaps comfortable—explanation for falling wages and rising inequality" (Lafer 2002). Skills training may be needed and can be effective, but it must be coupled with good economic policy (Baker 2020; Tankersley 2020). This means that any skills development must be aligned with labor market needs—that is, it must convey skills that are needed in actual jobs that have openings for new workers (Cleary, Kerrigan, and Van Noy 2017). If alignment efforts are not made, skills development can become a distraction from the real problem—a lack of jobs in the labor market.

Declining labor standards are not inevitable. Institutions have a role in mitigating the changes and their effects. Education systems, unions, collective bargaining units, and financial markets, as well as public investment, labor market regulations, and tax policies can all buffer against the increased inequality associated with technological progress and automation—changes that disproportionately affect workers without college degrees (Autor, Mindell, and Reynolds 2019). The current system for skills development is fractured and disconnected, but opportunities exist to shift the system toward a more coordinated one that creates coherent pathways for economic advancement (Schurman and Soares 2010).

While many who study work and workers may simply cast aside the idea of skills development as unimportant or unfixable, we argue that better systems for skills development must be funded and developed and that workers need to be empowered by—and exercise voice in—the process. With a broader view that simultaneously recognizes the limits and possibilities of education and training, skills development can help promote worker rights. This chapter examines both the underlying assumptions that form the basis of the US system for skills development and takes a bottom-up approach, looking at how policies and practices on the ground can be shaped to serve the interests of workers and set the foundation for broader, long-term change.

EXAMINING THE POLITICS OF SKILLING

Let us start with conceptual issues. To place this discussion in context, we compare the US skills development system with those of other advanced industrialized countries. Then we turn to a more detailed discussion of the US system. Finally, we examine the tensions inherent in the US system and the ways in which skills are conceptualized in it.

The US System in Comparative Perspective

The United States, labeled a liberal market economy in the varieties of capitalism (VoC) literature, depends mostly on market mechanisms to coordinate its labor market (Hall and Soskice 2001). This stands in stark contrast to the institutional arrangements of coordinated market economies, which rely on collaborative relationships facilitated by strong institutions. Most of Europe, with the exception of the United Kingdom, can be characterized broadly as coordinated. Typically, coordinated market economies have skills systems that are more stratified, feature stronger vocational training, and provide more effective channels for the collective agency of workers, as well as better outcomes for lower-income workers (Andersen and Van De Werfhorst 2010; Busemeyer and Trampusch 2011). In contrast, the United States typifies the extreme liberal market economy; in fact, in typologies that go beyond the bifurcation of the VoC paradigm specifically with regard to training systems, the United States is held up as the quintessential "liberal skill formation system" (Busemeyer and Trampusch 2011).

The US system has also undergone further liberalization as part of recent global neoliberal trends. This comparative context is important for two major reasons. First, alternative models for training represented by the world's rich democracies might offer insight into improvements that could be made to the US system. While this chapter's focus is bottom-up innovation borne of practice, it is important to keep in mind that there are indeed regulatory policy solutions. Countries across Europe have been experimenting with such solutions for decades, and researchers have demonstrated that they generally outperform the United States on measures such as equity, economic resilience, and long-term adaptability (Busemeyer and Trampusch 2011; Schulze-Cleven, Watson, and Zysman 2007). For example, Denmark's "flexicurity" approach to labor market policy has been put forward as a model for the United States to emulate, given that it prioritizes labor market flexibility like the United States while also guaranteeing social security for unemployed workers (Schulze-Cleven 2015).

Second, this comparative context is vital to our understanding of the historical origins of different national training systems, their potential for change, and the unique set of challenges they face in realizing that potential. The literature on comparative training regimes reveals that political power dynamics have variously allowed for or prevented the development of certain market-mediating training institutions. For example, both research on the relationship between a country's dominant type of unionism and the prevalence of apprenticeship, and research on the relationship between the different electoral systems of countries and the nature of their employer organizations, have reached the same key finding: that training institutions are interwoven with the rest of the institutions that comprise a nation's political economy and therefore are driven by similar power dynamics (Martin and Swank 2008; Thelen 2004). Thus, where we find weak or lacking institutions for training across the American landscape, we can assume that this absence is determined in part by the influence of business interests over those of workers—particularly low-income workers.

This overarching outlook guides much of what occurs within the United States and influences the conceptual ideas that drive skills development. Those ideas include the definitional parameters of the skills development system, the definition of skill underlying that system, and the goals of the various actors within the system as they respond to its incentives and disincentives. Within the United States, there are two concepts of workforce development: one narrowly defined, the other more broadly conceived. The traditional, narrow definition of workforce development is associated with decades of federal legislation written in response to crises and designed as a policy tool against abject poverty. Examples include the Manpower Development Training Act and the Work Incentive Program of the 1960s, the Comprehensive Employment and Training Act of the 1970s, and the Job Training Partnership Act of the 1980s (Gatta and Finegold 2010). With the Workforce Investment Act of 1998, which was later replaced by the Workforce Innovation and Opportunity Act (WIOA) in 2014, employers formally became the client of American workforce development policy, and unemployed workers the target participants, reflecting a "neoliberal trajectory" observed across advanced industrialized nations from the 1970s through the early 2000s (Baccaro and Howell 2011). The WIOA currently serves as the cornerstone for workforce development policy and practice in the United States. Notably, the WIOA includes an increased emphasis on regional coordination and planning through its mandate that states develop strategic plans accounting for the training requirements of state- and regional-level economic growth strategies. This requirement does not represent a move toward more institutional planning in American labor market policy. Instead, it marks a response to increasingly globalized competition for US industries and the formal integration of economic and workforce development goals (113th Congress 2014; Harper-Anderson 2008).

In contrast, the broad view of workforce development takes into account not only the systems and structures under the WIOA but also the formal education system, including secondary career and technical education; higher education, in particular community colleges; and other career and technical education actors. While these systems have typically operated separately in the United States, the number of touchpoints between them has expanded over time, and their strategic relevance has increased (Schurman and Soares 2010). With the education system struggling to meet the rapidly evolving needs of the 21st-century workplace, there is growing consensus around the need to better integrate academic learning and work-oriented training (Schurman and Soares 2010). Additionally, as the higher education system is forced to re-examine its financial model, modes of delivery, and audience amid the COVID-19 pandemic, a unique opportunity exists to reimagine higher education's relationship to the workforce training system. The ultimate goal is a more coordinated, holistic post-secondary education system capable of being academically rigorous while also being structurally flexible and responsive to the changing nature and needs of work (Schurman and Soares 2010). Yet, given the competitive rather than collaborative nature of the US skills development system, facilitating coordination will likely require more than a series of administrative, institutional, or legislative remedies; it will require changing American firm behavior (Ornston and Schulze-Cleven 2015).

Understanding the Tensions Between Stakeholders

Whether worker interests are advanced is in part determined by the competing goals of the various actors in the workforce development system, including employers, workers, occupational groups, educational providers, and the state. There are tensions among the respective goals of these various groups and the interests that shape them. The most obvious and studied tension occurs between workers and employers. Workers take a long-term view of their career and life goals, whereas employers seek short-term matches in skills between workers and immediate job openings. In the decades following World War II, employers typically had longer-term relationships with workers, particularly higher-paid workers, and were more likely to view long-term investments in skills development as being in line with their own interests (Cappelli 1999). In recent decades, the increased focus on short-term business gains by employers coupled with the decreased tenure of workers with employers has led many employers to all but abandon investment in worker training. Traditionally, employers have invested little in the training of lower paid workers because the incentive for retention of those employees is low. As a result, the interests of workers in skills development are left to be addressed only by public investments like those from the public workforce development system (Hansson 2008).

Where employer training is provided, it often focuses on a narrow set of "firm-specific" skills that are immediately relevant to a particular job rather than on the kind of general skills that can increase a worker's value in the marketplace (Becker 1994). Workers can benefit from these narrow opportunities for skills development only if there are institutional means to connect the learning opportunities to broader learning goals. The career pathways movement, as discussed further in the next section, is an attempt at creating space for those connections to develop. Alternately, employers may invest in general skills development through tuition reimbursement programs that allow workers to pursue degrees. This strategy is designed to retain workers, differentiate companies based on the skill level of their workers, and create high-performance work systems (Appelbaum, Bailey, Berg, and Kalleberg 2000; Barney 1991; Cappelli 2004). These kinds of investments are the exceptions, however. It is far more typical in recent times for employers to limit their training investment to a narrow set of skills only, if they make any such investment at all.

The broad trend of employers disinvesting in worker skills development has placed the burdens and costs of skills investment on educational institutions and workers themselves. In recognition of this, the US government has made investments in community college infrastructure to create workforce education and training focused on community needs—balancing employer interests with student goals (Mikelson, Eyester, Durham, and Cohen 2017). These investments have helped create institutional infrastructures that better support the interests of workers.

At the same time, the educational system is not without potential interests that can be at odds with the goals of workers and that serve to disempower them. For example, because the for-profit education sector has incentive to enroll as many learners as possible, those learners can be at risk of pursuing educational programs that are low quality and high cost and do not lead to the promised outcomes (Angulo 2016; Cottom 2017). Even in publicly funded institutions, the sector's trend toward "financialization" has been associated with less direct state funding and greater reliance on federally subsidized student loans (Schulze-Cleven and Olson 2017). Efforts to regulate and provide accountability to the educational sector can protect worker interests by removing bad actors and providing information to workers.

Further tensions in the workforce development system are reflected in the regulation of occupational training. Many fields require workers to have educational credentials and/or pass licensure examinations before they are able to practice in the field (Kleiner 2011). These requirements exist to ensure a minimum level of competence, but they also reflect the interests of occupational groups by keeping wages high for workers within the occupation and making entry more difficult for others (Collins 2019; Weeden 2002). The regulations could also work the other way, however: The formal structures created by licensure requirements may make entry easier by clarifying the process and removing informal entry processes (Redbird 2017). Moreover, while apprenticeships can be (positively) viewed as a worker-focused way of skilling that provides apprentice workers with some degree of power over their working conditions, occupations in which these opportunities are common, like construction, have a (negative) history of discrimination and closure (Waldinger and Bailey 1991).

Though the United States clearly faces challenges in workforce development, the openness and flexibility of the country's systems do present opportunities to workers. Unlike in a rigid system of occupational choice, where people make choices about their career path early in life and change can be challenging, workers in the US system have more flexibility in educational and occupational choices and can change paths (Powell, Coutrot, Graf, and Bernhard 2009).

Conceptualizing Skills

How we conceptualize skills has significant implications for workers. Even within the market-oriented American paradigm, there are various ways to view skills that can help shape skills development so that it more effectively empowers workers.

Through a positivist lens, skills are conceptualized as objectively observable, measurable, and thus tradable in the labor market. As a point of contrast, a Weberian perspective views skills as socially constructed and hierarchically driven by occupational competition, and a Marxist perspective sees skill as a site of capital–labor conflict (Attewell 1990).

In the positivist frame, the distinction between general skills (worker skills transferable to more than one employer) and specific skills (worker skills relevant to only one employer) has been instrumental for a scholarly comparison of training regimes. In the tradition of economics, human capital theory indicates that general skills (as opposed to firm-specific skills) empower workers because they provide flexibility for them in the labor market. However, we know from the varieties of capitalism literature that coordinated market economies have training systems that are more targeted to industries, occupations, or firms; often prioritize employment over job choice; and tend to produce more equitable outcomes for workers across the income spectrum (Andersen and Van De Werfhorst 2010; Busemeyer and Trampusch 2011; Estevez-Abe, Iversen, and Soskice 2001). The trade-offs associated with different types of skills are real for workers, and the institutional arrangements around employment and training in part determine how skills can be effectively leveraged to empower workers.

As the pace of technological change has dramatically increased, the valuation of certain skills has evolved alongside it. In the context of automation and "21st-century skills," scholars ask whether to attribute skills to people or to jobs/tasks (Ananiadou and Claro 2009; Attewell 1990). Some scholars have attributed skills to task bundles like expert thinking, complex communication, routine cognitive, routine manual, and nonroutine manual (Autor, Levy, and Murnane 2003). This framework has been used to understand how automation might alter the skills demands of workers. Alternatively, the growth of the service sector has elevated a people-centered approach for the measurement of skills, in particular around social and emotional competencies of workers, which could imply the commodification of their personal attributes (Gatta, Boushey, and Appelbaum 2009; Osher et al. 2016). In turn, the conceptualization of skills on which training regimes rely is high-stakes territory for workers. Let us now turn to reviewing reform strategies for the American skills development systems.

POLICIES AND PRACTICES TO PROMOTE WORKER INTERESTS

While the US system is fragmented, there is opportunity to "connect the dots" and more effectively serve the education and workforce development needs of individuals (Schurman and Soares 2010). Given the substantial returns to knowledge for workers and for the economy at large, the US system has the capacity not only to improve the access of workers to knowledge but also to do so in a way that advances their collective interests. To effectively connect the dots, the many different components of education and training must be brought together, including employer-sponsored training, community colleges and vocational school certificates and degrees, community college transfer degrees, four-year college and university degrees, and graduate and professional schools. We review strategies currently being implemented, including sector strategies, career pathways, job-quality initiatives, union training funds, credential system reforms, and systemic educational reforms as strategies that could increase the coherence of American training institutions.

Sector Strategies

With their focus on the demand side of skills, sector strategies use industry sectors as a guide for regional skills development and coordinate institutional actors to build a more cooperative system overall. Sector strategies focus on generating and coordinating strong local talent pipelines for a region's core industries or industry clusters in partnership with local employers and local education providers. Thus, sector strategies are designed to cater to a particular sector or occupation and to support the growth or competitiveness of a regional economy on a global scale (Prince, King, and Oldmixon 2017). The development of sector strategies in the United States is similar to industry-specific training regimes characteristic of coordinated market economies. These strategies are also analogous to the industry-based strategies Paul Osterman advocated in the volume *Creating Good Jobs* (2019). However, it is essential to recognize that sector strategies as implemented under the WIOA are the result of competitive pressures in the global market. They are not strategically intended to improve power dynamics between employers and workers or worker organizations. Nevertheless, the focus on global competition has important repercussions for workers and the framing and resourcing of skills development locally. Instead of prioritizing the individual needs of employers, sector strategies are now prioritizing the needs of globally competitive industry clusters, indicating "a good deal of competitive advantage lies outside companies ... and companies might actually benefit from having more local competitors" (Porter 2000: 16).

This reconfiguration of competitive advantage has been beneficial for American workers in a few ways. First, with firms competing as a cluster globally instead of with each other locally, they have incentive to invest cooperatively in their shared local labor market (Dyer and Singh 1998; Lavie 2008). Second, because regional coordination of investment requires collaboration, firms have been motivated to form strategic alliances with other firms and with local educational providers (Wassmer 2010). Third, firms in industry clusters have deemed skills transferable outside of any one individual firm a worthy investment for their collective competitive advantage. In sum, sector strategies value workers' skills and thus give workers more power in their local labor markets.

Career Pathways

Career pathways offer a strategy to rationalize the broader workforce development system to help workers advance in careers through a combination of education and work. Rather than a fragmented and disconnected system of education and training, career pathways are "well-articulated sequences of quality education and training offerings and supportive services that enable educationally under-prepared youth and adults to advance over time to successively higher levels of education and employment in a given industry sector or occupation" (Mortrude 2014: 1). The US Department of Labor (2020) lays out some key ideas about how career pathways should work. Credentials must be connected and transparent and include multiple entry and exit points between education and employment. They must also be "stackable" so learners can build on prior education as they pursue additional education. Further, career pathways systems should be constructed of intentionally designed programs that are clearly articulated, provide support for students, engage with industry, and align policy and practice. The essential goal of career pathways is to create real opportunities for advancement in a career for workers, so clear articulation across credentials is key. This approach seeks to add some structure to the inherent flexibility of the US system.[1]

The concept of career pathways has been broadly codified into federal legislation through the Perkins Career and Technical Education Act, the WIOA, and the Higher Education Act, which widely extended the idea. Many state systems have sought to organize their educational offerings and advising around the concept of career pathways systems by developing a systematic approach to the effort, including leading states in the movement such as Arkansas, California, Illinois, Kentucky, Massachusetts, Oregon, Virginia, Washington, and Wisconsin (Center for Postsecondary and Economic Success 2013). An essential premise of the career pathways movement is that learners can actually move along those pathways. This premise relies on a pair of assumptions. First, there must be adequate jobs along a pathway—not just a tiny number of positions that are unattainable to a large number of low-paid workers. Each credential in a pathway is a step toward more well-paying jobs. Second, the educational pathway must be attainable for learners. Career pathways assume that learners are able to attain the credentials along the pathway. Much has to be done within systems to make sure articulations happen and within institutions to provide real supports for learners.

Job-Quality Initiatives

The Aspen Institute defines a quality job as one that offers sufficient wages to cover basic living expenses, a safe working environment, stable and predictable work hours, and a package of benefits that facilitate a healthy, stable life (Job

Quality Fellows 2017). Because costs of basic needs can vary dramatically from region to region, tools like the MIT Living Wage Calculator are used by practitioners to understand how wage levels or benefits translate into a hypothetical basket of goods in a particular regional economy (Glasmeier 2017). At the higher end of the job-quality spectrum, metrics around career-building opportunities—including the overall economic mobility of workers—and engagement of workers in work and decision-making processes can also be considered measurable components of job quality.

At the level of the labor market, job-quality initiatives often focus on directing policy and worker training programs to industries and occupations creating "good jobs" (Holzer 2017; Osterman 2019). At the level of the firm, job-quality initiatives can take the shape of "high-road employment practices" or "high-performance work systems" (Cappelli and Neumark 2001; Osterman 2018b). These terms generally refer to the creation of "good jobs" via voluntary investments by firms in the skills of their workers and/or their capacity for involvement in work and workplace processes. Different firms are motivated to implement high-road employment practices for myriad values-based and economic reasons, including increased worker productivity, lower job turnover, and, in some, cases increased overall firm profit (Batt and Colvin 2011; Cappelli and Neumark 2001). The American Sustainable Business Council (no date), for example, created a public pledge for high-road employers, and worker organizations have pioneered similar efforts, some of which—such as the Good Work Code created by the National Domestic Workers Alliance—are directed at particular industries.

Job-quality initiatives in the form of regulation are powerful complements to traditional workforce development interventions because they can relieve the unreasonable burden placed on workers to improve the quality of their own jobs through training. Regulation can include increasing effective wages, improving access to benefits, improving worker protections and workplace standards, supporting worker empowerment, and creating government-sponsored or subsidized quality jobs (Loprest, Nightingale, Yang, and Brown 2019). As frequent intermediaries between employers and workers as well as allocators of subsidized government dollars, workforce development entities are often well positioned to contribute to framing job quality more holistically to include these regulatory thresholds—for example, through their approach to job placement of workers and to selection standards for partnering employers (Aspen Institute 2020).

Creating more skilled workers can be a central strategy to improve job quality. Recognizing that jobs are not fixed but rather are socially constructed, it is possible to create jobs that include greater skills, leading to greater productivity and the ability to command higher wages. Osterman (2018a) argues that this approach can improve the quality of jobs for low-wage long-term care workers. Through skills development, these workers can make their roles more skilled and productive by taking on more tasks typically held by nurses, opening up greater opportunities to lobby for increased wages.

Discussions around job quality are essential to those engaged in skills development. Where there are no jobs or poor-quality jobs, skills development can be a distraction from these more fundamental issues in the labor market. This can be particularly true during times of economic recession. Institutions that provide skills development need to find creative ways to engage in efforts to promote job quality. Some community college programs, for instance, have considered restricting the number of graduates in training programs for low-wage occupations so as to not flood the labor market with trained workers. Others may choose to partner only with employers who agree to provide an appropriate wage return for skills development or may engage in serious conversation with employers about how to better use skilled workers to increase productivity and compensate accordingly.

Union Training Funds

Unions are often overlooked in the literature as a provider and organizer of skilling and workforce development. However, unions around the country play an important role in workforce development. Some of these efforts, which Meléndez and Takahashi (2004) identify as indicative of the second wave of "new unionism," are geared specifically to serving disadvantaged populations. During this period, unions have begun to step away from the historically exclusionary, apprenticeship-based training and education efforts in the craft and building trades and toward a more inclusionary model aimed at empowering all workers through skills training.

A variety of goals exist for union training programs, including building career ladders for union members, providing training and pathways to employment for the disadvantaged, and building the ranks of unions and unionized companies. For workers, they can lead to both educational and career pathways in the long term and better jobs and wages in the short term. They have been found to empower the disadvantaged, especially women and minorities working in low-wage industries like service and healthcare.

Meléndez and Takahashi found that effective workforce development efforts by unions share common characteristics with other workforce development and labor market intermediaries, including "a knowledge of industrial needs, the ability to make job projections, an awareness of the needs of disadvantaged employees, the capacity to provide support services, strong ties to communities, adequate resources, and effective administration" (2004: 140–141). They also found that these efforts had benefits for employers—increasing skill levels in jobs and productivity and decreasing the high costs of turnover.

Unions benefit from collective agreements that can pay for training for incumbent workers. They can also develop partnerships that involve a multitude of community stakeholders, including community organizations, educational institutions, and government and local foundations. One such effort, the Philadelphia Hospital and Health Care District 1199C Training and Upgrading Fund, was created in 1974 as part of the first collective bargaining agreement signed by the Hospital and Health Care Workers Union 1199C, an affiliate of the National Union of Hospital and Health Care Employees, AFSCME, AFL-CIO (District 1199C, no date). The Training and Upgrading Fund serves both union and community members by providing training and education opportunities, from basic skills to career preparation to college degree pathways. Currently, with funding from Lumina Foundation, the union is working to create pathways for workers to acquire skills that they learn at work and that are assessed for credit toward a college degree through union training courses.

Credential System Reforms

In the United States, the credentialing system is vast and unregulated. With over 700,000 credentials, the marketplace is confusing, unstructured, and unregulated (Credential Engine, no date). Initiatives to promote credential quality are essential to promoting worker interests by making sure the credentials they attain are valuable. While the variety of credentials in the marketplace provides a great deal of choice, their quality is variable and often indiscernible to the credential seeker. Without efforts to ensure quality, this is a market of great risk for many individuals, and particularly those who do not have the power to access and navigate the credential market to their advantage. Different credentials lead to different occupational opportunities with varying economic returns—knowing what these opportunities are and how to seize them can make a great difference to workers in terms of social mobility.

Systems to promote credential quality are needed to ensure only valuable credentials are on the marketplace, acting as an important safeguard for workers. Credential quality models can guide institutional leaders and hold them accountable in the pursuit of credential quality while they guide policy and practice (Humphreys and Gaston 2019; Van Noy, McKay, and Michael 2019). Common measures of quality include societal and individual outcomes, credential or program design, student-centered policies and practices, processes to ensure market value, and a dynamic quality assurance system. Systems for translating credential quality models into policy and practice are in varying stages of development at various institutional levels. In educational institutions, traditional accreditors have focused on institutional elements of quality and only more recently have begun to examine learner outcomes. States are beginning to implement quality standards for nondegree credentials in addition to systems for quality through the WIOA (Counts 2017; Duke-Benfield, Wilson, Kermit, and Leventoff 2019; Education Strategy Group 2019). At the national level, the Credential Engine is an effort to gather information on credentials and make the process more transparent for learners. At minimum, these efforts are aimed at making better information on credentials available and/or to ensure that only high-quality credentials are available. These are basic elements to ensuring a functional and equitable workforce system that protects the rights of workers to a quality educational experience. More consistent standards around credentialing may also encourage employers to cooperate with one another and coordinate their training investments as part of sector strategy efforts.

Systemic Educational Reforms

Many within the educational system have come to recognize where these institutions have failed to meet the needs of learners. Given the vast and confusing workforce development system in the United States, workers are often confused about their options and look to educational institutions to help guide them. Unfortunately, most are not set up to help learners navigate their career options, and their systems and policies serve as barriers to credential completion. Current systemic reforms, particularly in community colleges, seek to address these issues to create a more equitable education system.

Institutions in the workforce development system can intentionally consider how to make information on education and career options clearer to workers trying to navigate these systems. How they present information and provide advising are potentially important influences on the decision making of workers. Research with community colleges has highlighted that informational resources on programs of study are often inconsistent, poorly organized, or unavailable, causing students confusion when navigating decisions at college (Jaggars and Fletcher 2014; Rosenbaum, Deil-Amen, and Person 2007). Additionally, the effectiveness of advising can be limited by low staffing levels and problems in service delivery, including conflicting advice from different advisors, a lack of individual support, and more emphasis on enrollments than program completion (Grubb 2001; Rosenbaum, Deil-Amen, and Person 2007). These deficiencies expose deep inequities among workers. Some institutions have engaged in strategies to counter these problems and create more opportunities for worker advancement. For example, two models aim to make better use of limited college advising staff. "Intrusive advising" links education and career information into the college experience, and "intentional advising" targets services to students' specific needs (Jaggars and Fletcher 2014; Kolenovic, Linderman, and Karp 2013; Rosenbaum, Deil-Amen, and Person 2007).

Numerous national reform initiatives within educational institutions promote student success and make sure greater numbers of students reach their goals. The

TAACCCT grant program sought to build a stronger infrastructure of workforce programs in community colleges to help workers gain skills with relevance in the labor market that can help them to both enter and advance in careers (US Department of Labor 2020). National initiatives such as the Aspen Institute Prize for Community College Excellence and Achieving the Dream highlight and promote institutional practices that support learner needs and lead to systemic institutional reforms (Achieving the Dream 2020; Aspen Institute 2020). The guided pathways reform movement seeks to reshape the institutional structure of community colleges to provide guidance and pathways for educational programs that clearly communicate what students need to be successful, rather than relying on the ability of students to navigate complex and confusing institutional structures on their own (Bailey, Jaggars, and Jenkins 2015).

CONCLUSION AND FUTURE DIRECTIONS

While the US workforce system is shaped by its reliance on market mechanisms, there are innovative, "bottom up" strategies being used to empower workers and, in some cases, to shift the whole system toward this goal. Given its form as an extreme liberal market economy, the US case illuminates the opportunities and limitations of market mechanisms as they pertain to the empowerment of workers. As the rest of the world trends toward increasing liberalization, the United States as a site of analysis can offer both important tools for practice and a cautionary tale. This chapter has focused on a few examples of how current policy and practice can be used to promote worker interests, both individually and collectively.

Recognizing that skills development is not a panacea for economic distress, it can offer relief for workers as they attempt to navigate the unstable and ever-shifting waters of the current economy. When designed more intentionally, skills development can provide some degree of protection for workers to help buffer the realities of the economy. This intentional approach must recognize the worker perspective. With that focus, those engaged in skills development can find ways within the current system to provide organization and structure that promotes the interests of workers. Recognizing that the current US system lacks this type of organization, the various collective efforts described in this chapter can serve to push back against the trend toward individualization that discounts the needs and rights of workers. Rather than a distraction from the realities of job loss and unemployment, skills development can be another strategy in the tool kit to support worker empowerment.

Future research needs to more carefully examine these strategies to better understand their implications for workers in terms of long-term impacts. Particularly given the current economic context of the United States reeling from the pandemic and undertaking a serious reckoning with racial injustice, these issues require thoughtful attention from the research community. Additional strategies may be identified and developed to further ensure that education and training realizes its potential and contributes to the goal of equity and worker empowerment.

ENDNOTE

1. In contrast, modularization offers an analogous movement in Germany but with the goal of increasing flexibility within the highly structured German system (Ertl 2002).

REFERENCES

113th Congress. 2014. Workforce Innovation and Opportunity Act. https://bit.ly/3qg3YER

Achieving the Dream. 2020. Website. Silver Spring, MD: Achieving the Dream. https://www.achievingthedream.org.

American Sustainable Business Council. No date. "Principles of High Road Employers." Washington, DC: American Sustainable Business Council. https://bit.ly/2MJOUSh

Ananiadou, Katerina, and Magdalean Claro. 2009. "21st Century Skills and Competencies for New Millennium Learners in OECD Countries." OECD Education Working Papers No. 41. Paris, France: Organisation for Economic Co-operation and Development.

Andersen, Robert, and Herman G. Van De Werfhorst. 2010. "Education and Occupational Status in 14 Countries: The Role of Educational Institutions and Labour Market Coordination: Education and Occupational Status in 14 Countries." *British Journal of Sociology* 61 (2): 336–355.

Angulo, A.J. 2016. *Diploma Mills: How For-Profit Colleges Stiffed Students, Taxpayers, and the American Dream.* Baltimore, MD: Johns Hopkins University Press.

Appelbaum, Eileen, Thomas Bailey, Peter Berg, and Arne L. Kalleberg. 2000. *Manufacturing Advantage: Why High-Performance Work Systems Pay Off.* Ithaca, NY: Cornell University Press.

Aspen Institute. 2020. "Community College Excellence Program." Washington, DC: Aspen Institute. https://highered.aspeninstitute.org

Attewell, Paul. 1990. "What Is Skill?" *Work and Occupations* 17 (4): 422–448. https://bit.ly/3rf378M

Autor, David H., Frank Levy, and Richard J. Murnane. 2003. "The Skill Content of Recent Technological Change: An Empirical Exploration." *The Quarterly Journal of Economics* 118 (4): 1279–1333.

Autor, David, David Mindell, and Elisabeth Reynolds. 2019. *The Work of the Future: Shaping Technology and Institutions.* Cambridge, MA: Massachusetts Institute of Technology.

Baccaro, Lucio, and Chris Howell. 2011. "A Common Neoliberal Trajectory: The Transformation of Industrial Relations in Advanced Capitalism." *Politics & Society* 39 (4): 521–563.

Bailey, Thomas, Shanna Smith Jaggars, and Davis Jenkins. 2015. *Redesigning America's Community Colleges: A Clearer Path to Student Success.* Cambridge, MA: Harvard University Press.

Baker, Dean. 2020 (Jul. 14). "It's Going to Be a Long and Harsh Recession: NYT Warns of Skills Gap." Washington, DC: Center for Economic Policy and Research.

Barney, Jay. 1991. "Firm Resources and Sustained Competitive Advantage." *Journal of Management* 17 (1): 99–120.

Batt, Rosemary, and Alexander J.S. Colvin. 2011. "An Employment Systems Approach to Turnover: Human Resources Practices, Quits, Dismissals, and Performance." *Academy of Management Journal* 54 (4): 695–717.

Baum, Sandy. 2014. *Higher Education Earnings Premium: Value, Variation, and Trends*. Washington, DC: Urban Institute.

Becker, Howard. 1994. *Human Capital: A Theoretical and Empirical Analysis with Special Reference to Education*, 3rd ed. Chicago, IL: University of Chicago Press.

Bessen, James. 2020. "Automation and Jobs: When Technology Boosts Employment." *Economic Policy* 30 (100): 589–626.

Brown, Phillip, Caroline Lloyd, and Manuel Souto-Otero. 2018. "The Prospects for Skills and Employment in an Age of Digital Disruption: A Cautionary Note." SKOPE Research Paper No. 127. Cardiff, UK: Centre on Skills, Knowledge and Organisational Performance.

Busemeyer, Marius, and Christine Trampusch. 2011. "The Comparative Political Economy of Collective Skill Formation." In *The Political Economy of Collective Skill Formation*, edited by Marius Busemeyer and Christine Trampusch, pp 3–10. New York, NY: Oxford University Press.

Cappelli, Peter. 1999. *The New Deal at Work: Managing the Market-Driven Workforce*. Cambridge, MA: Harvard Business School Press.

Cappelli, Peter. 2004. "Why Do Employers Pay for College?" *Journal of Econometrics* 121 (1–2): 213–241.

Cappelli, Peter, and David Neumark. 2001. "Do 'High-Performance' Work Practices Improve Establishment-Level Outcomes?" *ILR Review* 54 (4): 737–775.

Card, David, Francesco Devicienti, and Agata Maida. 2014. "Rent-Sharing, Holdup, and Wages: Evidence from Matched Panel Data." *Review of Economic Studies* 81: 84–111.

Case, Anne, and Angus Deaton. 2015. "Rising Morbidity and Mortality in Non-Hispanic Americans in the 21st Century." *Proceedings of the National Academy of Sciences* 112 (49): 15078–15083.

Center for Postsecondary and Economic Success. 2013. "A Framework for Measuring Career Pathways Innovation: A Working Paper." Washington, DC: Center for Law and Social Policy.

Cleary, Jennifer, Monica Reid Kerrigan, and Michelle Van Noy. 2017. "Towards a New Understanding of Labor Market Alignment." In *Higher Education: Handbook of Theory and Research*, edited by Michael B. Paulsen, pp. 577–629. Basel, Switzerland: Springer.

Collins, Randall. 2019. *The Credential Society: An Historical Sociology of Education and Stratification*. New York, NY: Columbia University Press.

Cottom, Tressie McMillan. 2017. *Lower ED: The Troubling Rise of For-Profit Colleges in the New Economy*. New York, NY: The New Press.

Counts, Donna. 2017. "WIOA 101: A Bird's Eye View of the State Implementation of the Workforce Innovation and Opportunity Act." Washington, DC: Council of State Governments.

Credential Engine. No date. "Credential Registry Overview." https://bit.ly/3bYolkR

District 1199C. No date. "History." Philadelphia: District 1199C Training & Upgrading Fund. https://bit.ly/3cgbsmv

Duke-Benfield, Amy Ellen, Bryan Wilson, Kaleba Kermit, and Jenna Leventoff. 2019. "Expanding Opportunities: Defining Quality Non-Degree Credentials for States." Washington, DC: National Skills Coalition.

Dyer, Jeffrey H., and Singh, Harbir. 1998. "The Relational View: Cooperative Strategy and Sources of Interorganizational Competitive Advantage." *Academy of Management Review* 2 (4): 660–679.

Education Strategy Group. 2019. "Building Credential Currency: Resources to Drive Attainment Across K-12, Higher Education and Workforce Development." https://bit.ly/38afD1Q

Ertl, Hubert. 2002. "The Concept of Modularization in Vocational Education and Training: The Debate in Germany and its Implications." *Oxford Review of Education* 28 (1): 53–73.

Estevez-Abe, Margarita, Torben Iversen, and David Soskice. 2001. "Social Protection and the Formation of Skills: A Reinterpretation of the Welfare State." In *Varieties of Capitalism: The Institutional Foundations of Comparative Advantage*, edited by Peter Hall and David Soskice, pp. 145–183. New York, NY: Oxford University Press.

Gatta, Mary, Heather Boushey, and Eileen Appelbaum. 2009. "High-Touch and Here-to-Stay: Future Skills Demands in U.S. Low Wage Service Occupations." *Sociology* 43 (5): 968–989.

Gatta, Mary, and David Finegold. 2010. "Meeting America's Skills Challenge." In *Transforming the U.S. Workforce Development System: Lessons From Research and Practice*, edited by David Finegold, Mary Gatta, Hal Salzman, and Susan J. Schurman, pp. 1–18. Champaign, IL: Labor and Employment Relations Association.

Glasmeier, Amy. 2017. "Living Wage Calculator." http://livingwage.mit.edu

Gould, Elsie, and Valerie Wilson. 2020. "Black Workers Face Two of the Most Lethal Preexisting Conditions for Coronavirus: Racism and Economic Inequality." Washington, DC: Economic Policy Institute.

Grubb, W. Norton. 2001. "Getting Into the World": Guidance and Counseling in Community Colleges. Report. New York, NY: Community College Research Center, Teachers College, Columbia University. https://bit.ly/3gw6RAj

Hall, Peter A., and David Soskice, eds. 2001. *Varieties of Capitalism: The Institutional Foundations of Comparative Advantage*. New York, NY: Oxford University Press.

Hansson, Bo. 2008. "Job-Related Training and Benefits for Individuals: A Review of Evidence and Explanations." OECD Education Working Papers No. 19. Paris, France: Organisation for Economic Co-operation and Development.

Harper-Anderson, Elsie. 2008. "Measuring the Connection Between Workforce Development and Economic Development: Examining the Role of Sectors for Local Outcomes." *Economic Development Quarterly* 22 (2): 119–135.

Holzer, Harry J. 2017. "The Role of Skills and Jobs in Transforming Communities." *Cityscape: A Journal of Policy and Development Research* 19 (1): 171–190.

Holzer, Harry J., Steven J. Davis, Michelle Miller-Adams, and Theresa Singleton. 2020 (Jul. 1). "How Job Training Matters." Webinar. Philadelphia, PA: Federal Reserve Bank of Philadelphia.

Humphreys, Debra, and Paul Gaston. 2019. "Unlocking the Nation's Potential: A Model to Advance Quality and Equity in Education Beyond High School." Indianapolis, IN: Lumina Foundation.

Jaggars, Shanna Smith, and Jeffrey Fletcher. 2014. "Redesigning the Student Intake and Information Provision Processes at a Large Comprehensive Community College." CCRC Working Paper No. 72. New York, NY: Community College Research Center, Teacher's College, Colombia University.

Job Quality Fellows Class of 2017–18. 2017 (Dec. 14). "The Importance of Job Quality: A Statement of Purpose." Washington, DC: Aspen Institute.

Kleiner, Morris M. 2011. "Occupational Licensing: Protecting the Public Interest or Protectionism?" Policy Paper No. 2011-009. Kalamazoo, MI: Upjohn Institute for Employment Research

Kolenovic, Zineta, Donna Linderman, and Melinda Merchur Karp. 2013. "Improving Student Outcomes via Comprehensive Supports: Three-Year Outcomes from CUNY's Accelerated Study in Associate Programs (ASAP)." *Community College Review* 41 (4): 271–291.

Lafer, Gordon. 2002. *The Job Training Charade*. Ithaca, NY: Cornell University Press.

Lavie, Dovev. 2008. "The Competitive Advantage of Interconnected Firms." In *21st Century Management: A Reference Handbook*, edited by Charles Wankel, pp. I-324–I-334. Thousand Oaks, CA: Sage.

Loprest, Pamela, Demetra Nightingale, Jenny R. Yang, and K. Steven Brown. 2019. "What Would It Take to Achieve Quality Jobs for All Workers?" Catalyst Brief. Washington, DC: Urban Institute.

Martin, Cathie Jo, and Duane Swank. 2008. "The Political Origins of Coordinated Capitalism: Business Organizations, Party Systems, and State Structure in the Age of Innocence." *American Political Science Review* 102 (2): 181–198.

Meléndez, Edwin, and Beverly Takahashi. 2004. "Union-Sponsored Workforce Development Initiatives." In *Communities and Workforce Development*, edited by Edwin Meléndez, pp. 119–150. Kalamazoo, MI: Upjohn Institute for Employment Research.

Mikelson, Kelly, Lauren Eyster, Christian Durham, and Elissa Cohen. 2017. "TAACCCT Goals, Design, and Evaluation: The Trade Adjustment Assistance Community College and Career Training Grant Program." Brief 1. Washington, DC: Urban Institute.

Manyika, James, Michael Chui, Mehdi Miremadi, Jacques Bughin, Katy George, Paul Willmott, and Martin Dewhurst. 2017. "A Future that Works: Automation, Employment, and Productivity." Executive Summary. San Francisco, CA: McKinsey Global Institute.

Mortrude, Judy. 2014. "Shared Vision, Strong Systems: The Alliance for Quality Career Pathways Framework Version 1.0." Washington, DC: The Center for Law and Social Policy.

Organisation for Economic Co-operation and Development. 2019. "The Future of Work: OECD Employment Outlook 2019." Paris, France: Organisation for Economic Co-operation and Development.

Ornston, Darius, and Tobias Schulze-Cleven. 2015. "Conceptualizing Cooperation: Coordination and Concentration as Two Logics of Collective Action." *Comparative Political Studies* 48 (5): 555–585.

Osher, David, Yael Kidron, Marc Brackett, Allison Dymnicki, Stephanie Jones, and Roger P. Weissberg. 2016. "Advancing the Science and Practice of Social and Emotional Learning: Looking Back and Moving Forward." *Review of Research in Education* 40 (1): 644–681.

Osterman, Paul. 2018a. "Improving Long-Term Care by Finally Respecting Home-Care Aides." *Hastings Center Report* 48 (Supp. 3): S67–S70.

Osterman, Paul. 2018b. "In Search of the High Road: Meaning and Evidence." *ILR Review* 71 (1): 3–34. Ithaca, NY: Cornell University Press.

Osterman, Paul, ed. 2019. *Creating Good Jobs: An Industry-Based Strategy*. Cambridge, MA: MIT Press.

Porter, Michael E. 2000. "Location, Competition, and Economic Development: Local Clusters in a Global Economy." *Economic Development Quarterly* 14 (1): 15–34.

Powell, Justin, Laurence Coutrot, Lukas Graf, and Nadine Bernhard. 2009. "Comparing the Relationship Between Vocational and Higher Education in Germany and France." WZB Discussion Paper SP I 2009-506. Berlin, Germany: Social Science Research Center.

Prince, Heath, Chris King, and Sarah Oldmixon. 2017. "Promoting the Adoption of Sector Strategies by Workforce Development Boards Under the Workforce Innovation and Opportunity Act." Austin, TX: Ray Marshall Center for the Study of Human Resources.

Redbird, Beth. 2017. "The New Closed Shop: Economic and Structural Effects of Occupational Licensure." *American Sociological Review* 82 (3): 600–624.

Rosenbaum, James E., Regina Deil-Amen, and Ann E. Person. 2007. *After Admission: From College Access to College Success*. New York, NY: Russell Sage Foundation.

Schulze-Cleven, Tobias. 2015. "Labor Market Policy: Toward a 'Flexicurity' Model in the United States?" In *Lessons From Europe? What Americans Can Learn From European Public Policies*, edited by R. Daniel Kelemen, pp. 77–96. Washington, DC: CQ Press.

Schulze-Cleven, Tobias, and Jennifer Olson. 2017. "Worlds of Higher Education Transformed: Toward Varieties of Academic Capitalism." *Higher Education* 73 (6): 813–831.

Schulze-Cleven, Tobias, Bartholomew C. Watson, and John Zysman. 2007. "How Wealthy Nations Can Stay Wealthy: Innovation and Adaptability in a Digital Era." *New Political Economy* 12 (4): 451–475.

Schurman, Susan, and Louis Soares. 2010. "Connecting the Dots: Creating a Postsecondary Education System for the 21st-Century Workforce." In *Transforming the U.S. Workforce Development System: Lessons from Research and Practice*, edited by David Finegold, Mary Gatta, Hal Salzman, and Susan J. Schurman, pp. 125–151. Champaign, IL: Labor and Employment Relations Association.

Tankersley, Jim. 2020 (Aug. 6). "The Real Reason the American Economy Boomed After World War II." *New York Times*. https://nyti.ms/3sTrIAv

Thelen, Kathleen. 2004. *How Institutions Evolve: The Political Economy of Skills in Germany, Britain, the United States and Japan*. New York, NY: Cambridge University Press.

US Department of Labor. 2020. "Trade Adjustment Assistance Community College and Career Training." https://bit.ly/389Bsyw

Van Noy, Michelle, Heather McKay, and Suzanne Michael. 2019. "Non-Degree Credential Quality: A Conceptual Framework to Guide Measurement." Piscataway, NJ: Education and Employment Research Center, Rutgers University.

Waldinger, Rodger, and Thomas Bailey. 1991. "The Continuing Significance of Race: Racial Conflict and Racial Discrimination in Construction." *Politics and Society* 19 (3): 291–323.

Wassmer, Ulrich. 2010. "Alliance Portfolios: A Review and Research Agenda." *Journal of Management* 36 (1): 141–171.

Weeden, Kim. 2002. "Why Do Some Occupations Pay More than Others? Social Closure and Earnings Inequality in the United States." *American Journal of Sociology* 108 (1): 55–101.

CONCLUSION

CHAPTER 14

In the Age of Crises:
Enlisting Universities in Support of Change

TOBIAS SCHULZE-CLEVEN

Rutgers University

ABSTRACT

This concluding chapter looks toward the future. Rather than summarizing the volume, it takes stock of the book as a product of the contemporary American academy and reflects on how labor studies can help enlist public research universities in support of building a human-centered future of work. American universities have long been intricate bundles of contradictions, but recent trends have left them at a crossroads: Will they be able to reform and connect with a progressive reading of the original land-grant vision to support a future in the interest of workers? Or will their practices further drift away from a public-serving mission as they succumb to neoliberal expectations? The chapter contends that the three constitutive features of labor studies—its focus on people's struggles, interdisciplinarity, and upholding workers' rights—illuminate crucial steps for realizing much-needed innovations in support of the revaluation agenda articulated in this volume.

INTRODUCTION

Facing the multiple systemic crises of contemporary societies head on, this volume has made the case for a labor studies perspective on the future of work. It has argued for the revaluation of work and workers as a means to increase sustainability and safeguard democracy. Moreover, it has emphasized the importance of collective action and the contribution of institutional innovation in the realm of reproductive labor for realizing this goal of revaluation. The volume has developed and substantiated these claims over its three different parts, while the two introductory chapters spelled out the benefits of centering insights from labor studies in the debate about the evolving world of work. Rather than further summarizing these contributions, this conclusion looks forward and inward, exploring the implications for higher education as the institutional home of most authors in this volume.

Taking stock of the book as a product of the contemporary American academy, the chapter reflects on how labor studies can help enlist public research universities in support of building a human-centered future of work.

The impact of universities on the future of work is a pressing issue. On the one hand, there is strong agreement among policy makers that universities have much to contribute to effectively addressing contemporary economic, political, and environmental crises. Given that universities are central nodes in the global knowledge economy, their teaching, research, and outreach missions serve essential roles in socioeconomic adjustment. One account even claims that the country's land-grant institutions—the "people's universities" as Abraham Lincoln called them—are "perhaps democracy's best hope" (Gavazzi and Gee 2018). Universities' mission statements echo these sentiments, frequently emphasizing excellence in the service of the public good. Whether it is supporting students' social mobility by improving their employment prospects or offering attractive working conditions to their own employees, universities frequently herald their constructive role in building a future that serves their various constituencies as well as the public interest. Many universities are clearly trying to deliver on these lofty goals and ideals.

On the other hand, there is significant skepticism about whether universities— as they are currently constituted—are sufficiently living up to their promises (e.g., Childress 2019; Newfield 2016). Critics have drawn up long lists of complaints about contemporary American higher education. On the political left, complaints focus on the role played by a differentiated university landscape in reproducing— and even increasing—social stratification, the tendency of university management to replace secure tenure-track employment with low-paid and precarious gig work, the contribution of rising tuition to the financialization of workers' lives, and the academy's enmeshment in processes of cultural and political colonialization. Commentators on the right, meanwhile, disparage universities as bastions of privilege on the wrong side of the "culture wars." They charge "liberal" professors with having allowed political correctness to run amok as they accommodate students' requests for "safe spaces" and "trigger warnings," threatening free speech and undermining American patriotism in the process. Even if one resists buying into any particular criticism and continues to acknowledge the many positive contributions of contemporary universities, it is hard to deny that their aspirations frequently outstrip reality.

This chapter emphasizes the importance of acknowledging the uncomfortable realities that have underpinned skepticism toward universities. Facing up to contemporary tensions within and around academia is the first step in better addressing them. Of course, universities have long been intricate bundles of contradictions, but recent trends have clearly left American universities—and public research institutions in particular—at a crossroads: Will they be able to reform and connect with a progressive reading of the original land-grant vision to support a future in the interest of workers? Or will their practices further drift away from a public-serving mission as they succumb to neoliberal expectations, moving toward an ever-deeper intertwining with the private sector and sustained deskilling of university labor?

Reforming universities with a focus on meeting collective needs and providing equality of individual opportunity will be an uphill struggle. Returning to the "good old days" is hardly a promising strategy, for while college was once more affordable for the average student and employment security was higher for many faculty, gender and racial barriers also greatly restricted who benefited. Moreover, given the changing political, economic, and ecological contexts, simply defending current organizational forms will do little to stop ongoing institutional drift. Rather, just as with respect to reproductive labor more generally, real innovations are needed. While labor studies cannot offer any quick-fix "solutions" to the contemporary crisis in higher education, the field can provide intellectual and practical guidance on how to support the revaluation agenda articulated in this volume. Below, I first elaborate on the contemporary crisis and then turn to the contribution of labor studies in addressing it.

AMERICAN UNIVERSITIES AT A CROSSROADS

Higher education has long played an outsized role in the provision of social citizenship in the United States. Following World War II, the G.I. Bill supported the higher education of returning soldiers, solidifying the country's international leadership in "massifying" higher education. While most of the early beneficiaries of federal financial support were White and male, higher education became more inclusive over time. For instance, the National Defense Education Act of 1958, the Higher Education Act of 1965, and the passage of Title IX in 1972 opened up higher education to women, who now make up the majority of students in colleges and universities (Rose 2018).

Publicly supported access to higher education has underpinned the social mobility of many people, and providing such opportunities continues to be a point of identification and satisfaction for many faculty, administrators, and staff. At my home institution, Rutgers–New Brunswick, many of my colleagues take pride in providing a high-quality university education for a large number of first-generation students and empowering them to climb the social ladder. As the university's communications department emphasizes, about 30% of Rutgers–New Brunswick students receive Pell grants (i.e., federally funded partial tuition scholarships for low-income students); in addition, "Rutgers' four- and six-year graduation rates are 24 percent and 21 percent above the national average, [while] ... its graduation rate for Black students is 38 percent higher" (Buccino 2021). Seeking to increase accessibility, universities have expanded offerings in online instruction, including massive open online courses (MOOCs) aimed at nontraditional students (Stevens 2018). Although the effective implementation of

MOOCs has proven to be difficult, given that the least prepared students usually most need the personal attention of faculty, online courses can still be a productive step in efforts to support a democratic and sustainable future of work. And yet far too many aspects of higher education today undermine the goal of centering workers' concerns in building the future of work.

Neoliberalism in Higher Education

The rise of neoliberalism in particular has left an indelible mark on the university sector. It is not that higher education—including its distinct functions of creating, sharing, and certifying knowledge—has been devalued. Quite to the contrary, as policy makers increasingly turned to markets, they embraced the power of higher education in the service of an expanding range of policy goals. Inspired by economists' human capital theory, education has become the one-size-fits-all solution to drive economic growth *and* support social integration, merging concerns that once motivated separate industrial and welfare policies (Stedward 2003). Yet this expansion of purpose also implied a significant narrowing in the understanding of education's transformative potential. As public discourses deemphasized the contributions of universities to cultural and political development, higher education has come to be viewed primarily as a means to improve the employability of individuals and the national competitiveness of countries. With day-to-day practices across colleges and universities shifting to emphasize the commodity character of education, the sector has become deeply implicated in neoliberalism's market-based transformation of social relations (Schulze-Cleven, Reitz, Maesse, and Angermuller 2017).

This transformation of higher education is part of a broader shift in welfare-state policy making, which has weakened social protections from market forces and embraced the provision of "welfare through work," a reorientation frequently likened to a shift from de-commodification to hyper-commodification (Lessenich 2008). Rather than treating people primarily as citizens, neoliberal public policies have come to view them both as suppliers of human capital (i.e., production inputs) and as sources of market demand. Reconceived as entrepreneurially oriented lifelong learners, individuals are expected to continually adapt their skill sets to changing economic demands, including by tapping into the ever more differentiated offerings that public policies encourage universities to provide (Jenson and Saint-Martin 2006; Schulze-Cleven 2011, 2020).

Stratification: Tuition and Debt

In the United States, with public funding significantly lagging the sector's expansion, many students now pay for (or at least co-finance) their college and university educations. The greater reliance on private—as opposed to public—funding is typically rationalized with reference to students' ability to reap the individual rewards of such investment in skill acquisition through higher earnings. Yet, given the differential financial endowments of students and their families, increases in tuition prices well above inflation have turned college from a potential equalizer of life chances into what one critic recently called the "great unleveler" (Mettler 2014): While the cost of attending a four-year public university increased only slightly from 6% to 9% of a family's annual income for the top fifth of the income spectrum between 1971 and 2010, for the bottom fifth of the income spectrum, it nearly tripled, from 42% to 114%. In line with relative college affordability, three fourths of affluent adults (i.e., those from the highest quartile of family income) graduate with a bachelor's degree by the time they are 24 years old, but graduation rates drop to one in three, fewer than one in five, and less than one in ten in each consecutive lower-income quartile. Of course, tuition is not the only factor driving these outcomes, and actual expenses frequently diverge from universities' sticker prices. Nevertheless, the social stratification of the student body in higher education is undeniable, particularly with respect to graduation rates, as opposed to mere attendance rates.

With under-resourced students attending high-charging universities, taking on debt has become a prominent feature of getting a university education. Nationally, the growth in the volume of outstanding student loans to $1.6 trillion in 2020 is widely viewed as a bubble. Having tripled over 13 years, the volume of student debt now eclipses credit card debt and car loans, remaining second only to mortgage debt. The chances of repayment are often slight for the 43 million borrowers. That is particularly true for those who fell prey to underdelivering, vocationally oriented for-profit education companies that the federal government has bankrolled via federally sponsored student loans and grants (and which came to enroll one in ten American undergraduates in 2009). At nonprofit colleges, nearly two thirds of graduating students had taken out student loans in 2019, leaving them with an average balance of almost $30,000, excluding borrowing by their parents. Last year, more than seven million student loan borrowers were in default, with almost two million additional borrowers having seriously fallen behind in payments (Lieber and Bernard 2020). Of borrowers who started college in 1995, only 41.3% had successfully paid off their student loans without defaulting two decades later (Woo et al. 2017: 12).

Graduate students in professional degree programs—including business, law, and medicine—often take on particularly high debt loads, which many observers see as less of a problem given these students' frequently very good earnings prospects. But, even here, not all is well. Take, for instance, the effects of the federal income-based loan repayment program. As currently formulated—exempting income up to 150% of federal poverty guidelines adjusted for household size, limiting payments to 10% of annual income above the exemption and offering loan forgiveness after 20 years (ten years if employed in public service)—it allows many professionals, including those earning six-figure salaries, not to repay all of their loans. This not only encourages more borrowing, it is also likely to make students less price sensitive and permit universities to further increase tuition (Delisle, Holt, and Blagg 2015). Moreover, these graduates' extreme debt levels continue to provide rationalizations for well-above-average annual increases in many professionals' salaries, which are already driving up income inequality in society. Admittedly, progress has been made in increasing the efficiency and effectiveness of the student loan system, with federal legislation in 2010 cutting out commercial banks and redirecting the savings to need-based financial aid. Yet some of the system's provisions remain quite punitive, including the barriers to disposing of crushing student loan debt through personal bankruptcy.

Internal Transformations

As signaled by popular critiques of universities' "corporatization" and diagnoses of movement toward "academic capitalism," the contemporary transformation of higher education extends deep into institutions themselves (e.g., Schrecker 2010; Slaughter and Rhoades 2004). From universities' management of academic labor to their strategies for gaining competitive advantage, practices in the academy increasingly mirror those pursued by private companies outside of education, many of which have fissured long-term employment relationships by reorganizing themselves around perceived core competences. Highlighted in descriptions of the "Uberfication" of the university and the rise of the "gig academy," there are even parallels to vanguard platform firms such as Uber and Amazon (Hall 2016; Kezar, DePaola, and Scott 2019). Universities have yet to match the abilities of those companies to source labor with high levels of control at low prices and to leverage market domination for rent extraction (Rahman and Thelen 2019). Nevertheless, the short lengths of many academic labor contracts, universities' embrace of technology, and their "knowledge hub" branding strategies all point in this direction. Paralleling developments in the private sector, neoliberal modes of imagining work within the university have reconceived academic labor in terms of faculty entrepreneurialism, thereby replacing self-conceptions anchored in professional, unionist or vocational norms (Steffen 2020).

Faculty pay has become considerably more dispersed since the 1980s. Research-focused faculty have often done quite well financially, but there are large disciplinary gaps. Professional fields such as law, business, medicine, and engineering tend to offer the highest salaries, well ahead of the hard sciences, where the ability to get outside grants has become crucial. Positions in the humanities usually pay the worst, particularly given the amount of education required. Growing cross-disciplinary inequality tends to be most visible in salaries for new assistant professors, with data for four-year colleges showing that those in business now earn almost twice as much as those in English or history (Jaschik 2016).[1] Moreover, teaching—the labor activity generating the tuition revenues on which universities rely—is increasingly provided by lower-paid faculty off the tenure track who tend to work on short-term and part-time contracts, frequently without social benefits such as health insurance. Crucially, women and people of color are disproportionately represented in these highly contingent positions (Nzingo 2020).

Admittedly, the declining share of tenure-track employment in higher education has been a feature of the American academy for decades. This trend has been driven by declining per-student financial support from state governments, universities' growing dependence on tuition income, and the introduction of new budgeting models such as "responsibility-centered management." It also reflects a long-standing pattern across society of trying to meet new functional challenges by unbundling tasks, moving toward a deeper division of labor, and allowing for greater specialization. Finally, it highlights and exacerbates the professoriate's decreasing collective power within universities, with the trend's unbridled continuation acting to weaken tenure as one of the central institutional pillars of faculty voice. Some observers interpret the associated flow of authority to university administration as merely a return to historical patterns (Bowen and Tobin 2015). That said, there is something distinctly new about contemporary shifts, not least because they have been accompanied by compensation increases for top administrators in particular, mirroring trends in the private sector where the average CEO to worker pay ratio has skyrocketed in recent decades.

Contemporary power relations in the American academy were on open display when COVID-19 hit in spring 2020. Responding to decreasing income—from tuition, auxiliary services such as housing, and state appropriations—universities embraced austerity and cutbacks. Many froze promised pay increases or retirement contributions for faculty and staff, and some even laid off tenured faculty. Adjunct faculty often did not see their contracts renewed. Although the cost savings of the latter move was often minimal, it was expedient and did not require management to renege on contractual obligations. In turn, while adjuncts as the most casualized parts of the academic workforce frequently had the least capacity for resilience during the pandemic-induced recession, they often were expected to make the greatest sacrifices.

The Changing Boundaries of Public and Private

Unsurprisingly, the for-profit companies active in higher education have been most radical in economizing on labor (Schulze-Cleven 2017). Offering no tenure-track employment at all, for-profit universities have tended to spend far more on marketing than on instruction, with some also excelling in using peer evaluations to place the burden of grading work on the student-customers themselves. For a while, the boom of online education and the growth of the adult market provided these companies with high profits. Yet, under the impact of investigations into fraud against both students and public authorities, some for-profit entities faced heavy fines, prominent businesses closed, and enrollment has declined significantly. In the search for new profit opportunities, big for-profit players such as Kaplan University and Bridgeport Education have since reinvented themselves as service platforms for nonprofit institutions seeking to open up new revenue streams in the online adult market.

This strategic reorientation fundamentally challenges former organizational boundaries in higher education, as well as the goals and practices attributed to different players within the sector. Private companies have entered into agreements with "hundreds of public and private nonprofit colleges"— Georgetown, Harvard, NYU, and Yale included—to provide marketing, recruitment, and technology services for university-branded online programs, "in exchange for a cut of revenues as high as 70 percent" (Carey 2020). Two public research universities have gone even further, incorporating large parts of for-profit companies into their organizations. In April 2018, Purdue University acquired the for-profit Kaplan University and used it to launch Purdue University Global (Lieberman 2019). Similarly, the University of Arizona Global Campus (UAGC) bought the for-profit Ashford University, which was once the core of scandal-plagued Bridgepoint Education. Now rebranded as Zovio, Ashford's former parent company also provides recruiting and marketing services for UAGC in exchange for tuition sharing (Carey 2020).

University managers have defended such partnerships and hybridization as supporting their public outreach mission and offering crucial levers to design a more socially inclusive "new American university" (Crow and Dabars 2015). Yet this approach comes with serious questions about both the quality of educational offerings and labor standards—including intellectual property protections—for academic workers. The use of pre-recorded lectures in online teaching is a case in point. Given their increasing role and essentially costless transfer, it is logical that universities would seek to tap into economies of scale. A recent story from Concordia University in Canada highlights the problematic potential implications of such practices: When the university's in-person classes were moved online in response to COVID-19, students were—unbeknownst to them—served recorded lectures by a deceased professor who had created them for a previously offered online course (Kneese 2021).

Higher Education and Social Power

Finally, it is important to underscore the contributions of contemporary universities to sustaining existing social hierarchies, including White supremacy. Universities and colleges have long played a role in engendering and upholding societies' patterns of racial domination. They did so most fundamentally by legitimating particular bodies of knowledge, but the links were frequently more direct. Manyt of the early American colleges benefited financially from slavery (Fuentes and White 2016; Wilder 2013). Moreover, the original land grants for America's public colleges were made possible by violence against and theft from Indigenous peoples that had inhabited land that the federal government granted to states for the purpose of expanding higher education. As critics emphasize, universities today remain "*large systems of authoritative control,*" acting through "standardization, gradation, accountancy, classification, credits and penalties" (Mbembe 2016: 30, emphasis in original). In these functions, they all too often fail to significantly challenge the multiple interlinked "forms of dehumanization, oppression, and exploitation" associated with capitalism, racism, and sexism (Maldonado-Torres 2012: 93).

Arguably, awareness of the university's role in sustaining and reproducing particular power structures has increased in some circles, particularly as post-colonial thought, feminism, and the Black radical tradition (e.g., Baldwin 1984; Chakrabarty 2008; Fanon 1967) have found broader audiences. Yet, while long-standing biases—including the conceptual foundations and empirical foci of entire academic fields and curricula, such as classics and Western civilization—are being recognized (e.g., Poser 2021), the realization of inclusive day-to-day practices in higher education remains a work in progress, whether with respect to race, gender, or class (e.g., Casselman 2021). Student consumerism, for instance, has frequently reinforced biases and discrimination against women faculty of color (Gutiérrez y Muhs, Nieman, González, and Harris 2012; Niemann, Gutiérrez y Muhs, and González 2020). Moreover, although universities have typically defended affirmative action in favor of historically disadvantaged groups, societies' embrace of "color blind" market rationales has frequently given legitimacy to conservative skeptics of actions that seek to counter long-standing patterns of subjugation. At the same time, neoliberal discourses and reforms have empowered for-profit corporations' targeting of "prospective students whose aspirations outstrip their available options for mobility" (Cottom 2017: 21), many of whom have been—given the stark racial wealth gap in the United States today—people of color.

Particularly in the past few years, there has been real progress in recognizing the value of diversity in higher education. But reform initiatives in the name of diversity without attention to equity and inclusion can remain "detached from histories of struggle for equality" and fail to challenge unequal distributions of resources (Ahmed 2007: 235). Moreover, if these programs do not seek to address claims about the historically grounded "colonialization of knowledge," they will not overcome some groups' perceptions of themselves as universities' "subaltern subjects" within a system likened to "neoapartheid" (Maldonado-Torres 2012: 91–93).[2]

UNIVERSITIES, LABOR STUDIES, AND THE FUTURE OF WORK

Given the complexity of the contemporary research university, including its service to a wide range of constituencies and its associated extension into many different parts of contemporary society, it is probably inevitable that it has multifaceted—even contradictory—effects on the future of work and workers. As early as the mid-1960s, the modern university appeared to have morphed into a "multiversity," and the growth of higher education since then has only promoted further "structural accretion"—i.e., the addition of functions without abandoning old ones (Kerr 1963; Smelser 2013). But there is ample scope to strengthen universities as forces of liberation (rather than instruments of domination) with respect to the future of work, in line with a progressive land-grant mission (Goldstein, Paprocki, and Osborne 2019). Simply embracing a labor studies frame will clearly not be sufficient for propelling forward much-needed innovations in support of the revaluation agenda developed in this volume, but it points to crucial steps for getting there.

Each of the three central features of labor studies—its focus on the struggles of working people, its practice of interdisciplinarity, and its normative commitment to upholding workers' rights—comes into play. As I argue in this volume's second chapter, labor studies has a strong edge over other approaches in informing debate on the future of work. Not only does the field bring into focus how institutions shape the character of distributional conflicts, but it also clarifies how collective action can productively address such conflicts in the name of realizing democratic values and increasing sustainability.

Productive Focus Within Analytical Breadth

The first payoff of labor studies with respect to higher education's role in building a desirable future of work is analytical. The field's interdisciplinarity allows for a broad perspective that incorporates insights from different and often siloed scholarly communities. From historical scholarship, the labor studies lens takes an appreciation of universities as crucial vehicles for the state and its citizens to relate to one another, with individual institutions serving as "parastates" that convey state interests by proxy (Loss 2014). The grounding of labor studies analyses in the actual historical record, moreover, guards against glorifying the past when seeking to illuminate contemporary tensions.

Economics provides labor studies with a recognition of cost dynamics in higher education. Given that higher education has long been a labor-intensive service, a fate it shares with other at least partially state-financed services (such as care for the ill, elderly, and children), annual productivity improvements at universities have lagged the more capital-intensive manufacturing sector. Representing a case of "Baumol's cost disease," this means that economy-wide wage increases tend to drive up the relative cost of higher education and other welfare state services, putting strong pressure on public budgets. Moreover, "Bowen cost effects" capture how universities tend to collect and spend as much money as possible in an attempt to rise within the university pecking order through investments in research prowess, real estate, and college sports.

From sociology, labor studies draws an understanding of universities' centrality to social organization and the peculiarities of their governance. Specifically, universities continue to act as "sieves for sorting and stratifying populations, incubators for the development of competent social actors, temples for the legitimation of official knowledge, and hubs connecting multiple institutional domains" (Stevens, Armstrong, and Arum 2008: 127). At the same time, they have retained "a substantial margin of jurisdiction over their own boundaries and internal affairs," with professional and associational governance curbing the effects of market pressures and government steering (Clark 1983; Eaton and Stevens 2020: 1; Stevens and Gebre-Medhin 2016).

Political science scholarship, finally, offers labor studies a handle on the interactions of different mechanisms for processing distributional conflicts—e.g., electoral politics, lobbying and interest group politics, collective bargaining, and social movement mobilization—and an awareness of the central role that the fiscal and regulatory strategies of states play in producing different varieties of academic capitalism (Schulze-Cleven 2017, 2020; Schulze-Cleven and Olson 2017).

Beyond incorporating these various disciplinary insights, labor studies has one crucial advantage: Its focus on work and workers allows for an analytical perspective that bridges a common division of scholarship in higher education between its changing relationship to society on the one hand and its internal transformation on the other, or between a demand-side student-centered lens (i.e., analyses of how the structural transformation of higher education is shaped by or affects the sector's "customers") and a supply-side faculty-centered lens (i.e., analyses that explore the changing fate and organizational politics of "providers"). Both the students that seek to leverage higher education for successful careers and the faculty (and other staff) that labor within the sector are workers. Given the normative commitment of labor studies to universal worker dignity, the field does not prioritize the fate of either group of workers but instead recognizes the increased precarity of both. While university management likes to emphasize that there are zero-sum distributional conflicts between academic workers and students, with wage increases for university staff and faculty automatically translating into tuition increases for students, labor studies shifts the focus to exploring the role that solidaristic collective action can play in designing positive-sum approaches to the challenges and problems discussed in this chapter.

Analysis-Based Practice

For many scholars of labor studies, this analytical orientation spills over into—and is fueled by—a practical orientation, whether in the classroom or in community-serving outreach activities. In line with the classic definition of publicly engaged scholarship, labor studies faculty tend to not merely reach out to different disciplinary publics, but they frequently also connect with broader publics outside of the university (Boyer [1990] 1997). Engaging these publics via "action research" that leverages the deepening of knowledge for advancing social justice (Levin and Greenwood 2017), labor studies seeks to empower underprivileged sections of the population in particular. Obviously, not all fields can take this approach, but there is arguably scope to bolster university–community linkages in this spirit.

At Rutgers' School of Management and Labor Relations, for instance, labor studies faculty have embraced this publicly engaged approach through a variety of centers: the Center for Global Work & Employment, the Center for Innovation in Worker Organization, the Center for the Study of Collaboration in Work and Society, the Center for Women & Work, the Center for Work and Health, the Education & Employment Research Center, the Institute for the Study of Employee Ownership and Profit Sharing, the NJ/NY Center for Employee Ownership, the Occupational Training and Education Consortium, and the Program for Disability Research. Frequently collaborating with the school's labor-focused continuing education arm, the Labor Education Action Research Network, the centers have laid important groundwork for pushing the conversation on the future of work in a worker-centered direction. Rutgers-based contributors to this volume report on some of the centers' findings, from sectoral bargaining for the common good to the scope for climate justice at work.

Three of the centers have been particularly active with respect to higher education's contribution to the future of work. Research at the Center for Global Work and Employment has probed the cross-national politics driving higher education reform, and the Education & Employment Research Center has evaluated education policy outcomes in the United States. Meanwhile, the Center for Innovation in Worker Organization has played a leading national role in convening stakeholders and facilitating knowledge transfer on bargaining for the common good in higher education.

It is a promising development that university leaders around the country are increasingly seeking to recommit higher education to public engagement, including by better recognizing the importance of such engagement in decisions about faculty promotions (Cantor 2020; O'Meara 2018). Such moves validate the founding principles of labor studies. The same is true for the growing recognition of how contemporary economic, political, and ecological crises have grown the scope for "post-normal" science that moves beyond academia's ivory tower in general and disciplinary silos in particular (Krauss, Schäfer, and von Storch 2012). As uncertainty has increased, so has the need for the kind of normatively anchored, theoretically integrated, problem-focused and context-sensitive scholarship that labor studies offers (Nowotny, Scott, and Gibbons 2001; Wallerstein 1999).

This is not to deny the labor studies field's own challenges. For instance, as labor studies focused on issues of class, it frequently failed to pay sufficient attention to the ineluctably racial character of capitalism (e.g., Du Bois [1946] 1969; Robinson 1983) and the mutual amplification of different forms of oppression (e.g., Matsuda, Lawrence, Delgado, and Crenshaw [1993] 2018; McGhee 2021). Yet this is changing. As Naomi R Williams and Sheri Davis-Faulkner argue in this volume, the embrace of an analytical lens informed by critical theorizing on race and intersectionality puts the field at the forefront of developing revisionist narratives about both the past and the future. Moreover, initiatives such as those spearheaded by Rutgers' School of Management and Labor Relations centers—and the Center for Innovation in Worker Organization in particular—translate such thinking into action. Spanning theory and practice, the interventions of labor studies faculty at the class–race–gender nexus provide actionable visions that can fill the potential vacuum created by exposing the biases of inherited forms of social organization. Addressing the fears of conservatives that it is easier to tear down collective standards than replace them with less-biased ones (e.g., Bauerlein 2020), this is a genuinely generative enterprise. Just like neighboring fields such as social work or public policy, labor studies can supply crucial ingredients for finding inclusive ways to define and pursue the "public good."

Toward Solidaristic Reform

With respect to higher education's impact on the future of work, labor studies can amplify progressive voices and help draw connections between the struggles of different groups of workers. Given the centrality of real-life stories for cultivating social change (Ganz 2009), directing attention to how contemporary universities shape different workers' struggles is crucial for spurring innovation in and around the university. Such discursive work can be accompanied by organization building that seeks to forge new social coalitions in support of solidaristic reforms. The prospects for successfully using labor studies and public engagement in support of "cultivating growth at the leading edges" of higher education are arguably good (Eatman and Peters 2015). After all, significant social mobilization is already under way, as indicated by several examples:

- The "free college" movement and mobilization to relieve student debt (e.g., Eaton 2017; Samuels 2013).
- Union organizing, including the city-focused "metro strategy" spearheaded by the Service Employees International Union to improve the work conditions of adjuncts and the surge in attempts by the United Auto Workers and others to institutionalize the collective voice of graduate student workers (e.g., Berry and Worthen 2014).
- Recent cross-sectional mobilization for solidarity and antiracism during the COVID-19 pandemic (Murch 2020), including faculty and graduate students at Rutgers joining the university's nonacademic workforce in advocating for a government-sponsored work-share approach, which would allow furloughed employees to recover lost income through temporarily increased partial unemployment benefits (Cohen 2020; Reitmeyer 2020).
- The turn to critical—and even "abolitionist"—university studies across the humanities (e.g., Boggs, Meyerhoff, Mitchell, and Schwartz-

Weinstein, no date; Williams 2012) committed to resisting, disrupting, and subverting the spread of neoliberalism (Harney and Moten 2013; la paperson 2017).

In emphasizing the shared experiences of workers within and outside of the academy, labor studies can help define common ground and collective demands across the different streams of mobilization for change, as recently happened in a campaign for a "New Deal for Higher Education" in the context of COVID-19 (Kahn, Mittelstadt, and Levenstein 2020). Such a reform program would significantly contribute to a more equitable, democratic, and sustainable future of work.

At times, labor studies provides this support from a somewhat precarious position in the academy. Dedicated state allocations for labor centers at universities have frequently been attacked, resulting in many labor centers being eliminated. Moreover, there is little agreement on the best place for labor studies programs within universities, leaving them spread out across the social sciences, business schools, law schools, and independent units. Pressure to merge with other units rarely goes away completely, and units' independence has frequently been maintained only by flanking traditional labor studies and industrial relations concerns with the expansion of curricular offerings in human resource management. At the same time, as Cedric de Leon, director of the Labor Center at the University of Massachusetts Amherst, recently emphasized, labor studies scholars have proven extremely adept at entrepreneurially exploiting contemporary higher education's "neoliberal predilections," whether it is by bringing in outside funding and tuition dollars to support organizational independence or by tapping into concerns with "social issues and identity politics to advance an intersectional approach to labor solidarity" (de Leon, personal communication).

Theoretically, practically, and even politically, there is thus much to build on. As university leaders respond to the rise of right-wing populism by calling on universities to reassert their values and build community (e.g., Holloway 2020a, 2020b), they would be well advised to leverage the traditional strengths of labor studies. Moreover, policy makers outside of higher education could support such engagement. Just as they have used performance funding to drive the liberalization of the sector (Dougherty and Natow 2020), they could change course and incentivize universities' turn to public empowerment. Not only is it possible to enlist universities in support of the changes that this volume has outlined for a human-centered future of work, but labor studies also offers crucial pointers on how to do so.

ENDNOTES

1. Admittedly, in some fields, disproportionate increases in spending on junior faculty have reduced salary ratios across rank.

2. Of course, even self-consciously "critical" scholarship on higher education can unwittingly shore up the very conditions it takes issue with within universities. Specifically, it may not connect to the concerns of the unrecognized—and potentially unassimilated—"undercommons" of universities, where counter-hegemonic behavior can create new possibilities through radical re-envisioning (Harney and Moten 2013).

REFERENCES

Ahmed, Sara. 2007. "The Language of Diversity." *Ethnic and Racial Studies* 30 (2): 235–256.

Baldwin, James. 1984 (Apr.) "On Being White … And Other Lies." *Essence*. https://bit.ly/3vPmo39 (from Anti-Racism Digital Library)

Bauerlein, Mark. 2020 (Feb. 19). "What Took the Place of Western Civ?" *Inside Higher Ed.*

Berry, Joe, and Helena Worthen. 2014 (Oct. 9). "22 States Where Adjunct Faculty are Organizing for Justice." *In These Times.*

Boggs, Abigail, Eli Meyerhoff, Nick Mitchell, and Zach Schwartz-Weinstein. No date. "Abolitionist University Studies: An Invitation." Abolition University. https://abolition.university/invitation

Bowen, William G., and Eugene M. Tobin. 2015. *Locus of Authority: The Evolution of Faculty Roles in the Governance of Higher Education.* Princeton, NJ: Princeton University Press.

Boyer, Ernest L. (1990) 1997. *Scholarship Reconsidered: Priorities of the Professoriate.* San Francisco, CA: Wiley.

Buccino, Neal. 2021 (Feb. 19). "Rutgers–New Brunswick Provost Shares Personal Connection to Access Week." *Rutgers Today.* https://bit.ly/3cYjTTP

Cantor, Nancy. 2020. "The Urgency of Recommitting Higher Education to the Public Good in 2020 and Beyond." Unpublished Paper. Newark, NJ: Rutgers University–Newark.

Carey, Kevin. 2020 (Aug. 11). "Proposed Merger Blurs the Line Between For-Profit Colleges and Public Universities." *New York Times.*

Casselman, Ben. 2021 (Feb. 23). "For Women in Economics, the Hostility Is Out in the Open." *New York Times.*

Chakrabarty, Dipesh. 2008. *Provincializing Europe: Postcolonial Thought and Historical Difference.* Princeton, NJ: Princeton University Press.

Childress, Herb. 2019. *The Adjunct Underclass: How America's Colleges Betrayed Their Faculty, Their Students, and Their Mission.* Chicago, IL: University of Chicago Press.

Clark, Burton R. 1983. *The Higher Education System: Academic Organization in Cross-National Perspective.* Berkeley, CA: University of California Press.

Cohen, Patricia. 2020 (Aug. 20). "This Plan Pays to Avoid Layoffs. Why Don't More Employers Use It?" *New York Times.*

Cottom, Tressie McMillan. 2017. *Lower Ed: The Troubling Rise of For-Profit Colleges in the New Economy.* New York, NY: New Press.

Crow, Michael M., and William B. Dabars. 2015. *Designing the New American University.* Baltimore, MD: Johns Hopkins University Press.

de Leon, Cedric. Director, Labor Center, University of Massachusetts Amherst. Personal communication.

Delisle, Jason, Alex Holt, and Kristin Blagg. 2015. "Measuring the Benefits of Income-Based Repayment for Graduate and Professional Students." In *Student Loans and the Dynamics of Debt*, edited by Brad Hershbein and Kevin M. Hollenbeck, pp. 415–446. Kalamazoo, MI: W.E. Upjohn Institute for Employment Research.

Dougherty, Kevin, and Rebecca S. Natow. 2020. "Performance-Based Funding for Higher Education: How Well Does Neoliberal Theory Capture Neoliberal Practice?" *Higher Education* 80 (3): 457–478.

Du Bois, W.E.B. (1946) 1969. *The World and Africa*. New York, NY: International Publishers.

Eatman, Timothy K., and Scott J. Peters. 2015. "Cultivating Growth at the Leading Edges: Public Engagement in Higher Education." *Diversity & Democracy* 18 (1). https://bit.ly/3c3bZZT

Eaton, Charlie. 2017. "Still Public: State Universities and America's New Student Debt Coalitions." *PS: Political Science and Politics* 50 (2): 408–412.

Eaton, Charlie, and Mitchell L. Stevens. 2020. "Universities as Peculiar Organizations." *Sociology Compass* 14 (3): e12768.

Fanon, Franz. 1967. *Black Skin, White Masks*. New York, NY: Grove Press.

Fuentes, Marisa J., and Deborah Gray White, eds. 2016. *Scarlet and Black: Slavery and Dispossession in Rutgers History*. New Brunswick, NJ: Rutgers University Press.

Ganz, Marshall. 2009 (Mar. 18–19). "Why Stories Matter: The Art and Craft of Social Change." *Sojourners*.

Gavazzi, Stephen M., and E. Gordon Gee. 2018. *Land-Grant Universities for the Future: Higher Education for the Public Good*. Baltimore. MD: Johns Hopkins University Press.

Goldstein, Jenny E., Kasia Paprocki, and Tracey Osborne. 2019. "A Manifesto for a Progressive Land-Grant Mission in an Authoritarian Populist Era." *Annals of the American Association of Geographers* 190 (2): 673–684.

Gutiérrez y Muhs, Gabriella, Yolanda Flores Niemann, Carmen G. González, and Angela P. Harris, eds. 2012. *Presumed Incompetent: The Intersection of Race and Class for Women in Academia*. Boulder, CO: University Press of Colorado.

Hall, Gary. 2016. *The Uberfication of the University*. Minneapolis, MN: University of Minnesota Press.

Harney, Stefano, and Fred Moten. 2013. *The Undercommons: Fugitive Planning & Black Study*. Wivenhoe, UK: Minor Compositions.

Holloway, Jonathan. 2020a (Jul. 17). "Universities Must Reassert their Values: Expertise is Essential, Now More than Ever." *Foreign Affairs*.

Holloway, Jonathan. 2020b (Aug. 31). "Innocence and Community." New Student Convocation Address, Rutgers University. https://bit.ly/3c4PB2c

Jaschik, Scott. 2016 (Mar. 28). "What You Teach Is What You Earn." *Inside Higher Ed*.

Jenson, Jane, and Denis Saint-Martin. 2006. "Building Blocks for a New Social Architecture: The LEGO Paradigm of an Active Society." *Policy & Politics* 34 (3): 429–451.

Kahn, Suzanne, Jennifer Mittelstadt, and Lisa Levenstein. 2020. "A True New Deal for Higher Education: How a Stimulus for Higher Ed Can Advance Progressive Policy Goals." Policy Brief. New York, NY: Roosevelt Institute.

Kerr, Clark. 1963. *The Uses of the University*. Cambridge. MA: Harvard University Press.

Kezar, Adrianna, Tom DePaola, and Daniel T. Scott. 2019. *The Gig Academy: Mapping Labor in the Neoliberal University*. Baltimore, MD: Johns Hopkins University Press.

Kneese, Tamara. 2021 (Jan. 27). "How a Dead Professor Is Teaching a University Art History Class." *Slate*.

Krauss, Werner, Mike S. Schäfer, and Hans von Storch. 2012. "Introduction: Post-Normal Climate Science." *Nature and Culture* 7 (2): 121–132.

la paperson. 2017. *A Third University Is Possible*. Minneapolis, MN: University of Minnesota Press.

Lessenich, Stephan. 2008. *Die Neuerfindung des Sozialen: Der Sozialstaat im flexiblen Kapitalismus*. Bielefeld, Germany: Transcript Verlag.

Levin, Morten, and Davydd J. Greenwood. 2016. *Creating a New Public University and Reviving Democracy*. New York, NY: Berghahn Books.

Lieber, Ron, and Tara Siegel Bernard. 2020 (Nov. 7). "For Millions Deep in Student Loan Debt, Bankruptcy Is No Easy Fix." *New York Times*.

Lieberman, Mark. 2019 (Jan. 9). "Purdue's Online Strategy, Beyond 'Global.'" *Inside Higher Ed*.

Loss, Christopher P. 2014. *Between Citizens and the State: The Politics of American Higher Education in the 20th Century*. Princeton, NJ: Princeton University Press.

Maldonado-Torres, Nelson. 2012. "The Crisis of the University in the Context of Neoapartheid." *Human Architecture: Journal of the Sociology of Self-Knowledge* 10 (1): 91–100.

Matsuda, Mari J., Charles R. Lawrence III, Richard Delgado, and Kimberlè Williams Crenshaw. (1993) 2018. *Words That Wound: Critical Race Theory, Assaultive Speech, and the First Amendment*. New York, NY: Routledge.

Mbembe, Achille Joseph. 2016. "Decolonizing the University: New Directions." *Arts & Humanities in Higher Education* 15 (1): 29–45.

McGhee, Heather. 2021. *The Sum of Us: What Racism Costs Everyone and How We Can Prosper Together*. New York, NY: One World.

Mettler, Suzanne. 2014 (Mar 1). "College, the Great Unleveler." *New York Times*.

Murch, Donna. 2020 (Fall). "Black Women, Mutual Aid, and Union Organizing in the Time of COVID-19." *Academe*.

Newfield, Christopher. 2016. *The Great Mistake: How We Wrecked Public Universities and How We Can Fix Them*. Baltimore, MD: Johns Hopkins University Press.

Niemann, Yolanda Flores, Gabriella Gutiérrez y Muhs, and Carmen G. González, eds. 2020. *Presumed Incompetent II: Race, Class, Power, and Resistance of Women in Academia*. Louisville, CO: University Press of Colorado.

Nowotny, Helga, Peter Scott, and Michael Gibbons. 2001. *Re-Thinking Science: Knowledge and the Public in an Age of Uncertainty*. Cambridge, UK: Polity.

Nzingo, Sekile M. 2020. *Lean Semester: How Higher Education Reproduces Inequity*. Baltimore, MD: Johns Hopkins University Press.

O'Meara, KerryAnn. 2018 (Aug. 22). "Accurately Assessing Engaged Scholarship." *Inside Higher Ed*.

Poser, Rachel. 2021 (Feb. 2). "He Wants to Save Classics from Whiteness. Can the Field Survive?" *New York Times*.

Rahman, K. Sabeel, and Kathleen Thelen. 2019. "The Rise of the Platform Business Model and the Transformation of Twenty-First-Century Capitalism." *Politics & Society* 47 (2): 177–204.

Reitmeyer, John. 2020 (May 15). "Plan to Partially Furlough Public Employees Awaits Governor's Signature." *NJ Spotlight*.

Robinson, Cedric J. 1983. *Black Marxism*. London, UK: Zed Press.

Rose, Deondra. 2018. *Citizens by Degree: Higher Education Policy and the Changing Gender Dynamics of American Citizenship*. New York, NY: Oxford University Press.

Samuels, Robert. 2013. *Why Public Higher Education Should Be Free: How to Decrease Cost and Increase Quality at American Universities*. New Brunswick, NJ: Rutgers University Press.

Schrecker, Ellen. 2010. *The Lost Soul of Higher Education: Corporatization, the Assault on Academic Freedom, and the End of the American University*. New York, NY: New Press.

Schulze-Cleven, Tobias. 2011. "Globale Agenda, Nationale Praktiken: Lebenslanges Lernen in Europa." In *Moving (Con)Texts: Produktion und Verbreitung von Ideen in der globalen Wissensökonomie*, edited by Johannes Angermuller, Jens Maesse and Jan Standke, pp. 230–270. Berlin, Germany: Logos.

Schulze-Cleven, Tobias. 2017. "Higher Education in the Knowledge Economy: Politics and Policies of Transformation." *PS: Political Science and Politics* 50 (2): 397–402.

Schulze-Cleven, Tobias. 2020. "Organizing Competition: Regulatory Welfare States in Higher Education." *The ANNALS of the American Academy of Political and Social Science* 691: 276–294.

Schulze-Cleven, Tobias, and Jennifer R. Olson. 2017. "Worlds of Higher Education Transformed: Toward Varieties of Academic Capitalism." *Higher Education* 73 (6): 813–831.

Schulze-Cleven, Tobias, Tilman Reitz, Jens Maesse, and Johannes Angermuller. 2017. "The New Political Economy of Higher Education: Between Distributional Conflicts and Discursive Stratification." *Higher Education* 73 (6): 795–812.

Slaughter, Sheila, and Gary Rhoades. 2004. *Academic Capitalism and the New Economy: Markets, State, and Higher Education*. Baltimore, MD: John Hopkins University Press.

Smelser, Neil J. 2013. *Dynamics of the Contemporary University: Growth, Accretion, and Conflict*. Berkeley, CA: University of California Press.

Stedward, Gail. 2003. "Education as Industrial Policy: New Labour's Marriage of the Social and the Economic." *Policy & Politics* 31 (2): 139–152.

Steffen, Heather. 2020. "Imagining Academic Labor in the US University." *New Literary History* 51 (1): 115–143.

Stevens, Mitchell L. 2018. "Research Universities and the Future of Work." *Issues in Science and Technology* 35 (1): 45–52.

Stevens, Mitchell L., Elizabeth A. Armstrong, and Richard Arum. 2008. "Sieve, Incubator, Temple, Hub: Empirical and Theoretical Advances in the Sociology of Higher Education." *Annual Review of Sociology* 34: 127–151.

Stevens, Mitchell L., and Ben Gebre-Medhin. 2016. "Association, Service, Market: Higher Education in American Political Development." *Annual Review of Sociology* 42: 121–142.

Wallerstein, Immanuel. 1999. *The End of the World as We Know It: Social Science for the Twenty-First Century*. Minneapolis, MN: University of Minnesota Press.

Wilder, Craig Steven. 2013. *Ebony & Ivy: Race, Slavery, and the Troubled History of America's Universities*. New York, NY: Bloomsbury Press.

Williams, Jeffrey J. 2012 (Feb. 19). "Deconstructing Academe: The Birth of Critical University Studies." *Chronicle of Higher Education*.

Woo, Jennie H., Alexander H. Bentz, Stephen Lew, Erin Dunlop Velez, Nichole Smith. 2017. "Repayment of Student Loans as of 2015 Among 1995–96 and 2003–04 First-Time Beginning Students: First Look." NCES Report 2018-410, National Center for Education Statistics, US Department of Education, Washington, DC.

ABOUT THE
CONTRIBUTORS

About the Contributors

EDITORS

Tobias Schulze-Cleven is an associate professor and co-director of the Center for Global Work and Employment at the School of Management and Labor Relations, Rutgers University–New Brunswick. His research examines the comparative political economy of labor markets and higher education in the rich democracies. Trained as a political scientist and working in a department of labor studies and employment relations, Schulze-Cleven engages across disciplines to understand the politics of work in the digital era. He has published in outlets such as *Comparative Political Studies, German Politics, Higher Education, Journal of Industrial Relations, New Political Economy,* and *Politics & Society.*

Todd E. Vachon is director of the Labor Education Action Research Network at Rutgers University's School of Management and Labor Relations. His research agenda seeks to understand the structural origins and consequences of inequality and the struggles of ordinary people to achieve greater equality and dignity through education, organizations, and movements. To this end, Vachon has published widely on labor and social movements, social stratification, and the intersection of work and environmental issues in journals such as *Socius, Social Science Research, Labor Studies Journal, Sociological Forum,* and the *Cambridge Journal of Regions, Economy and Society.*

CONTRIBUTORS

Robert Bruno is a professor of labor and employment relations at the University of Illinois Urbana-Champaign School of Labor and Employment Relations and director of the university's labor education program. He also oversees the university's labor policy analysis shop, the Project for Middle Class Renewal. Bruno is the author or co-author of four books—most recently, *A Fight for the Soul of Public Education: The Chicago Teachers Strike.* He has also authored over three dozen journal articles on labor studies and has either authored or co-authored more than 70 applied reports on various employment and labor policies.

J. Mijin Cha is an assistant professor of urban and environmental policy at Occidental College. She is also a fellow at the Worker Institute, Cornell University and a senior fellow at Data for Progress. Cha's research explores the intersection of inequality and climate change, particularly labor/climate coalitions. Her current research focus is on just transition—how to transition fossil fuel communities and workers equitably into a low-carbon future. Cha received her B.S. from Cornell University, J.D. from the University of California–Hastings, and L.L.M. and Ph.D. degrees from SOAS University of London.

Dorothy Sue Cobble is Distinguished Professor Emerita of history and labor studies at Rutgers University, where she specializes in the study of work, social movements, and social policy. She is the author of multiple prize-winning books and articles. Her most recent book, *For the Many: American Feminists and the Global Fight for Democratic Equality*, is a history of the 20th-century feminists who fought for the rights of women, workers, and the poor in the United States and abroad. Currently, she is writing about how US labor intellectuals of the past can help us reimagine a fairer, more inclusive America.

Sheri Davis-Faulkner is associate director for the Center for Innovation in Worker Organization, assistant professor in the School of Management and Labor Relations at Rutgers University, co-directing WILL Empower (Women Innovating Labor Leadership). She supports emerging leaders and executive leaders and studies women's labor leadership globally. She worked as union representative and grievance/arbitrations coordinator with an SEIU Justice for Janitors local. She is a Spelman alumna with a doctorate in American studies from Emory University. She is a member of and advisor for the Crunk Feminist Collective, Advancing Black Strategists Initiative, National Black Worker Center, and Philly Black Worker Center.

Victor G. Devinatz is Distinguished Professor of Management and was the Hobart and Marian Gardner Hinderliter Endowed Professor (2014–15) at Illinois State University, where he teaches courses in labor relations and human resource management. He has published articles in many scholarly journals, including *Labour/Le Travail, Labor History, Industrial Relations, Advances in Industrial and Labor Relations, Journal of Labor Research*, and *Labor Studies Journal*. Devinatz is a co-editor of *Labor Studies Journal* and currently writes a periodic labor column for *StreetWise*, a Chicago-based weekly newspaper. In 2003, he received a Merl E. Reed Research Fellowship in Southern Labor History.

Alysa Hannon is a doctoral student at Rutgers University's Labor (LSER) Department, where she studies the role of skills development systems in the empowerment of workers. Prior to the program, Hannon worked for ten years in economic and workforce development designing, implementing, and evaluating publicly funded programs in the United States and the Middle East. She has worked for the New York City Economic Development Corporation, the Center for Economic Forecasting at the University of California–Riverside, and USAID-funded Palestine StartUp Cup. She is a Fulbright Scholar and holds a B.S.F.S. and a certificate in international development from Georgetown University's School of Foreign Service.

William A. Herbert is Distinguished Lecturer and executive director of the National Center for the Study of Collective Bargaining in Higher Education and the Professions at Hunter College, City University of New York. He is also a faculty associate at the Roosevelt House Institute of Public Policy. His scholarship focuses on labor law and history, collective bargaining, unionization, and workplace privacy. He is a co-author of a recent study, "2020 Supplementary Directory of New Bargaining Agents and Contracts in Institutions of Higher Education, 2013–2019," and a chapter titled "Geoprivacy, Convenience, and the Pursuit of Anonymity in Digital Cities" in the forthcoming book, *Urban Informatics*.

David C. Jacobs is currently teaching at the Kogod School of Business at American University. He has written or co-edited five books, including two LERA research volumes and *The Internet, Organizational Change, and Labor* with Joel Yudken. His published work has covered such topics as pragmatism in business ethics and religion and labor. His creative contributions to curriculum and program development in business and society were recognized in his selection as a Faculty Pioneer Finalist by the Aspen Institute Business and Society Program in 2007. Jacobs is president-elect of the DC Chapter of the Labor and Employment Relations Association.

John E. McCarthy is an assistant professor in the Department of Labor Relations, Law, and History, School of Industrial and Labor Relations, Cornell University. Undertaken in the context of US public schools, one of his primary research streams focuses on how empowering workplace institutions, including labor–management partnerships, affects social networks within and between organizations and, in turn, shapes outcomes such as employee well-being, turnover, and performance. His research appears or is forthcoming in leading peer-reviewed journals including *ILR Review, British Journal of Industrial Relations, Industrial Relations, Journal of Applied Psychology*, and *Personnel Psychology*. McCarthy received his Ph.D. from the School of Management and Labor Relations at Rutgers University and was a Postdoctoral Fellow at MIT's Sloan School of Management.

Joseph A. McCartin is a professor of history and the executive director of the Kalmanovitz Initiative for Labor and the Working Poor at Georgetown University. He studies the intersection of politics, public policy, and worker organizations and movements. He is the author of more than 140 articles, chapters, and reviews in scholarly and popular publications and has authored, co-authored, or co-edited eight books, including, most recently, *Labor in America: A History* (9th edition), co-authored with Melvyn Dubofsky.

Heather A. McKay is the founding director of the Education and Employment Research Center at the School of Management and Labor Relations at Rutgers University. In that capacity, she conducts research and evaluations on community college programs, state and federal workforce development systems, and education and workforce policies. McKay completed her bachelor's degree at Bryn Mawr College. She has a master's degree in history as well a master's degree in global affairs from Rutgers University. In addition, she is a Ph.D. candidate in global affairs at Rutgers University.

Michael Merrill was dean of the Harry Van Arsdale Jr. Center for Labor Studies at SUNY Empire State College from 2002 to 2016, served as director of Rutgers LEARN (Labor Education Action Research Network) from 2016 to 2020, and is currently the education director of the Hudson County (New Jersey) Central Labor Council. He is completing a history of the rise and fall of capitalism in the United States. His study of Thomas Mann's *Joseph and His Brothers* will appear in the *Oxford Handbook of Ancient Egypt and the Hebrew Bible* (forthcoming).

Yana van der Meulen Rodgers is a professor in the Department of Labor Studies and Employment Relations at Rutgers University. She is also faculty director of the Center for Women and Work. Rodgers has worked regularly as a consultant for the World Bank, the United Nations, and the Asian Development Bank, and she was president of the International Association for Feminist Economics. She is an associate editor for the journals *World Development* and *Feminist Economics*. She earned her Ph.D. in economics from Harvard University and her B.A. in economics from Cornell University.

Saul A. Rubinstein is a professor at the Rutgers University School of Management and Labor Relations and is director of the Collaborative School Leadership Initiative. He received his Ph.D. from the Massachusetts Institute of Technology, his Ed.M. and M.B.A. from Harvard University, and his B.A. from Swarthmore College. His research and consulting have focused on management and unions that have created joint efforts to transform employment relations, work systems, and performance. His work over the past 15 years has focused on union–management collaborative efforts in public education and the impact of those partnerships on teaching and learning. He received the 2020 Outstanding Scholar–Practitioner Award from the Labor and Employment Relations Association.

Tod D. Rutherford is a professor in the Department of Geography and the Environment in the Maxwell School of Citizenship and Public Affairs at Syracuse University. His research focuses on North American and European trade unions, especially in the auto industry and labor market policy. He has published in *Transactions of the Institute of British Geographers, Economic and Industrial Democracy, Cambridge Journal of Regions, Economy and Society,* and *Regional Studies.*

Erica Smiley is the executive director of Jobs With Justice, where she has spearheaded strategic organizing and policy interventions for over 15 years. Serving as one of its lead architects, Smiley has been instrumental in developing the strategic vision of Jobs With Justice to build power for impacted working people through expanding their collective bargaining power as one way to redefine and claim their democracy. She has authored several related articles in the *New Labor Forum, Dissent* magazine, *Journal on Class, Race and Corporate Power,* and other publications.

Marilyn Sneiderman directs the Center for Innovation in Worker Organization at Rutgers University's School of Management and Labor Relations, bringing 30 years of experience in labor, community, and racial justice organizing. Previously, she directed the AFL-CIO's Department of Field Mobilization, where she launched the national "Union Cities" initiative to increase the capacity to support and win organizing, political, and policy campaigns throughout the United States. Sneiderman also served as education director for the Teamsters, community organizer for AFSCME, and on the faculty of the Meany Center, where she focused on leadership training, civil and women's rights, and labor/community organizing. She has published extensively on Bargaining for the Common Good, leadership, and organizing.

Joseph van der Naald is a doctoral candidate in the sociology program at the City University of New York Graduate School and University Center. He is also a graduate student researcher at the National Center for the Study of Higher Education and the Professions at Hunter College, CUNY; and co-author of the center's recent study, "2020 Supplementary Directory of New Bargaining Agents and Contracts in Institutions of Higher Education, 2013–2019." His doctoral dissertation will focus on public sector labor movements in the midwestern United States.

Michelle Van Noy is the associate director of the Education and Employment Research Center at the School of Management and Labor Relations at Rutgers University. She has over 20 years of experience conducting research on education and work. Her research focuses on community college workforce education, student decision making about majors and careers, and quality in nondegree credentials. She holds a Ph.D. in sociology and education from Columbia University, an M.S. in public policy from Rutgers, and a B.A. in psychology and Spanish from Rutgers.

Naomi R Williams is an assistant professor of labor studies at Rutgers University. Her research includes the history of social and economic movements of working people and the role of workers in shaping US political economy. Currently, Williams is revising a book manuscript on the transformation of class identity and politics in the second half of the 20th century.

Joel S. Yudken is principal, High Road Strategies LLC, an economic policy consultancy in Arlington, Virginia, where he focuses on manufacturing, energy, and workforce issues. Prior positions include sectoral economist for the AFL-CIO and manufacturing policy analyst for the AFL-CIO Industrial Union Council. He also served on the staff at the NIST Manufacturing Extension Partnership; the US House Committee on Banking, Financing and Urban Affairs; and the office of US Senator Barbara Boxer (D-CA). Yudken has written extensively on manufacturing, energy, workforce, and technology policy. He holds a bachelor's degree in electrical engineering from Rensselaer Polytechnic Institute and a master's of science in engineering-economic systems and Ph.D. in technology and society from Stanford University.

Elaine Zundl is the research project manager at The Shift Project at Harvard Kennedy School. Previously, she was the research director for the Center for Women and Work in the School of Management and Labor Relations at Rutgers University, where she worked on the development, implementation, and evaluation of research projects that highlight gender inequities in education and the labor force. At Rutgers, she also served as assistant dean at Douglass Residential College and director of the Douglass Project for Rutgers Women in Math, Science, and Engineering. Zundl has an M.A. in women's and gender studies from Rutgers University and is currently pursuing a Ph.D. in planning and public policy at Rutgers' Edward J. Bloustein School.

LERA Executive Board Members 2021–22

President
Wilma Liebman, former chair, National Labor Relations Board

President-Elect
Paul F. Clark, Pennsylvania State University

Past President
Adrienne Eaton, Rutgers University

Secretary-Treasurer
Andrew Weaver, University of Illinois Urbana-Champaign

Editor-in-Chief
J. Ryan Lamare, University of Illinois Urbana-Champaign

National Chapter Advisory Council Chair
William Canak, Middle Tennessee State University (retired)

Legal Counsel
Steven B. Rynecki

Executive Board Members
Daniel Altchek, Saul Ewing Arnstein & Lehr LLP
Peter Berg, Michigan State University
Robert Chiaravalli, Strategic Labor and HR, LLC
Julie Farb, AFL-CIO
Janet Gillman, Oregon Employment Relations Board
Shannon Gleeson, Cornell University
Kati Griffith, Cornell University
Beverly Harrison, Arbitrator/Mediator
Quinton Herbert, City of Baltimore
Erin Johansson, Jobs With Justice
Tamara Lee, Rutgers University
Kevin Legel, Ford Motor Company
Deborah Mueller, CSEA Local 1000, AFSCME
Jim Pruitt, Kaiser Permanente
Javier Ramirez, Federal Mediation and Conciliation Service
Christine Riordan, University of Illinois Urbana Champaign
Jake Rosenfeld, Washington University in St. Louis
Marc Weinstein, Florida International University

ILR AND LERA

A Long-Standing Partnership

COLLABORATING SINCE 1947
ilr.cornell.edu

Cornell's ILR School is transforming the future of work, employment and labor through our teaching, research and outreach to the community. As a leader in all aspects of labor and employment relations, ILR is a proud partner with LERA. ILR faculty and students are deeply engaged in this collaboration sharing ideas, contributing papers, chairing sessions and presenting on panels. Together, we've been at the heart of extraordinary changes in the workplace and in the lives of workers. We embrace multiple and diverse perspectives, encourage principled debate and collaborate across disciplines. And, we operate in the real world, drawing on the richness of the LERA community to drive positive impact for people and society, today and in the future.

Leading the Way with LERA

Rutgers School of Management and Labor Relations (SMLR) is proud to partner with LERA through an established tradition of leadership and service to the association across executive, editorial and committee roles. Through our academic programs, research initiatives, and outreach programs, Rutgers SMLR is a leading source of expertise on the world of work, building effective and sustainable organizations, and the changing employment relationship.

SMLR is pleased to collaborate with LERA to offer a unique lens to explore the evolution of work and the Future of Work(ers) through a focus on efforts and contributions of workers to achieve the promises of democracy and improve sustainability.

smlr.rutgers.edu

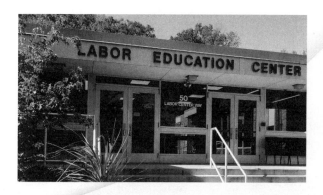

Empowering People. Transforming Communities.

Through educational offerings, original research, conferences, and public programs and activities, **Rutgers Labor Education Action Research Network (LEARN)** disseminates knowledge, skills, and ideas that strengthen the community at work; facilitate the organization of work on a more democratic basis; and address unjustified inequalities of power and wealth in the wider society.

Learn more about our certificate programs in labor relations, our classes for union leaders, and the various custom programs we develop for worker and social justice organizations.

**LABOR
EDUCATION
ACTION
RESEARCH
NETWORK**

smlr.rutgers.edu/LEARN